*America's Best Day Hiking Series*

# Hiking
# MISSOURI

## KEVIN M. LOHRAFF

**Human Kinetics**

**Library of Congress Cataloging-in-Publication Data**

Lohraff, Kevin, 1964-
    Hiking Missouri / Kevin Lohraff.
       p.  cm. -- (America's best day hiking series)
    ISBN 0-88011-893-8
    1. Hiking--Missouri--Guidebooks.   2. Trails--Missouri--Guidebooks.
3. Parks--Missouri--Guidebooks.   4. Natural history--Missouri-
-Guidebooks.  5. Missouri--Guidebooks.  I. Title.  II. Series.
    GV199.42.M8L65   1999                   98-46240
    917.7804'43--dc21                   CIP

ISBN: 0-88011-893-8

**Acquisitions Editor:** Patricia Sammann
**Managing Editor:** Coree Schutter
**Assistant Editor:** John Wentworth
**Copyeditor:** Bob Replinger
**Proofreader:** Pam Johnson
**Graphic Designer:** Robert Reuther
**Graphic Artist:** Francine Hamerski
**Cover Designer:** Jack Davis
**Photographer (cover):** Kevin M. Lohraff
**Photographers (interior):** Kevin M. Lohraff unless otherwise noted; Jane Epperson—pg. 170
**Illustrator:** Tim Shedelbower
**Printer:** Versa Press

Information for maps on pages 4, 8, 12, 16, 20, 24, 28, 32, 36, 40, 44, 58, 62, 66, 70, 78, 82, 94, 96, 100, 102, 106, 110, 114, 118, 132, 158, 162, 164, 168, 172, 182, 186, 190, 204, 210 was supplied by the Missouri Department of Natural Resources; page 17—adapted from Rocheport Area Merchant's Association; pages 48 and 74—adapted from the U.S. Fish and Wildlife Service; page 54 (Forest Park)—copyright by Gobberdiel Graphic Design; pages 86, 88, 92, 98, 122, 126, 136, 138, 140, 144, 148, 150, 152, 154, 176, 198, 202, 208—adapted from the U.S. Government Printing Office; page 195—copyright by J.C. Nichols Company.

Human Kinetics books are available at special discounts for bulk purchase. Special editions or book excerpts can also be created to specification. For details, contact the Special Sales Manager at Human Kinetics.

Printed in the United States of America       10  9  8  7  6  5  4  3

**Human Kinetics**
Web site: www.HumanKinetics.com

*United States:* Human Kinetics
P.O. Box 5076
Champaign, IL 61825-5076
800-747-4457
e-mail: humank@hkusa.com

*Canada:* Human Kinetics
475 Devonshire Road, Unit 100
Windsor, ON N8Y 2L5
800-465-7301 (in Canada only)
e-mail: orders@hkcanada.com

*Europe:* Human Kinetics
107 Bradford Road
Stanningley
Leeds LS28 6AT, United Kingdom
+44 (0)113 255 5665
e-mail: hk@hkeurope.com

*Australia:* Human Kinetics
57A Price Avenue
Lower Mitcham, South Australia 5062
08 8277 1555
e-mail: liahka@senet.com.au

*New Zealand:* Human Kinetics
P.O. Box 105-231, Auckland Central
09-523-3462
e-mail: hkp@ihug.co.nz

*To Jane, who loaned me cameras and camping gear, gave up weekends to print photos for the book, supplied me with pizza and brownies for hiking energy, and cared for Tina Cat while I was on the road. Thank you for being an obliging trail partner through flash floods, near-miss tornadoes, and the initial stages of dehydration. Thank you for advice on geology and photography, for manuscript editing, and for endless streams of much-needed encouragement.*

# Acknowledgments

My sincere thanks go to all the staff members at visitor centers, headquarters, and nature centers where I sought help. Everyone answered my incessant questions completely, many stopped what they were doing to help, and some hiked a trail with me. (Ron Papsdorf, Superintendent of Wallace State Park, even hiked with me in the rain.) Special thanks go to Dan Wedemeyer, Dan Drees, and Brian Wilcox of Meramec State Park—their dedication to Missouri's natural resources inspires me.

I appreciate Joan McKee for believing in me from the beginning of the project. Thank you to Tom Johnson for expert herpetological advice and for loaning me his photographic enlarger. Thank you to Kathy and Don Love for the use of their darkroom. Thanks to Tim Smith, Don Kurz, and Rick Thom for botanical advice and for reviewing parts of the manuscript.

I want to thank my family for their support, especially Betty Lohraff for some stay-up-late, hair-raising computer work. Thank you to Tom and Carole Bultmann for putting me up and for pulling my car out of the mud. Finally, my appreciation goes to the citizens of Missouri, whose support of the parks and soils tax has helped develop one of the finest state park systems in the nation.

# Contents

# How to Use This Book

Hiking is an antidote to modern life. It gives the body some much-needed (and enjoyable) exercise, and it gives the mind both rest and stimulation. It even lifts the spirit to connect again with this earth that we're a part of but seldom have time to think about. With the America's Best Day Hiking Series, we hope to provide you with an incentive to start or continue hiking, for the pleasure and the challenge of it.

Each book in the series offers information on more than 100 of the most interesting and scenic trails in a particular state, as well as notes about recreational, historical, and sightseeing destinations located near the trails. The assortment of trails ranges from short, easy hikes for occasional hikers and families with young children to longer, more rugged ones for the experienced trailblazer. None of the trails takes more than a day to hike, although some trails may be linked together to create a hike of several days.

The trails in *Hiking Missouri* are divided into four main areas—North, Southeast, South Central, and Southwest. Within each area, trails are listed from east to west. Divider pages signal the beginning of each new area, and those pages include information on the local topography, major rivers and lakes, flora and fauna, weather, and best features of the area.

The innovative format is designed to make exploring new parks and trails easy. Information on each park or other nature area always appears on a right-hand page. It begins with the park's name and a small state map that shows the park's general location. Bulleted highlights then point out the trails' most interesting features. A description of the park's history and terrain comes next, with practical information on how to get to the park and the park's hours, available facilities, permits and rules, and the address and phone number of a contact who can give you more information. The section entitled "Other Areas of Interest" briefly mentions nearby parks and recreational opportunities, with phone numbers to call for more information.

After the general information follows a selected list of trails in the park. The length and difficulty of hiking each is given, along with a brief description of its terrain. The difficulty rating, shown by boot icons, ranges from one (the easiest) to five (the most difficult).

On the other side of the page is a full-sized map of the park. Our book's larger format allows us to provide clear, readable maps that are easy to follow.

easiest 🥾 🥾 🥾 🥾 🥾 most difficult
       1   2   3   4   5

The next right- and left-hand pages are usually descriptions of the two best hikes in that park, along with a trail map at the bottom of each page (a few parks have only one hike, with just one map that primarily shows the trail). Each hike begins with information on the length and difficulty of the trail, and the estimated time to walk it, plus cautions to help you avoid possible annoyances or problems. The description of the trail provides more than directions; it's a guided tour of what you will see as you hike along. The scenery, wildlife, and history of the trail are all brought to life. Points of interest along the trail are numbered in brackets within the text, and those numbers are shown on the trail map to guide you. The approximate distance from the trailhead to each point of interest is given.

The park descriptions, maps, and trails are all kept as a unit within an even number of pages. Parks for which only one trail is highlighted take up only two pages; those with the regular two trails cover four pages. We've perforated the book's pages so you can remove them if you like, or you can copy them for your personal use. If you carry the pages with you as you hike, you might want to use a plastic sleeve to protect them from the elements. You also can make notes on these pages to remind you of your favorite parts of the park or trail.

If you want to find a park or trail quickly, use the trail finder that appears on the next pages. It gives essential information about each highlighted trail in the book, including the trail's length, difficulty, special features, and park facilities.

We hope the books in the America's Best Day Hiking Series inspire you to get out and enjoy a wide range of outdoor experiences. We've tried to find interesting trails from all parts of each state. Some are unexpected treasures—places you'd never dream exist in the state. Some may be favorites that you've already hiked and recommended to friends. But whether you live in a city or in the country, are away vacationing or are at home, some of these trails will be near you. Find one you like, strap on your hiking boots, and go!

# Trail Finder

## KEY

| RV camping | tent camping | swimming | canoeing |
| --- | --- | --- | --- |
| fishing | boating | picnicking | biking |

| Trail Sites and Trails | Park Facilities | Miles | Trail Difficulty Rating | Hills | Prairie/Grass | Forest | Lake | Wetlands | Overlook | River/Stream | Page # |
| --- | --- | --- | --- | --- | --- | --- | --- | --- | --- | --- | --- |
| **1 Cuivre River State Park** | RV, tent | | | | | | | | | | |
| Lone Spring | swimming, canoeing | 6 | 🥾🥾🥾 | ✓ | | ✓ | | | | ✓ | 5 |
| Big Sugar Creek—North Loop | boating, fishing, picnicking | 3.75 | 🥾🥾🥾 | ✓ | | ✓ | | | | ✓ | 6 |
| **2 Graham Cave State Park** | RV, tent | | | | | | | | | | |
| Indian Glade | canoeing, fishing | 2.25 | 🥾🥾🥾🥾🥾 | ✓ | ✓ | ✓ | | | | ✓ | 9 |
| Loutre River | boating, picnicking | 1.5 | 🥾🥾🥾 | ✓ | ✓ | ✓ | | | | ✓ | 10 |
| **3 Rock Bridge Memorial State Park** | fishing | | | | | | | | | | |
| Devil's Icebox | picnicking | 0.5 | 🥾🥾🥾 | ✓ | | ✓ | | | ✓ | ✓ | 13 |
| Spring Brook | biking | 2.5 | 🥾🥾🥾 | ✓ | | ✓ | | | | ✓ | 14 |
| **4 Katy Trail State Park** | | | | | | | | | | | |
| Historic Rocheport and MKT Tunnel | biking | 1.5 | 🥾 | | | | | | | ✓ | 17 |
| McBaine to Lewis and Clark Cave | | 9.75 | 🥾 | | | | | | | ✓ | 18 |
| **5 Mark Twain State Park and Historic Site** | RV, tent | | | | | | | | | | |
| Sugar Maple | swimming, canoeing, fishing | 0.5 | 🥾🥾 | ✓ | | ✓ | ✓ | | ✓ | ✓ | 21 |
| White Oak | boating, picnicking | 6 | 🥾🥾🥾 | ✓ | | ✓ | ✓ | | ✓ | ✓ | 22 |
| **6 Battle of Athens State Historic Site** | RV, tent | | | | | | | | | | |
| Yellow/Red Historic | canoeing, fishing | 1.75 | 🥾🥾🥾 | ✓ | | ✓ | | | ✓ | ✓ | 25 |
| Green/Blue River | boating, picnicking | 1.75 | 🥾🥾🥾 | ✓ | | ✓ | | | | ✓ | 26 |
| **7 Thousand Hills State Park** | All facilities | | | | | | | | | | |
| Redbud-Hickory-Oak | | 1.5 | 🥾🥾🥾 | ✓ | | ✓ | | | | ✓ | 29 |
| Thousand Hills | | 5 | 🥾🥾🥾 | ✓ | ✓ | ✓ | | | | ✓ | 30 |

Continued ☞

**Terrain/Landscape**

Continued ☞

# Terrain/Landscape

| No. | Trail Sites and Trails | Park Facilities | Miles | Trail Difficulty Rating | Hills | Prairie/Grass | Forest | Lake | Wetlands | Overlook | River/Stream | Page # |
|---|---|---|---|---|---|---|---|---|---|---|---|---|
| 18 | **Mingo National Wildlife Refuge** | | | | | | | | | | | |
| | Hartz Pond and Bluff | | 0.75 | 3 boots | ✓ | | ✓ | | ✓ | ✓ | | 75 |
| | Boardwalk Nature | | 1 | 1 boot | | | ✓ | | ✓ | ✓ | | 76 |
| 19 | **Lake Wappapello State Park** | All facilities | | | | | | | | | | |
| | Asher Creek | | 2 | 3 boots | ✓ | | ✓ | ✓ | | | ✓ | 79 |
| | Allison Cemetery | | 3.5 | 3 boots | ✓ | ✓ | ✓ | ✓ | | ✓ | | 80 |
| 20 | **Sam A. Baker State Park** | | | | | | | | | | | |
| | Mudlick—East Loop | | 7.15 | 5 boots | ✓ | ✓ | ✓ | | | ✓ | ✓ | 83 |
| | Shut-Ins | | 3 | 5 boots | ✓ | ✓ | ✓ | | | ✓ | ✓ | 84 |
| 21 | **Rock Pile Mountain Wilderness** | | | | | | | | | | | |
| | Rock Pile Mountain | | 7 | 4 boots | ✓ | ✓ | ✓ | | | | | 86 |
| 22 | **Silver Mines Recreation Area** | | | | | | | | | | | |
| | Air Conditioner | | 1.4 | 5 boots | ✓ | | ✓ | | | ✓ | ✓ | 89 |
| | Boulder Hike to Turkey Creek | | 1.65 | 4 boots | ✓ | | ✓ | | | ✓ | ✓ | 90 |
| 23 | **Crane Lake Recreation Area** | | | | | | | | | | | |
| | Crane Lake | | 5 | 4 boots | ✓ | ✓ | ✓ | ✓ | | ✓ | ✓ | 92 |
| 24 | **Taum Sauk Mountain State Park** | | | | | | | | | | | |
| | Mina Sauk Falls Trail and Ozark Trail to Devil's Toll Gate | | 5 | 5 boots | ✓ | ✓ | ✓ | | | ✓ | ✓ | 94 |
| 25 | **Johnson's Shut-Ins State Park** | | | | | | | | | | | |
| | Shut-Ins | | 2.5 | 5 boots | ✓ | ✓ | ✓ | | | ✓ | ✓ | 96 |
| 26 | **Bell Mountain Wilderness** | | | | | | | | | | | |
| | Bell Mountain | | 10 | 4 boots | ✓ | ✓ | ✓ | | | ✓ | ✓ | 98 |
| 27 | **Elephant Rocks State Park** | | | | | | | | | | | |
| | Elephant Rocks Braille | | 1 | 1 boot | | | ✓ | | | ✓ | | 100 |

*Continued* ☞

| Trail Sites and Trails | Park Facilities | Miles | Trail Difficulty Rating | Hills | Prairie/Grass | Forest | Lake | Wetlands | Overlook | River/Stream | Page # |
|---|---|---|---|---|---|---|---|---|---|---|---|
| **28 Hawn State Park** | | | | | | | | | | | |
| Pickle Creek | | 1.5 | 5 boots | ✓ | ✓ | ✓ | | | ✓ | ✓ | 103 |
| Whispering Pine | | 10 | 5 boots | ✓ | | ✓ | | | ✓ | ✓ | 104 |
| **29 St. Francois State Park** | | | | | | | | | | | |
| Mooner's Hollow | | 3 | 4 boots | ✓ | ✓ | ✓ | | ✓ | ✓ | ✓ | 107 |
| Swimming Deer | | 3 | 3 boots | ✓ | ✓ | ✓ | | | ✓ | ✓ | 108 |
| **30 Washington State Park** | | | | | | | | | | | |
| 1,000 Steps | | 1.5 | 4 boots | ✓ | | ✓ | | | ✓ | ✓ | 111 |
| Opossum Track | | 3 | 4 boots | ✓ | ✓ | ✓ | | | ✓ | ✓ | 112 |
| **31 Meramec State Park** | | | | | | | | | | | |
| Natural Wonders | | 1.3 | 2 boots | ✓ | ✓ | ✓ | | ✓ | | ✓ | 115 |
| Bluff View | | 1.5 | 3 boots | ✓ | | ✓ | | | ✓ | ✓ | 116 |
| **32 Onondaga Cave State Park** | | | | | | | | | | | |
| Blue Heron | | 1 | 1 boot | | | ✓ | ✓ | ✓ | | ✓ | 119 |
| Deer Run | | 2.5 | 3 boots | ✓ | ✓ | ✓ | | | ✓ | ✓ | 120 |
| **33 Big Spring** | | | | | | | | | | | |
| Big Spring | | 2.5 | 4 boots | ✓ | | ✓ | | ✓ | ✓ | ✓ | 123 |
| Giant Cane | | 0.5 | 3 boots | ✓ | | ✓ | | | ✓ | ✓ | 124 |
| **34 Peck Ranch Conservation Area** | | | | | | | | | | | |
| Ozark Trail to Stegall Mountain | | 4 | 5 boots | ✓ | ✓ | ✓ | | | ✓ | ✓ | 127 |
| Ozark Trail to Rocky Point Glade | | 6.4 | 3 boots | ✓ | ✓ | ✓ | | | | | 128 |
| **35 Grand Gulf State Park** | | | | | | | | | | | |
| Chasm Loop | | 0.25 | 2 boots | ✓ | | ✓ | | | ✓ | ✓ | 133 |
| Northwest Rim | | 0.9 | 2 boots | ✓ | | ✓ | | | | ✓ | 134 |
| **36 Greer Spring** | | | | | | | | | | | |
| Greer Spring | | 2 | 3 boots | ✓ | | ✓ | | | ✓ | ✓ | 136 |
| **37 McCormack Recreation Area** | | | | | | | | | | | |
| McCormack-Greer | | 8.5 | 4 boots | ✓ | ✓ | ✓ | ✓ | | ✓ | ✓ | 138 |

Continued ☞

*Continued* ☞

| | Trail Sites and Trails | Park Facilities | Miles | Trail Difficulty Rating | Hills | Prairie/Grass | Forest | Lake | Wetlands | Overlook | River/Stream | Page # |
|---|---|---|---|---|---|---|---|---|---|---|---|---|
| 49 | **Hercules Glades Wilderness** | (camping, tents) | | | | | | | | | | |
| | Coy Bald | (picnic) | 6.75 | 5 boots | ✓ | ✓ | ✓ | | | ✓ | ✓ | 177 |
| | Lookout Tower | (bicycle) | 4.5 | 5 boots | ✓ | ✓ | ✓ | | | ✓ | ✓ | 178 |
| 50 | **Pomme de Terre State Park** | (RV, tents) | | | | | | | | | | |
| | Indian Point | (swim, canoe) | 3 | 3 boots | ✓ | ✓ | ✓ | ✓ | | ✓ | | 183 |
| | Cedar Bluff | (boat, fish, picnic) | 2 | 2 boots | ✓ | ✓ | ✓ | ✓ | | ✓ | | 184 |
| 51 | **Harry S Truman State Park** | (RV, tents) | | | | | | | | | | |
| | Western Wallflower Savanna | (swim, canoe, fish) | 0.75 | 4 boots | ✓ | ✓ | ✓ | ✓ | | ✓ | | 187 |
| | Bluff Ridge | (boat, fish, picnic) | 2 | 4 boots | ✓ | ✓ | ✓ | ✓ | | ✓ | | 188 |
| 52 | **Knob Noster State Park** | (RV, tents) | | | | | | | | | | |
| | Hawk Nest and Clearfork Savanna | (canoe, fish, boat, picnic) | 2.5 | 3 boots | ✓ | ✓ | ✓ | ✓ | | | ✓ | 191 |
| | Discovery and North Loop | (bicycle) | 2.75 | 3 boots | ✓ | ✓ | ✓ | | ✓ | | ✓ | 192 |
| 53 | **Urban Kansas City** | (bicycle) | | | | | | | | | | |
| | Country Club Plaza | | 1 | 1 boot | | | | | | | | 195 |
| | Kansas City Sculpture Park | | 1 | 1 boot | | | | | | | | 196 |
| 54 | **Wilson's Creek National Battlefield** | (picnic, bicycle) | | | | | | | | | | |
| | Gibson Mill Site and Ray Cornfield | | 1.75 | 2 boots | | ✓ | ✓ | | | | ✓ | 199 |
| | Bloody Hill and Wire Road | | 2 | 2 boots | ✓ | ✓ | ✓ | | | | ✓ | 200 |
| 55 | **Piney Creek Wilderness** | (camping, tents, picnic, bicycle) | | | | | | | | | | |
| | Pineview Lookout Tower | | 3.75 | 6 boots | ✓ | ✓ | ✓ | | | ✓ | ✓ | 202 |
| 56 | **Roaring River State Park** | (RV, tents) | | | | | | | | | | |
| | Devil's Kitchen | (swim, fish) | 1.75 | 5 boots | ✓ | | ✓ | | | | ✓ | 205 |
| | Pibern | (picnic) | 1.75 | 5 boots | ✓ | | ✓ | | | | ✓ | 206 |
| 57 | **George Washington Carver National Monument** | (picnic) | | | | | | | | | | |
| | Carver | | 0.75 | 1 boot | | ✓ | ✓ | ✓ | | | ✓ | 208 |
| 58 | **Prairie State Park** | (camping, tents, picnic) | | | | | | | | | | |
| | Drover's | | 2.5 | 2 boots | ✓ | ✓ | | | | | ✓ | 211 |
| | Path of the Sky People and Sandstone | | 6.5 | 2 boots | ✓ | ✓ | | | | | ✓ | 212 |

# North

The north region of Missouri is defined as the area north of the Missouri River.

## Topography

The topography of the northern third of the state was greatly affected by at least two major glaciers that scraped and leveled most of the state north of the Missouri River. The last ice sheet retreated around 450,000 years ago, making this northern landscape much younger than unglaciated portions of the state. Because rivers and streams have had less time to carve and dissect the land, this area has less relief and lower elevation than southern regions.

Much of north Missouri's fertile soil is composed of loess, which is glacially deposited silt picked up by wind and deposited along the Missouri River Valley. Loess is highly cohesive, forming steep dunes and sheer, vertical walls at road cuts. Loess creates especially well developed dunelike topography, and loess hills are an unusual geologic feature in the state's northwest corner along the east side of the Missouri River. These great drifts of glacial dust are often 70 feet deep. Good examples are in the Squaw Creek and Rock Port areas.

While rolling plains dominate the topography of north Missouri, the Lincoln Hills are an exception. A narrow band of ridges along the Mississippi River, the Lincoln Hills have steep topography, bedrock exposures, rugged bluffs, and may have partially escaped glaciation.

## Major Rivers and Lakes

North Missouri is surrounded on three sides by the two largest continent-draining rivers in the country—the Missouri and Mississippi. The Missouri, which drains about one-sixth of the nation, marks the approximate southern reach of glaciers in Missouri and, in fact, was largely formed by outwash from glacier meltwater. The Missouri River forms the northwest boundary of the state and flows to St. Louis, where it joins the Mississippi River. The Missouri makes a 553-mile trek within the state, while the Mississippi River forms Missouri's entire 486-mile eastern boundary. No other natural feature has influenced the state's culture, history, and economy as much as these two rivers.

The Grand, Platte, Chariton, and Salt Rivers form major drainages in north Missouri, and the lower Des Moines River forms the state boundary in the northeast corner. Locust Creek is one of the last sizable stream segments in north Missouri that has not been channelized. Cuivre River drains the southern Lincoln Hills area. Major reservoirs include Smithville, Thomas Hill, and Long Branch Lakes. Mark Twain Lake, an impoundment of the Salt River, is north Missouri's largest reservoir.

## Common Plant Life

Before north Missouri was settled, vast tallgrass prairies covered half of the region's rolling plains. The rest of the landscape was oak savanna and deciduous forest in the uplands and river valleys. The Missouri River was a braided stream, with accompanying sloughs, islands, sandbars, wet prairies, oxbows, marshes, and wetland natural communities.

But north Missouri's gentle terrain and deep soils from glacial till and alluvium made it ideal for agriculture. Today, pasture and large fields of corn and soybeans dominate the landscape. Prairies are now found only in tiny fragments in cemeteries and along railroads. The Missouri River has been deepened and channelized, eliminating its backwater habitat. Locks and dams on the Mississippi River have converted it into a series of large pools, and most of the original riverine natural communities are no longer present.

Though fragmented, several deciduous forest and plant communities persist in the region's state parks, wildlife refuges, and conservation areas. Mesic (moderately moist) forests are the most common and include northern red oak, sugar maple, white oak, basswood, and pawpaw. Drier forests include shagbark hickory, post oak, and chinkapin oak. Forests along the rivers include cottonwood, bur oak, pecan, sycamore, shellbark hickory, and silver maple. Prairie grasses dominate in the dry prairies of the northwest, and silky aster, prairie larkspur, compass plant, and purple coneflower may also be found. A system of wetland communities is preserved along Locust Creek, and its wet prairie includes cordgrass, saw-toothed sunflower, false dragonhead, swamp milk-weed, and numerous sedges.

## Common Birds and Animals

Wildlife refuges in north Missouri, such as Squaw Creek, Swan Lake, Fountain Grove, and Ted Shanks, attract concentrations of birds and birdwatchers alike. Various ducks, geese, swans, pelicans, herons, egrets, wading birds, and other birds associated with water congregate in these areas by the hundreds of thousands, mostly during fall and spring migrations. Bald eagles also use these areas, as well as the major rivers, during winter months. Northern harriers may be seen gliding low over grass fields. Other common birds include the bobwhite, mourning dove, red-headed woodpecker, kingbird, common yel-lowthroat, dickcissel, meadowlark, and red-winged blackbird.

Other common animals include the coyote, white-tailed deer, red fox, raccoon, ground squirrel, and box turtle. Muskrat, beaver, massasauga rattlesnake, aquatic turtles, and water snakes are characteristic inhabitants of wet prairies and marshes.

## Climate

North Missouri is the first area in the state to show fall colors and the last area to warm up each spring. The mean average temperature is 54 degrees F in spring, 78 degrees F in summer, 56 degrees F in fall, and 24 degrees F in winter. The northwest corner has the driest climate in the state, with a mean annual precipitation of 35 inches. The rest of north Missouri averages between 36 and 39 inches annually.

## Best Features

- Unusual dunelike loess hills
- Loess hill prairies
- The two largest rivers in the nation
- The primeval roar of 10,000 geese lifting off a refuge marsh at sunrise in December
- Brilliant colors of sugar maples in autumn
- Natural marshes along the Missouri River
- Winter congregations of bald eagles
- Rich cove ravines along steep, north-facing slopes overlooking the Des Moines River
- A system of wetland natural communities along Locust Creek
- Native American petroglyphs at Thousand Hills State Park

# 1. Cuivre River State Park

- Give your legs a workout in the unusually rugged terrain of the Lincoln Hills.
- Hike next to Big Sugar Creek with alternating pools and riffles, gravel bars, and picturesque exposed bedrock and small bluffs.
- Listen for the loud and clear "Teacher! Teacher! Teacher!" of the ovenbird and the even louder guttural, toneless clucks of the yellow-billed cuckoo.

## Area Information

If Cuivre (pronounced "quiver") River State Park were in south Missouri, no one would question its rugged, wooded hills, deep valleys, clear-running creek, and karst features like caves, springs, and sinkholes—these are typical Ozark characteristics. But Cuivre River is surrounded by the glaciated plains of north Missouri. The park is situated at the southern edge of the Lincoln Hills, a band of uplifted limestone bedrock hills about 15 miles wide and 60 miles long, and they are responsible for the park's Ozark-like qualities.

Cuivre River was acquired in 1934 by the National Park Service as a recreation demonstration area and was primarily composed of abused farm areas. The site was developed to show the effects of good land use and provide an extensive recreation area for the people of St. Louis. Two of President Roosevelt's agencies, the CCC and WPA, built many of the park's facilities during the late 1930s. After World War II, Cuivre River was given to the state.

Cuivre River has largely recovered from its former abuses and now boasts three state natural areas and two state wild areas. Because of careful land stewardship and nature's ability to heal itself, Cuivre River's story is one of success.

**Directions:** Cuivre River is northwest of St. Louis off Highway 61 north. From the intersection of Highway 47 and Highway 61 in Troy, take Highway 47 north for 3.2 miles. Turn north on Highway 147, which takes you to the visitor center in 2 miles.

**Hours Open:** The site is open year-round. The visitor center is open from 8 A.M. to 4 P.M. Monday through Friday, from 10 A.M. to 5 P.M. on Saturday, and from 11 A.M. to 6 P.M. on Sunday. The visitor center is closed on Thanksgiving, Christmas, and Easter.

**Facilities:** The park offers a visitor center with exhibits, a campground, three group camps, an equestrian campground, an amphitheater, and picnic areas. Fishing, a boat ramp, and a swimming beach are available on 55-acre Lake Lincoln.

**Permits and Rules:** Horses are permitted only on designated equestrian trails. Bicycles are prohibited on all trails. Boats are restricted to using electric motors only. Pets must always be on leashes 10 feet long or shorter. Backpack camping is allowed on three of the park's longest trails, but campfires are prohibited on all trails.

**Further Information:** Park Superintendent, Cuivre River State Park, 678 State Road 147, Troy, MO 63379; 314-528-7247.

## Park Trails

**Mossy Hill Trail** 🥾🥾—1 mile—This trail follows a wooded valley and loops through an open forest with lots of mosses and reindeer lichen. It begins at the electric side of the campground.

**Lakeside Trail** 🥾🥾—4 miles—This trail follows the entire shoreline of Lincoln Lake and offers views of many wildflowers. It is accessible from the boat ramp or swimming beach.

**Big Sugar Creek Trail—South Loop** 🥾🥾🥾—4.5 miles—This trail winds along several sections of Big Sugar Creek. Horses are allowed on this section,

which may become unpleasant for hikers during wet periods.

**Frenchman's Bluff Trail** 🥾🥾🥾—2 miles—The trail begins behind the rest rooms at the equestrian campground, located 1 mile west of the visitor center, and takes you on top of a 120-foot-high bluff with tremendous vistas of the Cuivre River valley.

**Cuivre River Trail** 🥾🥾🥾—8 miles—This trail shares a trailhead with the Frenchman's Bluff Trail, traverses the entire length of Frenchman's Bluff, and descends into the Big Sugar Creek valley. This is the main equestrian trail, along with the south loop of the Big Sugar Creek Trail.

# Cuivre River State Park

N

Northwoods
Wild Area

Lone Spring
Trail

Big Sugar Creek

To Brussels

P

Northwoods
Native
Grasslands

KK

Camp
Derricotte

Camp
Sherwood
Forest

Big Sugar
Creek Trail
North Loop

P

Sac
Prairie

KK

61

Big Sugar
Creek
Wild Area

Lake
Lincoln

Cuivre River

To Troy

Camp
Cuivre

## LEGEND

| | | |
|---|---|---|
| ——— Major Road | 🚐 | Trailer Hook-ups |
| —╫— Minor Road | P | Trailer Parking |
| ········ Trail | 🏊 | Beach |
| ▨▨▨ Boundary | 🏇 | Horse Camp and Trail Head |
| 🏠 Visitor Center | ◉ | Amphitheater |
| ⛱ Picnic Area | ▣ | Overlook |
| ⛺ Picnic Shelter | | |
| ▲ Camping | | |

To Troy ←

147

47

To Winfield →

# Lone Spring Trail 👢👢👢

**Distance Round-Trip:** 6 miles

**Estimated Hiking Time:** 2.75 hours

*Even if you know exactly where it is and you walk right to it, the magical flow of a spring is always something of a surprise.*

**Caution:** Watch for traffic when crossing Highway KK; you'll cross it four times.

**Trail Directions:** Park in the lot at the north end of the park at the intersection of Highway KK and the main park road. The north half of this trail loops through the Northwoods Wild Area.

Begin from the parking lot **[1]**, cross Highway KK, and continue on the other side. When you reach the intersection at .08 mi. **[2]** turn left. This is a connector link marked with white arrows that will take you to the main trail. Immediately, you'll notice a landscape deeply scored. For thousands of years, water has cut through this limestone-laden area, draining into the Big Sugar Creek a half mile to the west. You'll pass hill after hill, each separated by a deep **V**.

At .30 mi. **[3]** is a trail registration box. Please fill out a registration card before continuing. Turn right here to continue, following yellow arrows in a clockwise direction. As the whine of car tires on the highway fades behind you, several things let you know you are approaching Big Sugar Creek. You will find yourself at the bottom of intersecting ravines, occasionally crossing small streams. The shade becomes denser and the forest smells more like a greenhouse. Notice the plants; pawpaw, bloodroot, ginger, and golden seal let you know you're in a shaded, moist, rich habitat.

A small, rocky stream soon appears on your right. Look for its small but lively inhabitants—whirligig beetles whirling on the surface and minnows schooling below. As you cross this stream at 1.05 mi. **[4]** look downstream and you'll see the wide, rocky bed of Big Sugar Creek. At the fork in the trail at 1.18 mi. **[5]** bear right. Emerging from the base of this ridge is the lone spring (1.20 mi.) **[6]** which will have a second, smaller outlet just eight feet to the right after a rainy period. Look for ginger and jack-in-the-pulpit just above the spring.

Another karst feature, a sinkhole, appears next to the trail on the right at 1.24 mi. **[7]**. Caused by the partial collapse of a cavern below, sinkholes sometimes hold water. Pickerelweed Pond, a state natural area in the park, features a sinkhole pond. The forest shows off its mighty white oaks and sugar maples as you hike through the heart of the Northwoods Wild Area. Ignore the spur to a camp at 1.46 mi. **[8]** and go straight. You'll cross several scenic streams and many ravines before reaching the connector link at 2.78 mi. **[9]** where you go straight.

Cross Highway KK at 2.89 mi. **[10]**. Cross several more streams and cross the park road at 4.2 mi. **[11]** near the entrance to Camp Dericotte. You'll soon emerge into an open forest with a tall canopy and a floor covered in violets, ginger, and ferns. Cross a wide stream at 5.0 mi. **[12]** with moss-covered boulders and tiny sand beaches. Just on the other side, look for a plant about shin-high with unusually wide, creased leaves. This is false hellebore, a plant rarely seen in bloom. Cross yet another stream and begin a hike uphill. Some ox-eye daisies will welcome you to Highway KK. Cross the highway at 5.54 mi. **[13]** and you'll soon return to **[3]**, where you turn right to return to the trailhead.

1. Start
2. Left turn
3. Trail registration
4. Small stream
5. Bear right
6. Lone spring
7. Sinkhole
8. Go straight
9. Go straight
10. Highway crossing
11. Road crossing
12. Stream crossing
13. Highway crossing

# Big Sugar Creek Trail— North Loop 🥾🥾🥾

**Distance Round-Trip:** 3.75 miles

**Estimated Hiking Time:** 2 hours

*After approaching what I thought was a stuffed animal lying in the trail I discovered a fresh fawn, camouflaged perfectly in the dappled shade. I snapped a quick photo and hiked on, knowing Mother was somewhere nearby, waiting for me to leave.*

**Caution:** Horses are not allowed on the north loop of this trail, but they are allowed on the connector link.

**Trail Directions:** Park in the lot for the trailhead on the west side of the main park road, halfway between Camp Sherwood Forest and Camp Dericotte. Begin hiking straight out from the parking lot **[1]** and you'll find a trail registration box at .05 mi. **[2]**. Please fill out a card.

Continue straight on the wide, old roadbed of the connector link, an easy, long descent. Look for red-spotted purple and great spangled fritillary butterflies socializing on the trail. At the bottom, go straight at the intersection at .90 mi. **[3],** marked with an orange marker. From here, follow blue arrows going clockwise. Turn right at .97 mi. **[4],** where the white trail goes straight. Here is a thickly vegetated floodplain of Big Sugar Creek. Notice the winged stems of white crownbeard, which may reach six feet tall before flowering. At 1.14 mi. **[5]** is an unusual tree with broad leaves in the shape of tulips. This is a tulip tree, an Appalachian hardwood that grew so big that pioneers hollowed out single logs to make long, lightweight canoes.

Just after passing the tulip tree, you'll see Big Sugar Creek on your left. Contrasted with the muddy and silty streams typical of north Missouri, Big Sugar Creek runs crystal clear over gravel and exposed limestone bedrock. Begin ascending the bluff over the river. Large dolomite boulders on the left complete the Ozark-like scene and invite you to climb them. As you turn away from the creek you enter an open forest crisscrossed with ravines and dominated by giant white oaks, sugar maples, and shagbark hickories. After you pass under a powerline, the habitat becomes drier. Here is dittany, fragrant sumac, and pussytoes. The trail swings to the left at 1.82 mi. **[6].** Pass under the powerline again, and it's down you go!

Hike on a shaded slope covered with Christmas and maidenhair ferns. At the bottom you'll find a sheltered cove, with limestone ledges on each side of you. Ravines intersect everywhere, pulling you in all directions, and you feel as if you've entered some type of geological crossroads. Cross an intermittent stream at 2.16 mi. **[7]**. You'll pass a pawpaw grove, some monster red oaks, and find a wet-weather spring in a ravine on your right.

Big Sugar Creek rolls right next to you at 2.52 mi. **[8],** where you can scan the slower pools for floating softshell turtles. Look carefully on rocks near the water for sunning water snakes. You'll see lots of their prey here—chubs, sunfish, and minnows. After you turn away from the creek you'll cross a small tributary at 2.64 mi. **[9]** and hike along it for a while. Steep slopes on both the left and right shelter moisture- and shade-loving plants like jack-in-the-pulpit, bloodroot, and ginger. After passing under a powerline, the trail puts you on top of a curving, dry ridgetop, and you feel as if you're hiking on the back of a big snake, with slopes falling away on each side. Turn right at the intersection at 3.16 mi. **[10]** and cross a final stream at 3.37 mi. **[11]** beneath basswood and sycamore trees. Turn left when you return to **[2]** to finish your hike.

1. Start
2. Trail registration
3. Go straight
4. Right turn
5. Tulip tree
6. Swing left
7. Stream crossing
8. Big Sugar Creek
9. Stream crossing
10. Right turn
11. Stream crossing

# 2.  Graham Cave State Park

- See the shelter cave that preserves evidence of human occupation as long ago as 7850 B.C., the first archaeological site in the nation to be designated a national historic landmark.
- Find a sandstone pirate's plank and fantastic wet-weather waterfalls over undercut stone ledges.
- Holler "Doodlebug! Doodlebug!" into an ant lion's pit to see if it's home.
- Hike on top of a geological rarity—a sandstone cave.
- Find the six-spotted tiger beetle, a metallic green beetle that runs and flies just ahead of you on the trail.

## Area Information

Caves in dolomite or limestone are common in Missouri (about five thousand by last count), but sandstone caves, like Graham Cave, are rare. Graham Cave was formed when softer, more soluble dolomite dissolved away from underneath a more resistant layer of St. Peter sandstone. This left an archlike cavity 120 feet wide and 16 feet high, extending about 100 feet into the hill. Two additional features of the cave—its location high enough on the hill to escape floods and its orientation almost due south, offering protection from northerly winter winds—set the stage for one of the greatest archaeological finds in the state.

Dr. Robert Graham came from Kentucky and settled in the area in 1816, buying rich bottomland along the Loutre River from Daniel Morgan Boone, one of Daniel Boone's sons, who became a property owner and land surveyor in the area with his father. In 1847 Graham bought the rocky tract that contained the cave, which remained in the Graham family. When archaeologists heard that the husband of Graham's great-granddaughter was bulldozing in the cave to enlarge it for his livestock, they persuaded him to stop and conducted excavations from 1949 through 1955. Their findings were astonishing—a

ten-thousand-year record of almost continuous human habitation in the cave. This was the oldest material and the best-preserved deposits found until that time. Because of the site's significance, portions have been left intact for future excavations.

**Directions:** From Danville, on I-70, take Highway TT west, which dead-ends at the park in two miles.

**Hours Open:**   The site is open year-round from 7 A.M. to sunset.

**Facilities:** A campground is available as well as picnic areas and playgrounds. Interpretive displays are located in the park office and in a shelter near the cave. A paved trail to the cave is available for people with disabilities. A boat ramp on the Loutre River offers access for boating and fishing.

**Permits and Rules:** Pets must always be leashed. As in all Missouri state parks, plants or animals may not be removed or damaged, although nuts, berries, and mushrooms may be collected for personal consumption.

**Further Information:** Park Superintendent, Graham Cave State Park, 217 Highway TT, Montgomery City, MO 63361; 573-564-3476.

## Other Areas of Interest

Located on some scenic hills along the Missouri River, the little town of **Hermann** preserves the culture of Missouri's early German immigrants. Vineyards, wineries, antique shops, galleries, and bed-and-breakfasts abound, and festivals in May and October feature German music, food, and the art of wine making. For more information call 573-751-4133.

**Deutschheim State Historic Site**, 109 West Second Street in Hermann, offers tours of two homes in the town's historic district. Tours of the Strehly House include the residence, the attached winery, and the first print shop in Hermann, which printed a German newspaper in the ground floor shop. A fee is charged for the tours. For more information call 573-486-2200.

# Graham Cave
# State Park

## L E G E N D

| | | | |
|---|---|---|---|
| —— | Road | ▬▬ | Boundary |
| ⋯⋯ | Trail | | |

🏠 Park Office

⛺ Graham Cave

△ Camping

◭ Camping With Electric

🔲 Picnic Area

🏛 Picnic Shelter

🔳 Interpretive Shelter

🚮 Trailer Dump Station

🚻 Restrooms

🥤 Water Fountain

🚤 Boat Ramp

🚰 Well

Indian Glade Trail

To
Montgomery City
8 Miles

TT

Loutre River Trail

Loutre River

N

# Indian Glade Trail

**Distance Round-Trip:** 2.25 miles

**Estimated Hiking Time:** 1.5 hours

*Archaeologically, Graham Cave is of national importance. Geologically, it is a rare and splendid example. Aesthetically, its elegant arch inspires wonder and delight.*

**Caution:** Watch for traffic when crossing the main park road.

**Trail Directions:** Park near the rest rooms in the campground; the trail begins at the signboard **[1]** across the road from the rest rooms. As you begin, notice the rocks. The thin, crumbly layers of stone on your left at .09 mi. **[2]** are limestone, but you'll find sandstone outcrops here too. Notice that the trail sometimes gets soft from the pure sand that collects there, eroded from sandstone.

Cross a small wooden bridge at .18 mi. **[3]**. Sandstone erodes into some strange-looking shapes—check out the pirate's plank jutting out from the trail over the valley on your right at .31 mi. **[4]**. Another fantastic feature will appear at .36 mi.—a wet-weather waterfall **[5]**. Note how the rock ledge is eroded and undercut—a characteristic of sandstone. Cross the wooden bridge over the waterfall and turn right at the intersection after crossing another bridge at .42 mi. **[6]**.

Look for shooting stars along the trail here, as well as maidenhair ferns and a plant that looks like a fern but isn't—lousewort. You'll cross the main park road at .68 mi. **[7]**. Venus's looking glass and spiderwort welcome you to a small glade at .80 mi. **[8]**. Prickly pear cactus is here, too, which produces big, beautiful, yellow blossoms in June and July. Take the trail to your right through the glade and take the wooden steps down. At the bottom of the steps, turn right at an amazingly contorted cedar tree. At .86 mi. **[9]** you'll come upon the graceful arch of Graham Cave. Several interpretive signs nearby explain segments of the cave's long history, including its geological origin, its occupation by prehistoric cultures as long ago as 7850 B.C., and its more recent use as a hog shed. Turn right, down the paved walkway, to continue.

At the bottom of the walkway is a parking lot. Find the trail on the opposite side of the lot to continue. When you find a dome of sandstone boulders at 1.08 mi. look around for perfectly round little depressions in the sand. These are ant lion pits **[10]**, which act as traps for ants and other small insects. Predatory insect larvae with long, spiny jaws wait at the bottom of each pit, just under the surface. Shouting their nickname "doodlebug" into their pit causes debris to fall from the sides, sometimes tricking the ant lion into motion.

A long sandstone wall clad in all manner of lichens, mosses, and ferns will soon accompany you for a while. At 1.33 mi. **[11]** you could take advantage of the spur to the interpretive shelter, with more displays on the cave and surrounding area—otherwise, turn right. Ignore the spur on your right crossed by logs at 1.35 mi. **[12]** and go straight. You'll soon find another undercut sandstone wet-weather waterfall. Ascend the steps here and turn right at the intersection at the top. You'll emerge onto the solid rock of Graham Cave's roof at 1.46 mi. **[13]**, an interesting place to ponder prehistoric peoples' activities below. Turn right here, up a steep, rocky hill. Cross the park road again at 1.61 mi. **[14]** and turn into the woods again behind the rest rooms. Turn right when you return to **[6]** to complete your hike.

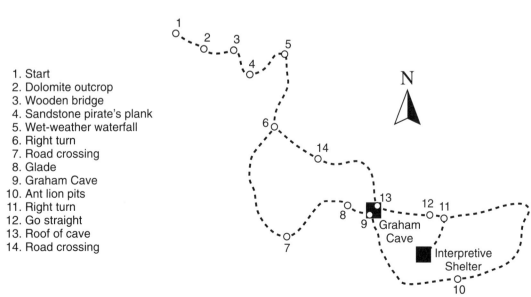

1. Start
2. Dolomite outcrop
3. Wooden bridge
4. Sandstone pirate's plank
5. Wet-weather waterfall
6. Right turn
7. Road crossing
8. Glade
9. Graham Cave
10. Ant lion pits
11. Right turn
12. Go straight
13. Roof of cave
14. Road crossing

# Loutre River Trail 👢👢👢

**Distance Round-Trip:** 1.5 miles

**Estimated Hiking Time:** 1 hour

*I pass a tropical pawpaw grove and descend onto the shadowy floodplain of the Loutre. Thick grapevines trail through the balmy air, suspended from the sprawling branches of enormous shagbark hickory trees. A spider monkey jumps from a treetop branch, startling a toucan, which lands just over my head . . . No, not really, but it was easy to imagine.*

**Caution:** Stay on the trail in the floodplain to avoid stinging nettles.

**Trail Directions:** Park in the campground and begin the trail at the signboard near the rest rooms **[1].** The trail takes you downhill over some sandstone boulders and occasional slabs of bedrock. Where outcrops appear on this sideslope they are often undercut, forming overhanging ledges. Tall red oaks, ash, and sugar maples produce dense and welcome shade.

Cross a small stream at .11 mi. **[2]** and go straight, ignoring the spurs to the left. Look for rattlesnake ferns here, as well as false Solomon's seal and moonseed. Turn left at the intersection at .19 mi. **[3].** You'll find a pawpaw grove at .27 mi. **[4],** identified by trees from 5 to 15 feet high with very large leaves that fan out like fingers on a spread hand. The only tropical tree that lives in Missouri, the pawpaw produces a four-inch peanut-shaped fruit in October that tastes like a banana.

At the bottom of the hill you descend into the Loutre River floodplain, where the trunks of the trees grow thicker and the lush vegetation grows taller. The breeze at the top of the hill that might have dissuaded the mosquitoes is now lacking. At .54 mi. **[5]** turn right on a wide mowed path and take one of several spurs down to the river. Sneak quietly to improve your chances of seeing herons stalking in the shallows, teal gathering in slack water, or kingfishers perching on snags. On a warm summer day you will probably see a myriad of butterflies assembled near the water, looking for moisture and mates.

Turn left after returning to the trail, which parallels the river for a while. If you see a brilliant green insect flying just ahead of you (great blue heron style) on the trail, you have discovered the six-spotted tiger beetle. They are plentiful on these sandy trails, their favorite haunts. Several views of the river open up through the trees, giving you chances to see aquatic turtles lying next to the water or longnose gar sunning just under the surface. Pass the connector link at .76 mi. **[6]** and go straight. Just after crossing a small stream you'll find a beautiful wet-weather waterfall at .90 mi. **[7],** its pool alive with crayfish, camouflaged with the bottom gravel.

A glade remnant appears on your left at 1.09 mi. **[8],** marked by exposed bedrock, native bluestem grasses, and several species of wildflowers. Turn right at 1.37 mi. **[9]** onto the pavement of the campground loop. Turn right to return to the trailhead.

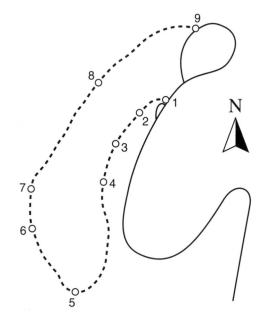

1. Start
2. Stream crossing
3. Left turn
4. Pawpaw grove
5. Spurs to river
6. Go straight
7. Wet-weather waterfall
8. Glade remnant
9. Right turn

# 3. Rock Bridge Memorial State Park

- Get a first-hand education in karst topography and enjoy a pleasant hike at the same time.
- Hike through the natural tunnel of a 63-foot-tall rock bridge, the remnant of an ancient cave passage, now collapsed.
- See a potpourri of karst features—a natural bridge, cave entrance, karst window, sinkholes, a pirated stream, and collapsed cave chasm—all on one short trail.

## Area Information

People have always been attracted to remarkable geologic features like the rock bridge at Rock Bridge Memorial State Park. A small town had sprung up near the bridge by the early 1800s. Over time, it included a grist mill, paper mill, blacksmith shop, general store, post office, and two whiskey distilleries. Although the settlement of Pierpont (French for "rock bridge") is no longer here, the geologic features continue to attract and intrigue visitors.

After your hikes, you can visit the Pierpont general store, just one mile south of here. Still with its wooden plank floor and still selling ice cream and soda, the store originally stood near the rock bridge but was moved after a fire in 1889.

Although the rock bridge is the centerpiece of the park, it is only a small remnant of something larger, though much less obvious—Devil's Icebox Cave. Even though perforated with sinkholes and partly destroyed by erosion, Devil's Icebox is still a living cave and, with over six miles of mapped passage, Missouri's sixth largest. The rock bridge and cave are part of a vast and ancient system of limestone, underground streams, air-filled passages, and surface drainage—a landscape known as karst topography. Come and explore!

**Directions:** The park is seven miles south of Columbia on Highway 163.

**Hours Open:** The park is open year-round from dawn until dusk.

**Facilities:** Picnic areas and playgrounds are near the park office. The site also offers bicycling, horseback riding, orienteering, and fishing in park ponds. Tours of Devil's Icebox Cave are given by reservation only for experienced and properly equipped groups.

**Permits and Rules:** Bicycling is allowed on most trails, but cyclists must heed the open or closed signs along the two main entrance roads to the park. The Trail Condition Hotline (573-442-2249) informs riders when the trails are temporarily closed because of wet conditions. Bicycling is never allowed in the Gans Creek Wild Area. Horseback riding is permitted only in the wild area from June 1 through October 31. Trail condition rules also apply to equestrians. No rock climbing, rappelling, or ATV use is permitted. Entry to Devil's Icebox Cave is prohibited except to those participating in park-led tours. All pets must be leashed. Bicyclists must wear helmets.

**Further Information:** Park Superintendent, Rock Bridge Memorial State Park, 5901 South Highway 163, Columbia, MO 65203; 573-449-7402.

## Park Trails

**Karst Trail** 🥾🥾—1.75 miles—The dozens of sinkholes seen from this trail are visible proof that this land (called a sinkhole plain) is resting on the roof of Devil's Icebox Cave. The trailhead is on Fox Lane, just .5 mile east of Pierpont store.

**Sinkhole Trail** 🥾🥾—1.5 miles—Hike past the ruins of a building foundation built into a stone outcrop at the historic site of Pierpont. The trail begins at the south end of the Devil's Icebox parking lot.

**Deer Run Trail** 🥾🥾🥾—3 miles—This trail takes you up and down wooded hills and along the banks of the Little Bonne Femme Creek. The trailhead is behind the rest rooms on the northernmost picnic loop.

**High Ridge Trail** 🥾🥾🥾—1.75 miles—The trail takes you alongside Clear Creek and onto an open hilltop with rolling, grassy slopes and great views of surrounding wooded hills. The trailhead is on Rock Quarry Road, .1 mile north of the driveway to the Devil's Icebox parking lot.

**Grassland Trail** 🥾—2 miles—Like the Karst and High Ridge Trails, this trail goes through areas being restored to native grassland by selective cutting and burning. The trailhead is on Rockbridge Lane, .8 mile south of the driveway to the Devil's Icebox parking lot.

Rock Bridge
Memorial State Park

N

Paxton
Trailhead

K

163

Deer Run
Trailhead

High
Ridge
Trail

Spring
Brook
Trailhead

Deer Run Trail

Gan's Creek
Trailhead

Devil's Icebox
Trailhead

Spring Brook Trail

Devil's
Icebox
Trail

S

S

Rock Bridge Lane

Grassland
Trailhead

Rock Bridge Lane

Grassland Trail

LEGEND

Paved Road

Gravel Road

Trail

Boundary

Park Office

Shelter

Devil's Icebox

Trailhead

Bridge

Cave

Silo

High Point Lane

# Devil's Icebox Trail 👢👢👢

**Distance Round-Trip:** .5 mile

**Estimated Hiking Time:** .75 hour

*As if looking down into a sinkhole to view an underground river wasn't bizarre enough, I then found that this cave stream is home to a pink planarian, a type of flatworm. Found nowhere else in the world, the pink planarian reproduces by splitting itself right down the middle!*

**Caution:** Watch your head when passing through the tunnel under the rock bridge.

**Trail Directions:** This is a self-guiding trail. Booklets that interpret the numbered stations along the trail are available at the park office for a small fee. Numbered features here do not coincide with numbers in the booklet. Park in the lot for the rock bridge and begin the trail **[1]** at the interpretive signs at the west end of the lot. Near the trailhead, you'll cross a pair of wooden bridges over streams. Blue-eyed Mary and wild sweet William color the streamsides while hackberry, boxelder, and Ohio buckeye trees shade the trail.

Some historians believe the rocky path at .05 mi. **[2]** is the roadbed of the Old Providence Plank Road, built in 1856 from Columbia to the Missouri River port of Providence and covered with wooden planks. Further evidence of Rock Bridge's cultural history appears on your right at .08 mi. Rock quarried from this hole in the rock wall **[3]** in the early 1800s was used for foundations and for a dam under the rock

bridge. Columbine now graces the vertical limestone walls. While the rock bridge invites you forward, a sign at .09 mi. describes the succession of mills that stood in this spot **[4]**.

Ascend the steps to your right to continue. At the top, you'll get a close look at limestone, which is relatively soft and porous. The abundance of this layered stone and the dissolving action of water over time are what have created Rock Bridge's fantastic karst features. From the rock bridge overlook at .18 mi. **[5]** you can look upstream and see the steep sides of the canyon that were once part of a cave passage. The bridge you are now standing on is the portion of the cavern's roof that did not collapse.

The Devil's Icebox overlook at .30 mi. **[6]** puts you on top of another cave roof, but this one is still intact. The sinkhole to your left, lined with lush mosses and ferns, is the only known entrance to Devil's Icebox Cave. The sinkhole on your right, called a karst window, offers a glimpse of the cave stream that has already traveled seven miles underground. Nearby, the stream returns to the surface before flowing under the rock bridge. Descend the steps to your left. If you are here on a warm day, you will suddenly realize the reason for this sinkhole's name. Ascend the steps and take the boardwalk on your left to continue.

You'll find several more views of sinkholes and the collapsed cave chasm before arriving at the entrance to the rock bridge's natural tunnel at .49 mi. **[7]**. Look on your right to see a part of the dam built in the early 1800s to provide waterpower for the mills and distilleries that once stood here. Go straight when you return to **[4]** to complete your hike.

1. Start
2. Old Providence Plank Road
3. Quarry
4. Old mill site
5. Rock Bridge overlook
6. Devil's Icebox overlook
7. Tunnel entrance

Parking

Rock Bridge

Devil's Icebox Cave

Devil's Icebox Sinkhole

Connor's Cave

N

# Spring Brook Trail 👢👢👢

**Distance Round-Trip:** 2.5 miles

**Estimated Hiking Time:** 1.5 hours

*Getting caught in a sudden rain shower in the woods isn't so bad. Gray tree frogs start up their musical trills, the aroma of nature's greenhouse rises to your nostrils, and wet-weather waterfalls contribute their short-lived, splashing music.*

**Caution:** A friendly, shallow, and refreshing wade is scheduled just before the two-mile mark. Do not attempt this river crossing during periods of high water. Also, watch out for bicyclists.

**Trail Directions:** Park at the picnic shelter near the park office and begin the trail **[1]** near the rest rooms. Go straight at the intersection at .02 mi. **[2]**. Pass a frightful honey locust tree on your right and continue through a thicket of cedars and brush. Turn left at the intersection at .35 mi. **[3]**. Soon you'll descend to a flat bottomland of the Little Bonne Femme Creek, where the massive trunks of cottonwoods and sycamores erupt from the carpet of lush floodplain plants.

Enjoy a scenic view of the winding creek from the bridge at .55 mi. **[4]**. You'll pass a wet-weather waterfall at .61 mi. **[5]**, nestled in a limestone outcrop on your right. Turn left just after you pass a bench at .80 mi. **[6]**. Jack-in-the-pulpits, as well as ginger, bloodroot, and wild geranium, adorn the rich slope on your right. Cross a wooden bridge at .97 mi. **[7]** and turn right. Cross a smaller bridge and go straight at the spur at 1.09 mi. **[8]**. Soon you'll be at the parking lot for the Devil's Icebox Trail **[9]**.

Begin the Devil's Icebox Trail, crossing the pair of wooden bridges. Turn right on the wide, unmarked rocky path at 1.21 mi. **[10]**, known as Old Providence Plank Road. The trail passes a variety of senior trees, some of which may have been here when the plank road was constructed in 1856. The trail travels alongside the boardwalk of the Devil's Icebox Trail for a short distance before veering off to the right. Go straight at the intersection at 1.35 mi. **[11]** and turn right at 1.46 mi. **[12]**. You'll pass through an old field with grassy openings. The thickets of blackberries, roses, and gooseberries indicate this area was probably once grazed; the plants that survived were the thorny ones that the cows passed over.

At a zigzag in the trail at 1.69 mi. **[13]** is a grove of persimmon trees. Look for tall, thin-trunked trees with knobby bark. Come fall, these trees produce a delectable fruit with such a flavor that entire cookbooks have been written about them. Although it looks like poison ivy, the shrub at the base of these trees is fragrant sumac, a plant that announces autumn by turning shades of yellow, deep violet, and scarlet. Turn left at the intersection at 1.74 mi. **[14]**. Cross a small stream and turn right at 1.89 mi. **[15]**, just after passing giant red oak and sycamore trees on your right. Now it's time for a little wade! Normally, the water here is only a few inches deep, and you might even find enough dry stepping-stones to cross the river **[16]** (1.90 mi.) without getting wet. Turn right when you get to the other side. Go straight at several spur intersections here. Turn right at 2.10 mi. **[17]** just after crossing a small stream and turn left when you return to **[3]** to finish your hike.

1. Start
2. Go straight
3. Left turn
4. Bridge
5. Wet-weather waterfall
6. Left turn
7. Right turn
8. Go straight
9. Devil's Icebox trailhead
10. Right turn
11. Go straight
12. Right turn
13. Persimmon grove
14. Left turn
15. Right turn
16. River crossing (wet)
17. Right turn

# 4. Katy Trail State Park

- Throw some diversity into your hiking and come hike "the Katy." It's scenic, flat as a board, and 233 miles long!
- Hike within a few feet of the mighty Missouri River while majestic river bluffs tower overhead.
- See the last remaining pictograph in the area painted by Native Americans on a sheer bluff face and described in Lewis and Clark's field notes of 1804.
- Wander through a 243-foot-long railroad tunnel constructed in 1892–93, the only tunnel on the Missouri-Kansas-Texas line.
- See Missouri's largest bur oak tree, a plant you have to hike *under* to appreciate.

## Area Information

Katy Trail State Park, while following the Missouri River for most of its route, is itself a river of magnificence, history, and recreation. Built on the former corridor of the Missouri-Kansas-Texas (MKT, or "Katy") Railroad, the park is 233 miles long and only 100 feet wide. Of more than 1,000 rail-to-trail conversions in the nation, it is one of the longest, stretching from Machens to Clinton. The Katy is designed specifically for hikers and bicyclists.

Pre–Civil War Rocheport ("port of rocks"), a trailhead for the Katy Trail, began in 1825 as an important crossing on the Boone's Lick Road trade route. Rocheport thrived as a river and ferry port and became a key shipping point between St. Louis and St. Joseph. Farming, grist milling, ice sales, and steamboat tourism were already in place when the MKT Railroad rolled into town in 1892, accelerating its economy. Rocheport is on the National Register of Historic Places.

The Katy Trail parallels the river route taken by the Lewis and Clark expedition, which in 1804 stopped in the area of Rocheport and the Big Moniteau Bluffs. Clark's field notes on June 7 mention "Several Courious Paintings and Carveings in the projecting rock of Limestone" and "spots within semi-circles, half-resembling the human eye," the latter descrip-

tion, no doubt, referring to the remaining pictograph visible above Lewis and Clark Cave.

**Directions:** Rocheport is west of Columbia off I-70. Take exit 115 and go north on Route BB for 2 miles into town. McBaine is southwest of Columbia. Take Highway 163 south for 3.4 miles. Take Highway K south an additional 7.3 miles. Turn right at McBaine at the sign for the park.

**Hours Open:** The trail is open only during daylight hours, year-round.

**Facilities:** Facilities vary at different trailheads. Rocheport caters to trail users, offering bike rentals, cafes, and bed-and-breakfasts, as well as rest rooms and drinking water. The McBaine trailhead has only rest rooms.

**Permits and Rules:** All motorized equipment is prohibited on the trail except motorized wheelchairs. Also prohibited are horses, camping, rock climbing, and shooting. Pets must be leashed.

**Further Information:** Missouri Department of Natural Resources, Division of State Parks, P.O. Box 176, Jefferson City, MO 65102; 800-334-6946. To reach the Rocheport Merchants Association call 573-698-2206.

## Other Areas of Interest

**Hartsburg** is another little river town revitalized by the Katy and offers hay rides, music, games, food, (and tons of pumpkins) at its increasingly popular fall Pumpkin Festival. Hartsburg is north of Jefferson City off Highway 63. For more information call the Missouri Division of Tourism at 573-751-4133.

**Les Bourgeois Winery** is on Route BB, just one mile south of Rocheport, and offers wine tasting and a bistro situated on a bluff overlooking the Missouri River. For more information call 573-698-3401.

**The Pinnacles Natural Area** features cliffs, arches, narrows, and pinnacles formed in limestone along three high-quality streams. A hiking trail traverses some of the pinnacles and explores the 27-acre hiking area, which is 11 miles north of Columbia off Highway 63. For more information call 573-449-2541.

## Park Trails

The Katy Trail provides infinite options for day hiking across the state, especially if a shuttle is

available. The trail is marked every mile with a signpost. Trailhead mileage charts and brochures are available from the Missouri Department of Natural Resources.

# Katy Trail State Park

Machens

St. Charles

Greens Bottom

Weldon Spring
Defiance
Matson

Augusta

Dutzow

Marthasville

Treloar

McKittrick

Portland

Mokane

Tebbetts

Wainwright

Hartsburg

McBaine

Rocheport

New Franklin

Boonville

Pilot
Grove

Clifton
City

Sedalia

Green
Ridge

Windsor

Calhoun

Clinton

70

61

40

47

19

54

63

50

5

135

65

13

N

## L E G E N D

— Road

······ Open Trail

- - - Undeveloped Trail

▬▬ County Boundary

★ Trailhead

◣ Undeveloped Trailhead

# Historic Rocheport and MKT Tunnel 🥾

**Distance Round-Trip:** 1.5 miles

**Estimated Hiking Time:** .75 hour

*Extend your hike on the Katy Trail. Bring your suitcase and stay at a bed and breakfast. Rocheport will charm you with its rich history, scenery, and hospitality.*

**Caution:** You won't find too many people driving fast in Rocheport but be careful at street crossings anyway.

**Trail Directions:** As you enter Rocheport from the interstate, turn left on Pike Street and park in the lot for the Katy Trail. The hike begins **[1]** at the far end of the lot, where monstrous cottonwood trees provide some shaded parking. The gray building here with the steeple was originally the Mt. Nebo Baptist Church **[2]**, built before the Civil War by black slaves for their use. Currently, the building is a restaurant, serving Rocheport visitors and residents alike.

Pass the Katy Depot **[3]** on your left and turn north on Pike Street, next to Trailside Cafe and Bike Rental. Turn left on Second Street, right on Clark Street, and left on Third Street. The School House Bed and Breakfast, at this corner, was built in 1914 as Rocheport's school for grades 1 through 12. The black slate floor of the entryway is made from the school's original blackboards. At .26 mi. **[4]** is the Community Hall, erected as a Baptist church in 1860. Pass several antique shops and galleries and turn right on Lewis Street.

The small, curious building coming into view on your right, erected in 1870, is the last remaining ice house in Rocheport **[5]** (.32 mi.). For business in the 1800s, as now, timing was everything. Ice blocks were cut from the Missouri River and Moniteau Creek in the winter and stored in ice houses between layers of sawdust and straw. Come summer, these ice houses held a lucrative commodity. The **A**-frame roof accommodated pulleys used to lift out the ice blocks. Turn right after returning to Third Street.

After one block turn left on Columbia Street. The United Methodist Church stands at .45 mi. **[6]**; its original building was constructed in 1844. Turn right on Second Street. The red granite stone on your left at .50 mi. **[7]** marks Rocheport as a major crossing on the Boone's Lick Road, an important trade route from an area to the north, where the sons of Daniel Boone recovered salt from natural salt springs in the early 1800s. Deer and other animals frequently licked minerals from these areas, which thus were called licks. Across the street is the Christian Church **[8]**, erected in 1847. The home of river captain John Kaiser **[9]** (.54 mi.), built around 1830, stands at this corner on your left. It is one of the few buildings in town that survived the major floods of the mid-1800s, the Civil War raids of the 1860s, and a disastrous fire in 1922.

Cross this intersection, continuing on Second Street. Turn left on Moniteau Street. The Friends of Rocheport Historical Museum at .66 mi. **[10]** contains artifacts from the area's rich cultural past. Turn right on the limestone gravel of the Katy Trail. After crossing a wooden bridge over Moniteau Creek you'll arrive at the yawning mouth of the MKT Tunnel at .82 mi. **[11]**. Hike through the tunnel to feel the drafts of cool air and see the original stonework, done in 1892 and 1893. To finish the trail, turn around toward Rocheport and stay on the Katy Trail until you return to the parking lot at the depot.

1. Start
2. Mt. Nebo Baptist Church
3. Katy Depot
4. Community Hall
5. Ice house
6. United Methodist Church
7. Boone's Lick Road marker
8. Christian Church
9. Kaiser-Dimmit home
10. Historical museum
11. MKT Tunnel

# McBaine to Lewis and Clark Cave 🥾

**Distance Round-Trip:** 9.75 miles

**Estimated Hiking Time:** 4 hours

*The biggest bur oak, all the indigo buntings, and the cave were interesting, but it was the lone pictograph high on the smooth rock bluff that intrigued me most. Who painted it, and what does it mean? How did they get up there . . . on that tiny ledge?*

**Caution:** Bring sunglasses and sunscreen (unless you are here in winter). The white limestone trail and the Missouri River reflect a lot of sunshine.

**Trail Directions:** Park in the lot for the Katy Trail in McBaine and begin hiking **[1]** on your right as you enter the trail. The terrain is easy, flat, and wide the whole way. The two advantages of this are that you'll not be surprised by hills at the end of the hike or (as long as you stay on the trail) come across ticks or chiggers.

The bridge over Perche Creek at .07 mi. **[2]** attests to the earnestness that railway engineers applied to bridge building. Handsome and strong, many of the bridges along the trail, built in the 1890s, remain today for use by hikers and bikers. The gravel roads at .20 mi. **[3]** lead to the constructed wetland cells that are the final stage of Columbia's innovative wastewater treatment program. After conventional treatment, the city's wastewater is pumped through a series of wetlands, where aquatic plants metabolize pollutants naturally. The clean water is then used to create wetland habitat for waterfowl at Eagle Bluffs Conservation Area. The MKT spur to Columbia at .25 mi. **[4]**, also a recycled abandoned railway, is 8.9 miles long.

As you continue, look through breaks in the trees into the large crop field on your left. You'll see three trees in this field, a sycamore and two bur oaks. Turn left at the intersection at 1.13 mi. **[5]** and keep your eyes on the tree on the left. This big field has a way of distorting your sense of proportion. The tree on the left, with the widest crown, may not look exceptionally big from a distance, but wait until you get under it. At over 350 years old, this is Missouri's state champion bur oak. Although a bur oak at Big Oak Tree State Park (see park #17) is nearly twice as tall,

this tree has the widest trunk and crown (1.28 mi.) **[6]**. Return to the main trail and turn left to continue. A plaque on the bridge at 3.48 mi. dates it at 1899.

Soon, the hill on your right becomes steeper and bluff faces start to appear through the trees. By 4.19 mi. the Big Moniteau Bluffs **[7]** are overhead and straight up and down. Vines of Virginia creeper, grape, and trumpet creeper string their way across the bluffs, taking advantage of the abundant sunshine. Somehow, the mighty Missouri River suddenly appears on your left. When the bluffs on the right get taller you are near your destination. Listen for rushing water; you will probably hear Lewis and Clark Cave before you see it. With its entrance hidden by some trailside trees, the cave is at 5.0 mi. **[8]**. Although trail users are not allowed in the cave, you can stand at the entrance, feel the cave air, and see the ferns, liverworts, and mosses living just above the cave stream. Step back onto the trail and look above the cave. The last Big Moniteau Bluffs pictograph is here, a red boomerang with a dot above it. Possibly intended for ancient river travelers, perhaps a symbol marking the cave, its meaning is a mystery. A bench and some large rocks here make a good spot for resting. Retrace your steps to return to the trailhead.

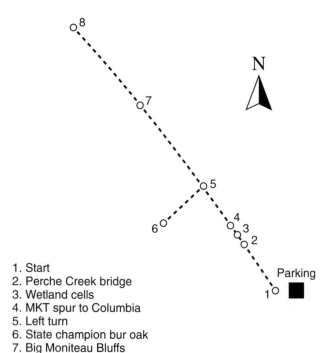

1. Start
2. Perche Creek bridge
3. Wetland cells
4. MKT spur to Columbia
5. Left turn
6. State champion bur oak
7. Big Moniteau Bluffs
8. Lewis and Clark Cave

# 5.  Mark Twain State Park and Historic Site

- Spy a giant aluminum butterfly, actually a hyperbolic paraboloid, from a Mark Twain Lake overlook.
- See the 420-square-foot cabin where a family of eight lived when Samuel was born.
- Spot the striking red-headed woodpecker in a lake cove "ghost forest."

## Area Information

John and Jane Clemens moved from Tennessee and had lived in their two-room cabin in Florida, Missouri, for only six months before Samuel was born on November 30, 1835. Writing under his pen name, Mark Twain, Clemens later wrote, ". . . I was postponed . . . to Missouri. Missouri was an unknown new state and needed attractions."

Established in 1924 to honor Monroe County's native son, Mark Twain State Park is the third oldest state park in Missouri and surrounds the historic site memorial museum. For decades, Mark Twain State Park consisted of rugged, forested hills overlooking the scenic Salt River, where Clemens spent his boyhood summers. But in 1983, 18,600-acre Mark Twain Lake was built, and now the park is reservoir based.

On seeing a picture of his birthplace cabin, Clemens wrote, "Heretofore I have always stated that it was a palace, but I shall be more guarded now." The soaring roof of Mark Twain Birthplace State Historic Site now protects this humble cabin, as well as a wealth of artifacts, exhibits, and Clemens family belongings in a museum, where visitors can come to contemplate Twain's wit, good-natured insight, and contribution to our national culture.

**Directions:** Travel east of Paris on Highway 154 for 12.3 miles. Turn north on Highway 107 for 2.7 miles. Turn east on Highway U for .4 mile to the historic site.

**Hours Open:** The site is open year-round except for Christmas, Thanksgiving, Easter, and New Year's Day. The historic site hours are 10 A.M. to 4 P.M. Monday through Saturday and noon to 6 P.M. on Sunday.

**Facilities:** The historic site offers a public reading room, museum exhibits, and tours for a small fee. The state park has campgrounds, picnic areas, overlooks, and facilities for fishing, swimming, and boating.

**Permits and Rules:** Pets must always be leashed.

**Further Information:** Park Superintendent, Mark Twain State Park, Route 1, Box 54, Stoutsville, MO 65283; 573-565-3440. To reach the historic site call 573-565-3449.

## Other Areas of Interest

Just across Highway U from the turnoff for the historic site is the **Florida Cemetery**, where several Clemens family members are buried including Samuel's sister, Margaret, and an uncle, John Quarles. A red granite monument stands in **Florida, Missouri,** at the original site of the birthplace cabin, just east of the historic site on Highway U.

The **Union Covered Bridge** is one of only four covered bridges remaining in the state and Missouri's only surviving example of the Burr-arch truss system. It is five miles west of Paris and four miles south on Highway C. For more information call the historic site.

U.S. Army Corps of Engineers' **Clarence Cannon Dam** offers multiple water recreation facilities, campgrounds, and hiking trails along Mark Twain Lake. For more information call 573-735-4097.

## Park Trails

**Historic Site Loop Trail** —.38 mile—The hike begins at the end of the paved road to the historic site and winds through an oak-savanna landscape on a peninsula between the lake and a cove.

# Mark Twain State Park and Historic Site

# Sugar Maple Trail 👢👢

**Distance Round-Trip:** .5 mile

**Estimated Hiking Time:** .25 hour

*Hike quietly when approaching the secluded lake cove and look for wood ducks, which nest in natural cavities of the dead standing trees. You'll see various woodpeckers, too. Scan the shoreline for deer, wild turkey, and red fox.*

**Caution:** During wet periods the trail will be muddy in the numerous small stream crossings.

**Trail Directions:** Find the trailhead for both the Sugar Maple Trail and the White Oak Trail near the scenic overlook in the Buzzard's Roost Picnic Area. For the first .29 mile both trails are the same. Begin at the trail sign **[1]**.

Once leveled by great sheets of ice, this area is more hilly and rugged than the surrounding level topography because of the carving action of the Salt River and its tributaries. The up-and-down hikes here are more reminiscent of the Ozarks than of north Missouri. At .03 mi. **[2]** cross a small drainage stream and go straight at the intersection. Take the small spur on your right at .05 mi. **[3]** to view Mark Twain Lake, created in 1983 by damming the Salt River. You can still see towering limestone bluffs carved by the river along some edges of the lake. The Buzzard's Roost area and other blufftop parts of the park that once overlooked the Salt River valley now overlook this 18,600-acre lake, created for hydroelectric power and recreation.

Return to the main trail and continue on your right. The trail turns into a fine lake overlook at .15 mi. **[4].** From here you can watch for ospreys in the summer or bald eagles in the winter. Turkey vultures (nicknamed buzzards) will usually be soaring in wide circles, quickly tilting their outstretched wings from side to side to keep balanced.

As you hike across the ends of these small ridges dissected by numerous drainage ravines, look for the orange yellow blossoms of hoary puccoon from March to June. Later, you'll find the purple flower spikes of lead plant, so named for its ashy gray leaves. Purple prairie clover also thrives in the more open areas of these dry, rocky woods.

Turn left at the intersection at .29 mi. **[5]** where the Sugar Maple Trail leaves the White Oak Trail. You'll hike through an open forest of mature white oaks, black oaks, and sugar maples, which put on a show of colors here in October. Turn left at .38 mi. **[6]** and turn right at **[2]** to return to the trail sign.

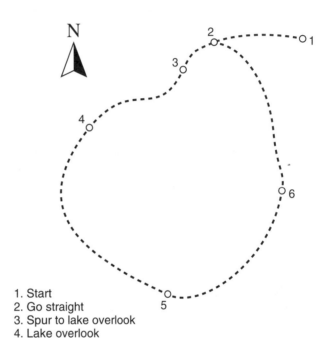

1. Start
2. Go straight
3. Spur to lake overlook
4. Lake overlook
5. Left turn
6. Left turn

# White Oak Trail

**Distance Round-Trip:** 6 miles

**Estimated Hiking Time:** 3 hours

*While hiking near the campground I came upon two furry baby red foxes, wrestling with each other on the trail. They didn't seem to mind me, but a bark from their nearby mother sent them scurrying into their den, tumbling over each other in their hurry.*

**Caution:** During wet periods the trail will be muddy in the numerous small stream crossings.

**Trail Directions:** Find the trailhead for both the Sugar Maple Trail and the White Oak Trail near the scenic overlook in the Buzzard's Roost Picnic Area. For the first .29 mile both trails are the same. The White Oak Trail may also be accessed in the campground for loop hikes of 2 and 3 miles. The main trail is marked in a counterclockwise direction with red arrows.

Begin at the trail sign **[1]** and go straight when you come to the intersection at .03 mi. **[2]**. At .15 mi. **[3]** you'll find the first of many splendid views of Mark Twain Lake. Turn right at .29 mi. **[4]** where the White Oak Trail leaves the Sugar Maple Trail. Go straight at the intersection at .37 mi. **[5]**.

Look beyond the Highway 107 bridge at the lake overlook at .93 mi. **[6]** and you'll see what looks like a giant aluminum butterfly, its wings spread in a graceful, wide V. This is the Mark Twain Birthplace

Historic Site building, specially engineered and constructed to protect the two-room clapboard cabin in which Samuel Clemens was born in 1835. Before or after hiking, be sure to stop in the historic site to see the cabin, a handwritten manuscript of *The Adventures of Tom Sawyer*, and other exhibits of Clemens's career.

The trail parallels the main body of the lake before bringing you to a cove. This is a fairly new lake, and many flooded trees have died but not yet fallen. Like many others, this cove is a ghost forest, and is a good place to look for the striking red-headed woodpecker, which prefers open, mature deciduous forests. Cross a small wooden bridge at the end of the cove before turning right at the intersection at 1.45 mi. **[7]**. Turn right again at the white connecting link at 2.29 mi. **[8]**.

After hiking past the last cove on the north shore of this peninsula, go straight at the intersection at 3.03 mi. **[9]** to begin hiking the south shore. From March through June, look for several patches of bluebells along the trail here, nodding their blue heads in the lake breezes. Turn right at the white connecting link at 3.40 mi. **[10]** and you'll soon cross the paved road to the boat ramp. Go straight at the intersection at 3.48 mi. **[11]**. Turn right at 4.01 mi. **[12]** after hiking over a ridge knob with views of several lake coves. You'll cross a woodchip path and the campground road before returning to **[7]**, where you turn right and enjoy more lake and forest views on your way back to the trailhead.

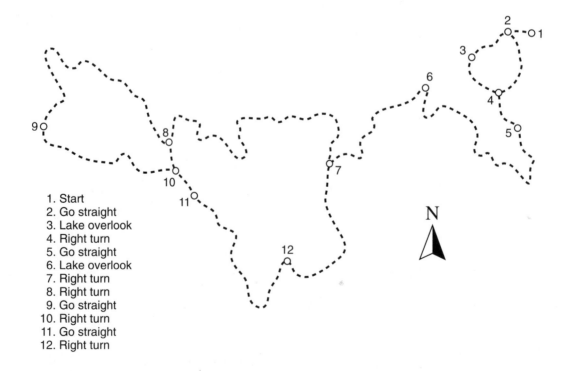

1. Start
2. Go straight
3. Lake overlook
4. Right turn
5. Go straight
6. Lake overlook
7. Right turn
8. Right turn
9. Go straight
10. Right turn
11. Go straight
12. Right turn

N

# 6.  Battle of Athens State Historic Site

- Walk around the 19th-century town of Athens, where a Confederate cannon (improvised from a hollow log) exploded with its first shot, where a 350-pound infantry captain (named Captain Small) successfully held the town's left flank despite his colleagues' defection, and where the Union forces (despite being besieged on three sides and outnumbered four to one) won the battle and assured Federal control of northeast Missouri for the remainder of the Civil War.

- Find the rare snow trillium, a glacial relict, in abundance in the rich, moist soils of the Des Moines River Ravines Natural Area.

- Tour the restored Thome-Benning home and see the holes in the walls where a Confederate cannonball ripped through the house and landed in the Des Moines River (or in Iowa) without hurting anybody.

- Come in March, April, or May to see acres (really) of blooming Dutchman's-breeches, many of them pink.

## Area Information

Anxiety gripped northeast Missouri in 1861. Despite the proximity of powerful Union forces in Iowa and Illinois, many residents were pro-Southern, and the question of secession had divided the area. People were choosing sides, sometimes splitting families. Ambushes and assassinations had begun. As secessionist forces grew more numerous and bold, Union leaders resolved to unify their troops under a single command. At a July 4 rally in Kahoka, the First Northeast Missouri Regiment was born. David Moore, a storekeeper from Wrightsville, was named commander. Immediately, Moore began enlisting volunteers.

Moore chose Athens as the place to garrison his troops, confiscating the homes and businesses of the many Southern sympathizers who lived there. He and his 500 soldiers had not long occupied Athens before they were warned early on the morning of August 5 that an attack of 2,000 Rebel soldiers was imminent. Moore began lining up his troops to face the attack, and by 5:30 A.M. the Union Home Guard found themselves surrounded by the Confederate State Guard on three sides, with the wide and swift Des Moines River at their backs. For two hours, cannons roared and muskets barked, finally leaving the Confederates retreating in such a hurry that they abandoned their horses and weapons.

Except for the old street grid and building foundations, it would be hard to tell Athens was once a thriving town with 50 businesses. Apart from the cannonball hole and the history books, it would also be hard to tell it was the site of an important Civil War skirmish.

**Directions:** If you put your finger on a map on the northeasternmost tip of Missouri, Battle of Athens State Historic Site is under your finger. From Kahoka take Highway 81 north for 12.5 miles. Turn east on Highway CC for 3.7 miles. Turn left on a gravel road at the sign for the site.

**Hours Open:** The site is open year-round. The park office is open from 8 A.M. to 5 P.M.

**Facilities:** A wooded campground, picnic area, and playground are at the site. Rest rooms and drinking water are available in the campground but not showers. Fishing and boating are available on a small lake or the Des Moines River. Guided tours of the Thome-Benning Home (Cannonball House) are offered year-round for a small fee. Battle of Athens reenactments are held in early August every third year.

**Permits and Rules:** Pets must always be leashed.

**Further Information:** Site Administrator, Battle of Athens State Historic Site, RR 1, Box 26, Revere, MO 63465; 660-877-3871.

# Battle of Athens State Historic Site

LEGEND

| | | | |
|---|---|---|---|
| Road | | Monument | |
| Trail | | Thome Mill Ruins | |
| Boundary | | Overlook | |
| Boardwalk | | Athens Cemetery | |
| State Boundary | | Camping | |
| Historic House | | Picnic Area | |
| | | Picnic Shelter | |
| | | Playground | |

IOWA

MISSOURI

Des Moines River

Blue Trail

Green Trail

Yellow Trail

Red Trail

Lake

Thome-Benning Home

McKee House

Isaac Gray House

Widow Jane Gray Home

Service Area

N

CC

# Yellow/Red Historic Trail 👢👢👢

**Distance Round-Trip:** 1.75 miles

**Estimated Hiking Time:** 1 hour

*Hike through Athens, a bustling pre–Civil War town now nearly ghostlike. Let your imagination run as you walk on the remnants of the old street grid next to the foundations of homes long gone, and see where an early Civil War showdown raged for almost two hours.*

**Caution:** There are several stream crossings, and the Stallion Branch may be difficult to cross after a rainy period.

**Trail Directions:** As you enter the park, you'll see the signboard designating the trail at the edge of the forest where the road bends, just after you pass the driveway to the lake. There is no parking area at this trailhead, but you are allowed to park on the main park road. Be sure to keep vehicles on the pavement.

Begin at the trail sign with a yellow arrow **[1]**. If you are here in the spring, you'll start among a profusion of blooming Dutchman's-breeches, anemone, and toothwort—a display that you'll find is not restricted to the trailhead! Go straight at the intersection at .05 mi. **[2]**. Turn right at .13 mi. **[3]** to begin the loop marked with red arrows. Turn left at .23 mi. **[4]**, just before you reach a small, rocky stream. At .37 mi. **[5]** cross a small stream and continue the trail on the right. Go straight at the intersection at .44 mi. **[6]**.

Cross the Stallion Branch at .53 mi. **[7]** and continue the trail on the other side. It was in the dense brush here, on August 5, 1861, around 5:30 in the morning that about 60 Union soldiers clashed with advancing Rebel forces and successfully held the west flank of Athens, then occupied by the Union Home Guard. At the Yellow/Red intersection at .57 mi. **[8]** turn right and walk up a hill. Soon you'll emerge in a large field. Turn to the right slightly and head for the McKee House, a white two-story home with red trim. This house **[9]** (.73 mi.) was used as headquarters for the Union forces during Colonel Moore's occupation of Athens. Turn left here. The cream-colored house at .81 mi. is the Thome-Benning Home, also called the Cannonball House **[10]** because

it still bears the holes where a Confederate cannon-ball shot through it. Check here or at the park office if you are interested in a guided tour of the home. As you face the front of the Cannonball House, turn left on St. Louis Street to continue the trail.

Take the Overlook boardwalk at .87 mi. **[11]** to see the ruins of the Thome Mill, once housing a gristmill, sawmill, and woolen factory. After the Overlook, turn right on St. Louis Street and ignore the red trail sign on your right. Follow the edge of the field around until you see where you entered the field from the forest. Turn back into the forest here and hike down the hill. At 1.14 mi. you'll be back at the Yellow/Red intersection at **[8]**.

Turn right here and cross the Stallion Branch again. At 1.26 mi. go straight at this intersection **[12]**. At 1.33 mi. turn left at the Des Moines River **[13]** and turn left again at the Blue/Red intersection **[14]** at 1.42 mi. Go straight at the intersection at 1.57 mi. **[15]** and soon you'll be back at **[3]**, where you turn right to finish the trail.

1. Start
2. Go straight
3. Right turn
4. Left turn
5. Stream crossing
6. Go straight
7. Stream crossing
8. Right turn
9. McKee House
10. Cannonball House
11. Overlook boardwalk
12. Go straight
13. Des Moines River
14. Left turn
15. Go straight

# Green/Blue River Trail 👢👢👢

**Distance Round-Trip:** 1.75 miles

**Estimated Hiking Time:** 1 hour

*From early on, you'll have fun with the roller-coaster pattern of ridge, stream, ridge, stream, ridge . . . These steep slopes, called cove ravines, hide a botanist's paradise of unusually rich flora including many ferns, doll's eyes, and snow trillium, a glacial relict found nowhere else in the state.*

**Caution:** The many streams may be difficult to cross after a rainy period.

**Trail Directions:** Drive to the end of the main park road and park next to the playground in the picnic area. The trailhead **[1]** is just across the road and is marked with a sign with a green arrow. The trail begins in a rolling, open forest among Ohio buckeye and big white oak and ash trees. Because of their unusual qualities and because they harbor rare and

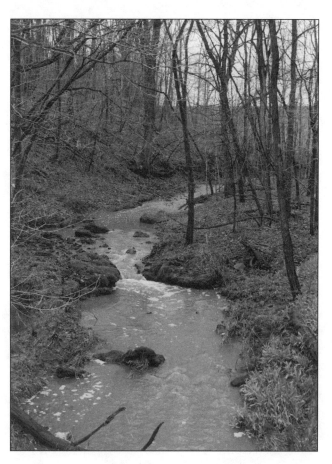

diverse plant life, 40 acres of these cove ravines have been designated as the Des Moines River Ravines Natural Area. You'll get to hike over the backs of these ravines now, and you'll see the ends of them later, next to the river. On the forest floor are wake robins, bloodroot, and trout lilies—all lovers of rich, moist woods. You might notice there are many single, flowerless trout lily leaves. Flowers arise only from two-leaved plants. The plant is also known as thousandleaf because of the abundance of leaves and scarcity of flowers.

At .27 mi. **[2]** cross the first of many small streams that have been eroding these cove ravines for eons. Between crossing streams and climbing ridges you will see entire groves of giant shagbark hickories on either side of the trail. You might not want to count them, but you'll cross no fewer than five more small streams before arriving at the intersection at .73 mi. **[3],** where you turn left. Turn left again at .88 mi. **[4].** For the next three-quarters of a mile you'll get to hike between the Des Moines River and the ends of all those ridges you just hiked over. You'll also get to see where all the water goes from the streams you just crossed. In several places these streams widen at their mouths, no longer confined to the steep ravines of the forest, and large, moss-covered boulders become wet-weather waterfalls. The rare snow trillium, blooming in March, can be found on this section of the trail in abundance.

At 1.53 mi. **[5]** a small spring erupts from under a rock with a gooseberry bush on top. Go up the wooden steps **[6]** at 1.65 mi. and you'll emerge in a field. When you come to the pavement, turn left to return to the trailhead.

1. Start
2. Stream crossings
3. Left turn
4. Left turn
5. Spring
6. Wooden steps

# 7. Thousand Hills State Park

- Visit the petroglyph site and see realistic depictions of opossum, deer, and snakes carved into sandstone as long as 1,500 years ago.
- Discover wolf trees on the Thousand Hills trail.
- Near Forest Lake listen for the rattle of kingfishers, the clear whistles of osprey, and the mournful yodels of loons.
- Explore the trails in the forest and discover the reason for the park's name.
- Hike through a grove of rare trees in Missouri—the big-toothed aspen.

## Area Information

Half of northern Missouri was once covered in prairie. Just west of Kirksville, however, lies a rugged belt of hills that runs north and south between rolling expanses of prairie lands. These hills supported a mosaic of mixed oak-hickory woodlands, tallgrass prairie openings, and savannas—grasslands with trees interspersed much farther apart than in the forest. Remnants of these natural communities can be seen from the park's hiking trails.

Many early settlers bypassed this rugged terrain, but a young doctor named George Laughlin developed a large farm here and named it Thousand Hills Farm. Later, the Laughlin heirs donated 1,100 acres of the old farm to the city of Kirksville to construct a freshwater reservoir for the town's growing population. Additional land was bought, and in 1952 a 600-acre reservoir was made by damming Big Creek. The whole tract was turned over to the state, which dedicated Thousand Hills State Park in 1953.

**Directions:** From Kirksville take Highway 6 west for 3.4 miles. Turn south on Highway 157 for 2 miles to the park entrance.

**Hours Open:** The park is open daily from 7 A.M. to 10 P.M. from April 1 through October 31. It is open from 7 A.M. to sunset during the other months. The park office is open weekdays from 7 A.M. to 3:30 P.M.

**Facilities:** Forest Lake offers all kinds of water recreation, including sailing, waterskiing, canoeing, boating, and fishing. A swimming beach is along the shore, as well as a fully equipped marina from which visitors can rent many types of boats. The park includes a campground, as well as rental cabins overlooking the lake, an interpretive shelter protecting the petroglyphs, numerous picnic areas, an amphitheater, and a dining lodge famous for its good food and scenic views of the lake.

**Permits and Rules:** Pets must always be leashed. Alcoholic drinks are prohibited on parking areas and swimming beaches in all state parks. Jet skis are prohibited on Forest Lake, and motorboat horsepower is limited to 90. Bicycles are permitted only on the Thousand Hills Trail.

**Further Information:** Park Superintendent, Thousand Hills State Park, Route 3, Box 126, Kirksville, MO 63501; 660-665-6995. For information on cabins, the marina, or the dining lodge call 660-665-7119.

# Thousand Hills State Park

To Route 6
5 Miles

157

N

Hickory
Trail

Redbud
Trail

Oak
Trail

Thousand Hills Trail

Forest Lake

226

### L E G E N D

| | | | |
|---|---|---|---|
| —— | Road | ★ | Trailhead |
| ······ | Trail | ◭ | Camping |
| —— | Boundary | | Cabins |
| | Park Office | | Bath House |
| | Restrooms | | Amphitheater |
| | Picnic Area | | Dining Lodge |
| | Shelter | | Boathouse |
| | Petroglyph Shelter | | Dam |

# Redbud-Hickory-Oak Trails

**Distance Round-Trip:** 1.5 miles

**Estimated Hiking Time:** 1 hour

*You never know what you'll see at Thousand Hills State Park. While hiking these trails near Forest Lake I saw a pair of osprey, a pair of beaver, and three common loons yodeling and laughing at each other across the cove.*

**Caution:** The trail near the lake will be muddy after a rain.

**Trail Directions:** As you enter the park, you'll find a main park road on your right just after you pass the park office. Turn right here (toward the day-use area) and go .9 mile. Parking is available here. The trailhead for the Redbud Trail is just across the road.

Begin at the trail sign **[1]** for the Redbud Trail and you'll soon be hiking between a western cove of Forest Lake and a grove of pines that whisper among themselves at the slightest breeze. Go straight at the intersection at .17 mi. **[2]**. As you hike, you'll notice that the lake cove tapers into the woods, offering privacy for more elusive wildlife. Watch for osprey perching in large trees or hovering over the water, watching for fish. Because fish are their only prey, these elegant birds are also called fish hawks. You might notice some nearby trees chewed by beaver. Also look for herons stalking the shoreline shallows.

Cross a small stream at .35 mi. **[3]** and turn left. You'll find a stream splashing its way over several "falls" created by a series of large rock layers in the stream bed at .45 mi. **[4]**. Go straight here and hike along the stream until the trail cuts away to the right and ascends a hill. Look and listen for woodpeckers in this second-growth forest of northern red oak,

white oak, and shagbark hickory. Go straight at .65 mi. **[5]** and discover the reason for the park's name. In several places here you can count 10 or more different hills, all seeming to come and go in different directions. Cross a small wooden bridge and turn left at the intersection at .77 mi. **[6]**.

When you come upon the trail sign for the Hickory Trail go straight and cross the park road at .88 mi. **[7]**. Continue at the Oak Trail sign, just behind the rest rooms. One of the common understory trees here is redbud. If you are here in April you won't be able to miss it—pink or lavender flowers cover almost every branch of the tree. The flowers make a slightly sweet (though not very filling) trailside nibble. At 1.08 mi. **[8]** you'll find a wooden bench. Turn right here and make your way down a short but rather steep hill. Walk toward the rest rooms and go straight. At 1.16 mi. **[9]** you'll meet the main park road, where you turn right and follow the road to return to the parking lot.

1. Start
2. Go straight
3. Left turn
4. Wet-weather waterfall
5. Go straight
6. Left turn
7. Road crossing
8. Wooden bench
9. Right turn

# Thousand Hills Trail 👢👢👢

**Distance Round-Trip:** 5 miles

**Estimated Hiking Time:** 2.5 hours

*Savannas are grasslands interspersed with trees. Lacking a shrub layer, they form a parklike transition area where prairie and forest intermingle. Savannas need fire to maintain their composition. Missouri may have had 13 million acres of savanna before settlement, but today they are absent from most areas of the state.*

**Caution:** The trail includes several stream crossings, and Big Creek may be impassable after heavy rain. *Note:* Check with park personnel about a hiking and biking trail that connects other park trails with the Thousand Hills Trail. As of spring 1998 this connector trail was planned but not completed. If there is no connecting trail, you'll have to drive 7.5 miles out of the park to the Thousand Hills trailhead, which begins on the Big Creek Conservation Area.

**Trail Directions:** Exit the park, turn right on Route 6, and go .7 mile. Turn right and go 2.3 miles. Turn right on Osteopathy Street and go 1.8 miles. Turn right on Michigan Street and go .3 mile. Turn left on Boundary Avenue and go 1.2 miles. Turn right at the sign for Rainbow Basin Ski Resort and go 1.2 miles, where the road dead-ends. Here are signs for Big Creek Conservation Area and the Thousand Hills trailhead.

Begin on a wide, mowed path **[1]**. You'll cross several streams and two wooden bridges. On these hilltops are remnants of hill prairies evidenced by native grasses such as big bluestem and Indian grass. At .33 mi. **[2]** turn right at the intersection. Cross Big Creek at .50 mi. **[3]**.

A sprawling white oak marks a bend in the trail at .62 mi. **[4]**. These wolf trees have 180-degree-wide crowns that nearly reach the ground. Once monarchs of expansive savannas, wolf trees didn't have to compete for sunlight. The trees on the north-facing

slope at .76 mi. are remarkable as well. These are the rare big-toothed aspen **[5]**. Turn left at the intersection at .92 mi. **[6]** and you'll soon pass another wolf tree on your left. The trail bends to the right when you reach the first cove of Forest Lake **[7]** (1.57 mi.), which has settled into such natural beauty that it's hard to tell it's human-made. The trail follows the shore, offering a continuum of scenic views.

On your right at 1.83 mi. **[8]** is a prairie remnant. Though now choked with shrubs, sumac, and blackberries, native grasses still dominate the ground cover. Cross a small stream at the end of the lake cove and continue on your left. Turn right, away from the lake, at 2.78 mi. **[9]**. At 3.30 mi. you will hike through a savanna remnant **[10]**. Notice the old trees have wide-spreading limbs while the young, crowded trees must compete for sunlight. Turn left at the intersection at 3.97 mi. **[6]** to hike back to the trailhead.

1. Start
2. Right turn
3. Big Creek
4. Wolf tree
5. Big-toothed aspen grove
6. Left turn
7. Forest Lake
8. Prairie remnant
9. Right turn
10. Savanna remnant

# 8.  Pershing State Park

- Hike an educational, award-winning trail—an outdoor visitor-center-as-you-go.
- Bring your binoculars to help you make out the red eye of the red-eyed vireo or the black bill of the black-billed cuckoo—over 100 birds make their homes here.
- Hike in rare, natural wetland communities—bottomland forests, wet prairies, marshes, and swamps.
- Feel the spongy stalks of river bulrush, a marsh plant that must get its oxygen from its stalks instead of its roots.
- From an observation tower, feel the breeze on your face from across the largest natural wet prairie in northern Missouri—one mile wide and two miles long.

## Area Information

Growing up in the 1860s and 1870s in Laclede, Missouri, John J. Pershing found nuts and hunted in the wild countryside around his home, fishing and swimming in nearby Locust Creek. Later, he became the commanding general of the American Expeditionary Forces during World War I, eventually becoming the highest ranking military officer in American history.

In 1930, a ranch southwest of Laclede, still rich with its tall forests, open prairies, and wild streams was chosen as a memorial park to the still-living hero. The state acquired initial park acreage in 1937 for Pershing State Park, which now totals 2,909 acres. Creators of the educational Wetland Boardwalk won a Renaissance Award from the Missouri Department of Natural Resources, which acknowledges outstanding works within Missouri state parks.

A major portion of the park is in the Locust Creek floodplain. Annual flooding and other natural processes of the meandering, unchannelized river here has formed a wealth of wetland habitats. Oxbow lakes, sloughs, and swamps are formed and re-formed. Entire communities of plants inhabit wet prairies and marshes. The old-growth bottomland forest is one of the highest quality forests in the state and has been officially designated a state natural area. In the 1870s this area would have been wildland typical of north Missouri. Today, however, surrounded by human-made drainage ditches, channelized rivers, and seemingly endless miles of row crops, the park is a rare gem.

**Directions:** Pershing State Park is on Highway 130, two miles southwest of Laclede.

**Hours Open:** The site is open year-round.

**Facilities:** The park offers a campground, picnic areas, and four small lakes for swimming and fishing. Fishing is also available in Locust Creek.

**Permits and Rules:** Pets must always be leashed. Boats with electric motors are allowed on the lakes but must be carried on.

**Further Information:** Park Superintendent, Pershing State Park, 29277 Highway 130, Laclede, MO 64651; 660-963-2299.

## Other Areas of Interest

**General John J. Pershing Boyhood Home State Historic Site** is three miles northeast of the park on Highway 5. Guided tours of the house are available for a fee.

**Locust Creek Covered Bridge** is one of only four surviving covered bridges in the state and is the longest of the four. Built in 1868, the bridge is three miles west of Laclede on Highway 36, then one mile northeast on a gravel road. For more information on either site call Pershing State Park.

Both **Fountain Grove Conservation Area** and **Swan Lake National Wildlife Refuge,** just south of the park, offer exceptional viewing opportunities for migrating waterfowl. Swan Lake has one of the largest concentrations of Canada geese in North America. For more information call 660-938-4124 (Fountain Grove) and 660-856-3323 (Swan Lake).

## Park Trails

**Locust Creek Backpack Trail** 👢👢—5.5 miles— This trail starts at the Locust Creek overlook on the Wetland Boardwalk Trail and follows the natural levee of the creek into Fountain Grove Conservation Area. The trail is prone to periodic flooding and will be seasonally overgrown in places, as well.

# Pershing State Park

# Wetland Boardwalk Trail 🥾

**Distance Round-Trip:** 1.5 miles

**Estimated Hiking Time:** 1 hour

*The observation tower lets you view the largest remaining wet prairie in northern Missouri. Sedges make it a vibrant sea of green in spring, and 12-foot-high wildflowers splash it with yellow and gold by fall.*

**Caution:** The trail is wheelchair accessible, yet seasonal flooding sometimes leaves it underwater. Check with park staff for conditions. Unless you are here during the winter, repellent for mosquitoes and biting flies is advised. Also, stay on the boardwalk to avoid abundant stinging nettle and poison ivy.

**Trail Directions:** Park near the interpretive signs in the parking lot for the boardwalk trail, across the main park road from the park office. The trail begins **[1]** at the iron bridge over Locust Creek. The portion of Locust Creek that runs through the park is one of the only sections of sizable streams in north Missouri that has not been channelized. Flowing and meandering along its natural course, the creek's periodic flooding is the single most important influence on the landscape of the park.

Cross the bridge and you'll see one of the many interpretive signs on the boardwalk that explain wetland communities, their formation, and the plants and animals that depend on them. The natural levee at .19 mi. **[2]** was formed by the creek's deposition of sand. The slightly higher elevation and well-drained sandy soil provide a drier habitat for plants than saturated soil. The elevation drops slightly at .37 mi. **[3]**. Water stands on the ground for much of winter and spring here, leaving little oxygen in the soil. Specially adapted plants and trees in this bottomland forest include knotweed, pin oak, shellbark hickory, and swamp white oak.

A wooden bench at .41 mi. **[4]** makes a great place to stop and listen for the cooing of black-billed cuckoos or the buzzing, rising trill of the northern parula. Resident and migrating birds alike find an oasis in this towering forest. Go straight at the intersection at .44 mi. **[5]**. Another wetland community, a shrub swamp, is at .59 mi. **[6].** Plants that live here, like duckweed and tickseed, have extraordinary adaptations to cope with the abundance of water and the scarcity of oxygen. An overlook of Locust Creek is at .84 mi. **[7]**.

At the entrance to the 1,040-acre wet prairie **[8]** (1.00 mi.) an interpretive sign explains that, paradoxically, the other major natural force that maintains these wetlands besides flooding is fire. The observation tower at 1.09 miles **[9]** lets you experience the vastness of the prairie, home to wild iris, false dragonhead, and saw-toothed sunflower. Note the water-filled oxbow of Locust Creek transformed to a marsh **[10]** at 1.15 mi. Feel the spongy stalks of the river bulrush, specially adapted for gathering oxygen from the air. At 1.26 mi. you'll return to the intersection at **[5]**, where you turn left to return to the bridge.

1. Start
2. Natural levee
3. Bottomland forest
4. Wooden bench
5. Go straight
6. Shrub swamp
7. Locust Creek overlook
8. Wet prairie
9. Observation tower
10. Marsh

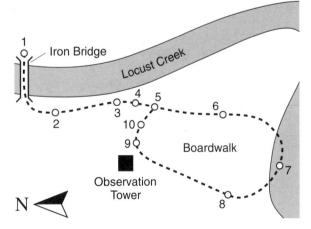

# Lake Trail 👢

**Distance Round-Trip:** .5 mile

**Estimated Hiking Time:** .25 hour

*Spend a quiet 15 minutes strolling around this picturesque little lake and watch the small natural dramas unfold. A katydid jumps into the lake from near your feet and is inhaled by a bluegill with a slurp. A shagbark kerplunks a nut into the water from an overhanging limb, sending a nearby squirrel racing across dry leaves.*

**Caution:** Stay on the trail to avoid damage to fragile mosses and lichens.

**Trail Directions:** Park in the lot for the small lake on the left, 1.3 mi. into the park off Highway 36. Begin at the parking lot **[1]** and follow the trail counter-clockwise around the lake. As you begin the section between the lake and the park road, scan the water for wood ducks or teal huddled in small coves. Look for green herons perched motionless on tree limbs or exposed tree roots near the water, and watch for red-eared sliders and other aquatic turtles basking on logs. Near the parking lot, you'll find evidence of beaver teeth on trees near the water.

In the spring or summer, you may be surprised by frogs springing into the water beside you, later exposing bulging eyes between floating leaves of aquatic plants. At .12 mi. **[2]** you'll cross a wooden bridge over the end of the lake. Look in the water for young largemouth bass chasing schools of small bluegill in the shallow water. Watch for zipping dragonflies, hovering nearby and landing on the bridge railing.

Just after crossing another wooden bridge, you'll enter a forest of mixed oaks and hickories. Mounds of reindeer lichen grow between rounded tufts of moss that bubble up from the forest floor like pin cushions at .17 mi. **[3].** Reindeer lichen, like all lichens, is a composite organism formed from fungi and algae, though the lichen formed does not resemble either of the components. The fungus maintains a moist habitat for the algae, which produces food by photosynthesis that both organisms use. This mutually advantageous relationship is known as symbiosis. On rainy and humid days, reindeer lichen is soft and spongy. On sunny, dry days, it is brittle and crunchy.

Cross another wooden bridge at .18 mi. **[4]** and notice all the beaver stumps nearby. Look for fragrant sumac and leadplant near the trail—two plants that prefer dry, upland habitats. If you are here in early spring, look for wine-red, fernlike leaves of lousewort or wood betony. This plant produces stalks of yellow blossoms in April and May. At .24 mi. **[5]** you'll cross another wooden bridge over a drainage stream to the lake. Notice the Christmas ferns lining the drainage. Named because they are green at Christmas, Christmas ferns are actually green all year long. Turn left at the intersection with a gravel road at .27 mi. **[6]** and turn left again at the elevated wooden bridge at .30 mi. **[7].**

Just after crossing yet another wooden bridge, ignore the two spurs on your right that lead to a picnic area at .39 mi. **[8],** and go straight at both of them. You'll wind through the woods between the lake and park road before returning to the parking lot and finishing your lake hike.

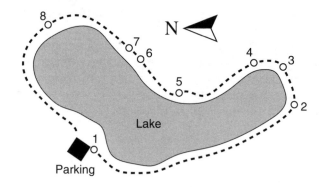

1. Start
2. Wooden bridge
3. Reindeer lichen
4. Beaver stumps
5. Wooden bridge
6. Left turn
7. Left turn
8. Go straight

# 9. Crowder State Park

- Meet the Kentucky coffee tree—the only tree in Missouri whose compound leaves grow up to three feet long.
- How can you tell a possum track from a raccoon's? Brush up on your wildlife tracks, then come test your skills on the River Forks trail.
- Examine a tree that is growing sideways.
- Look around for the occasional ostrich in the forest (ostrich fern, that is).

## Area Information

With its winding and shaded entrance road, wooded hillsides, and picturesque lake, Crowder State Park poses a classic park landscape and serves as a scenic memorial to Major General Enoch H. Crowder, the Missourian who founded the nation's Selective Service System, better known as the military draft.

Crowder State Park, with its hilly forests, steep-walled valleys, and well-shaded sandstone ledges, is a natural attraction in northern Missouri, a region that has been converted mainly to agricultural uses. It was probably, in fact, the rugged drainages of the adjoining Thompson River that helped protect the thick forests from the saw and the plow.

Today, under the protection and management of the state park system, mature and sprawling white oak, red oak, and sugar maple thrive in the glacial till and loess soil of the park. Giant cottonwoods tower in the bottomland forests along the Thompson River, and yellow lady slipper orchids and ferns adorn moist, rocky ledges.

**Directions:** The park is four miles west of Trenton on Highway 146.

**Hours Open:** The park is open daily from 7 A.M. to 10 P.M.

**Facilities:** All types of campsites are available at Crowder, including primitive camping for scout groups and a large group camp with enclosed buildings for use by nonprofit organizations. Crowder Lake offers fishing, boating, swimming, a sandy beach, and a nearby bathhouse. The park contains numerous picnic areas, an enclosed shelter, grills, playground equipment, and a paved tennis court.

**Permits and Rules:** No gas-powered motors are allowed on Crowder Lake, but electric motors are permitted. Horses are allowed only on the River Forks trail. Pets must always be leashed.

**Further Information:** Park Superintendent, Crowder State Park, 76 Highway 128, Trenton, MO 64683; 816-359-6473.

## Park Trails

**Redbud Trail** 🥾🥾🥾—1.75 miles—Park in the Scout Area across the road from the park office. The trail has several stream crossings and limestone shelves on hillsides with wild ginger and maidenhair ferns. Exit the trail at the tennis court and walk uphill (right) toward the trailhead.

# Crowder State Park

### LEGEND
| | |
|---|---|
| —— | Paved Road |
| ···· | Trail |
| ▬▬ | Boundary |
| 🏠 | Park Office |
| ⛺ | Camping |
| ⛺ᴳ | Organized Group Camp |
| ⛺ | Scout Area |
| ⌐ | Shelter House |
| 🏠 | Enclosed Shelter House |
| 🏠 | Thompson House |
| 🎾 | Tennis Court |
| 🏊 | Swimming Beach, Shower House, and Restroom |

Thompson River

Tall Oaks Trail

Crowder Lake

River Forks Trail

N

128

146

# River Forks Trail 🥾🥾🥾

**Distance Round-Trip:** 2.5 miles

**Estimated Hiking Time:** 1.25 hours

*Human fishers know that river confluences are good places to fish. Animal anglers know it, too. At the two-river junction on this trail I saw an osprey plunge completely underwater, feet first. Soon it emerged and pulled itself (and its finny prey) back into the air with long, powerful wing strokes. A belted kingfisher chattered by just then, as if in congratulations.*

**Caution:** The first mile of this trail will be muddy after wet weather.

**Trail Directions:** Park at the swimming beach parking lot at the northeast corner of Crowder Lake and find the trailhead [1] near the northeast corner of the lot. The trail starts as a wide dirt path lined with tall black walnut, sugar maple, basswood, and sycamore trees, closing a beautiful canopy over the trail. Look for animal tracks on the trail; no matter what time of the year you are here, this part of the trail will probably be well trod by white-tailed deer. North Missouri is known for its large numbers of deer, and this trail, which parallels crop field and forest edge, is a likely wildlife highway.

Look on your left at .51 mi. just a few feet off the trail for several trees with flaky, papery bark. These

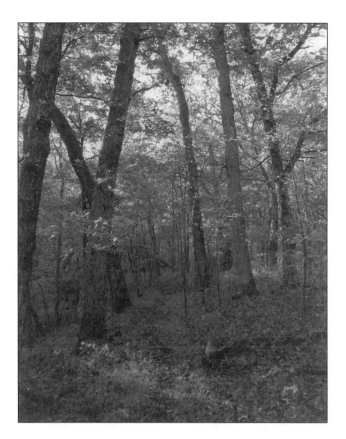

are Kentucky coffee trees [2]. Early settlers ground the seeds of this tree to make a passable (though not very popular) substitute for coffee. With compound leaves up to three feet long, the Kentucky coffee tree produces the largest leaf of all Missouri trees.

Enjoy the view at .86 mi. at the junction of the Thompson River with the Weldon Fork [3]. This is a likely spot to see wood ducks taking to the air, crying "Weet! Weet! Weet!" Also look for statuesque shorebirds in the shallows. Nearby dead trees provide favorite perches for belted kingfishers and osprey. If the water is low, the muddy river bed would be another good place to look for animal tracks. Deer, heron, raccoon, coyote, and mink are likely. Note the multitude of young trees on the river banks—willows, cottonwood, and sycamore. These are natural erosion controllers. Turn right, uphill, to continue the trail.

Turn right at the switchback at .98 mi. [4] and find a shagbark hickory [5] at 1.36 mi. At 1.53 mi. [6] turn right and begin to go downhill. At 1.73 mi. [7] you will cross an intermittent stream. Turn right at the intersection at 1.97 mi. [8] and you will find some picnic tables from an old camp. Continue on the right to find your way back to the trailhead.

1. Start
2. Kentucky coffee trees
3. River junction
4. Right turn
5. Shagbark hickory
6. Right turn
7. Stream
8. Right turn

# Tall Oaks Trail 👢👢

**Distance Round-Trip:** 3.6 miles

**Estimated Hiking Time:** 2 hours

*On this trail the landscape will change channels on you and your feet. You will hike next to a lake, under tall oaks, through a hay field, into a creek bottom, and back to the lake. Enjoy the diversity!*

**Caution:** The trail will be muddy in the stream bottom after a rain and stinging nettles encroach the trail there; long pants are in order. Intermittent streams crossing the trail may not be dry. Watch for traffic at park road crossings.

**Trail Directions:** Park in the swimming beach parking lot. Walk across the dam of Crowder Lake and find the trailhead **[1]** at the northwest corner of the lake. Begin the trail to the left of the trail sign. Stop for a moment and listen for the sound of beaver teeth in wood—at least one beaver in the area has a habit of dropping trees right across the trail! You will find some beaver stumps at .08 mi. **[2]**.

Cross a couple of intermittent streams and go straight when a road crosses the trail at .22 mi. **[3]**. Go straight also at the spur on the left at .50 mi. **[4]**. A remarkable example of a bent tree is on your right at .53 mi. **[5]**. Note how the trunk grows horizontally while all the limbs grow straight up. This tree was probably bent over when it was a sapling when a larger tree (now rotted away) fell on it and trapped it. The bent tree survived in its sideways condition and still grows that way today, a testimony to its resilience.

Go straight at the road crossing **[6]** at .73 mi., and soon the forest will have a different look and feel. Walk under towering oaks with broad, creeping limbs. See the twisted bark of old trees, some with lightning scars, and notice the trunk cavities at their bases, filled with black, tannic water. Soon you will find yourself on a shelf, with a rocky stream below you on your left and a rocky slope ascending on your right. At 1.38 mi. **[7]** you will come across a rugged limestone wall in the forest. Note how the rocks fracture into flat, stepping-stone shapes. Early settlers used these natural foundation stones for their buildings.

At 1.58 mi. **[8]** you will emerge into a large hay field—a good place to look for deer beds and soaring hawks. Follow the mown path through the field and reenter the forest at 1.74 mi. **[9]**. Ignore the intersecting paths near the powerline and continue straight. Soon you will cross a log bridge at 1.99 mi. **[10]** and enter a stream bottom. Check out the monstrous cottonwood tree at 2.21 mi. **[11]** with grooves in the bark so deep you can lay your finger inside. Cross a gravel road at 2.92 mi. **[12]** and continue straight. Finally, you climb out of the creek bottom, the trail opens up again, and you find yourself on another shelf at 3.3 mi. **[13]**, skirting a hill on your right. Find a gigantic black maple at 3.36 mi. **[14]**, which will probably require two people's arms to go around.

Turn right at the intersection at 3.37 mi. **[15]** and start counting your steps. At about 25 paces, take the small trail on the left **[16]** (3.39 mi.). (If you come out at the brown buildings of the group camp you missed this last turn.) Go straight at an intersection **[17]** at 3.47 mi. and soon you will be back at the trailhead.

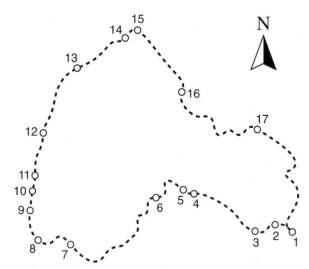

1. Start
2. Beaver stumps
3. Go straight
4. Go straight
5. Bent tree
6. Go straight
7. Limestone wall
8. Hay field
9. Reenter forest
10. Log bridge
11. Cottonwood
12. Road crossing
13. Shelf
14. Black maple
15. Right turn
16. Left turn
17. Go straight

# 10.  Wallace State Park

- Enjoy the solitude and beauty of a forested oasis in the midst of rolling farmland.
- Hike next to some limestone shelves in Deer Creek, a site believed to be a Mormon trail crossing of the early 19th century.
- Discover the beauty and utility of the Osage orange tree.
- Stand in a thicket of American bladdernut.

## Area Information

While hiking one of the forest trails at Wallace State Park, it's easy to imagine you are in the Ozarks, where rugged and rocky terrain is the norm and trails intersect dozens of small, rocky streams. But you are in the glaciated plains of northwest Missouri, where fertile farmlands dominate the landscape. You are also only an hour's drive from the heart of Kansas City.

Wallace was only the second state park, after Mark Twain, to be acquired north of the Missouri River, where land was considerably more expensive than in the Ozarks. Bought from the Wallace family in 1932, the park became one of the first recreational areas in northwest Missouri. The area is rich in the history of the Mormons, who flooded by the thousands into the surrounding counties after Joseph Smith arrived in March 1838 and proclaimed Far West, only four miles east of the Wallace farm, their new gathering place. Far West quickly became second in population among western Missouri cities, until non-Mormon settlers drove the Saints to Nauvoo, Illinois, and later to the Great Salt Lake in Utah.

Today, Wallace State Park preserves about 500 acres of forested hills, including a mile of the valley of Deer Creek. The hillsides are covered with white, black, and red oaks, as well as hickories, black walnut, and redbud. A turkey vulture roost and nest site are located just south of Lake Allaman. Common springtime plants include trout lilies, May apples, touch-me-nots, and Dutchman's-breeches.

**Directions:** Travel six miles south of Cameron on Interstate 35 and exit onto Highway 121. The park entrance is two miles off the interstate.

**Hours Open:** The park is open between 7 A.M. and 10 P.M. and is open year-round.

**Facilities:** The park offers four campgrounds, including sites with or without electricity and sites for organized travel camping groups. Lake Allaman offers fishing, boating for carry-on boats only, and a sandy beach for swimming. Shady picnic areas abound.

**Permits and Rules:** Pets must always be leashed. Electric motors only are allowed for boats, and horses are prohibited on all trails.

**Further Information:** Park Superintendent, Wallace State Park, 10621 NE Highway 121, Cameron, MO 64429; 816-632-3745.

## Other Areas of Interest

**Trice-Dedman Memorial Woods**, a 60-acre remnant old-growth oak woodland, is one of the best examples of presettlement forest in northwest Missouri. A one-mile hiking trail leads the visitor through an impressive stand of white oaks, many of which are 175 years old. The preserve is owned by the Nature Conservancy and managed by the Missouri Department of Natural Resources. For more information call Wallace State Park at 816-632-3745 or the Nature Conservancy at 314-968-1105.

**Watkins Mill State Park** provides a scenic area for recreation, including a four-mile paved biking and hiking path around Watkins Mill Lake. **Watkins Woolen Mill State Historic Site**, a national historic landmark, is the only 19th-century American woolen mill with its original machinery still intact. For more information call 816-296-3357 or 816-580-3387.

## Park Trails

**Rocky Ford Trail** 👢👢—.75 mile—Hike next to Deer Creek and see large limestone shelves in the streambed that serve as a crossing, or "ford." The shelves at .28 mi. are thought to be a Mormon trail crossing from the early 19th century.

**Skunk Hollow Trail** 👢👢—.5 mile—This pleasant and shady trail takes you by some large shagbark hickories and an intermittent stream with a small waterfall (when wet). Park at the entrance to the travel campground and walk to the trailhead near campsite #80.

# Wallace State Park

LEGEND

- ——— Road
- —✛— Fire Access Road
- ......... Trail 1
- ——— Boundary

| Symbol | Name | Symbol | Name | Symbol | Name |
|---|---|---|---|---|---|
| | Park Office | | Shelter | | Trailer Disposal Station |
| | Gate | | Amphitheater | | Water Tower |
| | Information Kiosk | | Parking | | |
| | Camping | | Restrooms | | |
| | Scout Area | | Portable Restrooms | | |
| | Telephone | | | | |

# Deer Run Trail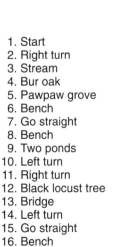

**Distance Round-Trip:** 3.5 miles

**Estimated Hiking Time:** 1.5 hours

*The pawpaw is Missouri's only tropical tree. When you walk under a grove of them it's easy to imagine you are somewhere where palm trees grow, too. The handsome leaves—oval, pointed at the tip, and up to 12 inches long—fan out from stems like fingers from hands (just the way many palms do).*

**Caution:** Several streams may be difficult to cross after heavy rains.

**Trail Directions:** Park at the picnic shelter at the northwest corner of Lake Allaman and walk across the dam. The trailhead is at the southwest corner of the lake. Two opportunities for shortcuts on this trail provide length options of 1, 2, or 3.5 miles. Deer footprint signs guide you around the 2-mile route.

Begin at the trailhead **[1]** and turn right at the first intersection **[2]** at .04 mi. Soon you will come to an intermittent stream **[3]** (.08 mi.). You are likely to see a patch of jewelweed by the stream if you are here during spring or early summer. If you are here in late summer, however, don't be surprised to see only bare stalks—jewelweed is one of the white-tailed deer's favorite late-summer foods.

Take a few steps and identify a stately bur oak **[4]** on your left (.10 mi.). This one is particularly easy to identify because it has a label on it. When they aren't labeled, you can identify them by their characteristic acorn, which is broad, has a scaly cap, and has a hairy fringe around the outside of the cap. The bur oak prefers bottomland soils and produces the largest acorn in Missouri. Look up as you walk under a pawpaw grove **[5]** at .18 mi. to experience the delightful illusion of walking under so many palm trees.

Find a wooden bench **[6]** at .21 mi. and decide whether to take the shortcut option **[7]** at .23 mi. Go straight to continue the trail and find another bench **[8]** at .63 mi. You will come upon two ponds **[9]** on the left at .90 and .95 mi. The elevated nest boxes in the second pond are for wood ducks, which are undoubtedly one of the most brilliantly colored birds in North America. Once nearly extirpated from Missouri, the wood duck is now one of the state's most common waterfowl.

Just after you pass the second pond you can turn right at the intersection **[10]** (.96 mi.) to return to the trailhead. Turn left here to continue the trail and begin the Deer Creek Loop. At the intersection **[11]** at 1.37 mi. turn right and soon you will be hiking next to Deer Creek. Note the large black locust tree **[12]** on your right at 1.75 mi. The black locust has only small spines on its twigs, while the similar honey locust has clusters of long spines on its bark. Because black locust wood is extremely hard and durable, colonists and settlers used it for fence posts and corner posts for buildings.

Just after you cross a small, wooden bridge **[13]** at 2.23 mi., a thicket of American bladdernut grows on both sides of the trail. This shrub has compound leaves with three leaflets and curious, three-lobed hanging lanterns, encapsulating shiny seeds. Even after the leaves fall, the capsules hang on until midwinter. Note the patch of maidenhair ferns on your right and turn left at the intersection **[14]** at 2.51 mi. Meet the shortcut intersection **[15]** at 2.72 mi. and go straight. Find a bench **[16]** at 3.01 mi. and ignore the spur to the creek. At the five-way intersection **[17]** at 3.19 mi. take the extreme right trail. Turn left at the intersection **[18]** at 3.30 mi. to return to the trailhead.

1. Start
2. Right turn
3. Stream
4. Bur oak
5. Pawpaw grove
6. Bench
7. Go straight
8. Bench
9. Two ponds
10. Left turn
11. Right turn
12. Black locust tree
13. Bridge
14. Left turn
15. Go straight
16. Bench
17. Right turn
18. Left turn

# Old Quarry Trail 👢👢

**Distance Round-Trip:** 1.25 miles

**Estimated Hiking Time:** .75 hour

*In October I found dozens of hedge apples lying on the ground near the trailhead. I watched a big fox squirrel tear into one, rolling it around and ripping it to shreds. Proportionately, this would be like somebody eating something the size of, say, a kitchen stove.*

**Caution:** Don't stand under an Osage orange tree on windy days in October. Osage oranges can be bigger than Texas grapefruit, and much harder.

**Trail Directions:** Park outside the gate at the scout area and walk down the gravel road a quarter of a mile to find the trailhead on the right. It's OK to hike this trail even if the scout area is being used. As you begin, notice all the Osage orange trees in the scout area and across the road from the trailhead. Archery bows made from the wood of these trees were highly prized by the Osage and other Native Americans and were traded in distant regions where the Osage orange doesn't grow. Early settlers fenced the plains and prairies with rows of these spiny trees before the introduction of barbed wire. They also extracted a yellow dye for clothing from the root bark. The tree is still used today for archery bows and fence posts. The fruits, heavy yellow-green balls, are eaten by wildlife as well as livestock, giving rise to two other common names—hedge apple and horse apple.

Begin the trail at the trailhead **[1]** and turn right at the first intersection **[2]** at .02 mi. At .12 mi. the dangerous-looking tree on your left with the long, clustered spines on the bark is the honey locust **[3]**, so named for the sweet, edible pulp found in the seed pods around the seeds.

Come to the shortcut **[4]** at .15 mi. and turn left to continue the trail. If you count about 125 paces from this intersection you'll find the trail's namesake, an old quarry **[5]** at .22 mi. on the left. Long ago on this small rock outcrop a local settler might have pried out enough limestone rocks to make a small building foundation or fruit-cellar entrance. You won't find any titanic bulldozers or earth movers at this quarry. In fact, you may have to look hard to see the quarry at all.

Note the big white oak tree **[6]** at .24 mi. Both Native Americans and wildlife preferred white oak acorns because they ripen in a single season and have a mild flavor. The acorns of the red oaks, on the other hand, are bitter and require two years to mature. You can identify the white oak in winter by noticing that the bark on the upper limbs is usually flakier than the bark on the trunk.

At .34 mi. the trail brings you to the edge of a hay field **[7]**, a good place for deer to graze and sleep and for turkeys to come out of the woods to find grasshoppers and other insects. Turn right to follow the trail along the edge of the forest.

Turn right at .51 mi. **[8]** to reenter the forest. Pass the shortcut **[9]** at .53 mi. and go straight. Cross a small wooden bridge **[10]** at .60 mi. and finish the trail at the scout area at .66 mi. **[11].** From here, take the gravel road to the right to return to the trailhead (.72 mi.) or turn left to return to your car. Even though the trail is only .75 mile, include the .25-mile trip each way from your car to make the trail 1.25 miles, round-trip.

1. Start
2. Right turn
3. Honey locust
4. Left turn
5. Old quarry
6. White oak
7. Right turn
8. Right turn
9. Go straight
10. Bridge
11. Finish

# 11.  Weston Bend State Park

- View the Missouri River and the Kansas plains and hike on a blufftop trail at the same time.
- Meet loess (pronounced "luss").
- Hike down to the state's second largest river, the Missouri, and meet the Big Muddy at its own level.
- Bring your camera and enjoy expansive views of the Missouri River and some of the state's best fall colors, as well.

## Area Information

In the late 1830s, the town of Weston, Missouri, sprung up and grew rapidly. Settlers quickly discovered that the soil of the surrounding river hills was extremely fertile. This fine-grained soil, called loess, was ground by retreating glaciers and deposited by the wind. The two main plantation crops of the antebellum upper South were tobacco and hemp, and both crops flourished in Weston's wind-blown, silty soil.

Located at a natural harbor on the great bend of the Missouri River now known as Weston Bend, Weston became a major river port. Trade was established with Fort Leavenworth, just across the river, and Weston became a major outfitting station for settlers heading west. Steamboat traffic added to the commercial boom. Tremendous quantities of tobacco and hemp were exported, and by 1858, Weston was recognized as the largest hemp port in the world.

The hemp industry died in the late 1800s, but the tobacco economy still flourishes today. Four tobacco-drying barns are still standing in Weston Bend State

Park. One of them has been converted to a picnic shelter and another is still actively used to teach visitors about tobacco production and the state's tobacco heritage.

**Directions:** The park is on the Missouri River, just northwest of Kansas City, and is 1 mile south of Weston on Highway 45. The park entrance is .4 mile south of the intersection of Highways 45 and 273.

**Hours Open:** The park is open year-round from 7 A.M. to 9 P.M., but the trails are open only until sunset.

**Facilities:** The park features views of the Missouri River from an overlook that is accessible to persons with disabilities. The park offers a campground, picnic tables, shelter houses, and playground equipment. Fishing is available in the Missouri River.

**Permits and Rules:** Bicycles are restricted to paved areas. Horses, roller skates, and skateboards are prohibited in all areas. Pets must always be leashed.

**Further Information:** Park Superintendent, Weston Bend State Park, P.O. Box 115, 16600 Highway 45 North, Weston, MO 64098; 816-640-5443.

## Other Areas of Interest

Visit the natural Missouri river oxbow lake that William Clark named Gosling Lake in 1804 for its abundance of waterfowl. It's at **Lewis and Clark State Park**, which commemorates one of the most successful exploratory journeys of all time, the Lewis and Clark expedition. The park is 20 miles southwest of St. Joseph, on Highway 138. For more information call the park superintendent at 816-579-5564.

## Park Trails

**Missouri River Trail** —.5 mile—Park in the lot for the North Ridge Trail. Walk around the iron gate, over the gravel road, and find the trailhead on the other side of the railroad tracks. This trail offers the opportunity to stand next to the Missouri River.

**Bear Creek Trail** —.5 mile—The trailhead for this trail is the same as for the Missouri River Trail. Hike quietly to increase your chances to see wildlife.

**North Ridge Trail** —2 miles—This new trail ascends a hill into the forest and winds through some vegetation thickets on the ridgetop.

**Barn Trail** —.5 mile—This is a mowed-path trail that winds through some woods and onto the park road just south of the park office. Begin the trail at the south end of the parking lot for the tobacco barn, across the road from the park office.

**McCormick Trail** —.4 mile—This mowed-path trail takes you through an old field and offers the chance to see wild turkeys and other birds. Park at the tobacco barn and begin the trail at the sharp curve in the road between the park office and the campground.

Weston Bend State Park

To Weston

To U.S. 59
St. Joseph

11

273

45

McCormick
Trail

North Ridge Trail

Bear Creek

Bear Creek Trail

Missouri River Trail

Missouri River

Barn Trail

Harpst Valley Trail

Harpst Pass

West Ridge Trail

Hiking/Bicycle Trail

Bee Creek

45

To Kansas City

LEGEND
━━━ Road
═╤═ Gravel Road
········ Paved Trail
------ Unpaved Trail
—·—·— Mowed Trail
+++ Railroad
▬▬▬ Boundary

🏠 Office
🏠 Contact Station
⛺ Camping
🏠 Shelter
★ Trailhead
🚻 Restrooms
📷 Overlook
🪑 Bench
🏠 Barn

N

# West Ridge and Harpst Valley Trails 👢👢

**Distance Round-Trip:** 2.5 miles

**Estimated Hiking Time:** 1.25 hours

*While some hiking trails have an overlook or two, this trail **is** an overlook. For the first mile, the trail is lined with dozens of views of the state's second largest river, the Missouri, and the Kansas plains beyond. Vistas explode in front of you while you hike, and the views keep getting better as you go.*

**Caution:** It's best to stay on the trail because the soil here (loess) is crumbly and easily eroded. Also, watch for bicycle traffic when the trail joins the Hiking/Bicycle trail.

**Trail Directions:** Park in the lot for the Overlook and find the trailhead about 30 yards up the asphalt path leading to the Overlook. (Don't forget to stop at the Overlook, too.) Begin at the trail board **[1]**. If you are here in the fall, you will soon find yourself under a blinding barrage of yellow sugar maple leaves over the trail and on both sides of it. If you are here in the summer, you will enjoy the dense shade these leaves provide. Ignore the occasional side spurs and follow the blue arrows on this trail.

At .31 mi. come to a four-way junction **[2]**. Take a left to complete the Harpst Pass and Harpst Valley loop (1 mile) and return to the trailhead. To continue the West Ridge trail go straight. Take a look at the purplish white, arching canes on both sides of the trail at .33 mi. These are wild raspberry vines **[3]**. If you are here in June or July look closely for the purplish black berries, highly prized for making jelly, pie, syrup, wine, or for nibbling trailside!

Hike among many mature sugar maple trees with flaky bark and knobby, outreaching limbs. The bluff on your right is so steep you can look down on the tops of some of these big trees. The best (and unique) feature of this trail is that you can have overlook

views of the Missouri River and hike at the same time. You are even traveling in the same direction as the river, although the water is moving a little faster. Turn right at the small overlook spur at 1.0 mi. **[4]** for the best view of all. The Kansas plains seem to go on forever, with the horizon interrupted only by an occasional church steeple surrounded by a cluster of rooftops. Wheat fields lie between patches of trees. If it weren't for the flatness, you'd think you were on an Alpine peak, looking down on so many European hamlets.

After you return to the main trail, you will hike downhill and away from the river. See how the dark, rich loess soil erodes into straight-up-and-down ravine sides as you descend. At 1.33 mi. you will be in a cool, lush valley **[5]**. See how the plants grow thicker and taller here than on the dry ridgetop. At 1.53 mi. **[6]** turn left on the asphalt, where the West Ridge trail meets the paved Hiking/Bicycle trail. Find a red bench **[7]** at 2.0 mi. At 2.25 mi. leave the paved trail and walk behind the yellow bench **[8]**. Follow the signs to take the Harpst Valley trail and complete the West Ridge loop.

1. Start
2. Go straight
3. Wild raspberries
4. Overlook spur
5. Valley
6. Left turn
7. Red bench
8. Yellow bench

# Hiking/Bicycle Trail 👢👢

**Distance Round-Trip:** 3 miles

**Estimated Hiking Time:** 1.5 hours

*It was fall. The sky was a bleary gray, and had been for days. Yet every time I hiked under some sugar maples, with their stunningly bright yellow leaves, I thought for sure that the sun had finally come blasting through the clouds.*

**Caution:** Watch out for bicycles. Bicyclists are restricted to counterclockwise use on this trail, so at least you'll know from which direction to expect them.

**Trail Directions:** The parking lot for this trail is .3 mile from the park entrance, on the left. This paved trail includes mileage marks every quarter mile, so it's a good trail to check the accuracy of your pedometer. The trail is accessible to persons with disabilities, although it climbs some fairly steep hills.

Begin the trail at the west side of the parking lot **[1]**. Start in some open woods with a small stream on your right and cross a small bridge **[2]** at .20 mi. There are several interesting trees in this section. The tree at .45 mi. with six trunks is a black cherry **[3]**. The small cherries are black when ripe and are a favorite among robins, orioles, and catbirds. Note the remarkable cottonwood tree **[4]** on your left at .53 mi.

The tree that looks like a porcupine at .63 mi. is the honey locust **[5]**, which is responsible for the dark brown, curlicue seed pods you often see on trails. The tree on your right at .73 mi. with the orange bark and spiny branches is the Osage orange tree **[6]**.

At .82 mi. you will find a yellow bench **[7]**, along with the Harpst Pass and Harpst Valley trail intersection. If you are here in the fall, keep your eyes (and nose) open for clusters of small, wild grapes that have fallen onto the trail from the vines above. These are fragrant when ripe, and tasty, too! At 1.0 mi. see the octopus-tangle of grapevines **[8]** on your left. If you are lucky enough to find some ripe grapes, you could sit on the red bench **[9]** at 1.1 mi. to eat them.

Find a white bench **[10]** and the West Ridge trail intersection at 1.53 mi. Find another red bench **[11]** at 1.77 mi. An outcrop of boulders **[12]** at 1.85 mi. underneath a sugar maple canopy provides some good photographic subjects, with or without people. The last bench is blue **[13]**, at 2.17 mi.

Soon, you will enter another landscape. The maple and cottonwood canopy gives way to open sky. You walk uphill and begin to feel breeze on your face as you walk out onto some Missouri River loess hills. At 2.5 mi. the hilltop prairie **[14]** goes on in both directions as far as the eye can see. Watch for kestrels, hovering while searching for mice in the grass below. Look for cottontail rabbits bounding into thickets of blackberry and sumac. The last part of the trail winds through the prairie before returning you to the parking lot.

1. Start
2. Bridge
3. Black cherry tree
4. Cottonwood tree
5. Honey locust tree
6. Osage orange tree
7. Yellow bench
8. Grapevines
9. Red bench
10. White bench
11. Red bench
12. Boulders
13. Blue bench
14. Hilltop prairie

# 12.  Squaw Creek National Wildlife Refuge

- Hike where the ruckus of half a million snow geese and ducks replaces the sound of hiking boots shuffling through dead leaves.
- Bring your binoculars and bird field guides to help you identify everything from pintails to gadwalls, dowitchers to snipe, pheasants to snow geese, as well as the occasional swan.
- From an observation tower scope out the refuge, where white pelicans are the first heralds of fall in September and three hundred bald eagles arrive by early winter.
- Hike on a loess bluff hill, a rare geologic formation of wind-deposited soil from the past glacial period.

## Area Information

Unique wildlife viewing and hiking opportunities abound at Squaw Creek. One of four national wildlife refuges in Missouri, Squaw Creek was established in 1935 by President Franklin D. Roosevelt as a resting and feeding area for migratory birds and other wildlife. The 7,178-acre refuge includes a mosaic of wildlife habitat—open marsh, moist soil, flooded timber, cordgrass prairie, and forest.

Squaw Creek's main attraction is the migratory waterfowl that stop over every spring and fall in phenomenal numbers. During peak season, sometime in November or December, as many as 450,000 snow geese and 100,000 ducks feed and rest in the vast marshes. The diversity of habitat promotes a diversity of species—321 species of birds have been identified here so far. Come in spring for the best shorebird viewing. Come in fall to see pelicans, geese, ducks, and eagles.

Overlooking the refuge from the east like ancient guardians of the flocks are the rare loess bluff hills. Loess (a fine-grained fertile soil deposited by the wind) in itself is not uncommon, but these steep-sided mounds of loess are found in only a few other places in the world. In the words of early 20th-century natural historian Bohumil Shimek, the loess bluff hills "appear like a giant swell of a stormy sea which has been suddenly fixed." To make them even more exceptional, on top of these bluffs are some of the last remnants of the once vast native prairie.

One way to enjoy Squaw Creek's variety of landscapes and wildlife is to drive its auto tour route—another way is to hike its trails. One of the trails leads you to an observation tower in a marsh, where you can see bald eagles keeping watch for sick and injured waterfowl. Another takes you to the top of a loess bluff hill, where you can hear the wind in the native prairie grasses as you look out over the bustling refuge.

**Directions:** Drive about 35 miles northwest of St. Joseph on I-29. Take exit 79 and head southwest on Highway 159. The visitor center is about 2.25 miles on your left.

**Hours Open:** The refuge is open sunrise to sunset, year-round. The visitor center is open Monday through Friday from 7:30 A.M. to 4 P.M.

**Facilities:** The refuge offers a visitors center, a 10-mile auto tour route, several observation towers (including some that are accessible to persons with disabilities and some with scopes), and a picnic area.

**Permits and Rules:** Camping, overnight parking, collecting, and firearms are prohibited. Fishing is permitted. Pets are allowed but must be on a leash.

**Further Information:** Refuge Manager, Squaw Creek National Wildlife Refuge, P.O. Box 101, Mound City, MO 64470; 660-442-3187.

## Other Areas of Interest

Camping is available at **Big Lake State Park,** eight miles west of Squaw Creek. The park also offers a swimming pool, cabins, and a modern motel. For more information call 816-442-3770.

**St. Joseph** is home to the Pony Express Stables, Jesse James Home Museum, and hosts of other museums, theaters, mansions, and historic attractions. For more information call 816-232-4626.

# Squaw Creek
# National Wildlife Refuge

Omaha
100 Miles

Mound City

Exit 84

118

159

29

Davis Creek

E

Bigelow

Squaw Creek

Mallard
Marsh

Bluff
Pool

Pintail
Pool

Snow
Goose
Pool

Long
Slough

Cattail
Pool

Eagle
Pool

Pelican
Pool

159

Exit 79

St. Joseph
40 Miles

Loess Bluff
Trail

Eagle
Overlook
Trail

### L E G E N D
— Road
····· Trail
▬ Boundary

🏠 Headquarters

🗼 Observation
Tower

P Parking

Rulo, NE

Big Lake
State Park

N

# Loess Bluff Trail 🥾🥾🥾

**Distance Round-Trip:** 1 mile

**Estimated Hiking Time:** .75 hour

*Early on, you may notice nothing unusual about this trail. A gray squirrel scurries over dry oak leaves. A crow calls somewhere overhead . . . But wait. The 191 limestone steps near the end will kick your heartbeat into overdrive as they lift you to the top of one of Missouri's rarest natural features—a loess bluff prairie remnant.*

**Caution:** Loess is crumbly and easily eroded. Stay on the trail, especially on the blufftop. Also, the trail meanders alongside an active honeybee colony.

**Trail Directions:** You might want to stop in the visitor center and pick up a trail guide, which explains interesting features noted on the trail with numbered posts. Begin the trail at the signboard **[1]** directly behind the visitor center. Ignore spurs to the left and right at .03 mi. **[2]** and continue straight. At .04 mi. **[3]** you will find a planted plot that previews some of the plants found on the trail at the blufftop. The Indian grass, little bluestem, and side-oats grama found here are a sample of plants found in the vast prairies that covered about a third of the state during presettlement times. A folk remedy for warts is to soak the wart in water that's been standing in a cavity of a tree. You may find the ingredient for this remedy in a tree cavity at .13 mi. **[4]**, which is, incidentally, about the size of a witch's cauldron.

Continue under many black walnut, hackberry, and pawpaw trees, start to climb uphill, and find a wooden bench at .24 mi. **[5]**. Watch out for the active honeybee colony in an oak tree on your right at .33 mi. **[6]**. Soon you will find the first of the 191 limestone steps that will take you to the loess blufftop. These stones were carried by hand by Civilian Conservation Corps workers, who built the trail in 1936. As you ascend, you may find some of the light-colored steps dotted with small blue, waxy berries.

These are the fruit of the eastern red cedar, the only evergreen tree native to northwest Missouri. Because of its abundance, its evergreen nature, and its aroma, the cedar was (and still is) a popular choice for a Christmas tree.

At the blufftop (after step #191) you may find a good use for the bench in the stone shelter **[7]** at .42 mi. As you continue, notice how a slope's aspect (its position in relation to direction) influences its vegetation. Prairie grasses and forbs dominate the left side of the trail because these south-facing slopes receive lots of sunlight and are warmer and drier. Conversely, trees dominate the shadier, damper north-aspect slopes on the right.

The overlook **[8]** at .50 mi. offers unusual vistas in all directions. Look out over the Squaw Creek Refuge, where muskrat houses in the marsh look like hundreds of ladybugs, floating on a calm, open ocean. From here, on a clear day, you can look across the refuge into Nebraska, and farther south, into Kansas. Look behind you at the loess hills, which occur in only a few places on earth. The sunny slopes grow vigorous stands of native prairie grasses, which turn a warm orange brown in the winter. The backbone ridges seem to hold back the crowded trees on the other side in the same manner as electric fences hold back cattle. Relax and enjoy the sights; the return hike is easier. Retrace your steps to return to the trailhead.

1. Start
2. Go straight
3. Native grasses
4. Tree cavity
5. Bench
6. Bee tree
7. Stone shelter
8. Overlook

# Eagle Overlook Trail 🥾

**Distance Round-Trip:** 1.35 miles

**Estimated Hiking Time:** .75 hour

*You will feel as if you stepped into a wildlife movie as you hike out into a 1,500-acre marsh on a narrow strip of land and watch the nature scenes unfold. American lotus looms for what seems like miles, and a large crayfish scuttles away as you approach the water. You are looking for bald eagles perching in nearby trees when you spot a white pelican, silently and gracefully passing just overhead.*

**Caution:** This trail is on a levee that is about 2 miles along a 10-mile auto tour route around the refuge. The road is *one way*, so if you take your vehicle to get to the trailhead be sure you have enough gas to go the distance. The auto route will take at least a half hour.

**Trail Directions:** Pick up an auto tour guide from the visitor center and locate the route, which begins across Highway 159 from the visitor center. Drive (or hike) about 2 miles (going clockwise) along the auto tour route, which is a gravel road that goes around most of the refuge. You will find the trail signboard just past the Eagle Pool water-control gates on the right, on a levee between Eagle and Pelican pools. Parking is available here along the side of the road.

It's interesting to observe the refuge from an overlook or look into it from the road, but this trail goes farther and gives you the privilege of hiking into the refuge. As you hike on this skinny isthmus, glance often into the skies. You may watch a dozen teal glide down and make an elegant water-ski landing, or you may witness a thousand snow geese boil up like a loud, gray cloud, take flight for a few confusing moments, and settle back down quietly.

Begin at the signboard **[1]**. Probably one of the first things you'll notice is the great number of brushy, domed muskrat houses **[2]** in the water on both sides of the trail. The walls of these houses are made of nearby aquatic vegetation, are about one foot thick,

and keep the inside cool in summer and warm in winter. The muskrat enters the dry interior of the house through an underwater tunnel. Keep watch for ducks, geese, eagles, snakes, turtles, and other animals that commonly use the houses for basking or idling.

Some of the aquatic plants nearby that wildlife use for food and shelter are arrowhead, cattail, and river bulrush. The American lotus **[3],** found in the water on both sides of the trail, has plate-sized leaves that lie on top of the water and a large, dish-shaped seed pod. If you are here during summer, look for the radiant, saucer-sized yellow blooms. Some lotus seeds found in the Orient have the distinction of being the oldest, still viable seeds in the world—over 900 years old.

As you continue the trail, notice the odd loess bluff hills **[4],** which dominate the horizon on the right. From this distance, the warmer, drier southern slopes look shaved, contrasted with the northern slopes, which are crowded with trees. These hills are made of silty soil that was deposited by the wind after being ground fine by retreating glaciers. Loess bluff hills are found in only a few places on earth.

At .67 mi. is an observation tower **[5],** which is a good vantage point to watch ducks, geese, deer, coyotes, and the occasional swan. Further hiking on the levee is prohibited, so you must retrace your steps to return to the trailhead. On the way back, check the shore next to the water for a highway of muskrat, raccoon, and other wildlife tracks, as well as burrowing crayfish tunnels.

1. Start
2. Muskrat houses
3. American lotus
4. Loess bluff hills
5. Observation tower

# Southeast

The southeast region of Missouri comprises the area south of the Missouri River and east of Highway 19.

## Topography

In almost every way possible, this part of Missouri is the most diverse. It contains the highest and lowest points in the state and areas of the most relief and the least. It contains the oldest exposed land mass and the youngest. Desertlike glades are home to dwarfed, scrubby trees, while swamps and wet forests in the Bootheel produce some of the largest trees in the nation. Topographically, the region can be divided into three areas—Ozark, Ozark border, and Mississippi Lowlands.

The Ozark Highlands, which cover almost the lower half of Missouri (40 percent of the state), compose the western half of the southeast region of Missouri. The Ozarks are an unglaciated area of greater relief and elevation than surrounding areas. Characteristic features include steep topography, thin, rocky, residual soils, deep erosion by streams, and extensive forests. While glaciers, seas, or floods repeatedly covered surrounding areas, the Ozarks have remained exposed for 250 million years. The St. Francois Mountains, in the center of the southeast region, are igneous in origin and considered the geologic core of the Ozarks. Exposed granites and rhyolites are around 1.5 billion years old—some of the oldest rocks on the continent.

The Ozark border, an area along the lower Missouri and Mississippi Rivers, is a transition zone between the Ozarks and the big rivers. The rugged hills resemble the Ozark landscape, but the soils are influenced by the rivers and are much deeper and more productive. The Mississippi Lowlands, often referred to as the Bootheel region, are a sharp contrast to the rugged, rocky Ozarks. Except for Crowley's Ridge, a disjunct series of forested, low hills that rise in a diagonal line just above the Bootheel, the Mississippi Lowlands are a flat, alluvial plain with slight relief. Once the northern boundary of the Gulf of Mexico, much of the area is less than 100 meters above sea level. Missouri's lowest point occurs at the Bootheel's southwest tip.

## Major Rivers and Lakes

The southeast region is bordered on the north by the Missouri River and on the east by the Mississippi River. The St. Francis River carries the distinction of forming the western boundary of the Bootheel. Nearly all the region's rivers are rock bottomed and clear, and most are popular for floating and fishing. At the top of the region, the Meramec River is the most biologically diverse in the Midwest. The Current and Jacks Fork are managed by the National Park Service as the Ozark National Scenic Riverways because of their high-quality waters, scenic beauty, and recreation opportunities. The Eleven Point, farther south, is another spring-fed, scenic river favored by canoeists. To the east, the Black, St. Francis, and Castor Rivers begin in the St. Francois Mountains and include sections of shut-ins, where rushing water sculpts and polishes igneous boulders in the streambed. National and regional kayak races are held on the St. Francis River in spring. The Bootheel is a massive grid of channels built to drain the low-lying area for agriculture, and the lower end of the Castor River was channelized to serve as a drainage canal.

The region includes two reservoirs—Clearwater Lake, formed by impounding the Black River, and Wappapello Lake, an impoundment of the St. Francis River. The swamps, marshes, and other wetlands at Mingo National Wildlife Refuge were formed in an abandoned channel of the Mississippi River when the river shifted east about 18,000 years ago.

## Common Plant Life

With the exception of prairies, virtually every plant and forest community in Missouri can be found in this diverse region. The Ozarks have been altered the least, and presettlement vegetation of pine and pine-oak forests still dominate. Much of the Ozark border has been converted to pastures and crop fields, but fragmented forests and forested bottomlands still persist. The Mississippi Lowlands lost almost all their original natural communities of extensive swamps, bottomland forests, and associated wetlands. Starting around 1900, bottomland forests were cleared and canals were constructed to drain the swamps for fields of soybeans, wheat, corn, rice, and cotton. The conversion was almost total. Today, only tiny fragments of swamp and bottomland forest are preserved. Except for the Bootheel, the southeast and south-central regions are the most heavily forested in the state. Besides mixed forests of oak, pine, and hickory, sheltered cove ravines along the Mississippi River hide trees more typical of Appalachian habitats—cucumber tree, tulip tree, and American beech.

Dry igneous forests and glades characterize the St. Francois Mountains and include blackjack oak, post oak, black hickory, and shortleaf pine. Common plants are Indian grass, little bluestem, buttonweed, reindeer lichen, sundrops, milkwort, and fameflower. Dolomite glades are common on the hills of the Ozarks and Ozark border and include little bluestem, sideoats grama, prairie dropseed, black-eyed Susan, Missouri evening primrose, calamint, and yellow coneflower. Gravel bar communities in the Ozarks commonly include shrubs like witch hazel, buttonbush, ninebark, swamp dogwood, and black willow, as well as wildflowers like blue star, cardinal flower, and mistflower. Bald cypress, tupelo gum, water hickory, and pumpkin ash dominate Bootheel swamps. Wet bottomland forests include bur oak, swamp white oak, water oak, swamp cottonwood, deciduous holly, swamp rose, and lizard's tail.

## Common Birds and Animals

Many animals that use glades live in adjacent forests, but several have adapted to live in the dry, desertlike habitat. While on glades with large rocks, look for eastern collared lizards, which turn bright blue and green (males) during breeding times. Other glade reptiles include the fence lizard, six-lined racerunner, eastern coachwhip snake, and flathead snake.

Birds commonly seen in upland forests are wild turkey, great horned owl, screech owl, various woodpeckers, yellow-throated warbler, nuthatch, summer tanager, titmouse, and red-eyed vireo. Other animals include the bobcat, gray fox, white-tailed deer, raccoon, opossum, squirrel, chipmunk, and various bats. Black bears are slowly returning to Missouri by expanding their range from Arkansas and are occasionally seen in more remote portions of the Ozarks.

Birds of bottomland forests and swamps include the barred owl, teal, ruddy duck, great blue heron, green heron, pileated woodpecker, Louisiana water thrush, prothonotary warbler, and cerulean warbler. Other animals include the muskrat, beaver, raccoon, water snake, river cooter, painted turtle, and stinkpot.

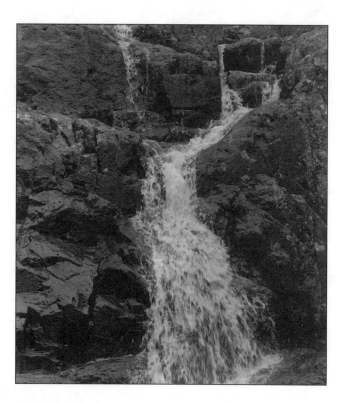

## Climate

The Bootheel area has the highest average temperature and precipitation in the state. Bootheel temperatures average 60 degrees F in spring, 79 degrees F in summer, 60 degrees F in fall, and 34 degrees F in winter. Precipitation here averages 51 inches annually. The rest of the southeast region's temperatures average 57 degrees F in spring, 78 degrees F in summer, 58 degrees F in fall, and 31 degrees F in winter. Precipitation varies greatly from top to bottom of this region; the average is 44 inches annually.

Finally, it is noteworthy that Taum Sauk Mountain, the state's highest point, is high enough to have a microclimate of its own. Its winter weather is like that of Kirksville in northeast Missouri, and summer temperatures rarely reach 90 degrees F.

## Best Features

- Incredibly huge trees at Big Oak Tree State Park
- Forested swamps in the Bootheel
- Large and fabulously decorated caves
- Vast igneous glades with astounding vistas
- Mina Sauk Falls, the state's highest waterfall
- Refreshing water and scenic beauty of Johnson's Shut-Ins
- Numerous beautiful springs, including the largest single-outlet spring in the nation

# 13. Urban St. Louis

- Walk up to the Arch, feel its warm stainless steel sides, and experience Arch vertigo for yourself.
- Ride in a five-person capsule to the top of the 630-foot-tall Arch, the tallest human-made monument in the Western Hemisphere with a 25-mile view on a clear day.
- Hike past grizzly bears, polar bears, gazelles, and a Southern pudu, the world's smallest deer, which is only shin-high when standing!

## Area Information

In 1764, Pierre LaClede, a French trader from New Orleans, set up a post on the Mississippi River just a few miles south of where the Missouri River flows into the Mississippi from the west. He chose a good spot. St. Louis was a thriving fur-trading settlement by the time President Thomas Jefferson bought the Louisiana Territory from France. In 1804 Lewis and Clark began their exploration of the unknown West from St. Louis and returned with reports of the new land's wealth. Land-hungry settlers in the East flocked to St. Louis and outfitted for journeys west, and St. Louis became, literally and commercially, the gateway to the West.

In 1947 a national architectural competition was held to create a design for the Jefferson National Expansion Memorial, a monument to commemorate Thomas Jefferson's purchase of the Louisiana Territory and the wave of westward expansion that followed. An ambitious design by Eero Saarinen was chosen—the mightiest freestanding arch ever built, taller than any symbolic monument except the Eiffel Tower. Remarkably, no inner frame or skeleton holds up the Arch; its steel panels, composed of equilateral triangles, bear the Arch's entire weight. The Arch grounds and museum are administered by the National Park Service.

Forest Park was dedicated in 1876 as a carriage park and was the site for the 1904 World's Fair, an event that attracted 20 million visitors. Over 1,500 plaster-of-paris buildings were constructed for the fair. The second largest urban park in the nation, Forest Park is used by over 10 million visitors a year, who come to its lawns, lakes, museums, and zoo to play and relax.

**Directions:** Take any major highway in Missouri east toward St. Louis and you'll end up at the Arch. On I-70 east, take exit 250A. Follow signs to the Arch or the riverfront. Forest Park is four miles west of the Arch on I-64/Highway 40. Take Hampton Avenue north into the park and follow the signs to the art museum.

**Hours Open:** The Arch grounds are open from 6 A.M. to 11 P.M. year-round. The visitor center and museum are open daily from 8 A.M. to 10 P.M. in the summer and from 9 A.M. to 6 P.M. in the winter. A 10 P.M. curfew is enforced in Forest Park. The St. Louis Zoo is always free and is open daily from 9 A.M. to 5 P.M., except for Christmas and New Year's Day.

**Facilities:** The visitor center underneath the Arch offers tram rides to the top, the Museum of Westward Expansion, two theaters, and a bookstore. Ranger-led tours of the Old Courthouse are available. Forest Park facilities include a skating rink, tennis courts, science center, golf courses, musical theater, conservatory, boat rentals, zoo, art museum, fishing, and sledding.

**Permits and Rules:** Smoking or pets are not allowed in the Arch visitor center or Old Courthouse. While on Arch grounds, pets must be leashed.

**Further Information:** Superintendent, Jefferson National Expansion Memorial, 11 North Fourth Street, St. Louis, MO 63102; 314-982-1410. For information on Forest Park call 314-535-1503 or 314-367-7275.

## St. Louis

LEGEND

— Paved Road
⋯⋯ Trail
⭐1 Arch
⭐2 Busch Memorial Stadium
⭐3 Kiel Center
⭐4 Union Station
⭐5 Old Cathedral
⭐6 Old Courthouse
⭐7 Convention Center
⭐8 New Federal Building
⭐9 Federal Building
⭐10 City Hall

## Forest Park

LEGEND

— Road
⋯⋯ Bike Path
⋯⋯ Trail
P Parking

⭐1 History Museum
⭐2 F. Park Forever
⭐3 Lindell Pavilion
⭐4 Cabanne House
⭐5 Skating Rink
⭐6 Tennis Courts
⭐7 Science Center
⭐8 Golf & Tennis Club
⭐9 Park Office
⭐10 Jewel Box
⭐11 Opera House
⭐12 Boat House
⭐13 W. Fair Pavilion
⭐14 Zoo
⭐15 Art Museum
⭐16 Golf Course
⭐17 Tennis Center
⭐18 Turtle Park

# Arch Area 👢👢

**Distance Round-Trip:** 2 miles

**Estimated Hiking Time:** 1.25 hours

*Hold both ends of a necklace about nine inches apart, allowing the loop to hang freely. You are holding a catenary curve—the exact design (though upside-down) of the Arch.*

**Caution:** Cross streets with care and only at corners; Memorial Drive is a major artery.

**Trail Directions:** Park in the garage for the Arch or in one of the lots along the river. A fee is charged for parking. Begin your hike at the north leg of the Arch **[1]**, a good place to pat its stainless steel sides. (You'll see many people doing this.) Feel the warmth of the steel. As the two legs of the arch were being built, engineers took measurements at night to avoid variations caused by the sun's heat. Now look up. If there are any clouds at all, you'll be able to experience Arch vertigo, the remarkable illusion that the monument is falling over. In reality, the Arch sways a little in the wind but only as far as four inches off center since it was built in 1965.

Hike northward, away from the Arch, along a curved walkway lined with ash trees. Bear right at two forks in the trail. You'll step out onto the William Clark overlook at .23 mi. **[2]**. The Eads Bridge, the first one on your left, was completed in 1874 and was St. Louis's first bridge over the Mississippi. Granite for its massive piers came from quarries in the Elephant Rocks area, south of Potosi. The silver ship in front of you is the *Admiral.* Once the largest river excursion ship in the nation, it is now permanently moored as a casino.

Turn right, descend the steps, and walk under some bald cypress trees. You'll reach the grand staircase at .44 mi. **[3]**, a favorite place for meeting, sunning, and watching activities by the water. Continue straight and pass some steamboat replicas moored to the levee that serve as excursion ships and restaurants. When you reach the world's only floating McDonald's on your left, ascend the steps and walk across the walkway. Climb a final set of steps to reach the Meriwether Lewis overlook at .83 mi. **[4]**, with great views of the river, the Arch, and the assembly of skyscrapers behind it.

Turn around, descend the first set of steps, and turn left. Turn right at the fork at .93 mi. **[5]** and walk toward the Arch. Just before reaching the south leg,

turn left, toward the cathedral with the green steeple. This is the Basilica of St. Louis, the King, and is affectionately known as the Old Cathedral (1.20 mi.) **[6]**. The oldest Catholic church west of the Mississippi, the cathedral was founded in 1770. It's okay to step quietly inside. From here, turn right on Memorial Drive, pass the Old Cathedral Museum, and turn left onto Market Street. Luther Ely Smith Plaza, on your right, was named for the St. Louisan who proposed the memorial in 1933 that is now realized as the Arch. Cross Fourth Street and enter the Old Courthouse if it's open.

The Old Courthouse (1.4 mi.) **[7]** was the site of slave auctions, the Dred Scott trial, and is interpreted by museum galleries and ranger-led tours. Walk under the magnificent rotunda and exit the building opposite the side you entered. Just across Broadway is a red granite monument marking the beginning of Boone's Lick Road (1.5 mi.) **[8]**, the nation's first westward trail this side of the Mississippi. Walk through Kiener Plaza toward the fountain with the bronze statue, *The Runner,* in its center (1.6 mi.) **[9]**. At the far side of the fountain, turn and face the Old Courthouse for an unexpectedly splendid view of the Arch, which has a way of complimenting its surrounding structures, both old and new. Turn right on Chestnut Street, which borders Kiener Plaza on the north. Stay on Chestnut until it leads you to the north leg of the Arch, where you started.

1. Start
2. William Clark overlook
3. Grand staircase
4. Meriwether Lewis overlook
5. Right turn
6. Old Cathedral
7. Old Courthouse
8. Boone's Lick Road monument
9. *The Runner*

# Forest Park 🥾

**Distance Round-Trip:** 2.5 miles

**Estimated Hiking Time:** 1.5 hours

*I liked watching the polar bears' antics and strolling through the 1904 Flight Cage, but I liked the Southern pudu best, a 14-inch-high deer that makes its living pushing over small trees!*

**Caution:** Watch for bicycle and car traffic, and don't feed the bears! (or the hammerkops!)

**Trail Directions:** Park on any of the streets near the art museum (parking is free) and begin your hike at the statue of Saint Louis on his horse, in front of the art museum **[1]**. As you face the lake at the bottom of the hill, the Grand Basin, turn right and hike down Fine Arts Drive. Just after you cross the paved bicycle path, make a gentle curve to your right through the shaded park and look for a building with blue tiles and animal figures on its side. This is the zoo entrance.

Enter the St. Louis Zoo at the Living World Entrance, with educational, interactive exhibits (.30 mi.) **[2]**. (If the zoo is closed, walk around to the zoo Hampton exit at its southeast end to resume the hike.) Walk through the Living World and go down the steps outside. Turn left on the main zoo path to the Bear Pits (.44 mi.) **[3]**. Pass the black bears, spectacled bears, grizzly bears, and polar bears, and remain on the main zoo path. Pass the Kiener Memorial Entrance on your left and make your way toward the black walk-through bird cage. Enter the 1904 Flight Cage at .70 mi. **[4]**.

Built by the Smithsonian Institution as an attraction for the 1904 World's Fair held in Forest Park, the giant cage's continuing popularity led to its purchase by St. Louis, and eventually to the formation of the St. Louis Zoo in 1913. Look for white-faced whistling ducks and white-headed buffalo weavers. You can't miss the pink flamingos; they're pink and loud.

Turn left at all forks in the trail after exiting the Flight Cage and you'll arrive at the antelope fields on your right at .80 mi. **[5]**. Here are gazelles, kudus, and the Southern pudu, the world's smallest (and one of its rarest) deer, standing only 14 inches high. Stay on

the main path until you reach the Hampton exit at .95 mi. **[6]**, where you exit the zoo, cross Concourse Drive, and continue on Carr Lane Drive. Turn right at 1.04 mi. **[7]** on Wells Drive and turn left on McKinley Drive. Take the sidewalk to the art-deco glass house on your right. This is the Jewel Box (1.32 mi.) **[8]**, a 1936 greenhouse must-see for anyone interested in houseplants or botany.

Return to McKinley Drive, continue on your right, and go through several intersections. The building on your right, just as you cross a canal, is the Municipal Theater, better known as the Muny (1.67 mi.) **[9]**. This has been an outdoor theater since 1919 and has hosted such entertainers as W.C. Fields, Grace Kelly, and Bob Hope. Curve to the left and you'll be on Government Street. The lake on your right is Post Dispatch Lake (1.88 mi.) **[10]**, where boats of all types are available for rent when weather permits. The shelter on the hilltop on your left is the World's Fair Pavilion, often used, like the Jewel Box, for weddings and other special events. Cross Washington Drive and stay on Government. Turn right at 2.21 mi. **[11]** on Fine Arts Drive to return to the Saint.

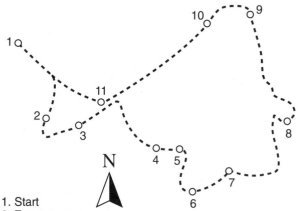

1. Start
2. Zoo entrance
3. Bear Pits
4. 1904 Flight Cage
5. Antelope fields
6. Hampton exit
7. Right turn
8. Jewel Box
9. The Muny
10. Post Dispatch Lake
11. Right turn

# 14. Dr. Edmund A. Babler Memorial State Park

- Discover spicebush, an aromatic shrub you can smell when you brush against it on the trail. A tea made from its bark or fruit has been used to treat everything from colds to dysentery to intestinal worms!
- Observe an ant metropolis next to the trail.
- Hike through a grove of pawpaws, the only food plant for caterpillars of a distinctive woodland butterfly, the zebra swallowtail.
- Find at least three official state species on one trail.

## Area Information

Dr. Edmund A. Babler Memorial State Park is named after Edmund A. Babler, a renowned and beloved St. Louis physician. After Babler died suddenly from pneumonia at age 54 in 1930, his two brothers, Jacob and Henry, gave the park to the state as a living memorial.

The park, only a 20-minute drive from downtown St. Louis, is an interesting blend of urban and rural characteristics. Manicured lawns and trees surround the full-length bronze statue of Dr. Babler, and the wide entry avenue with its impressive stone gateway is reminiscent of a metropolitan plaza. Yet Babler is home to unusually tall and rich forests of oak, basswood, sugar maple, and walnut, a quality owing to its geographic location.

Situated in a transition area between the rugged Ozarks to the south and the expansive glacial plains to the north, Babler State Park has both highly dissected ridges and rich soil. Located only about two miles from the Missouri River floodplain, the park's rugged landscape was covered with deep deposits of windblown glacial dust—a fertile soil called loess. It is these loess deposits and deep sheltered valleys that have nurtured Babler's rich forest communities.

An area near the campground is a designated state natural area, featuring an old-growth white oak and sugar maple forest that has remained relatively undisturbed since presettlement times. When dedicated in 1938, Babler was a long drive into the country from St. Louis. Now it is a much-needed green oasis amid an ever-growing suburban landscape.

**Directions:** Babler State Park is in west St. Louis County. From the intersection of Highways 100 and 109 in Wildwood, turn north on Highway 109 for 3.7 miles. Turn left into the entrance gates.

**Hours Open:** The park is open from 7 A.M. to 9 P.M. year-round. The visitor center is open from 8:30 A.M. to 4 P.M. Monday through Friday and from 9 A.M. to 4 P.M. on weekends. The visitor center is closed on Christmas, New Year's Day, Easter, and Thanksgiving.

**Facilities:** The park offers a campground, picnic areas, horseback-riding rentals and trails, bicycle trails, a tennis court, swimming pool, visitor center with exhibits, amphitheater, and an outdoor education center designed to accommodate campers with disabilities.

**Permits and Rules:** Hikers are permitted on hiking, bicycle, and horse trails, but bicycles are permitted only on paved trails and roads. Horses are permitted only on equestrian trails. Pets must always be leashed.

**Further Information:** Park Superintendent, Dr. Edmund A. Babler Memorial State Park, 800 Guy Park Drive, Chesterfield, MO 63005; 314-458-3813.

## Park Trails

**Dogwood Trail** 👢👢👢—2 miles—This trail gives a good sampling of the park's upland forests, ravines, and moist forests. Two sections are united with a horse trail. It shares a trailhead with the Woodbine Trail.

**Woodbine Trail** 👢👢👢—1.75 miles—Hike next to a stand of towering sweet gum trees, past a CCC-era stone building, and through some lush, wooded ravines. A portion of the trail is shared by bicyclists. The trailhead is at the Nature Trail parking area, off Guy Park Drive.

# Dr. Edmund A. Babler
# Memorial State Park

N

Division of Youth Services

Walnut Grove Shelter

Dogwood Trail

Cochran Shelter

Wild Horse Creek Rd.

Wirth Drive

Nature Trail Parking Area

Hawthorn Trail

Alta Shelter

Guy Park Drive

Wood-bine Trail

Cochran Drive

109

Virginia Day Memorial Trail

Bike Trail

Jacob L. Babler Outdoor Education Center

Rieger Rd.

L E G E N D

| | | | |
|---|---|---|---|
| —— Road | Visitor Center | Trailhead | P Parking |
| Park Service Road | Camping | Shelter | Horse Trailer Parking Only |
| ····· Trail | Swimming Pool | Stables | |
| Boundary | | | |
| Area Closed To General Public | | | |

# Virginia Day Memorial Trail 🥾🥾

**Distance Round-Trip:** 1.5 miles

**Estimated Hiking Time:** .75 hour

*Trace is an old word for trail. People traversing new territory followed the tracks, bent grasses, or other barely perceptible traces of those who had gone before them. Consequently, traces evolved into trails, literally and semantically.*

**Caution:** The trail is hard packed, moist, shaded, and slippery in places. Also, watch out for land snails on the trail to avoid stepping on them; they are abundant here.

**Trail Directions:** Park at the visitor center and find the trailhead across the road, off a paved loop **[1]**. What little sunlight makes it through the tall canopies of white oak, red oak, and sugar maple is usually blocked by shorter basswood, dogwood, and redbud. Right away, the trail introduces you to one of the park's most outstanding natural features—dense shade.

Turn right at the three-way intersection at .13 mi. **[2]** and again at .17 mi. **[3]**. If you are here in spring you will be treated to a wildflower display 10 to 20 feet tall in the form of blooming dogwood and redbud. Look for the umbrellas of mayapples here, adding their shade to the rich forest floor. Turn right at the intersection at .31 mi. **[4]**. The patch of shrubs growing on both sides of the trail at .46 mi. **[5]** looks like poison ivy but it isn't—it's fragrant sumac. Although both plants have "leaves of three," poison ivy's middle leaflet has a longer stem than the others. Fragrant sumac's middle leaflet stem is either very short or absent.

As you descend into a shaded valley notice how the Christmas ferns increase. Pawpaws are more numerous here too, their giant, unlobed leaves

providing a pleasant contrast to the lacy fern leaves below. Turn left at the spur intersection at .66 mi. **[6]**. In the low areas, especially at the big bend at .88 mi. **[7]**, look for spicebush that tends to encroach on the trail. This aromatic shrub produces shiny green fruit in May that turns bright red by October. The fruit was used during the Revolutionary War as a substitute for allspice, and the shrub's leaves were used as a tea during the Civil War. Listen for the trills of tree frogs here and watch out for land snails, feeding on the thin layers of algae and moss on the shaded trail.

Cross a wooden bridge over an intermittent stream at 1.30 mi. **[8]**. When you return to the intersection at **[2]** turn right to complete your hike.

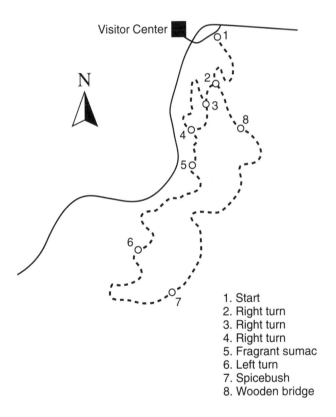

1. Start
2. Right turn
3. Right turn
4. Right turn
5. Fragrant sumac
6. Left turn
7. Spicebush
8. Wooden bridge

# Hawthorn Trail 🥾🥾

**Distance Round-Trip:** 1.15 miles

**Estimated Hiking Time:** .75 hour

*You'll find at least one kind of hawthorn here (of the state's 79 hawthorn species), representative of Missouri's state flower. You'll also find the state tree (flowering dogwood) and the state fossil (crinoid). You may even find the state insect (honeybee) on the glade and the state bird (bluebird) near the trailhead. Chances of spotting Missouri's state aquatic animal (paddlefish), however, are low.*

**Caution:** Check for ticks after passing through the glade.

**Trail Directions:** Park at the Alta picnic shelter, located on Wirth Drive, on the west side of the park. Begin the trail at the signboard **[1]** across the road from the south end of the parking lot.

You'll cross a horse trail near the trailhead and continue on a dry, wooded ridgetop. White oaks and sugar maples are plentiful, as well as flowering dogwood and redbud. Look for sassafras, with three types of leaves on the same tree. Some leaves have no lobes (football shaped), some have one lobe (mitten shaped), and others have two lobes (trident shaped).

Turn left at the intersection at .10 mi. **[2].** At around .25 mi. **[3]** start looking next to the trail on the right side for low mounds of granular soil, dotted with small holes. These are the tops of underground colonies of ants. The main "city" is about 6 feet wide and 75 feet long. The hundreds of thousands of ants that live here are important members of the forest community. Small reptiles and amphibians often feed on ants, as do birds and other insects. If you are here on a warm day you will probably see a steady stream of worker ants (all females) emerge from a hole, drop a load of soil, and return to the tunnel.

A post oak with limbs hanging over the trail marks a rocky, sunny opening in the forest—a limestone glade remnant (.54 mi.) **[4].** Notice all the bluestem grass here, interrupted by patches of yellow wing-stem sunflowers and spiderwort. Bright red fruit of the fragrant sumac adds its color, too. To the left, next to the forest, are several hawthorn trees. Close observation of the exposed slabs of limestone bedrock on the trail will reveal fossils of crinoids and other sea creatures. At the north end of the glade is the former state champion gum bumelia. Normally a glade tree of small, stunted stature, this one's girth is over three feet!

After you reenter the forest, some boulders on your left at .65 mi. **[5]** provide glimpses of the outlying rugged ridges through the trees. Small patches of ferns appear on your right and big patches of may-apples cascade down the slope on your left. Be watching for the metallic green six-spotted tiger beetle, running and flying ahead of you on the trail. If you've seen zebra swallowtails (medium-sized black-and-white striped butterflies) in the park, it's because of the abundance of pawpaws, a small, tropical-looking tree of moist woods. The pawpaw is the only food plant for zebra swallowtail caterpillars. At .90 mi. **[6]** is a grove of pawpaws on both sides of the trail. Check the leaves for caterpillar holes. Turn left at **[2]** to return to the trailhead.

1. Start
2. Left turn
3. Ant metropolis
4. Limestone glade
   remnant
5. Overlook
6. Pawpaw grove

# 15. Mastodon State Historic Site

- What was nine feet high at the shoulder, weighed five tons, and had eight-foot-long tusks? (Big hint: A full-sized replica of this animal's skeleton is at Mastodon State Historic Site.)
- Visit the archeological site that yielded the first solid evidence that humans coexisted with mastodons 12,000 years ago.
- Hike on top of an ancient ocean bed on a natural sidewalk in the forest.
- Stroll quietly on a trail above a gravel-bottomed stream to spy on stonerollers, hornyhead chubs, and northern hog suckers.

## Area Information

In the early 1800s, bones of many now-extinct animals were found just south of St. Louis, in what is now known as the Kimmswick Bone Bed. An early discoverer, Albert C. Koch, assembled a colossal collage of animal bones and named his creation the Missouri Leviathan. Describing his creature as "swift as the descending eagle and terrible as the angel of the night," Koch toured the spectacle across the United States, sometimes with a three-piece band playing in its rib cage. Koch's leviathan turned out to be an American mastodon, an elephant-like beast that browsed on trees and roamed what is now Missouri during the ice age that occurred from 35,000 to 10,000 years ago.

Over the span of a century, the bones from more than 60 mastodons were reportedly taken from the Kimmswick Bone Bed, which became known as one of the most extensive Pleistocene bone beds in the country. In 1970, four local women led a movement to preserve the bone bed, enabling the state to buy the site in 1976. Archeological history was made at the site in 1979 when a large stone spear point was found with the bones of American mastodons, providing the first undisputed evidence of the association of human being and mastodon in North America. For the first time, it could be considered that early human's contact with mastodons and other large mammals at the end of the ice age may have contributed to their extinction.

As you enter the museum at Mastodon State Historic Site, a sign invites you to "Please—touch this tooth," and on top of the display is a genuine young adult mastodon molar. As you run your fingers over the tooth's six mountainlike ridges, you are reenacting a human-mastodon contact that was proven to have taken place on this spot 12,000 years ago.

**Directions:** At the south edge of St. Louis, take exit 186 (Imperial/Kimmswick) off Highway 55. Turn north on West Outer Road, and go .9 mile to the museum.

**Hours Open:** The picnic area is open from 8 A.M. to dusk, year-round. The museum is open from 9 A.M. to 4:30 P.M. Monday through Saturday and from noon to 4:30 P.M. on Sunday, year-round. The museum is closed on Easter, Thanksgiving, Christmas, and New Year's Day.

**Facilities:** The site features a museum with animal and human artifacts, interpretive exhibits, and an audio-visual area. A small fee is collected for entrance to the museum. Excavations have been closed to protect the bone bed, but an interpretive kiosk at the Kimmswick Bone Bed explains the site's past excavations. Picnic tables are available at the museum and the picnic area.

**Permits and Rules:** Wading is allowed in Rock Creek at the picnic area. Alcoholic beverages are prohibited on the parking lots or creek beaches. Camping is permitted only by special groups with permission of the site administrator. Pets must be leashed. Collection of plants, wildlife, fossils, or artifacts is prohibited. Hikers may not leave marked trails.

**Further Information:** Historic Site Administrator, Mastodon State Historic Site, 1050 Museum Drive, Imperial, MO 63052; 314-464-2976.

## Other Areas of Interest

Just southwest of Mastodon, off Highway 21, **Sandy Creek Covered Bridge State Historic Site** features a bridge built in 1872 and rebuilt in 1887—one of only four covered bridges remaining in the state. The site includes a picnic area and an interpretive shelter about covered bridges. For more information call Mastodon State Historic Site.

## Site Trails

**Wildflower Trail** 👢👢👢—.5 mile—This trail takes you down several flights of steps across an old limestone quarry and down to the base of the limestone bluff where the famous human artifacts and mastodon bones were discovered. An interpretive kiosk is at the site. The trail begins behind the museum.

# Mastodon State Historic Site

LEGEND

Road
Trail
Boundary

Visitor Center and Park Office
Scout Camping
Picnic Area
Pit Toilet

# Limestone Hill Trail 👢👢👢👢

**Distance Round-Trip:** 2.25 miles

**Estimated Hiking Time:** 1.25 hours

*I liked the rough, limestone boulders that protruded from the ravined slopes, just before the long bluff walk. Tiny orange and red mushrooms shaped like little funnels poked through the dark green moss on the boulders and were as brilliant as any spring wildflower.*

**Caution:** Use caution when crossing Seckman Road; vehicles can be fast and numerous. Also, the trail is sometimes slippery, due to small, loose rocks on hills and algae-covered bedrock.

**Trail Directions:** The Limestone Hill Trail and the Spring Branch Trail share a trailhead, located in the picnic area, just west of the visitor center. From the entrance to the visitor center, turn south on West Outer Road for .2 mile. Turn west on Seckman Road for .9 mile and turn left at the sign for the picnic area. The trailhead is at the corner of the first parking lot on your right.

Begin at the sign for the trailhead **[1]** and turn right at the intersection at .01 mi. **[2]**. At .02 mi. **[3]** are the remnants of the Bollefer family springhouse. Turn right at the fork in the trail, just past the springhouse, and cross Seckman Road at .05 mi. **[4]**. Turn left at the intersection at .06 mi. **[5]**. Notice the thorns up and down the trunks of the honey locust trees on your right. New, bright green thorns are mixed in clusters with older brown ones. Many of the vines climbing the sugar maple trees are trumpet creeper, which produces orange red, trumpet-shaped blossoms in July and August.

Hike onto a natural sidewalk at .10 mi. **[6]**, made of limestone bedrock. Composed of layers of sediment from the bottom of ancient oceans, limestone often reveals its layers as it erodes. Notice the limestone bluffs on your right. Enough soil has accumulated in their eroded cracks to support ebony spleenwort and other ferns. Sometimes you can see the layers in perfectly parallel, horizontal lines. Soon you'll begin some switchbacks up a steep and rocky hill through an aged cedar forest, with a few white oaks mixed in. A resting bench provides a good place to stop and notice the knobby and distorted trunks of many of the old cedars, reminiscent of the coniferous forests that were here when mastodons roamed the area.

The trail ascends a good exercise hill under some big ash trees, and the drainage valleys on each side of the trail become more evident. Ignore the spur on your right at .46 mi. **[7]** and go straight. Turn right at the intersection at .48 mi. **[8]**. Bear left at the wide, rocky fork in the trail at .59 mi. **[9]**. Several red mulberry trees grow on this ridgetop. Box turtles are quick to find their fallen fruit, which resembles a blackberry, in early summer. Pass a resting bench on your left and ignore the spur on your right at .82 mi. **[10]**. Now it's an easy downhill hike.

Notice the fierce competition for space by shrubs and young trees under the powerline at 1.21 mi. **[11]**. Follow the yellow arrows and turn right at the intersection at 1.34 mi. **[12]**. The trail passes through a beautiful, shaded forest with deep ravines and rough, protruding boulders. An intermittent stream trickles at the bottom on your left. Just after the trail swings to the right, a scenic limestone bluff appears at 1.40 mi. **[13]**. Smooth cliffbrake and alum root adorn its weathered sides, while wild grape and trumpet creeper vines connect it to the tree canopy. At one point, the trail puts you in a squeeze between the bluff and a hackberry trunk.

The bluff continues at your right shoulder for quite a distance. Look for delicate columbine and an assortment of ferns. Wild hydrangea sprouts where water trickles from small cracks. A small stream crossing the trail marks the end of your bluff walk. You'll find a spur to the entrance of the picnic area on your left at 2.15 mi. **[14]**. Turn left at this spur or at **[5]** to finish your hike.

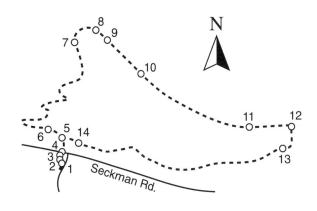

| | |
|---|---|
| 1. Start | 8. Right turn |
| 2. Right turn | 9. Bear left |
| 3. Springhouse remnants | 10. Go straight |
| 4. Road crossing | 11. Powerline |
| 5. Left turn | 12. Right turn |
| 6. Natural sidewalk | 13. Limestone bluff |
| 7. Go straight | 14. Spur to picnic area |

# Spring Branch Trail 🥾

**Distance Round-Trip:** .75 mile

**Estimated Hiking Time:** .5 hour

*I walked around the old springhouse, feeling its stone walls. I imagined the sturdy door that must have been in place once, keeping raccoons out of precious milk, hand-churned butter, and Mason jars filled with green beans, dill pickles, and gooseberries.*

**Caution:** The area is prone to occasional flooding, because of Rock Creek and the spring branch.

**Trail Directions:** The Limestone Hill Trail and the Spring Branch Trail share a trailhead, located in the picnic area, just west of the visitor center. From the entrance to the visitor center, turn south on West Outer Road for .2 mile. Turn west on Seckman Road for .9 mile and turn left at the sign for the picnic area. The trailhead is at the corner of the first parking lot on your right.

Begin at the sign for the trailhead **[1]**. Turn left at the intersection at .01 mi. **[2]** and cross the small, wooden bridge over the spring branch of Bollefer Spring, named for a family that once lived in the area. Bushy, green mats of plants in the stream are watercress, an indicator of springwater and a highly favored wild edible. A traditional wilted salad recipe calls for watercress, hot bacon grease, vinegar, and sugar. Across the bridge, follow the trail to the left along the spring branch. Enormous cottonwood and sycamore tree trunks make the stream look smaller than it really is.

At .07 mi. **[3]** is a four-way intersection. Take the second trail from the left, which will take you behind the picnic shelter. Look for boxelder trees here, which have leaves that resemble poison ivy and often have small, green sprouts growing from the trunk. Boxelder trees can grow in many habitats but are not good choices for landscaping around homes because of inevitable periodic infestations of red and black boxelder bugs. Soon you'll pass another picnic area on your left. Turn right at .20 mi. **[4]** at the wooden bridge and you'll see Rock Creek, a tributary to the Mississippi River, riffling and churning on your left. Several spurs off the trail down to gravel washes and sandbars give testimony to the creek's use as a summertime wading and splashing hole.

As the trail parallels the creek, look into the water and you'll notice a variety of fish. Look for stonerollers, four- or five-inch-long fish that push small stones around on the creek bottom, grazing on algae underneath. These curious fish have the odd habit of occasionally flipping vertically out of the water on warm days in late fall. Northern hog suckers live here, too, and resemble small, motionless sharks when seen from above. As you continue, a sprawling catalpa tree looms over the creek near a stand of horsetail, a slender and ancient water-loving plant.

At .42 mi. **[5]**, just before reaching some private homes on the right, turn right on the wide, mowed path. Here the trail winds through a young forest of boxelder and hackberry trees near the park boundary on your left. Listen for the mewing calls of the gray catbird, which, like the mockingbird, is often associated with residential areas.

Turn right at the intersection at .58 mi. **[6]** and cross a small, wooden bridge over the Bollefer Spring branch. The limestone remnants of the Bollefer family springhouse come into view at .70 mi. **[7]**. Taking advantage of the cool year-round temperature of springwater (around 56 to 58 degrees in Missouri), families built springhouses, usually of stone, over springs or spring branches to cool perishable foods like milk and butter in the days before indoor refrigeration. In a few steps you'll return to **[2]**, where you turn left to complete your hike.

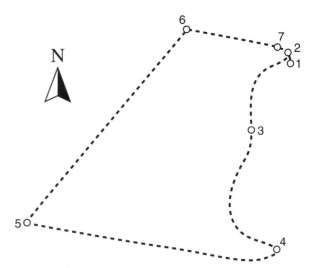

1. Start
2. Left turn
3. Four-way intersection
4. Right turn
5. Right turn
6. Right turn
7. Bollefer family springhouse

# 16. Trail of Tears State Park

- Stand on 600-foot-high Mississippi River blufftops with spectacular views of Ol' Man River and the Illinois floodplain.
- Get your blood pumping on some beautiful trails with some serious topographic relief.
- Look for doll's eyes.
- Find a cucumber magnolia.

## Area Information

It's easy to appreciate Trail of Tears State Park for its natural resources and its scenic beauty. Rich, moist forest bottoms are contrasted with sharp ridges and deep ravines. Blufftop overlooks offer dramatic views of the Mississippi, Missouri's largest river. The mixed hardwood forests of the park have been preserved with much of their original integrity, and two areas with special designations, Indian Creek Wild Area and Vancill Hollow Natural Area, offer their own natural features. One of these is a rare forest containing American beech, tulip trees, and cucumber magnolia, species more characteristic of the Appalachian Mountains than of the Ozarks.

But the park has a more somber cultural history. When the federal Indian Removal Act was passed in 1830, 13,000 Cherokee Native Americans were forced to leave their ancient homelands east of the Mississippi River and travel 1,200 miles to reservations in the west. During the bitter winter of 1838–39, a quarter of the entire Cherokee tribe died. "Trail of Tears" refers to routes used during this forced exodus.

The park interpretive center's main purpose is to teach visitors about this tragedy.

**Directions:** Trail of Tears State Park is on the Mississippi River, just north of Cape Girardeau. Go 10 miles east of Fruitland on Highway 177.

**Hours Open:** The site is open year-round.

**Facilities:** The park offers a visitor center, amphitheater, and picnicking; camping (including electric, nonelectric, and camping for special groups and backpackers), boating, and fishing on the Mississippi River; and boating, fishing, and swimming on 20-acre Lake Boutin. Most trails are for hikers only, but the Peewah Trail is open to hikers, backpackers, and equestrians.

**Permits and Rules:** Camping by backpackers on the Peewah Trail is allowed, but campfires are prohibited there. Bicycles are prohibited on all trails. Boats with electric motors only are allowed on Lake Boutin. Pets must always be leashed.

**Further Information:** Park Superintendent, Trail of Tears State Park, 429 Moccasin Springs Road, Jackson, MO 63755; 573-334-1711.

## Other Areas of Interest

Visit the **Burfordville Bridge**, the oldest of only four covered bridges remaining in the state. It is located at **Bollinger Mill State Historic Site**, off Highway 34, near Burfordville. Picnicking is available near the covered bridge, and guided tours of the mill are offered for a fee. For more information call 573-243-4591.

## Park Trails

**Nature Trail** 👢👢—.5 mile—This loop trail, which begins behind the interpretive center and travels behind the seats of the amphitheater, has many pawpaws and ferns.

**Lake Trail** 👢👢👢—1.5 miles—See some giant tulip trees and hike next to Lake Boutin. Begin at the showerhouse at the nonelectric campground loop and finish across the road from the showerhouse.

# Trail of Tears State Park

Indian Creek

Indian Creek Wild Area

Peewah Trail

Mississippi River

Vancill Hollow Natural Area

Sheppard Point Trail

177

N

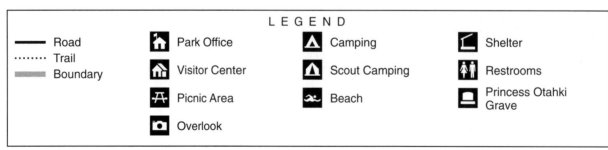

L E G E N D

| | | | |
|---|---|---|---|
| —— Road | Park Office | Camping | Shelter |
| ······ Trail | Visitor Center | Scout Camping | Restrooms |
| Boundary | Picnic Area | Beach | Princess Otahki Grave |
| | Overlook | | |

# Sheppard Point Trail

**Distance Round-Trip:** 2 miles

**Estimated Hiking Time:** 1.25 hours

*Hike this trail in an hour and a half or less and you will be in for a real sweat-er. The naturalist in the visitor center told me she had it down to 45 minutes!*

**Caution:** The four intermittent streams that cross the trail may be wet. The scenic overlook is perched on some very high bluffs. Also, there are loose rocks on some steep ascents.

**Trail Directions:** The trailhead sign [1] is at a small parking area, just off the main road, northeast of Princess Otahki's grave. The trail begins just left of this sign. At .08 mi. stop to look at the unusual ferns on your right. These are broad beech ferns [2], the only ferns in Missouri whose central stem (rachis) is winged throughout its entire length.

The large trees with smooth bark are beech trees. At .11 mi. look at the leaves on the big tree on the trail's left side. The leaf shape gives the tree its name—the tulip tree [3]. Another tree on this trail in the same family as the tulip tree is the cucumber magnolia, so named because its fruit is green and erect when developing. The cucumber magnolia's leaves look like pawpaw leaves, but they are not as pointed nor do they have the pawpaw leaves' unpleasant odor. The higher rainfall here, along with the protective high bluffs and deep ravines combine with the winter-ameliorating effects of the Mississippi River to produce a climate and habitat more typical of Tennessee, North Carolina, and Virginia. Unless you are accustomed to hiking in the Appalachian region of the United States, these three trees may not be familiar to you.

These beautiful ravines cut through moist, rich soil. On this trail you will see a lot of wild ginger, bloodroot, jack-in-the-pulpit, and Christmas ferns. If you come in August or September, look for doll's eyes on both sides of the trail. This is a medium-large plant with strange-looking fruit—pure white balls the size of large peas, held erect on red stems. There are even black pupils in the eyes!

At .27 mi. [4] turn left and follow the yellow arrows. You will find a giant sassafras tree at .44 mi. [5]. Just for fun, put your outstretched hands around the base—it will take more than four hand-lengths to span it! In the early 1500s, Spanish explorers mistook the aromatic sassafras for a cinnamon tree, and it became a major colonial export, second only to tobacco. Before sassafras oil was found to be a potential carcinogen in the 1960s, the fragrant oil was used commercially to flavor root beer, chewing gum, and toothpaste.

Cross a couple of intermittent streams at .70 mi. and .76 mi. [6] and find a lot of jewelweed, a favorite flower of hummingbirds. You are close to the Mississippi now and from here you will begin a steep ascent to the blufftops.

At .90 mi. reach a flat boulder [7] that offers a magnificent view of the largest river in the state and its Illinois floodplain. In winter look for soaring bald eagles. During summer months you can spot the graceful and rare Mississippi kite, gliding and swooping for insects.

Begin your descent back to water level and find a couple more intermittent streams at 1.03 mi. and 1.13 mi. [8]. Enjoy the flat walking in the stream bottom because at 1.31 mi. [9] the trail makes another steep incline. Some small, loose rocks here cause unsure footing. At 1.49 mi. you will reach the intersection you came across earlier [4]. Bear left to retrace your steps and return to the trailhead.

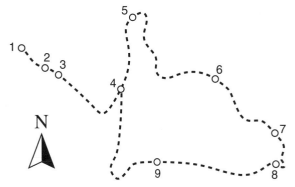

1. Start
2. Broad beech ferns
3. Tulip tree
4. Left turn
5. Giant sassafras tree
6. Intermittent streams
7. Boulder overlook
8. Intermittent streams
9. Rocky incline

# Peewah Trail 👢👢👢👢👢

**Distance Round-Trip:** 8.75 miles

**Estimated Hiking Time:** 4.75 hours

*Peewah is a Native American word meaning "come follow in this direction." Actually, following someone on this trail wouldn't be a bad idea—then you wouldn't have to carry a spider web stick.*

**Caution:** There is some loose footing on steep ascents, and the overlooks are on some high bluffs. Stinging nettles encroach the trail in creek bottoms, and the intermittent streams may be wet.

**Trail Directions:** Find the parking lot for the Peewah trailhead on Overlook Road, about halfway between Lake Boutin and the overlook. Hikers are encouraged to register at the trailhead before they begin, especially if they plan to stay overnight. There are two backpack camps on this trail.

Begin at the trailhead **[1]**. If you are here in late August, September, or October, you might as well pick up a stick right now and practice waving it in front of you—you will find no shortage of harmless spiders with a propensity for building extensive webs about face-high. Don't turn back, though—the blufftop views are worth a little arachnid annoyance.

Follow the yellow arrows until you come to the yellow-green intersection at .33 mi. **[2]**, where you turn right. This is a spur, marked by green arrows, that takes you to a tremendous bluff overlook. Go straight at the intersection at .65 mi. **[3]** to continue to the overlook. At the overlook **[4]** (.69 mi.), take your time to gaze at the Mighty Mississippi and Illinois land beyond. When you are ready to move, retrace your steps to the yellow-green intersection **[2]** and turn right to follow the yellow arrows.

At 1.09 mi. **[5]** come to the yellow-yellow intersection and turn left. At 1.60 mi. **[6]** come to the yellow-red intersection and turn right to continue the yellow loop and find more exercise and more overlooks.

Cross a couple of intermittent streams and watch out for stinging nettles encroaching the trail. At 2.40 mi. **[7]** you will step into a streambed. The continuing trail may be hard to see, but it is directly across the stream from the bank where you are standing now.

Climb the hill to the blufftop, and spectacular views of the Mississippi will begin to emerge on your left. At 3.83 mi. **[8]** take the spur to the left to find a 600-foot overlook with the most impressive views of all **[9]** (3.93 mi.). In winter look for bald eagles perched in large trees near the river.

Backtrack on the spur to return to **[8]** and complete the yellow loop by turning left. At 4.36 mi. ignore the intersecting green path on your left and continue to 4.43 mi. to the yellow-yellow intersection **[5]** where you were earlier. If you are officially tuckered, go straight to return to the trailhead. If you are ready for more, turn right.

Come to the yellow-yellow intersection at 4.84 mi. **[6]**. In just a few steps you'll come to the red-red intersection **[10]** (4.86 mi.) where you will bear left to begin the red loop. At 5.54 mi. **[11]** is the white connector intersection. Turn right to shorten the red loop or bear left to continue it. At around 6 mi. you will hike under some majestic tulip trees. You are now in Indian Creek Wild Area. At 6.47 mi. **[12]** is a white spur to Indian Creek. Bear right to continue the red loop. Cross a streambed at 6.65 mi. **[13]**, pass the white connector at 6.95 mi. **[14]**, and finish the red loop back at **[10]** (7.86 mi.). Turn left to return to the yellow loop, turn right at **[5]** (8.28 mi.), and turn right again at **[2]** (8.38 mi.) to return to the trailhead.

1. Start
2. Right turn
3. Go straight
4. Overlook
5. Left turn
6. Right turn
7. Streambed
8. Spur to overlook
9. Overlook
10. Bear left
11. White connector
12. Spur to Indian Creek
13. Streambed
14. White connector

# 17.  Big Oak Tree State Park

- Stand beneath six state champion trees, two of which are national champions.
- Find yourself in the heart of a genuine swamp (from the convenience of a wheelchair-accessible boardwalk).
- Find the tallest tree in Missouri.

## Area Information

In many ways, no other Missouri park can boast what Big Oak Tree can. Within the park's 1,005 fertile acres are enormous trees, six of which are state champions (the largest individuals of their species). Of these six state champions, two of them, the pumpkin ash and the persimmon, are national champions. With a tree canopy averaging 120 feet, and with several trees more than 140 feet tall, the park is often called the Park of Champions.

Big Oak Tree State Park is one of the last remaining examples of the vast bottomland forest that once covered 2 million acres of the Bootheel region. Standing like an island in the midst of a vast agricultural area, it is registered as a national natural landmark. Also, a 940-acre part of the park is a Missouri natural area. Missouri natural areas are permanently protected and managed to preserve their natural qualities.

Big Oak Tree showcases the bottomland forest and swamp. These two communities, now two of the rarest types in Missouri's natural landscape, depend on periodic flood cycles. The park also includes an 80-acre portion that is virgin wet-mesic bottomland forest.

Majestic trees—giant oaks, hickories, bald cypress, and swamp cottonwood—dominate the scene. The rich soils support patches of giant cane, which can reach 25 feet in height, and poison ivy vines as big around as a person's leg. The swamp rabbit, a rare species, lives in the area. Big Oak Tree has a national reputation among bird watchers.

**Directions:** Follow Highway 102 south of East Prairie for 14 miles. Brown signs direct you to the park office and the park.

**Hours Open:** The site is open year-round and designed for day use. However, it is not accessible during flood periods. Call the park before you come to ensure access to the park and interpretive center, which have irregular hours.

**Facilities:** Big Oak Tree State Park features an interpretive center, an interpretive boardwalk into the swamp, picnic shelters, and boating, canoeing, and fishing on 22-acre Big Oak Lake.

**Permits and Rules:** Except for special youth outings, camping is not allowed. Pets must always be leashed.

**Further Information:** Park Superintendent, Big Oak Tree State Park, Route 2, Box 343, East Prairie, MO 63845; 573-649-3149 or 573-649-9066.

## Other Areas of Interest

Just to the east of Big Oak Tree State Park is **Towosahgy State Historic Site,** which preserves the remains of a Native American village. Inhabited between A.D. 1000 and A.D. 1400 by people of the Mississippian Culture, the village was also an important ceremonial center. Interpretation for the site is planned. For more information call 573-649-3149 (Big Oak Tree State Park).

The **Hunter-Dawson Home State Historic Site** is a 15-room mansion that reflects the lifestyle of Missouri Bootheel gentry before the Civil War. The home features Georgian, Greek Revival, and Italianate architecture, original furniture, nine fireplaces, and guided tours. For more information call 573-748-5340.

# Big Oak Tree State Park

Park Entrance

Shumard Oak

Rusty Blackhaw

Persimmon

Virgin Forest

Bottomland Trail

P

Giant Cane

Tip-Up Mound

Boardwalk Trail

Bur Oak

Big Oak Lake

LEGEND

— Road
···· Trail
— Natural Area Boundary
— Boundary
P Parking
Picnic Shelter
Rest Stop
Trees
Wildlife Observation Deck
Point of Interest
Interpretive Center

Bent Tree

Pumpkin Ash

Eastern Cottonwood

Graveyard Forest

Swamp

N

Black Willow

# Boardwalk Trail 🥾

**Distance Round-Trip:** 1.25 miles

**Estimated Hiking Time:** 1 hour

*A pileated woodpecker pierces the swamp air with a shrill cry, a barred owl's "who-cooks-for-you?" resonates between tree trunks, and unexplained splashes in the calm water remind you that you are not alone.*

**Caution:** Swamps are notorious for mosquitoes; bring repellent. Also, there are two good reasons to call the park before you visit: First, the whole park floods once or twice a year, sometimes placing the boardwalk 10 feet under water, and second, park staff will open the interpretive center for you if you call just before you come.

**Trail Directions:** The trailhead [1] is in the southwest corner of the parking lot for the boardwalk and interpretive center. This is a self-guiding trail, so pick up a trail guide, which explains points of interest labeled along the trail. However, numbered features on the trail do not correspond to numbered features in this book.

After a few steps you will come upon the pentagonal interpretive center [2] on your left. Built 19 feet off the ground, it testifies to the regular floods that have maintained for centuries this now-rare natural community. The center houses a cross section of a 400-year-old bur oak, the park's namesake. Walk under a gigantic pawpaw tree (Missouri banana) leaning over the boardwalk and you will come upon a stand of giant cane at .05 mi. [3]. The cane in this park provides a nesting habitat for Swainson's warbler.

At .13 mi. [4] look for a tip-up mound on the left. When a tree falls over, its roots bring to the surface these large mounds of soil. In poorly drained soils like these, such depressions are often filled with water.

At .15 mi. [5] look up. The massive branches of the tallest tree in Missouri are towering 142 feet over your head. This bur oak, with a trunk circumference of 17 feet, 7 inches, is a remaining example of the impressive giants that formerly spread over two million acres of lowland area in Missouri's Bootheel.

Two wooden benches at .34 mi. [6] mark the halfway point on the boardwalk. At .41 mi. [7] look on the left for what look like wooden stalagmites growing from the forest floor. These are knobby growths from the root systems of bald cypress trees. Although their function is not known for certain, it is thought that these growths, called knees, might serve as oxygen-absorbing structures for the trees. Also notice that the cypress trunks are buttressed. Their flared trunks keep them from falling over in the saturated, mucky soil.

At .43 mi. [8] you will see the largest pumpkin ash tree in the nation. If you haven't seen standing water yet, you probably will soon. Characteristic plants in the swamp include buttonbush, swamp privet, young water locust, and black willow trees. The green "scum" on the water is actually millions of floating duckweed plants.

At the end of the boardwalk at .60 mi. [9] is the state champion black willow tree and two wooden benches. If you hear something like a loud, lone monkey, it is probably the state's largest woodpecker, the pileated. If you hear a hoarse and abrupt "Bwaaawk!" it is probably the great blue heron. Also look for wood ducks skimming through the duckweed and turtles lying on little log islands. Retrace your steps to return to the trailhead.

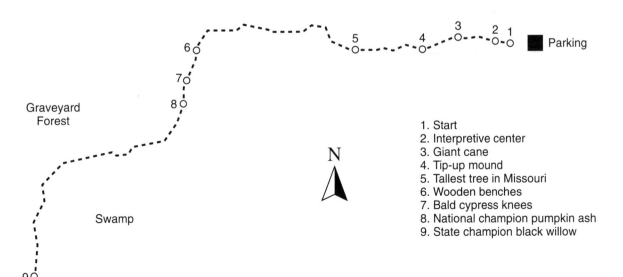

1. Start
2. Interpretive center
3. Giant cane
4. Tip-up mound
5. Tallest tree in Missouri
6. Wooden benches
7. Bald cypress knees
8. National champion pumpkin ash
9. State champion black willow

# Bottomland Trail 🥾

**Distance Round-Trip:** 1.4 miles

**Estimated Hiking Time:** 1 hour

*This trail brings you right up to some of the largest trees in the state and nation. Have you heard of the Druids, the ancient people who worshipped trees? You may not feel like worshipping these trees after you finish this trail, but I guarantee you will not leave unaffected by them.*

**Caution:** Be careful if you admire the towering tops of these giant trees and walk at the same time; poison ivy and stinging nettle are common on either side of the trail. As with the Boardwalk Trail, be sure to call the park before you come to make sure it isn't flooded. Also, if you forget mosquito repellent on all your other hikes this year, don't forget it on this one.

**Trail Directions:** Find the Bottomland Trail sign **[1]** directly across the road from the parking lot for the Boardwalk Trail. You are about to enter what is probably the highest concentration of Big (capital *B*) trees in the state. Nickname this trail the Trail of Giants.

After only a few steps, notice the big tree on your right with the bark that pulls away from the trunk in thin strips **[2]**. This is a shellbark hickory. The nuts, the largest of all Missouri hickories, are almost the size of baseballs. At .17 mi. **[3]** you will encounter the state champion swamp chestnut oak, with a trunk over 20 feet around and a height of 142 feet. These trees have a way of making you feel mighty small.

At .29 mi. **[4]** is a small spur on your right that takes you to Big Oak Lake. Turn left to continue the trail. At .48 mi. **[5]** is a bald cypress tree whose trunk is starting to flare at the base. Just 5 feet away is a pumpkin ash with a trunk circumference of over 11 feet. Notice the uniform, deep grooves of the ash bark. Take a few more steps and contrast the ash bark with the bark of the big tree on your left (.50 mi.) **[6]**. This is a hackberry showing its characteristic bark—very smooth background with raised, corky bumps. The hackberry's fruit, similar to wild black cherries, is a favorite of songbirds.

If you are here on a breezy day you may notice white, fleecy tufts in the air or in puffy piles on the trail. These are the seeds of the cottonwood tree, and at .63 mi. **[7]** is a cottonwood with a circumference of over 12 feet. Sometimes these seeds travel for miles on the wind and make it look as if it's snowing in summer.

Look closely around the cypress knees and you may see what look like little mud smokestacks. These are the burrow entrances, or "chimneys," of the devil crayfish. The burrows extend to groundwater, sometimes to a depth of 15 feet.

Walk under a giant sweet gum tree **[8]** at .72 mi. (look for the spiky "gum balls" on the trail) and find the state champion possum haw (also called deciduous holly) **[9]** about 20 yards off the trail on your right at .78 mi. Walk through a stand of native cane (bamboo) **[10]** at .83 mi. and exit the forest at 1.13 mi. **[11]**. Take the short spur on your right to visit the state champion shumard oak tree **[12]** and retrace your steps to the forest exit. Follow the mown path through the picnic area and look at the giant persimmon tree on your left at 1.26 mi. **[13]**. With a trunk circumference of six feet, nine inches, this is the largest persimmon tree in the country. Continue the path and finish the trail back at the trail sign.

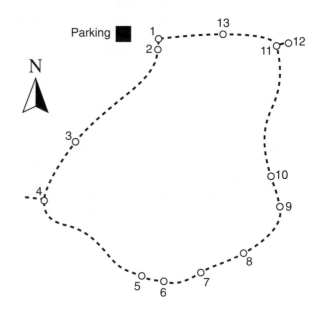

1. Start
2. Shellbark hickory
3. State champion swamp chestnut oak
4. Spur to lake
5. Bald cypress
6. Hackberry
7. Cottonwood
8. Sweet gum
9. State champion possum haw
10. Native cane
11. Forest exit
12. State champion shumard oak
13. National champion persimmon

# 18. Mingo National Wildlife Refuge

- From the convenience and safety of a boardwalk, hike through a swamp that survived 40 years of attempts to drain it.

- Hike out onto an observation tower in a vast marsh and look for egrets, herons, and ducks while listening for the splashes of turtles, fish, muskrats, and beaver.

- Bring your binoculars to help you see the colorful but often tiny songbirds that frequent the canopies of towering bottomland trees.

- Bring your tree guide to help you identify and learn more about the unusual trees that live in the swamp.

## Area Information

Mingo National Wildlife Refuge is part of a system of refuges administered by the U.S. Fish and Wildlife Service and dedicated to the preservation of wildlife. Situated among marshes and hardwood swamps on the Mississippi Flyway, Mingo is an important refuge for migrating waterfowl. The refuge is managed to provide open water, protection, and ample food for ducks, geese, swans, and other wildlife.

Mingo was formed in an abandoned channel of the Mississippi River when the river shifted east about 18,000 years ago. Then, like now, the swamp was a refuge for wildlife of many kinds. Native Americans lived nearby and hunted the swamp, but legends regarded the swamp as a spooky place. *Mingo,* in fact, means "treacherous" or "unreliable" in local Indian language.

Settlers of the late 1800s quickly exploited the swamp for its centuries-old cypress and tupelo logs, then set out to drain the swamp for farming. Drainage attempts continued through the Great Depression but with only limited success. The result was economic and ecological bankruptcy. In 1945, Mingo got a new

start as a national wildlife refuge, and much of the swamp's natural productivity has been restored. Today, careful management practices provide an important refuge for wildlife and excellent wildlife viewing opportunities for the public.

**Directions:** From the intersection of Highways 67 and 60 in Poplar Bluff, turn east on Highway 60 for 14.8 miles. Turn north on Highway 51 for 14.1 miles and turn left at the sign for the visitor center.

**Hours Open:** The refuge is open one hour before sunrise to a half hour after sunset from March 15 through September 30. During the remainder of the year, visitors should check with regulations provided at the visitor center. The visitor center is open from 8 A.M. to 4 P.M. Monday through Friday, year-round, and from 9 A.M. to 4 P.M. on Saturdays and Sundays in the spring and fall.

**Facilities:** The refuge offers a visitor center with exhibits, displays, and audiovisual programs, four wildlife observation towers, a 25-mile auto-tour route, two picnic areas, and a boat ramp. Canoeing, fishing, and limited hunting are also available.

**Permits and Rules:** The visitor center and hiking trails are free, but a three-dollar daily entrance fee is required for each vehicle entering the refuge from March 15 through November 30. The use or possession of gas-powered boat motors is prohibited on all refuge waters. Electric trolling motors are permitted, but only outside the wilderness area. Fishing is possible from March 15 through September 30, and certain types of hunting are allowed on designated portions. Consult the refuge manager on current regulations.

**Further Information:** Refuge Manager, Mingo National Wildlife Refuge, 24279 State Highway 51, Puxico, MO 63960; 573-222-3589.

# Mingo National Wildlife Refuge

To Duck Creek
7 Miles

51

Red Mill Dr.

Bluff Rd.

51

To Puxico
1 Mile

One-way

One-way

Visitor Center Exit Rd.

Bluff Rd.

Hartz
Pond

Boardwalk Nature Trail

To Flat
Banks

Bluff Trail

N

LEGEND

—— Road

······ Trail

Entrance Fee Information

Visitor Center

# Hartz Pond and Bluff Trail

🥾🥾🥾

**Distance Round-Trip:** .75 mile

**Estimated Hiking Time:** .75 hour

*Don't be alarmed if the occasional dragonfly zips and hovers near your head, crinkling and rattling its cellophane wings. It is chasing your enemy, the mosquito, which it catches and eats on the wing.*

**Caution:** While not as numerous here as in the swamp, mosquitoes will still be present.

**Trail Directions:** Park in the lot for the visitor center and find the trailhead at the southeast corner of the lot. Begin at the signboard **[1]** and hike beneath the small, compound leaves of black walnut. Look for the smooth, knobby bark of persimmon and the bumpy, corky bark of hackberry. Hike quietly to increase your chances of spotting wildlife at Hartz Pond, which will come into view at .08 mi. **[2].** Look for ducks or muskrats bobbing or swimming on the surface. Watch for the high, arching leaps of bullfrogs into the water and scan the surface for their bulging, bubblelike eyes. Don't forget to check logs and the pond banks for sunning turtles.

Turn left to make your way clockwise around the pond. Two moisture-loving trees are on the pond bank—look for the star-shaped leaves of sweet gum and the feathery, fernlike leaves of bald cypress. The cypress has adapted to living in standing water, and you can see many of them in Mingo's swamps and marshes. You'll pass patches of several kinds of ferns before crossing a wooden bridge. When you return to **[2]**, turn left to return to **[1]**.

Back in the parking lot, turn left and walk on the paved walkway to the visitor center. Notice the beautiful kaleidoscope of varied leaves overhead. Yellow green, pumpkin-shaped leaves of basswood contrast with the small leaves of black walnut and the wavy-edged leaves of swamp chestnut oak. At .31 mi. **[3]** arrive at the visitor center, which offers exhibits and a slide show about the refuge. Find the signboard for the Bluff Trail at the west end of the building and begin the trail next to a rock wall.

You'll reach the Rockhouse overlook at .37 mi. **[4]**, with fabulous vistas of Rockhouse marsh. Here, at the north boundary of the Mississippi Lowlands, a contrast between two landscapes becomes evident. Looking over the flat marsh in the foreground, the ridges and domes of the Ozark foothills form the horizon in the distant north. Bear right at the fork in the trail at .41 mi. **[5].** Just after the trail makes a sharp right, you'll hike next to limestone boulders covered with wild hydrangea, ebony spleenwort, and other ferns. As the trail turns more rugged and rocky and a steep slope dips on your left, you'll think you're in the Ozarks and forget all about Mingo, a marsh and swamp refuge.

At .53 mi. the limestone boulders turn into big bluffs at your right shoulder, and the swamp **[6]** comes into view below you on the left. Wild ginger, ferns, and several colors of mushrooms decorate the forest floor. Passing beneath immense bottomland trees, you can look down on the tropical leaves of pawpaw on your left. At .64 mi. **[7]** turn right at the spur to the Boardwalk Trail. The trail zigzags up a good exercise hill before bringing you to the intersection at .73 mi. **[8]**, where you turn left to return to the parking lot.

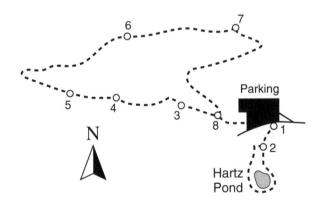

1. Start
2. Hartz Pond
3. Visitor center
4. Rockhouse overlook
5. Bear right
6. Swamp
7. Right turn
8. Left turn

# Boardwalk Nature Trail 🥾

**Distance Round-Trip:** 1 mile

**Estimated Hiking Time:** .75 hour

*There is something primeval about a swamp . . . we know their facts, yet their legends persist. We are attracted to them, yet an uneasiness hangs like the sultry air in their shadows.*

**Caution:** Unless you are here in the winter, do not even attempt to hike this trail without mosquito repellent.

**Trail Directions:** Exit the visitor center parking lot and make the first left. Turn left at the stop sign and turn right into the parking lot for the Boardwalk Trail. Interpretive brochures are available at the trailhead for this self-guiding trail. Numbered stations along the trail do not correspond to numbered features in this book.

Before you begin, notice the trees with long, thin leaves shading the parking lot. These are willow oaks, moisture-loving trees restricted to swampy habitats. Start at the trailhead **[1]** in the northwest corner of the lot and turn right at the first intersection at .01 mi. **[2]**. The trail begins in a swamp, although you may not see standing water here right now. Water levels in swamps fluctuate naturally, according to the seasons and rainfall. Flooding water may persist for months. The trees and plants thriving here are specially adapted to this wetland habitat.

As the boardwalk makes a pleasant drumming sound underfoot, listen above for the drumming of woodpeckers. At .20 mi. **[3]** a sturdy bench makes a good spot to listen for the songs of warblers and many other songbirds that find refuge at Mingo. Turn left on the paved walkway at .24 mi. **[4]**. The standing water on your right is one of the ditches dug in the 1920s in an unsuccessful attempt to drain the swamp for farming. At .38 mi. **[5]** turn right on the arched bridge over the drainage ditch. Notice the bald cypress trees near the bridge. These wetland trees often have an enlarged, or buttressed, trunk that is thought to give the tree greater stability in saturated, soft soils. Notice the knobby stumps all around the trees; these are cypress knees, extensions of the tree that are thought to carry oxygen to its waterlogged roots.

Go over the bridge and continue to the observation tower. As you exit the swamp and enter the marsh, look near the boardwalk for buttonbush, an aquatic shrub with white, globe-shaped flowers about the size of Ping-Pong balls. As the trail goes over the remnants of a beaver lodge at .47 mi. **[6]**, notice that aluminum sheeting has been installed on the upright posts of the boardwalk in attempts to beaver-proof them. At .56 mi. **[7]** is the observation tower, complete with a shaded bench and a free viewing scope. Although the greatest number of ducks, geese, swans, and eagles frequent this marsh from November to March, various birds and wildlife can be seen from the tower all year long. Spend some time gazing at the wide, open marsh, dotted with monstrous cypress trees. Return to **[5]** and turn right.

Just after passing a bench on the left, turn left on the boardwalk at .83 mi. **[8]** to enter a darker section of the swamp. Half-submerged twisted tree limbs arch out of the water like sea serpents. Look for water snakes gliding over the surface and listen for unexplained splashes just under the boardwalk. Turn left at the spur to the Bluff Trail at .88 mi. **[9]**. Two more swamp trees grow close to the boardwalk. A water tupelo is on the left at .92 mi. **[10]**. Notice it has a flared trunk like the bald cypress. Look for the spines on the trunk of the water locust at .93 mi. **[11]**. It resembles the honey locust, a close relative. Turn right at **[2]** to finish your swamp hike.

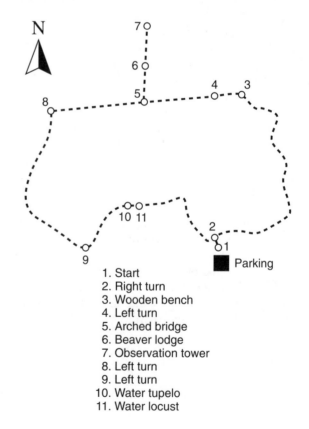

1. Start
2. Right turn
3. Wooden bench
4. Left turn
5. Arched bridge
6. Beaver lodge
7. Observation tower
8. Left turn
9. Left turn
10. Water tupelo
11. Water locust

# 19.  Lake Wappapello State Park

- Wait until the leaves have fallen and bring your binoculars to scan the sycamore trees near the lake—not for birds, but for plants! Wappapello is one of the few places in Missouri where you can find wild mistletoe.
- Come in the winter to look for eagles, ospreys, and a variety of ducks in the arm of the lake by Asher Creek, a designated winter waterfowl refuge.
- Imagine what the devil's walking stick might look like, then find this unusual, slender tree growing next to the trail.

## Area Information

The peninsula on which Lake Wappapello State Park is now situated was once part of the rich southeastern Ozark foothills used as hunting grounds by various Native American tribes. The St. Francis River flowed freely through the pine-clad ridges then, before dropping into the Mississippi Lowlands farther south.

Pioneers arrived in the early 1800s and began lumbering and farming. Named after a Shawnee chief who had hunted in the area, the town of Wappapello was established as a Frisco railway station. In 1941, the U.S. Army Corps of Engineers completed a dam on the St. Francis River, the first of many large corps dams in Missouri, and 8,400-acre Wappapello Lake was the result. Wappapello and Table Rock State Park are the oldest of the corps' reservoir parks in the system.

The hills surrounding the lake are steep and covered in a diverse mix of trees and plants. Typical Ozark flora of white oak, hickories, and shortleaf pine is joined by species of the Mississippi Lowlands like sweet gum and devil's walking stick. American beech, tulip tree, and mistletoe add their unusual flavor to the park's environment. The Wappapello landscape is much different today from what it was in the time of the Shawnee chief's or even the pioneers'. A resilient and diverse area, it still has much to offer.

**Directions:** From the intersection of Highways 60 and 67 in Poplar Bluff, take Highway 67 north for 13.3 miles. Follow Highway 172 east for 8.3 miles to the park office.

**Hours Open:** Day-use areas of the park are open from 7 A.M. to 10 P.M. The park office is open from 8 A.M. to 4 P.M. Monday through Thursday, from 8 A.M. to 6 P.M. on Friday, and from 8 A.M. to 5 P.M. on Saturday.

**Facilities:** The park offers picnic areas, an amphitheater, rental cabins, and campgrounds that feature many campsites next to the lake. A sand swimming beach and boat ramp are available, as well as fishing, boating, and water skiing on the lake.

**Permits and Rules:** Bicycles and horses are allowed on the Lake Wappapello Trail but are prohibited on all other trails. Camping is permitted by backpackers only along portions of the Lake Wappapello Trail. Campfires and cutting implements are prohibited on all trails. Pets must always be on leashes 10 feet long or shorter.

**Further Information:** Park Superintendent, Lake Wappapello State Park, Route 2, Box 102, Williamsville, MO 63967; 573-297-3232 (park office) or 573-297-3247 (cabin reservations).

## Other Areas of Interest

The **U.S. Army Corps of Engineers** operates 12 recreation areas and landings on Lake Wappapello that primarily feature water recreation and camping. The corps' visitor center, located on Highway T near the dam, offers nature walks and tours of the gatehouse. For more information call the visitor center at 573-222-8773.

A Civil War battle was fought at the old town of **Greenville**, located 20 miles north of Wappapello on Highway 67. Pioneer history is brought to life here in special events including Old Greenville Black Powder Rendezvous and Old Greenville Days. For more information call 573-222-8773.

## Park Trails

**Lake Wappapello Trail** 👢👢👢👢—15 miles—This loop trail, designed for hiking, backpacking, bicycle, and equestrian use, extends beyond the park boundaries over varied and rugged terrain. Sections of the trail, identified on a park trail map, are closed to camping. The trailhead is .3 mile west of the park office on Highway 172.

**Lake View Trail** 👢👢—.5 mile—Open to hikers only, this trail offers excellent views of the lake from the south shore of Allison Peninsula. It begins in the day-use area west of the cabins.

# Lake Wappapello
# State Park

N

Lake
Wappapello

Day Use
Area

Day Use
Area

172

Day Use
Area

Asher
Creek
Trail

Allison
Cemetery
Trail

L E G E N D

| | | | | | | |
|---|---|---|---|---|---|---|
| ——— | Road | 🏚 Cabins | 🚹🚺 Restrooms | | 🛶 Boat Launch |
| ······ | Trail | 🏠 Change House | Latrine | | 🏊 Beach |
| ——— | Boundary | 🚿 Bath House | Picnic Shelter | | Sanitation Station |
| ▲ | Camping | | | | |

# Asher Creek Trail

**Distance Round-Trip:** 2 miles

**Estimated Hiking Time:** 1.25 hours

*It was in the middle of a warm afternoon, and I had already spooked three deer from the trail by the lake's edge. Later, a fourth one ran up the slope above me, stopping to stamp its front leg on the ground and issue a few explosive, bull-like snorts.*

**Caution:** Stay on the trail to avoid several large patches of poison ivy.

**Trail Directions:** Pull into the driveway marked with a campground sign, located .3 mile southeast of the park office. Turn right at every opportunity until you reach the lake. The trailhead is next to the lake, behind campsite #57.

Begin at the signboard **[1]** and follow red arrows and markers clockwise on this trail. The trail follows the lake shoreline here on the side of a dry, rocky slope. Beside Ozark hickories and oaks are sweet gum, trees more common in the Mississippi Lowlands. The trees with papery, flaky bark growing at the water's edge are river birch. If you are here in the fall or winter, watch the nearby skies and water for ducks and geese that stop at Wappapello on their migration routes. The cove in front of you is a designated winter waterfowl refuge.

At .25 mi. **[2]** is an intersection with a connector link; go straight as the trail swings to the right. Reach a second connector at .47 mi. **[3]**; go straight here also. The trail swings to the left just after crossing a wooden bridge over a small stream. Note the diversity of trees here and see if you can distinguish them by their bark alone. White oaks have light bark with loose scales that rub off on your hands. Dark brown, fissured bark of sweet gum might be confused with that of southern red oak or cherrybark oak. The bark of shagbark hickory and river birch is a giveaway!

Note the large, tulip-shaped leaves of the tree on your left at .61 mi. **[4]**. This is a tulip tree, a species more common in the Appalachian region of the United States. If you find a tree with corky wings on its twigs, you have either discovered a winged elm or a sweet gum tree. Winged elms have small leaves with serrated edges. Sweet gum leaves are star-shaped and have five lobes.

Soon the trail veers to the right, opening more views of the lake and the surrounding steep hills and knobs. Look for the hornbeam tree, also called musclewood, named for its smooth trunk, fluted into musclelike ridges. Just after the trail veers right again, away from the lake, turn right at .86 mi. **[5]** and climb a hill into the woods. You'll find blueberries, fragrant sumac, and wild grape in this drier, rockier habitat. Look for bright yellow orange chantarelle mushrooms, which come up in profusion the summer after a prescribed fire. Go straight at the intersection with the connector link at 1.4 mi. **[6]**. Turn left at the intersection at 1.72 mi. **[7]** to return to the trailhead.

1. Start
2. Go straight
3. Go straight
4. Tulip tree
5. Right turn
6. Go straight
7. Left turn

# Allison Cemetery Trail 👢👢👢

**Distance Round-Trip:** 3.5 miles

**Estimated Hiking Time:** 1.75 hours

*After hearing so much about the devil's walking stick in the park, I was on a mission to find it. What would it look like? Where would it be? Why would he leave it? Would he want it back?*

**Caution:** Watch for traffic when you cross the main park road.

**Trail Directions:** Drive to the end of the main park road and park at the end of the cabin area, located 1.7 miles east of the park office. Begin at the signboard **[1]** and walk downhill toward the lake. Near the bottom of the hill, turn right at the intersection at .06 mi. **[2]** and follow green arrows in a clockwise direction from here on.

The trail takes you between the lake and a wooded slope on your right, shaded by a tall canopy of tulip, white oak, and sugar maple leaves. As you descend into a cooler, protected draw, you'll pass through a grove of pawpaws and patches of Christmas ferns. After the trail swings to the right at .48 mi., look for a shrub near the trail whose five shiny, dark green leaflets look like an outspread hand. This is the red buckeye **[3]**, a shrub restricted to southeast Missouri and noted for its red flowers and its shiny, dark brown seeds. Some Ozark old-timers carry buckeye seeds in their pockets for good luck.

The patch of strange-looking, flat-topped small trees at .61 mi. **[4]** is devil's walking stick, or Hercules club—the evil reference, no doubt, deriving from the myriad of sharp spines protruding from the tree's trunk. Listen for the blows and snorts of white-tailed deer, as they discover your whereabouts just moments before you discover theirs. An overlook of the lake opens at .67 mi. **[5]**, as the trail veers to the right. Just after hiking around a small cove, you'll find several glade remnants at 1.0 mi. **[6]**, complete with little bluestem grass, leadplant, and black-eyed Susans. Go straight at the connector link option at 1.11 mi. **[7]**.

After traversing several rocky draws, turn right at 1.39 mi. **[8]**, at the intersection with the Lake View Trail. At 1.42 mi. **[9]** hike to the right of the picnic shelter and reenter the forest on the trail behind the rest rooms. Turn left at the bottom of the wooden steps. Cross the main park road at 1.68 mi. **[10]** and turn left at the intersection with the connector link at

1.81 mi. **[11]**. The 1,854 acres that make up the state park were owned by the Allison family from after the Civil War until the early 20th century. Now known as Allison Peninsula, the area became surrounded by water after the creation of Lake Wappapello in 1941. You are now hiking on an old roadbed that leads to the Allison family cemetery, at the peninsula's tip.

Go straight at the intersection at 2.31 mi. **[12]** if you choose to take the spur to the cemetery. You'll find a smooth-barked tree at 2.37 mi. **[13]**, an American beech. A clearing in the trees on your right reveals the old gravestones at 2.40 mi. **[14]**. A bench overlooks the lake just ahead, a site known for its remarkable sunset views. Return to **[12]** and turn left. Just after passing a musclewood tree on your right, you'll reach two connector intersections at 3.10 mi. Go straight at **[15]** and turn left at **[16]**. As the trail joins an old roadbed, continue on the left. Turn left when you approach the sewage lagoon at 3.14 mi. **[17]** and reenter the forest at the trail sign. Turn right when you return to **[2]** and you'll find your car at the top of the hill.

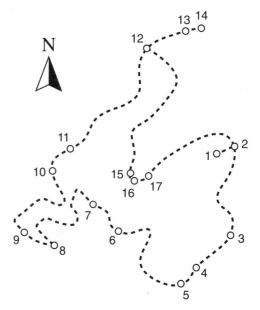

| | |
|---|---|
| 1. Start | 10. Road crossing |
| 2. Right turn | 11. Left turn |
| 3. Red buckeye | 12. Spur to cemetery |
| 4. Devil's walking stick | 13. American beech |
| 5. Lake overlook | 14. Allison cemetery |
| 6. Glade remnants | 15. Go straight |
| 7. Go straight | 16. Left turn |
| 8. Right turn | 17. Left turn |
| 9. Picnic shelter | |

# 20. Sam A. Baker State Park

- Climb to 1,313 feet above sea level at the top of Mudlick Mountain, an exposed igneous dome in one of the oldest mountain regions in North America—the St. Francois Mountains.

- Challenge your hiking skills on difficult, though interesting, terrain—talus fields, also known as rock glaciers.

- Hike on a national recreation trail through one of the most significant undisturbed natural landscapes in Missouri, the 4,420-acre Mudlick Mountain Wild Area.

- In the spring look for the uncommon yellow-wood tree, whose large, fragrant blossom clusters often overhang small streams.

- Visit the only park whose entire area is a historic district.

- See gnarled, knobby, 200-year-old oak trees that illustrate the effects of ice storms, violent winds, and repeated lightning strikes on their mountaintop home.

## Area Information

Named in honor of a Missouri governor and well-known educator, Sam A. Baker State Park is one of the state's first-generation parks, having the first portion of its 5,164 acres acquired in 1926. At the southern edge of the scenic St. Francois Mountains, the park features Mudlick Mountain, one of the highest and most distinctive igneous domes in the region.

Mudlick Mountain originated some 1.5 billion years ago, when volcanoes dominated the landscape of southeast Missouri and created some of the oldest and hardest exposed rock on the continent. After warm oceans completely buried the ancient mountains under hundreds of feet of sedimentary rock, down-cutting streams, wind, and rain gradually began exposing the resistant, igneous knobs. These conical, domelike hills remain, some over 1,000 feet high, covered with mixed hardwood and pine forests and surrounded by boulder-strewn slopes and narrow, winding valleys.

Big Creek is a clear, rocky Ozark stream that forms most of the eastern boundary of the park. Its valley is one of Missouri's largest and deepest canyonlike gorges, with shut-ins, glades, and sheer rock bluffs. Big Creek flows into the St. Francis River at the southeast end of the park. Both streams offer park visitors recreation opportunities as well as beauty.

**Directions:** The park is in southeast Missouri, four miles north of Patterson on Highway 143.

**Hours Open:** The site is open year-round. The nature center is open from 8 A.M. to 8 P.M. Sunday through Thursday and from 8 A.M. to 10 P.M. Friday and Saturday.

**Facilities:** The park offers a campground, equestrian camp, nature center, rental cabins, dining lodge, general store, canoe rentals, amphitheater, picnic areas, and boat ramp. Swimming, fishing, and boating are available on Big Creek and St. Francis River.

**Permits and Rules:** Horses are allowed on most of the Mudlick Trail. Camping is permitted on the Mudlick Trail but only by backpackers. Three hiking shelters are open for overnight use from October 1 to May 15—first come, first served. Except in the shelters, campfires are prohibited. Bicycles are not allowed on any trail. All pets must be kept on leashes.

**Further Information:** Park Superintendent, Sam A. Baker State Park, Route 1, Box 114, Patterson, MO 63956; 573-856-4411 (park office) or 573-856-4223 (cabin reservations).

## Park Trails

**Mudlick Trail—West Section** —7.75 miles—From the hiking shelters, this segment delves into Mudlick Hollow, ascends Green Mountain, traverses the park's west border, descends into Logan Creek valley, and climbs the southern edge of Mudlick Mountain. There are no trailheads on this section. The west section and the east loop together compose the entire Mudlick Trail (12 miles).

Sam A. Baker
State Park

N

Horse
Difficult

Private
Property

Hollow Pass Trail
(Horse Friendly)

Shut-Ins Trail

Big Creek

143

Mudlick
Mountain

Fire
Tower

Mudlick Trail – East Loop

Miller's
Ridge

Mudlick
Mountain

St. Francis River

143

To Ozark
Trail

L E G E N D

| | | | |
|---|---|---|---|
| ── | Road | ◭ | Camping |
| ═╪═ | Old Road | 🐎 | Equestrian Camping |
| ⋯⋯ | Trail | P | Equestrian Day Use Parking |
| ▬ | Boundary | ◿ | Hiking Shelter |
| 🏠 | Visitor Center and Park Office | ◿ | Shut-Ins Area |
| 🏛 | Lodge | ★ | Trailhead |
| S | Store | ⌂ | Picnic Area |
| 🏚 | Cabins | | |

# Mudlick Trail—East Loop

**Distance Round-Trip:** 7.15 miles

**Estimated Hiking Time:** 3.75 hours

*Precambrian volcanoes, inundating oceans, tectonic compression . . . beneath the serenity of this wilderness lie the products of nature's most cataclysmic events.*

**Caution:** Talus is difficult terrain to hike; wear sturdy boots and keep their laces tight to help prevent a twisted ankle.

**Trail Directions:** Park in the lot for the trailhead **[1]**, across the highway from the dining lodge and slightly toward the Big Creek bridge. Fill out a registration card before you begin. Follow yellow arrows and markers on this trail.

If you're here on a warm day, you'll feel the temperature drop as you descend into the floodplain of Big Creek. Just after crossing a wooden bridge over a clear, small stream, turn left at the intersection at .09 mi. **[2]**. At .18 mi. **[3]** cross an old road. Turn right at the three-way intersection at .32 mi. **[4]**, where an oak-hickory forest dotted with sugar maples replaces floodplain trees. At .63 mi. **[5]** is the first of many stream crossings through deep-cut ravines. Like most other rock in the St. Francois Mountain region, this extremely hard and old rock began as molten lava.

As you continue on the wide, rocky trail, look for ebony spleenwort, a fern whose fronds stand nearly straight up. At 1.20 mi. **[6]** a little stone cabin, hiking shelter #1, appears through the trees. Built of local dellenite, this is one of three shelters on this trail

built by the CCC in the early 1930s. Take the spur to the rock ledge in front of the cabin for an outstanding view of Big Creek's canyon. Turn right after returning to the main trail and you'll soon be on a sweat-er hill. (You probably won't reach the top without sweating.) Pass shelter #2 and turn left at the intersection at 1.73 mi. **[7]**, at shelter #3.

Turn left at 2.20 mi. **[8]** on the spur to the mountain summit and fire tower. Turn left on the limestone gravel road and you'll reach the mountaintop at 2.45 mi. **[9]**. The CCC-era fire tower is not open to the public, but here is a good place to relax. Many old oaks with missing limbs and twisted, scarred trunks tell their tales of 200 years of tornadoes, snow, ice, and lightning.

Return to **[8]** and turn left. When the trail turns into a jumble of rocks of all sizes you have entered a talus field (2.90 mi.) **[10]**. Talus is rock that has broken off from bluffs or bedrock above and tumbled downslope.

Cross an old road at 3.48 mi. **[11]** and arrive at a connector link at 3.71 mi. **[12]**. Going straight will shorten the hike by 2.35 mi. Turn right to continue. Go up and over Miller's Ridge while your feet get some relief on this wide, grassy, old roadbed that's free of talus. Find an old field at 3.99 mi. **[13]**, now grown up in persimmon groves and blackberry briars. Go up and over the south end of Mudlick Mountain. Turn left at the intersection at 4.62 mi. **[14]** and hit the rocky trail again. You'll pass several glade openings at 4.94 mi. **[15]**. Turn left at the spur to the equestrian camp at 5.11 mi. **[16]**. You'll soon enter another talus field. You'll cross several streams that splash around some of these boulders. Turn left at 6.02 mi. **[17]** and turn right at 6.08 mi. **[18]**. Cross the fire-tower road at 6.30 mi. **[19]** and pass under a powerline. Turn right when you return to **[4]** to finish your hike.

1. Start
2. Left turn
3. Road crossing
4. Right turn
5. Stream crossing
6. Hiking shelter #1
7. Left turn
8. Spur to summit
9. Peak of Mudlick Mountain
10. Talus field
11. Road crossing
12. Right turn
13. Old field
14. Left turn
15. Glade openings
16. Left turn
17. Left turn
18. Right turn
19. Road crossing

# Shut-Ins Trail 👢👢👢👢👢

**Distance Round-Trip:** 3 miles

**Estimated Hiking Time:** 2 hours

*Pass through a junglelike creek bottom (complete with bamboo) next to wet-weather waterfalls that splash their way down boulders, creating little open terrariums of mosses and ferns. Listen for the deep "Chug . . . chug, chug" of green frogs in the stream's pools as you hike to the overlook.*

**Caution:** The trail to the overlook is steep and covered with small, loose rocks.

**Trail Directions:** Park at the dining lodge; the trailhead is just behind it. Begin at the signboard **[1]**. If you're here on a warm day, you'll probably hear shouts of joy and exhilaration from children and adults alike as they swim and play in Big Creek, a clear-water, rock-bottom stream that forms the majority of the eastern boundary of the park. The trail follows Big Creek a short distance near the trailhead. Follow blue arrows on this trail.

Descend some wooden steps and follow the trail under the Big Creek bridge. At the intersection at .09 mi. **[2]** turn left. Pawpaw, slippery elm, and massive sugar maple trees of the Big Creek floodplain cover the trail with dense shade. Cross a wooden bridge at .14 mi. **[3]** over a small stream and notice the washboard appearance of the weathering bedrock on the streambank. Go straight at the following trail intersection and at the old road crossing at .17 mi. **[4]**. Descend some switchbacks and turn left at the bottom.

Dellenite boulders protrude from the steep slope on the left, and giant grapevines hang from tall black walnut and hackberry trees. Thick vegetation and calm, humid air contribute to the junglelike atmosphere. The trail passes through a stand of 12-foot-tall canes of native bamboo at .25 mi. **[5]**. Now uncommon, this member of the grass family was abundant in Missouri's presettlement wetland and riverine habitats. At .40 mi. **[6]** take the spur to the left to find massive boulders and talus tumbled into a gorgelike ravine, crisscrossed by several wet-weather waterfalls. The towering tree here with star-shaped leaves is a sweet gum. You might have seen its seed balls on the trail. These "gum balls" have a long, cherrylike stem and prickly spikes.

Turn left after returning to the main trail. After a flood or heavy rain you may come across a slough that covers part of the trail. In different places, the trail's surface is gravel, silt, or sand—materials deposited by the flooding creek. If it's dry enough, walk up the streambed on your left at 1.02 mi. **[7]** to see another wet-weather waterfall tumbling down mossy boulders. At medium flow, its water falls into a small pool and disappears! Return to the main trail and turn left.

At 1.15 mi. **[8]** turn left just after crossing a small stream. Follow the sound of running water and ascend some steps to begin the trail's grand finale—a blood-pumper hill to an overlook of the Big Creek canyon. Look for brown fence lizards scurrying on this talus slope. You'll find several glade remnants along the way. Bear left at the fork in the trail at 1.36 mi. **[9]**. When you reach the stone cabin (hiking shelter #1), walk toward the rock ledge in front of the shelter for a vista of the forested, mountainous landscape (1.5 mi.) **[10]**. From here, you have the option of descending the Mudlick Trail (yellow arrows) or retracing your steps to return to the dining lodge.

1. Start
2. Left turn
3. Wooden bridge
4. Go straight
5. Native bamboo
6. Spur to ravine
7. Spur to disappearing waterfall
8. Left turn
9. Bear left
10. Overlook

# 21. Rock Pile Mountain Wilderness

- See the ancient circle of granite stones believed to be of human origin, at the crest of Rock Pile Mountain.
- Hike in the uncommon solitude of a 4,000-acre federally designated wilderness.
- Hike across a broken ridge from one mountain to another.
- On Rock Pile Mountain, find stark bedrock glades that look like a landscape on another planet.
- Watch for harmless hognose snakes, which may puff up with air, flare like a cobra, or just roll over and play possum.

## Area Information

The St. Francois Mountains began as molten rock around 1.5 billion years ago, when volcanoes dominated the southeast region of Missouri. Magma cooled slowly and hardened into solid masses of igneous rock. After millions of years of inundation by warm seas, which deposited hundreds of feet of sedimentary rock on top of the igneous rock, uplift and erosion uncovered the ancient granites, andesites, and rhyolites, among others. Contrasted with the porous, highly erodible sedimentary rock, these igneous rocks—gray to dark blue or purple, dark red, or pink— are among the hardest and oldest on the continent.

Rock Pile Mountain Wilderness was designated by act of Congress on December 22, 1980, to be managed under the provisions of the Wilderness Act of 1964. One of seven wildernesses in Missouri on the Mark Twain National Forest, it is managed by the U.S. Forest Service. Located in the St. Francois Mountains region of the Ozarks, the 4,131-acre wilderness is characterized by steep, rocky slopes, deep ravines,

igneous outcrops and glades, and dense forests of oak, hickory, and pine.

Rock Pile's namesake is an ancient circle (or remnants of several circles) of granite stones, piled at the crest of the mountain. Around the turn of the century early white settlers noted the structure to be about four feet high, but human disturbance has reduced it to its present level. Although we know few details of the site, the stones may be remnants of Native American burial cairns or ceremonial structures.

**Directions:** From Fredericktown, take Highway 67 south 5.9 miles to County Road C, where you turn right. Take Highway C 5.1 miles to County Road 406, where you turn right. Go 2.5 miles to FR 2124, where you turn left. The road ends at 1 mile at the parking lot for the trailhead.

**Hours Open:** The wilderness is always open.

**Facilities:** There are no facilities.

**Permits and Rules:** Wilderness regulations are designed to reduce human impact that could damage or destroy the wilderness resource. Prohibited activities include littering, leaving a fire without completely extinguishing it, cutting live or dead standing trees, using bicycles or motorized equipment, and building rock fire rings or other structures. Camping is permitted, but fires must be kept low and small. Hunting is permitted but not near the trail. Avoid using trail ribbons and tread lightly so nature can endure and replenish. Also, strict laws prohibit the disturbance of archeological sites and artifacts on federal property.

**Further Information:** District Ranger, U.S. Forest Service, Potosi/Fredericktown District, P.O. Box 188, Potosi, MO 63664; 573-438-5427.

## Area Trails

Rock Pile Mountain Wilderness and adjacent Forest Service property contain numerous old roads and trails open to the public. The trail heading west from

[7] on the featured trail leads to shut-ins on Cave Branch Creek, caves and bluffs along the St. Francis River, and Chimney Rock Bluff, a variety of fractured and weathered features in sedimentary rock. A compass and topo map are recommended.

# Rock Pile Mountain Trail

**Distance Round-Trip:** 7 miles

**Estimated Hiking Time:** 3.5 hours

*After staring from several different angles at the old stones that formed the curious, misshapen circle, my mind was in high gear. Was this a burial place? A ceremonial structure? Who? When? Why?*

**Caution:** Loose and protruding rocks cover several steep sections. Refrain from climbing on the rock cairns or disturbing them in any way. Bring a compass and topo map if you choose to extend this hike or do some cross-country exploring.

**Trail Directions:** Park in the lot for the trailhead on top of Little Grass Mountain and walk to the north end of the lot. The trail begins to the left (west) of a granite boulder with "ROCK PILE MTN. WILDERNESS" engraved in it **[1]**. As the trail begins a C-shaped curve, you'll find a registration box at .06 mi. **[2]**. Please register before you continue.

You'll now descend a rocky hill where granite and rhyolite boulders are dark red, gray, or dark purple, and speckled with different-sized mineral crystals (porphyritic). You'll pass through a scenic, open forest of oaks, hickories, and occasional pines, where tumbled-down boulders fill steep ravines and igneous outcrops protrude from the forest floor. At .53 mi. **[3]** the trail bends right, and you begin hiking across a series of ridgetops to Rock Pile Mountain.

As you hike, listen for a variety of woodpecker calls and drummings. Woodpeckers hammer on hollow trees, not only to search for food and to hollow out nesting cavities but also to communicate with other woodpeckers. The flat terrain and the mature trees here have allowed a buildup of soil, and the trail is now relatively free of rocks. The trail goes uphill and gets rocky again, and you'll find a series of igneous glades at 1.60 mi. **[4],** with tall big bluestem grass and large, rounded boulders.

At 2.20 mi. **[5]** you'll find a small pond on your right, with bur reed and dozens of frogs, many of which are southern leopard frogs. Leopard frogs are easy to identify at night in March and April because their breeding call is a distinctive quacklike chuckle. As you hike on an old road, watch for round antlion pits, iridescent turkey breast feathers, or long, barred turkey wing feathers. Go straight at the four-way intersection at 2.62 mi. **[6]** and turn left at the three-way intersection at 3.09 mi. **[7]**.

After turning right at the intersection at 3.16 mi. **[8]** you'll be back in the company of rocks. A big outcrop on your right invites you to climb on it. As you begin your ascent to Rock Pile Mountain, you'll find a different rock on the trail—ashy gray on the outside and black inside—still with a porphyritic structure. After a final ascent, you'll reach the peak and find the ancient circle of stones on your right that gave the mountain its name (3.52 mi.) **[9]**. With the rock pile on your right, turn left to discover another strange (though not human-made) structure. Climb on huge, billowing rocks that look as if they flowed from the earth like lava. A little exploration reveals that this lunarlike landscape caps much of the mountaintop. After examining Rock Pile's rocky curiosities, retrace your steps to finish your hike.

## Rock Pile Mountain Wilderness

Little Grass Mountain

Trail Creek Rd

1. Start
2. Registration box
3. Right turn
4. Igneous glades
5. Small pond
6. Go straight
7. Left turn
8. Right turn
9. Circle of stones

Rock Pile Mountain

LEGEND
— Road
······ Trail
▨ Boundary

N

# 22.  Silver Mines Recreation Area

- Hike alongside a mile-long stretch of shut-ins in one of the state's most scenic rivers, the St. Francis.

- Discover potholes—not in the asphalt road but in the ancient, sculpted, igneous boulders of the streambed.

- Hike on pine-covered bluffs next to massive granite boulders and on top of billowing outcrops of pink bedrock.

- Sit in the "air conditioner," a trailside log structure left over from an old silver mine where the temperature stays around 60 degrees, year-round.

- See a curved dam across the St. Francis River, built of granite blocks in 1879.

- Find a pack rat's lair.

## Area Information

Silver Mines Recreation Area is located on the St. Francis River at the site of a historic mining operation, where the Einstein Mining Company began recovering lead and silver from the area's granite bluffs in 1877. Two years later, the company constructed a dam across the river to divert water to power machinery for mining operations. The town of Silver Mountain sprang up on the ridge just above the mine and included a post office, school, blacksmith shop, several stores, and around 850 citizens. Granite, one of the hardest rocks known, did not yield its treasures easily, however, and the mine soon shut down, with total production recorded at 50 tons of lead and 3,000 ounces of silver.

The St. Francois Mountains, which surround the recreation area, are sometimes referred to as the geologic core of the Ozarks. Igneous rock exposures, some of the oldest on the continent, are dated at well over a billion years old. Granite and felsite masses contain extensive veins of minerals. Besides silver, lead, and tungsten ores found in quartz veins, more than 20 minerals have been identified in the area.

The narrow, deep valley of the St. Francis River with its 200-foot bluffs reveals the erosive action the water has carried on for millennia. Constricted in a series of rocky narrows locally known as shut-ins, the river has created a natural playground of sculpted and polished rocks, with small waterfalls, waterslides, and calm pools. The St. Francis River is the only river in Missouri classified as white water, and the high water of spring attracts kayakers from around the nation for Olympic trials as well as annual and regional races.

Silver Mines Recreation Area, in the Potosi/Fredericktown District of the Mark Twain National Forest, is managed by the U.S. Forest Service. With its unique blend of history, geology, scenery, and recreation, Silver Mines is a sure bet for outdoor fun.

**Directions:** From the south end of Ironton, take Highway 72 east 14.3 miles to the second intersection with Highway D. (Pass the first intersection at 2.4 miles.) Turn southwest on Highway D for 3 miles and turn right at the sign for the area. Go straight until the road dead-ends in a parking lot for the footbridge over the St. Francis River.

**Hours Open:** The site is open year-round. The campground is open from 6 A.M. to 10 P.M.

**Facilities:** The site offers three campgrounds, a group camp, and three picnic areas. Water and rest rooms are available in the campgrounds, but there are no showers. Fishing, wading, and carry-on canoeing are available on the St. Francis River.

**Permits and Rules:** A two-dollar fee is required per day per vehicle. The Forest Service advises against climbing on the dam or hiking across it. Hunting is prohibited within the recreation area, and all pets must be leashed.

**Further Information:** District Ranger, U.S. Forest Service, Potosi/Fredericktown District, P.O. Box 188, Potosi, MO 63664; 573-438-5427.

## Other Areas of Interest

Just upstream from Silver Mines, **Millstream Gardens Conservation Area** features more shut-ins of the St. Francis River and includes a state natural area. The area also offers a one-mile asphalt hiking trail (wheelchair accessible), picnic areas, demonstration sites, an archery range, and a hand-launch boat ramp on the river. The site, eight miles west of Fredericktown on Highway 72, is managed by the Missouri Department of Conservation. For more information call 573-290-5730.

Silver Mines Recreation Area

To Millstream Gardens

Low Water Crossing

Turkey Creek

Foot Bridge

Spring Branch Campground

St. Francis River

Summit Campground

Prospect Campground

N

Boulder Hike to Turkey Creek

Air Conditioner Trail

Foot Bridge

To Hwy. 72

Riverside Campground

LEGEND

—— Road

········ Trail

🔺 Camping

🔺 Group Camping

🔺 Picnic Area

🅿 Parking

⭐ Einstein Silver Mines

🔺 Air Conditioner

〰 Dam

🚪 Gate

# Air Conditioner Trail 👢👢👢👢👢

**Distance Round-Trip:** 1.4 miles

**Estimated Hiking Time:** 1 hour

*Hike this trail on a muggy, summer day and be rewarded with a walk-in air conditioner, complete with wooden benches and shade, compliments of the Einstein Mining Company.*

**Caution:** Several steep slopes, especially near the dam, have loose rocks.

**Trail Directions:** Park in the lot for the concrete footbridge over the St. Francis River, at the south end of the area. Begin the trail by starting across the footbridge **[1]**. Halfway across, at .03 mi. **[2]**, this bridge offers an in-the-river view of unusually beautiful shut-ins, where the swirling waters of the St. Francis churn around, over, and around huge igneous boulders, smoothing and sculpting them into abstract forms. Water rushes down natural waterslides, cascading into white, bubbly pools below. When the river is low, shallow pools form in depressions in the bedrock, creating little aquariums full of life. Look for small longear sunfish, chubs, and crayfish in these ephemeral pools.

Across the bridge, pass a picnic area on your left and turn right on the trail, into the woods at .10 mi. **[3]**. You'll hike uphill among outcrops of igneous boulders, splashed green with lichens. Higher on the hill, rounded outcrops of bedrock like the backs of elephants or rhinos bulge through the forest floor between columnlike trunks of shortleaf pine. Take the spur on your right at .35 mi. **[4]** past a ravine filled with boulders to an overlook of the river. From this view of the river bend, far below, look upstream to see the stone block dam built by the Einstein Mining Company in 1879 to divert the river to a turbine that powered machinery for hoisting and crushing ore. Downstream, the river continues its ceaseless journey over and around Precambrian granite and felsite boulders, some of the hardest and oldest rocks on the continent. Turn right after returning to the main trail.

The trail continues through gardens of boulders, where sensitive ferns and mosses emerge from vertical cracks. The rocks themselves look like living, growing things because of their ever-present green lichen coats. Besides the rocks, the abundance of hickory nuts in the fall, collecting on the trail faster than the squirrels can carry them away, may further complicate trail navigation. Turn right at the fork in the trail at .54 mi. **[5]** and you'll soon reach the air conditioner at .60 mi. **[6]**, a roofed log structure over a gated mine shaft. Sit on one of the benches and feel the cool air billowing out of the shaft, which extends into the ridge behind.

Follow the small stream emerging from the shaft, past some cattails and willows. Hike downhill on some loose rocks, toward the river, and you'll arrive at the base of the concave side of the stone dam at .70 mi. **[7]**. Look for aquatic snakes, sunning themselves on the dam blocks near the water. Watch for suckers coasting across the bottom of this large pool and look for turtles and smallmouth bass near the surface. A large section of the steep valley wall across from you is solid rock, displaying dramatic diagonal fractures and several colors of its igneous composition. Retrace your steps to return to the trailhead.

1. Start
2. Shut-ins
3. Right turn
4. Spur to river overlook
5. Right turn
6. Air conditioner
7. Stone dam

# Boulder Hike to Turkey Creek
👢👢👢👢

**Distance Round-Trip:** 1.65 miles

**Estimated Hiking Time:** 1 hour

*While hiking, I kept thinking of the miners, just across the river, and their search for silver and lead, long ago. Today, people come searching for fun, relaxation, and the beauty of the shut-ins.*

**Caution:** Several steep slopes, especially near the dam, have loose rocks.

**Trail Directions:** Park in the lot for the concrete footbridge over the St. Francis River, at the south end of the area. The trail follows the east bank of the river and overlooks almost the entire one-mile stretch of shut-ins. Begin the trail near the rest rooms **[1]**.

Like the Air Conditioner Trail, this trail traverses igneous boulders in various shades of pink, gray, or gray purple. The sound of small waterfalls and cascades of the shut-ins rise up the steep valley wall on your left, while rounded boulders decorated with green lichens growing in circular, targetlike patterns protrude from the slope on your right. Take the spur on your left at .18 mi. **[2]** on a giant slab of contoured, pink bedrock that slopes downhill toward the river.

At the end of the bedrock, with the splashing and churning waters of the shut-ins in front of you, look on your right, in the bedrock of the streambed, for a round hole about the size of a washtub. This is a good example of a pothole, created when river sediment scoured a depression in the bedrock. As larger stones settled in the depression and tumbled in the currents, they gradually enlarged the depression, carving it rounder and deeper. Look for smaller potholes and remnants of potholes that have eroded out of shape. Turn left after returning to the main trail.

As you gain elevation, pine trees become more common and the boulders more imposing, sometimes perched like small houses next to the trail. Take the steep and rocky spur at .38 mi. **[3]** to the stone dam. If you are here in spring or fall, watch for ospreys (fish hawks) perched in trees near the water, and listen for their call—a series of loud, clear whistles. In winter, look for bald eagles. Any time, you might see great blue herons, little green herons, and kingfishers. The smooth, sculpted bedrock makes a good place to relax in the sun or listen to the stereo sound of multiple riffles of the shut-ins. Turn left after returning to the main trail.

Soon, the large boulders near the trail turn into rock walls. Take a close look into some of the cracks and small ledges of the rocks at .45 mi. **[4]** and you'll likely see messy nests of twigs, leaves, nutshells, and bones, made by eastern wood rats. Nicknamed pack rats for their habit of collecting shiny objects like foil candy wrappers, pull tabs, and bottle caps, these nocturnal rodents sometimes use the same disorderly nest their entire life, constructing multiple levels and including underground passages. Ignore the spur at .47 mi. **[5]** and go straight. After passing two more spurs at .55 mi. **[6]**, you'll find an interesting spheroidal boulder on the trail.

As you climb even higher on this bluff, several rock ledges allow you to step to the edge and view the shut-ins through gaps in the trees. The sound is a hushed roar now, far below, and blends with the whispers in the pine trees around you. Ignore the spur on your right at .73 mi. **[7]** and go straight. You'll hike next to another assortment of huge granite boulders and rock walls that line the trail and march off onto the slope above you. Sensitive ferns, mosses, and several kinds of lichens adorn these rocks. After a descent, you'll find an arched bridge over Turkey Creek, which joins the St. Francis here at .83 mi. **[8]**. A pleasant picnic area just across the bridge makes a good place to relax before retracing your steps to the trailhead.

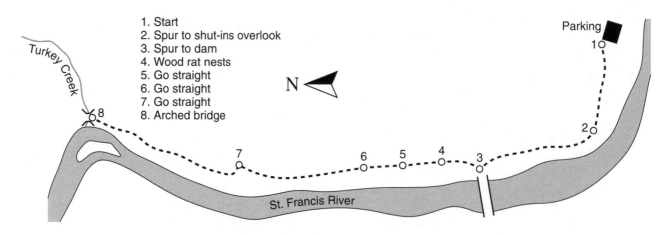

1. Start
2. Spur to shut-ins overlook
3. Spur to dam
4. Wood rat nests
5. Go straight
6. Go straight
7. Go straight
8. Arched bridge

N

Turkey Creek

Parking

St. Francis River

# 23. Crane Lake Recreation Area

- Stand on huge, rounded boulders on open, igneous glades and take in panoramic views of placid Crane Lake and rocky glades on distant ridges.
- On the glades, keep an eye out for basking reptiles, including six-lined racerunners and eastern collared lizards.
- Hear the music making of a myriad of orthopterans (grasshoppers, crickets, and katydids) in the tall vegetation of an old field.
- In the fall, find a big patch of strongly fragrant ladies' tresses orchids.
- Hike across the pillowlike, sculpted igneous boulders of the shut-ins on Crane Pond Creek.

## Area Information

Crane Lake is nestled between several ridges of the St. Francois Mountains, a 5,000-square-mile landscape that is one of the oldest mountain ranges in North America. Often considered the geologic core of the Ozarks, the St. Francois Mountains originated around 1.5 billion years ago as molten rock, which cooled and hardened into the ancient igneous rocks that typify this region.

Besides igneous rock exposures, Crane Lake has other features characteristic of the area, including ridgetop glades and shut-ins, which are gorgelike streambeds filled with bedrock and boulders, created when a stream forced its way through resistant outcrops of igneous rock. The site also boasts scenic ridgetop overlooks, a variety of Ozark habitats, and a picturesque and peaceful lake.

Crane Lake was originally created by an earthen dam constructed across the shut-ins of Crane Pond Creek. After the original dam failed in 1968, a concrete dam was installed in 1971–1972 to impound about 100 acres of water. The U.S. Forest Service bought the lake and surrounding area in 1973. Crane Lake Trail is one of only five national recreation trails in the state. This special designation identifies the

trail as an outstanding recreation resource and qualifies it for public recognition through U.S. Department of the Interior publications and news releases.

**Directions:** From Ironton, take Highway 21 south 15.1 miles to Chloride, where you turn east on Iron County Road #124 (just past Doe Run iron smelter). Go 3.8 miles and turn right at the sign for the area. Go 2.1 miles to a fork in the road, where you turn left into the parking lot for the boat ramp.

**Hours Open:** The area is always open.

**Facilities:** A boat ramp is available, making 100-acre Crane Lake accessible for fishing, canoeing, and boating. Picnic tables are provided, as well as grills and a toilet. Crane Lake Trail is open to hiking and biking, and a portion of the trail is open to equestrian use. The area can also be used to access the Marble Creek Section of the Ozark Trail.

**Permits and Rules:** No camping is allowed. Horses are only allowed on the southwest half of the trail and along the lake's west shore. Motorized vehicles are prohibited on the trail. Boat motors are restricted to electric trolling motors. Pets must be leashed.

**Further Information:** District Ranger, U.S. Forest Service, Potosi/Fredericktown District, P.O. Box 188, Potosi, MO 63664; 573-438-5427. For more information on the Ozark Trail, call the Missouri Department of Natural Resources at 573-751-2479.

## Other Areas of Interest

**Marble Creek Recreation Area,** also managed by the U.S. Forest Service, offers camping, picnicking, and wading and fishing in Marble Creek. The remains of a grist mill dam and building foundation are visible. The area is named for deposits of attractively colored dolomite that were mined and used in the building trade as "Taum Sauk Marble." The area is a trailhead for the Ozark Trail. The site is nine miles northeast of Crane Lake, just off County Highway E. For more information call 573-438-5427.

## Area Trails

### Marble Creek Section of the Ozark Trail

—8 miles—While not all of this 21-mile section is complete, the 8-mile portion that connects

Crane Lake with Marble Creek Recreation Area is finished and is open to the public. The trail traverses Reader Hollow, glades, bottoms, ridges, and offers views of Kelly and Patterson Mountains before finishing at Marble Creek's parking area.

# Crane Lake Trail

**Distance Round-Trip:** 5 miles

**Estimated Hiking Time:** 2.75 hours

*"It's kind of a booger to get to . . . kinda outa the way. But it's a mighty purty place."—resident of Chloride, describing Crane Lake.*

**Caution:** Vegetation crowds the trail in the creek bottom, so consider wearing long pants.

**Trail Directions:** Park in the lot for the picnic area and boat ramp. The trail begins between two chert boulders at the edge of the parking lot [1]. After passing through the picnic area, the trail takes you along the shore for fantastic views of the tranquil lake. Fingers of pine-clad ridges reach down to touch the water, and the sun plays with ripples near the edge like so many sparkling jewels.

At .72 mi. [2] you'll cross a small stream that feeds the lake's east bay. As the trail bends right at 1.15 mi. [3] white and tan sedimentary rocks are replaced by dark gray and purple igneous rocks, which form an interesting contrast with the patterns of green lichens that grow on them. The forest suddenly gives way to open glades at 1.30 mi. [4] with huge, rounded, igneous boulders. A fabulous vista of the lake soon opens over your right shoulder. Watch for eastern collared lizards sunning on the rocks.

As you descend into the valley of Crane Pond Creek, you'll pass several walls of pink boulders next to the trail. After crossing a few intermittent streams, you'll emerge into a large, old field at 1.86 mi. [5].

Watch for soaring birds of prey here and listen for their clear, whistlelike calls. Turn right at the intersection with the Ozark Trail, at 2.04 mi. [6]. The streambed at 2.11 mi. [7] is an eclectic rock collection, with specimens of varied colors, textures, and formation. Blue lobelia and brown-eyed Susans bloom next to the stream.

At 2.20 mi. [8] cross two streambeds of Crane Pond Creek. Turn right at 2.24 mi. [9], just across the second streambed, which may be flowing with spring water. In a weedy bottom, turn left at the intersection at 2.35 mi. [10], away from the creek. Next, you'll hike along an old farm field on an old road, lined with white oaks and shagbark hickories. Just after turning right at the fork in the trail at 2.49 mi. [11], look for blooming ladies' tresses orchids (August through November), a strongly fragrant orchid with small, white flowers spiraled on a stem about a foot tall. After passing through rocky woods, you'll find more igneous glades and overlooks at 2.87 mi. [12], with views across the chasmlike valley of Crane Pond Creek, far below.

Turn right at 3.06 mi. [13] and again at the dam at 3.10 mi. [14]. This spur leads to the shut-ins of Crane Pond Creek. Explore the billowing, sculpted rocks of the shut-ins at 3.14 mi. [15]. After returning to the dam, follow the shoreline to continue. After crossing a small stream that feeds the south bay, turn right at the intersection with an old road at 3.55 mi. [16]. The trail now hugs the shoreline. After crossing a concrete bridge at 4.82 mi. [17], go straight on the gravel road. Turn right at the intersection with the county road at 4.90 mi. [18] to return to the trailhead.

1. Start
2. Stream crossing
3. Igneous rocks
4. Glades and overlook
5. Old field
6. Right turn
7. Rocky streambed
8. Creek crossing
9. Right turn
10. Left turn
11. Right turn
12. Glades and overlooks
13. Right turn
14. Spur to shut-ins
15. Shut-ins
16. Right turn
17. Concrete bridge
18. Right turn

## Crane Lake Recreation Area

**LEGEND**

— Road
······· Trail
Picnic Area
Boat Launch
Springs
Dam
Parking

# 24.  Taum Sauk Mountain State Park

- Stand at the summit of Taum Sauk Mountain, the highest point in Missouri.
- Hike next to the 132-foot cascades of Mina Sauk Falls, the highest waterfall in the state.
- If you dare, gain admittance through Devil's Toll Gate, a narrow gap in a ridge of rock 50 feet long and 30 feet high, located in the state's deepest valley.
- Hike in the state's largest designated natural area, the 7,028-acre St. Francois Mountains Natural Area.
- Emerge from the forest onto rocky glades with tremendous views of the seemingly endless layers of the forested Ozark Highlands.

## Area Information

The 5,000-square-mile St. Francois Mountains include 30 forested peaks and constitute the great geologic dome of the Ozark interior. At the apex of this dome is Taum Sauk Mountain, the state's highest point, at 1,772 feet above sea level. Rock exposures give evidence of the area's geologic origins, which can be traced to volcanic activity around 1.5 billion years ago.

The character of the area can best be described as wilderness. Probably no other place in the state is home to as many plants, animals, and geologic features in their unspoiled state. Rich forests of oak, hickory, and shortleaf pine are interspersed with extensive glades, allowing unobstructed views of the rugged, expansive landscape. Prairie blazing star and rattlesnake master contribute their color to the red rocks of the glades, while fire pink, wild crocus, and ferns adorn the woodlands.

Zigzagging its way through the area's steep terrain is a portion of the Ozark Trail, which will be 500 miles long when complete. It begins in St. Louis, follows a scenic route through the Ozarks of southern Missouri, and will join the Ozark Highlands Trail of Arkansas.

**Directions:** From Ironton, go 6.5 miles south on Highway 21. Turn west on Highway CC, which dead-ends in 4 miles at Taum Sauk Mountain State Park.

**Hours Open:** The park is open year-round.

**Facilities:** The site offers basic camping, picnic areas, pit latrines, and drinking water. A fire tower, maintained by the Missouri Department of Conservation, is located on Highway CC one mile from the campground and is open to the public for climbing during daylight hours.

**Permits and Rules:** The Mina Sauk Falls Trail and the Taum Sauk Section of the Ozark Trail are open to foot traffic only. Standard wilderness ethics apply, which include staying on the trail, leaving plants, animals, and rocks undisturbed, and carrying out everything you brought in.

**Further Information:** Park Superintendent, Taum Sauk Mountain State Park, HCR1, Box 126, Middlebrook, MO 63656; 573-546-2450. For more information on the Ozark Trail call 573-751-2479.

## Other Areas of Interest

Ameren UE Company operates a museum at **Taum Sauk Reservoir Power Plant** with exhibits on geology, Native Americans, wildlife, and local industry. It is located on Highway AA, about four miles south of Highway CC. For more information call 573-637-2281.

## Park Trails

**Taum Sauk Section—Ozark Trail** 👢👢👢👢👢—12.8 miles—Although the entire Taum Sauk section is 33 miles long, the segment from Taum Sauk Mountain to Johnson's Shut-Ins State Park is only 12.8 miles long and offers ambitious day hikers an unforgettable hike.

# Mina Sauk Falls Trail and Ozark Trail to Devil's Toll Gate 👢👢👢👢👢

**Distance Round-Trip:** 5 miles

**Estimated Hiking Time:** 3.25 hours

*Hike Missouri's trail of superlatives. This five-mile hike includes the state's highest mountain, deepest valley, tallest waterfall, oldest rocks, and a portion of its longest trail (when completed), all within Missouri's largest designated natural area.*

**Caution:** There is no shortage of rocks on this trail. Some are sharp and many are loose.

**Trail Directions:** Begin the hike **[1]** near the signs at the edge of the parking lot at Taum Sauk Mountain. The trail begins as a sidewalk to the state's highest point. From there (obviously) it's a steady decline to the bottom. At .16 mi. **[2]** turn left on the spur to the peak of Taum Sauk, marked with a red granite monument stating that you are now 1,772.68 feet above mean sea level. Return to the main trail and turn left. Turn right at the intersection at .24 mi. **[3]**.

The first of many glades opens at .47 mi. **[4]**. Blue and green lichens add their colors to the red volcanic rock. This rock, rhyolite, is well over a billion years old. Prescribed fires set by park staff have allowed native plants, including rattlesnake master, to thrive in abundance here. Back in the forest, fire invigorates wildflowers like the brilliant fire pink and the deep blue wild crocus, found along the entire trail. An-

other glade starts at .70 mi., and the views of outlying forested domes keep getting better until .94 mi. **[5]**, where the best view of all will stop you in your tracks. Mountain after mountain is layered in uninterrupted succession, the farther ones increasingly shrouded in blue gray haze.

Go straight at 1.36 mi. **[6]** at the trail sign, which directs you to the top of the main cascade of Mina Sauk Falls. A wet-season waterfall, Mina Sauk flows most often during spring and fall. In all, the falls drop 132 feet in a series of cascades, splashing down one volcanic rock ledge after another. For a better view of Mina Sauk near the bottom, return to the trail sign and turn left on the Ozark Trail, toward Devil's Toll Gate. At 1.46 mi. **[7]** you will reach the base of the falls, where you can feel the mist on your face and become engulfed in the water's timeless roar. Cross the rocky stream here and turn right at the fork at 1.61 mi. **[8]**.

The trail soon parallels Taum Sauk Creek. Although not in its lowest point, you are now in Missouri's deepest valley **[9]** (1.87 mi.), measuring one thousand feet from top to bottom. Turn left at the intersection at 2.19 mi. **[10]**, just after crossing a rocky stream. Suddenly, an igneous rock ridge rises through the trees, leaving only an eight-foot gap through which the trail passes. Return to Mina Sauk Falls after experiencing Devil's Toll Gate **[11]** (2.32).

Turn right at **[6]** and pass several more cascades of Mina Sauk Falls. The trail treats you to the music of the stream as you pass several glades on your left, including some with remarkable vistas of the Ozark landscape. Turn left at the intersection at 4.49 mi. **[12]**. Turn right when you return to **[3]** to finish your hike.

## Taum Sauk Mountain State Park

1. Start
2. State's highest point
3. Right turn
4. Glade
5. Glade overlook
6. State's highest waterfall
7. Base of falls
8. Right turn
9. State's deepest valley
10. Left turn
11. Devil's Toll Gate
12. Left turn

Johnson's Shut-ins State Park

Mina Sauk Falls Trail

Mina Sauk Falls

Ozark Trail

N

L E G E N D
— Road
•••••• Trail
— Boundary
⭐ Trailhead
🔺 Devil's Toll Gate

# 25. Johnson's Shut-Ins State Park

- Sit in a natural, river-carved Jacuzzi and let the cool, clear waters of the Black River splash and bubble all around you.
- Learn about shut-ins, yet another Ozark geologic curiosity.
- Explore the diversity of 8,470-acre Johnson's Shut-Ins State Park, home of East Fork Wild Area and three state-designated natural areas.
- Hike in Missouri's most botanically rich area; 1,008 species of trees, shrubs, grasses, wildflowers, and ferns have been identified here so far.
- Meet Ozark witch hazel, a beautiful gravel bar shrub with a habit of blooming in January, often while there's snow on the ground.

## Area Information

Locally called shut-ins, this canyonlike gorge was formed when the swift water of the Black River was forced to pass through a valley of rhyolite, a volcanic rock that is extremely hard and erosion resistant. The river churned and swirled over the ancient igneous rock for eons, slowly scouring potholes, chutes, and spectacular cascades. Although the state has other shut-ins, Johnson's Shut-Ins are Missouri's most outstanding example.

Also remarkable is the park's wild and diverse character. The East Fork Wild Area includes bottomland woods, upland ridges, bluffs, wet meadows, and igneous glades with outstanding vistas. Dolomite glades are rare in the St. Francois Mountains, but the one here provides habitat for a group of specialized plants. Also, a combination of seasonally ponded rainwater and calcareous seepage promotes an unusual eight-acre fen.

Come on a hot summer day and you'll quickly appreciate Johnson's Shut-Ins' most popular feature.

Sitting and wading in the cool water among the smooth volcanic rocks is both a unique outdoor experience and a refreshing way to cool off. Johnson's Shut-Ins is probably Missouri's best-known park—and for many reasons. Come and find out your favorites.

**Directions:** The park is eight miles north of Lesterville on Highway N.

**Hours Open:** The entrance gate is open from 7 A.M. to 11 P.M. year-round. However, the park is limited to 100 cars, so if you want to come on a summer weekend plan to arrive early in the morning. Better yet, reserve a campsite. (Campsites may be reserved no later than two weeks in advance.) The park office is open from 8 A.M. to 4:30 P.M. Monday through Friday, and the shut-ins area is open for day use only.

**Facilities:** The park offers a campground, amphitheater, park store, picnic areas, and fishing and swimming in the East Fork Black River. Rock climbing, rappelling, and scuba diving are allowed by permit.

**Permits and Rules:** Food, drinks, and pets are prohibited in the shut-ins area or on the trail. In all other areas pets must be kept on leashes 10 feet in length or shorter. Daily permits from the park office are required for rock climbing, rappelling, and scuba diving. Diving and jumping from rocks in the shut-ins area are prohibited. Canoes, kayaks, or other boats are not allowed on the river within the park.

**Further Information:** Park Superintendent, Johnson's Shut-Ins State Park, HCR1, Box 126, Middlebrook, MO 63656; 573-546-2450. For more information on Missouri natural areas, call or write for a free directory from the Missouri Department of Conservation, Natural History Section, P.O. Box 180, Jefferson City, MO 65102; 573-751-4115.

## Park Trails

**Taum Sauk Section—Ozark Trail** 🥾🥾🥾🥾🥾— 33 miles—This section passes through Johnson's Shut-Ins State Park about midway. Bell Mountain Wilderness, to the northwest of the park, and Taum Sauk Mountain State Park, to the east, are each about 12.5 miles away.

# Shut-Ins Trail 👢👢👢👢👢

**Distance Round-Trip:** 2.5 miles

**Estimated Hiking Time:** 1.75 hours

*As you sit in the shut-ins, with the water bouncing and gurgling all around you, it's easy to imagine you are one of the many igneous boulders getting the same treatment. The main difference is that you've only been here for an hour or so, while the boulders have been here about 1.5 billion years!*

**Caution:** The rocks in the shut-ins are slippery, even when dry. Wear sneakers if you choose to wade in. Avoid white water and forgo jumping or diving from rocks.

**Trail Directions:** Begin the trail **[1]** at the interpretive signs in the south end of the main parking lot, near the park office. Cross a wooden boardwalk and stay on the paved trail. You'll follow blue arrows on this trail going clockwise. The first quarter mile to the shut-ins overlook is wheelchair accessible. Go straight at the intersection at .14 mi. **[2].**

By now you should hear the roar of the park's namesake. At .19 mi. **[3]** on your left is the first of several spurs to the shut-ins. Even if you don't plan to get wet, take at least one of these spurs to witness, up close, the turbulent, swirling water on these ancient rocks. Of course, the best way to experience the shut-ins is to join the rocks and get wet! Soon you'll reach the overlook boardwalk. Another spur to the shut-ins is at .33 mi. **[4].** Climb the steps for a higher-level overlook **[5]** at .36 mi., where you can see the blue green river water turn white as it plunges, and the blue gray rhyolite rocks turn red as they get wet.

At .49 mi. **[6]** is another overlook and spur to the shut-ins. The trail turns steeper and rockier. Turn left at the connector link at .63 mi. **[7].** Just after following a zigzag in the trail, you'll see what looks like an avalanche. This is a talus slope **[8]** (.85 mi.). All these rocks broke off the bluff above and rolled down the hill, perhaps thousands of years ago. The trail parallels the river for a while, giving you a chance to look for Ozark witch hazel. This is a shrub that grows next to rocky streams or in the gravel of the streambed. It has egg-shaped leaves with wavy edges and is the source for witch hazel extract, used in astringents and shaving lotions.

Turn left at the intersection at 1.20 mi. **[9].** You'll cross a couple of small, rocky streams before turning right at 1.36 mi. **[10],** where the Ozark Trail departs on its way to Bell Mountain. Cross a stream at a wet-weather waterfall and turn left. Hike uphill, toward a larger waterfall at 1.42 mi. **[11]** where you turn right. This upper trail passes through several glades, and the one at 1.50 mi. **[12]** offers a scenic view of the shut-ins as well as the surrounding mountains. Go straight at both the intersection at 2.00 mi. **[13]** and the connector link at 2.13 mi. **[14].** Hike downhill until you return to **[2],** where you turn left to return to the trailhead.

## Johnson's Shut-Ins State Park

1. Start
2. Go straight
3. Spur to shut-ins
4. Spur to shut-ins
5. Shut-ins overlook
6. Spur to shut-ins
7. Left turn
8. Talus slope
9. Left turn
10. Right turn
11. Wet-weather waterfall
12. Glade
13. Go straight
14. Go straight

LEGEND

| | | | |
|---|---|---|---|
| —— | Road | 🏕 | Picnic Area |
| ······ | Trail | 👫 | Restrooms |
| ▬▬ | Boundary | 📷 | Scenic Overlook |
| 🏠 | Park Office | 🎹 | Playground |
| P | Parking | 🍴 | Amphitheater |
| ▲ | Camping | | |
| ⬆ | Scout Area | ▤ | Gate |

# 26. Bell Mountain Wilderness

- Hike in the uncommon solitude of a U.S. Forest Service wilderness area.
- Find so many huckleberry bushes you won't have to venture off the trail to find ripe fruit (June through August).
- Hike on igneous glades—natural communities under extreme drought stress that turn into minideserts in the summer.
- Climb a mountain with panoramic views from the top without a house, barn, or road in sight.

## Area Information

The expression "as old as the hills" has geologic meaning in the Ozarks, which have been an exposed land mass for over 250 million years. Bell Mountain Wilderness is 9,027 acres in the St. Francois Mountains, one of the oldest landforms in North America—at least 1.3 billion years. Like the other six wilderness areas in Mark Twain National Forest, Bell Mountain required an act of Congress to be designated. Generally, a U.S. Forest Service wilderness must be at least 5,000 acres, basically roadless, and show little evidence of human works. It is a natural area affected primarily by the forces of nature. Some wilderness areas are classified as airsheds and are protected by laws to prevent their deterioration.

Most of Bell Mountain is rugged, dry, rocky, and forested by a variety of oaks and hickories, with interspersed shortleaf pine. Mature forest species such as pileated woodpeckers, woodthrush, and ovenbirds thrive here. Igneous glades and rock outcrops are common and add to the diversity of wildlife habitat and scenery. Blackjack oak, winged elm, and native grasses live on the glades, which are havens for snakes, lizards, and plants specially adapted to the hot, dry conditions. Even though Bell Mountain's big rocks are fun to hike around and the uninterrupted views from the mountaintop are stupendous, its best feature is its peacefulness.

**Directions:** From Potosi take Highway 21 south to Highway 32. Turn west on Highway 32 for 7 miles to Highway A. Turn south on Highway A for 5.6 miles. The parking lot for trailhead #2 is on the right. To get to trailhead #1, turn south on Highway A for .5 miles and turn left on Farm Road #2228 (gravel) for 1.9 miles. The parking lot is on the right.

**Hours Open:** The wilderness is always open.

**Facilities:** There are no facilities.

**Permits and Rules:** Hunting is allowed but not within 150 yards of the trail. Horses and bikes are allowed; ATVs are prohibited. Camping is allowed, but users must observe regulations designed to protect the wilderness beauty. Choose a campsite away from the trail and avoid constructing a fire ring. Cut no standing trees (live or dead), extinguish all campfires, and scatter their evidence before leaving. Leave no litter, trail-marking ribbons, or other evidence of your presence.

**Further Information:** District Ranger, U.S Forest Service, Potosi/Fredericktown District, P.O. Box 188, Potosi, MO 63664; 573-438-5427.

## Other Areas of Interest

**Council Bluff Lake** is a 440-acre impoundment of the Big River and offers boating, canoeing, fishing, camping, picnicking, and swimming. From Bell Mountain, return to Highway 32 and turn west. Go north on Highway DD 3.2 miles and turn right. For more information call 573-438-5427.

## Area Trails

**Lindsey Mountain Trail** 👢👢👢 —4.3 miles—Just east of the Bell Mountain Trail, this trail offers two good exercise climbs and the opportunity to hike up another mountain (1,600 feet) in wilderness solitude. Large boulders are scattered on the mountain, and the trail is difficult to follow near the end. To reach the trailhead, continue on Farm Road #2228 for 2.7 miles past trailhead #1. Turn right on Farm Road #2359. This road dead-ends in 2 miles at the Lindsey Mountain trailhead.

# Bell Mountain Trail 👢👢👢👢

**Distance Round-Trip:** 10 miles

**Estimated Hiking Time:** 5 hours

*What would the world be, once bereft of wet and of wildness? Let them be left, oh let them be left, wildness and wet, long live the weeds and the wilderness yet.—Gerard Manley Hopkins*

**Caution:** Rocks are found on most parts of the trail. Hunting is allowed in national forests. Bring a compass and topo map if you choose to extend this hike or explore off the trail.

**Trail Directions:** Park in the lot for trailhead #2, which is directly off Highway A. The northern trailhead for the Taum Sauk section of the Ozark Trail is also here, and the first 1.92 miles of the Bell Mountain Trail is also a portion of this Ozark Trail section. This linear hike can be extended; it's about 9 miles between trailheads. A 3-mile loop section in the middle down to Joe's Creek also adds options.

Begin by taking the trail directly north out of the parking lot **[1]**. This parallels Highway A for a short distance. Turn right at .03 mi. **[2]** and cross Highway A. The trail gains a little elevation here so you might huff and puff a bit. For compensation you'll have trailside scenery of lichen-covered igneous boulders and bountiful wildflowers. Larger rhyolite outcroppings shade small seeps and damp areas, and provide habitat for mosses, ferns, and water-loving sedges. This is the

most difficult part of the trail as you complete several switchbacks up the side of the mountain.

As you near the end of the first mile the trail finally levels off at the top of the ridge. For the next mile, vistas of neighboring Ozark mountains appear through rocky openings in the forest. One of several igneous glades appears on your right at 1.20 mi. **[3]**. The jumble of huge boulders and rock fragments makes natural overlook decks. Notice the stunted trees and shrubs here—this exposed bedrock turns into a solar oven in the summer.

At 1.92 mi. **[4]** is an important intersection. Beware the trail to the right (south); the next trailhead is 13 miles away! Turn left (north) to continue the Bell Mountain trail. At 2.91 mi. **[5]** go straight. Soon you'll see evidence of early settlers of Bell Mountain—a farm pond and an old pasture, now thick with blackberries, sumac, and buckbrush. Turn left at the intersection at 3.29 mi. **[6]**. Your feet will enjoy the temporary lack of rocks on the trail. A gradual ascent will bring you to the peak of Bell Mountain at 4.35 mi. **[7]**. Take the short spur behind the campsite to find a superb spot to snack, relax, and take in views of the world from 1,702 feet up.

After you return to the trail visit the post oaks **[8]** on the glade at 4.63 mi. Their twisted trunks and contorted branches bespeak their hard lives on this thin, dry, rocky soil. Hike through several more glade openings before turning around at the entrance gate to the forest—some larger-than-usual boulders at the outer edge of the last glade (4.95 mi.) **[9]**.

## Bell Mountain Wilderness

**LEGEND**
— Road
······ Trail
▬ Boundary
**P** Parking
⭐ Trailhead

1. Start
2. Right turn
3. Igneous glade
4. Left turn
5. Go straight
6. Left turn
7. Peak of Bell Mountain
8. Post oaks
9. Boulders

# 27.  Elephant Rocks State Park

- See and touch the pink elephants, some of the most curious geological wonders in Missouri and among the oldest rocks on the earth's surface.

- Hike on the first trail in the state designed especially for people with visual and physical disabilities.

- Find a wealth of life in the short-lived pools of the *tinajitas*.

- Learn how the elephants were formed 1.3 billion years ago, how quarry workers split them in the late 1800s, and how weather is eroding them today.

- Hike among the Precambrian elephants and let your imagination go wild.

## Area Information

Although these titanic, spheroidal granite boulders currently dominate the summit of a bedrock dome, they began as a solid mass deep beneath the earth's surface. Originating as molten rock, magma was pushed up toward the surface where it cooled slowly, forming solid granite. Cracks developed in the granite, producing stacks of huge, oblong blocks. Through a combination of mountain-forming uplift and hundreds of millions of years of erosion, the blocks were eventually brought to the surface, where they began to face, as they still do, the effects of weather. Rainwater, freezing, thawing, wind, and sun all play their parts to break down the rocks. Even plants and trees growing in cracks help break them apart. As these agents wear at the corners and edges of the rocks, the rounded shapes of the elephants begin to appear.

The economic value of granite, one of the hardest rocks known, was quickly recognized. Several quarries are located within the park, and just outside the park is the oldest granite quarry in the state, opening in 1869. These quarries supplied granite for paving stones for some of St. Louis's streets, for massive blocks for the piers of the Eads Bridge at St. Louis, and for the state capitols of Iowa and Illinois. Fortunately, the legacy of these ancient rocks is preserved today. They are tangible parts of the geological core of the Ozarks. Come hike among the elephants, an old and peaceful herd.

**Directions:** The park is at the northwest edge of Graniteville on Highway 21. The entrance is 1.2 miles north of the intersection of Highway 21 and Highway N.

**Hours Open:** The site is open year-round from sunrise to sunset.

**Facilities:** Picnic areas, rest rooms, a small fishing lake, and drinking water are available.

**Permits and Rules:** No bicycles, roller blades, or rock-climbing equipment is allowed in the park. Rock collecting and camping are prohibited. No disposable containers are allowed on the trail. Hikers must stay on the trail. Pets must always be leashed.

**Further Information:** Elephant Rocks State Park, P.O. Box 509, Pilot Knob, MO 63663; 573-546-3454 (Fort Davidson State Historic Site).

## Other Areas of Interest

Earthwork remnants of a Civil War fort occupied by Union forces are still visible at **Fort Davidson State Historic Site**. A visitor center interprets the historic September 27, 1864, battle, and the site includes a picnic area and playgrounds. The fort is on Highway V in Pilot Knob, just north of Ironton. For more information call 573-546-3454.

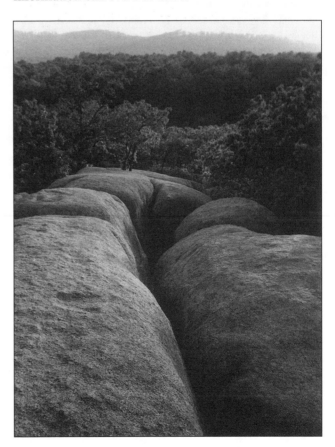

# Elephant Rocks Braille Trail 🥾

**Distance Round-Trip:** 1 mile

**Estimated Hiking Time:** 1 hour

*Rock, animal, vegetable . . . they're all mixed up at Elephant Rocks State Park. You'll never know what will loom up through the trees next. Is that a nose? Is that a mouth? Watch out! That is most certainly a pachyderm!*

**Caution:** Bring repellent for summer evening hikes among the elephants; *tinajitas* can produce mosquitoes.

**Trail Directions:** Begin the trail **[1]** at the large interpretive signs at the north end of the parking lot. The paved trail is ideal for park visitors who are disabled or elderly. The signs here, as well as ones along the hike, describe the origin of the massive spheroidal granite boulders and explain why they look the way they do. Some of the oldest and hardest rocks on the earth, these elephants have a long and interesting history.

As you begin, the rounded contours of the first elephants loom through the trees. Turn right at the intersection at .05 mi. **[2].** Because of its outstanding geologic value, the seven-acre site encircled by this trail is a designated state natural area. Although it is tempting to explore, please stay on the trail to avoid broadening unauthorized paths. Later, a boardwalk will take you to the top of the mountain where you can roam at will among the elephants.

Along the way there are plenty of low, smooth boulders (baby elephants) that make great natural benches. At .29 mi. **[3]** is a circular bench made from red granite blocks. Take the overlook spur to your left at .37 mi. **[4]** to view an interesting jumble of sprawling white oaks and piles of red granite left from quarry work. On the horizon are the forested igneous domes of the St. Francois mountains. Continue on your left after returning to the main trail.

Turn left at the spur at .50 mi. **[5]** to walk among the elephants. At this summit you will see the names of early quarry workers engraved in some of the boulders. This was often done on the date they became master stonecutters. At the feet of the elephants look for *tinajitas*—natural depressions in the rock sometimes filled with temporary pools of water. Grasses and mosses find homes here, and frogs, toads,

and insects often lay their eggs in the water. Turn left after returning to the main trail. Turn left again at .59 mi. **[6]** to pass through Fat Man's Squeeze, a natural fracture between two boulders. Turn right at .62 mi. **[7]** to walk beside some piles of granite blocks, some of which still bear holes drilled by quarry workers. Turn right at **[6]** to pass again through the Squeeze.

At .73 mi. **[8]** is an overlook of a water-filled quarry, where granite blocks were extracted to pave streets in St. Louis and other U.S. cities. An iron wedge used to split the granite still remains in a stone at .77 mi. **[9].** Turn left at the fork at .82 mi. **[10]** and turn right at **[2]** to finish the trail.

## Elephant Rocks State Park

LEGEND
— Road        🅰 Picnic Area
····· Trail
▬ Boundary    🅿 Parking

1. Start
2. Right turn
3. Red granite bench
4. Overlook spur
5. Spur to elephants
6. Left turn
7. Right turn
8. Quarry overlook
9. Iron wedge
10. Left turn

# 28.  Hawn State Park

- See, hear, and smell the lofty pine trees and feel their needles cushioning the trail.
- Spend some peaceful time in a botanically and geologically rich state park that contains four designated state natural areas and a wild area.
- Find one of Missouri's showiest flowering shrubs, the wild azalea, in abundance on the park's sandstone ledges.
- Hike within the state's finest concentration of distinctive Lamotte sandstone features—sculpted outcrops, terraced cliffs, overhanging shelves, shattered blocks, bedrock slabs, and oddly shaped boulders (called hoodoos).
- See the narrow canyons and overhangs that provide cool refuge for some of Missouri's rarest and most restricted plants including glacial relics like Canadian white violet, partridge berry, and hay-scented fern.

## Area Information

Located in the LaMotte sandstone basin, Hawn State Park is a superb example of the eastern Ozark sandstone country. LaMotte, a very old, coarse-grained sandstone lends its distinctive character to the park. Because of the sandstone's unique ability to hold groundwater moisture and to produce acidic, sandy soils, the park is home to many unusual and rare plants, some of which are found nowhere else in Missouri.

Sandy-bottomed and tea-colored Pickle Creek, with its diverse life and beauty, is the primary feature of Pickle Creek Natural Area. Its narrow shut-ins are some of the few places in Missouri where sandstone and igneous rocks come into contact at the surface. The stream's steep valleys are lined with sandstone cliffs, undercut ledges, and shaded ravines. Three other natural areas within the park feature 17 species of ferns, rare orchids, sandstone glades, and some of the finest native shortleaf pine forests in the state.

**Directions:** The park is about halfway between Ste. Genevieve and Farmington off Highway 32, on Highway 144.

**Hours Open:** The park gate is open from 7:30 A.M. to 9 P.M. year-round. The park office is open Wednesday through Sunday from noon to 4 P.M. from April through November.

**Facilities:** A campground and picnic areas are available, as well as a playground and amphitheater.

**Permits and Rules:** Much of the flora of the park is unusual and fragile. Stay on the trails and refrain from climbing on rocks and ledges. Entry into Orchid Valley Natural Area is by permit only. Pets must always be leashed. Backpack camping is allowed on the Whispering Pine Trail, but campfires are prohibited there. All trail users must register at the trailhead.

**Further Information:** Park Superintendent, Hawn State Park, 12096 Park Drive, Ste. Genevieve, MO 63670; 573-883-3603. For a free directory of Missouri natural areas contact the Missouri Department of Conservation, Natural History Section, P.O. Box 180, Jefferson City, MO 65102; 573-751-4115.

## Other Areas of Interest

A 2-mile hiking trail loops through **Pickle Springs Natural Area**, revealing more interesting sandstone features like boxed canyons, cliffs, leaning boulders, hoodoos, and a double arch. To reach the area from Hawn, turn west on Highway 32 for 5 miles, turn left on Highway AA for 1.6 miles, and turn left again on Dorlac Road for .5 mile. For more information call 573-290-5730.

**Sainte Genevieve**, northeast of the park, is the oldest incorporated community in Missouri, founded sometime between 1723 and 1735. Originally settled by French explorers who traveled up the Mississippi River, the town became an important river port. Guided tours are available for a fee at the **Felix Valle House State Historic Site**, which preserves the home of Felix Valle and the headquarters for his company that dealt in furs and Indian trade goods in Missouri and Arkansas. For more information call 573-883-7102.

# Hawn State Park

To Route 32

Hawn Park Rd.

144

Pickle Creek Trail

Pickle Creek

Whispering Pine Trail

North Loop

Evans Knob

South Loop

N

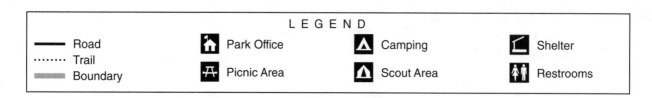

L E G E N D

| | | | | | | |
|---|---|---|---|---|---|---|
| —— Road | | Park Office | | Camping | | Shelter |
| ···· Trail | | Picnic Area | | Scout Area | | Restrooms |
| ▬▬ Boundary | | | | | | |

# Pickle Creek Trail 👢👢👢👢👢

**Distance Round-Trip:** 1.5 miles

**Estimated Hiking Time:** 1 hour

*Pickle Creek flows with life. Black-winged damsel-flies with alarmingly blue bodies flit near the banks. A northern water snake slowly eases down a natural rock waterslide. Tiny black tadpoles dot the bottom of shallow pools, while whirligig beetles nervously scurry on the surface.*

**Caution:** Watch your step as the trail takes you over jumbles of rocks of all different shapes and sizes.

**Trail Directions:** This trail follows Pickle Creek for the first half, then crosses the creek and uses a section of the Whispering Pine Trail for the return route. Park near the picnic shelter between the park office and campground. The trailhead **[1]** is just west of the Whispering Pine trailhead, near the picnic shelter. You'll begin the hike in a natural community that was familiar to Missouri settlers but is rare today—a pine savanna **[2]**. The large pines here are widely spaced, allowing sunlight to reach the ground where native grasses and wildflowers thrive instead of underbrush and thickets. As with other types of savannas, pre-scribed fires maintain the area's parklike open appearance.

You'll soon be hiking with riffling Pickle Creek on your left and a steep, rocky slope on your right (.16 mi.) **[3]**. Because of its natural beauty, interesting geology, unusual plants, and diverse aquatic life, this section of Pickle Creek has been designated both a state natural area and an outstanding state water resource. Notice the sand on the trail and on tiny beaches along the creek. This sand eroded from the sandstone bedrock and boulders on the slopes above. Sometimes pine needles build up on sandy patches on the trail, making a cushiony layer for hiking feet. Look for the flattened stems of winged elm, a common small tree here. A talus slope of pink granite rocks is at .26 mi. **[4]**.

Pickle Creek carved through the sandstone and became entrenched between some igneous boulders at .35 mi., creating a shut-in **[5]**. You may be surprised to walk out onto the bedrock glade at .56 mi. **[6]**, which looks like a sheet of flowing lava. While

you're looking at the interesting textures and colors of this once-molten igneous rock, look for lichen grasshoppers, which camouflage themselves as lichens and remain unseen until they jump. Brown fence lizards may make an appearance, too.

At the intersection at .66 mi. **[7]** turn left and cross Pickle Creek. Once across, turn left on the Whispering Pine Trail, signed with red arrows and markers. A blood-pumping hill takes you to a blufftop overlook at .89 mi. **[8]** where the scenery is rich, both near and far. Massive sandstone boulders have fractured and tilted, jamming against those farther downhill. Some of the boulders wear frilly hats of ferns and blueberry bushes, while others dress more moderately in mosses and lichens. Pine-clad ridges and knobs fill all distant views.

Turn right at 1.18 mi. **[9]** and go straight at the fork in the trail at 1.44 mi. **[10]**. Just after descending a steep hill on a sandy trail with many rocks and roots, turn left at 1.5 mi. **[11]** and go over two wooden bridges. You are now at the trailhead for the Whispering Pine Trail. Turn left to return to the picnic shelter.

1. Start
2. Pine savanna
3. Pickle Creek
4. Talus slope
5. Shut-in
6. Bedrock glade
7. Creek crossing
8. Blufftop overlook
9. Right turn
10. Go straight
11. Left turn

# Whispering Pine Trail 👢👢👢👢👢

**Distance Round-Trip:** 10 miles

**Estimated Hiking Time:** 7 hours

*A pine forest is a glorious place to hike. The stately pines are beautiful to see, and their fallen needles soften hard and rocky trails. Whether moistened in new rain or warmed in the sun, their waving boughs fan their unforgettable fragrance. All the while, the slightest breeze plays their timeless music.*

**Caution:** Some trail sections are rife with rocks. Follow trail markers closely to keep your orientation.

**Trail Directions:** Park in the picnic area between the park office and campground. A signboard marks the trailhead. The trail consists of two loops; the north loop is six miles long (marked with red arrows) and the south loop covers four miles (blue arrows). Fill out a registration card at the trailhead before your hike.

Begin by crossing two wooden bridges **[1]** and turn right at the intersection at .04 mi. **[2]**. A rocky and rooty climb will lift you to several overlooks among sandstone boulders, blueberry bushes, and many ferns. As you descend, listen for the shut-ins of Pickle Creek below. Cross the creek at .85 mi. **[3]** and turn left on the trail on the other side. The cool, clear water splashing around the smooth igneous boulders of the shut-in **[4]** at .94 mi. will invite you in for a dip. As you continue, the character of the creek changes dramatically. No longer forced around resistant, igneous rock, the creek becomes wide and shallow over a sandy bottom, revealing its clear, tea-colored water.

Make a couple of stream crossings and complete a switchback over a sandstone bluff at 2.09 mi. **[5]**. You'll pass a white spur to a backpack camp at 3.00 mi. Climb a steep dome at 3.25 mi. **[6]**, ignoring several paths on the way, and enjoy the views from the top. Turn right at 3.50 mi. **[7]** to begin the south loop. Pass a white spur to a camp at 4.44 mi. At 4.52 mi. **[8]** on your right you'll see a patch of cinnamon ferns.

Many of the Lamotte sandstone boulders at 5.36 mi. **[9]** exhibit cross-bedding, showing that layers of sand were cemented together at different times. Just after passing under a powerline, you'll meet the River Aux Vases **[10]** (5.77 mi.) as it meanders at the base of a steep bluff. Cool, shaded, and moist, this terraced rock face is a living fern garden. The stream has undercut the bluff in places, creating mysterious overhangs.

The trail parallels the stream for a while, and several more overhanging shelves appear next to the water, creating terrarium-like gardens. Everywhere, the water is alive with chubs, sunfish, and schools of minnows. When a boulder next to the stream appears to be blocking the trail at 5.90 mi. **[11]** you can either scamper over the boulder to continue or go around it, up the hill. If you go around, don't climb too far up the hill. Return to the stream to continue.

Pass a white spur to a camp at 6.61 mi. and you'll soon be hiking under a nearly pure stand of shortleaf pines. Turn right at 7.45 mi. **[12]** to return to the north loop. When your heart rate speeds up again you are probably climbing Evans Knob (8.10 mi.) **[13]**. After the sharp bend in the trail near the campground you'll be treated to some final overlooks of the Pickle Creek valley at 9.15 mi. **[14]**. Turn right when you return to **[2]** to finish your hike.

1. Start
2. Right turn
3. Creek crossing
4. Shut-in
5. Switchback
6. Dome overlook
7. Right turn
8. Cinnamon ferns
9. Sandstone boulders
10. River Aux Vases
11. Boulder block
12. Right turn
13. Evans Knob
14. Final overlooks

N

# 29. St. Francois State Park

- Explore the Pike Run Hills, a rough, rugged, and remote section of the Ozarks that became the favorite refuge for one of Missouri's most notorious Civil War guerrillas.
- Stroll through Mooner's Hollow, named for the moonshine stills that flourished in the 1920s in the isolated hills, rich with cold, clear springwater.
- Hike next to Coonville Creek, a premier Ozark headwater stream that is a designated outstanding state resource water, a state natural area, and is buffered by a state designated wild area.

## Area Information

Like most places, the history of St. Francois State Park includes a rock. Soft, porous dolomite composes most of the area's bedrock, which has been whittled and carved for eons by water draining to the Big River. This has left a rugged landscape, with deeply dissected forests, steep bluffs, caves, and numerous streams. South-facing upper slopes are dry, thin-soiled glades and savannas, while narrow, shaded valleys are kept even cooler and moister by spring-fed seepages.

Like most places, too, the park's physical characteristics have influenced its ecological and cultural history. Long ago, as the last glacier receded to northern climes, taking a cooler climate with it, it left behind a few plants that have since been protected in their unusually cool and moist environments. These rare northern plants, such as bog coneflower, swamp wood betony, and queen-of-the-prairie, depend on coldwater seeps and fens for their fragile existence.

People, too, have found refuge in these steep ridges known as the Pike Run Hills. Sam Hildebrand, a deadly Civil War rebel bushwhacker bent on revenging his three brothers' deaths, reputedly hid out in a small cave, still concealed in the park. Later, the isolated and deep coves of the hills hid the small,

primitive stills of Ozark moonshiners, who found one of their product's main ingredients, clear springwater, in abundance. Today, St. Francois State Park offers the beauty and renewal of an unspoiled, natural setting. For these qualities, it remains a beautiful refuge.

**Directions:** From the intersection of Highways 47 and 67 in Bonne Terre, turn north on Highway 67 for 4.3 miles. Turn right at the sign for the park.

**Hours Open:** The park is open year-round from 7 A.M. to 10 P.M. in the summer and from 8 A.M. to 9 P.M. in the winter.

**Facilities:** A campground is available, as well as picnic areas, a park office, and an amphitheater. Swimming, fishing, and boating are available on Big River, which forms the southern boundary of the park. Boat accesses (carry-on only) are located near both picnic areas. Horse riding is permitted on the Pike Run Trail but discouraged during wet periods.

**Permits and Rules:** Pets must always be leashed. Bicycles are prohibited on all trails. Camping is permitted only by backpackers on Pike Run Trail, but campfires are prohibited there.

**Further Information:** Park Superintendent, St. Francois State Park, 8929 Highway 67 North, Bonne Terre, MO 63628; 573-358-2173.

## Other Areas of Interest

**St. Joe State Park**, Missouri's second largest, features 1,800 acres for off-road-vehicle use. Also available are a 23-mile equestrian trail, an 11-mile paved bicycle and hiking trail, and swimming, fishing, boating, and picnicking. The park is in Park Hills, just south of St. Francois State Park. For more information call 573-431-1069.

**Missouri Mines State Historic Site**, also in Park Hills, includes a museum that interprets the Old Lead Belt of Missouri. Guided tours are available for a fee. For more information call 573-431-6226.

## Park Trails

**Pike Run Trail** 🥾🥾🥾—11 miles—Divided into a 6.7-mile south loop and a 4.3-mile north loop, this trail explores much of the scenic 2,101-acre Coonville Creek Wild Area. The trail is open to hikers, back-

packers, and equestrians, and begins .1 mile north of the campground entrance.

**Missouri Trail** 🥾🥾—.5 mile—This is a linear trail that begins at the east end of the campground loop, behind campsite #30, and ends at the west end. It passes through a diversity of plant habitats.

St. Francois
State Park

N

To De Soto
20 Miles

67

Coonville Creek

Pike Run Trail
North Loop

Mooner's Hollow Trail

Coonville
Creek
Wild Area

Pike Run Trail
South Loop

67

To
Bonne Terre
5 Miles

Swimming Deer Trail

Big River

LEGEND

| | | | | |
|---|---|---|---|---|
| —— Road | | 🏠 Park Office | 🛉 Picnic Area | 🏊 Beach |
| ···· Trail | | | | |
| ▓▓ Boundary | | ⛺ Camping | 🏠 Picnic Shelter | 🏇 Equestrian Staging Area |
| | | 🚮 Trailer Sanitation Disposal Station | 🛁 Bath House | |

# Mooner's Hollow Trail 👢👢👢👢

**Distance Round-Trip:** 3 miles

**Estimated Hiking Time:** 1.75 hours

*A typical moonshine recipe called for cornmeal, rye, and homemade malt, in more or less exact proportions. Most mooners made their own stills from copper sheet and tubing, and a product with a decent reputation would bring a dollar a gallon.*

**Caution:** Smooth bedrock on the trail is sometimes slippery because of moist algae and mosses.

**Trail Directions:** The trail begins near picnic shelter #1, located in the first picnic area in the park, just past the park office. Coonville Creek is fed by numerous seeps and small springs, as you will soon see for yourself, and its cherty, gravel bottom is easy to see beneath the stream's crystal-clear waters. As you cross Coonville Creek on a wooden bridge **[1]**, you'll hear the soothing music of its small riffles below—a refreshing sound anyway, but especially if you've just come away from the anxious scurry of Highway 67.

Just across the bridge, a sign welcomes you to Coonville Creek Wild Area, a 2,101-acre area of forested ridges, hollows, glades, and stream valleys protected for its qualities of wilderness and unconfined solitude. Turn left just behind the wild area sign. Coonville Creek now accompanies you on the left for the first mile, offering many chances to scan its slower, deeper pools for some of the 18 kinds of fish that live here. Breeding males of the orangethroat darter and southern redbelly dace are among the most beautiful fish anywhere, splashing brown creek gravel in the spring with brilliant orange, crimson red, and lemon yellow.

After you pass several small gladelike openings on the right, you'll hike over dolomite boulders blanketed with liverleaf, smooth cliffbrake, and mosses. Cross the first of many intermittent tributaries to Coonville Creek at .26 mi. **[2].** Ignore the spur on the left at .27 mi. **[3]** and go straight. A picturesque aquatic scene appears at .34 mi. **[4]** next to the trail, with robust clumps of heart-leaved plantain emerging from rolling riffles. Tufts of sedges and slender boughs of willow arch gracefully over the water.

Some wooden steps will soon lift you to a glade. Keep going and you'll hike out onto flat bedrock at .55 mi. **[5],** with a panoramic vista of three ridges of the Pike Run Hills in front of you. A glorious glade awaits behind you, with pale-purple coneflowers, prairie dock, and rose gentian. Pinch the stems of the grasses at the base; little bluestem grass has very flat stems while big bluestem grass has oval stems.

Just after crossing a moss- and fern-cloaked tributary, the trail crosses Coonville Creek at .94 mi. **[6].** Midstream, find a stable stepping-stone and stop. Look upstream to see magnificent cascades of water, flowing down layer upon layer of stair-stepped bedrock. Look downstream to see half-submerged blocks of rock, gravel bars, and miniature islands with umbrella-like tufts of sedges. Hike beneath some musclewood trees, growing just on the other side of the creek, and pass several small seeps, or wet meadows. Formed by cool, upwelling groundwater, these small wetlands support rare queen-of-the-prairie and grass pink orchids.

After climbing a good exercise hill, the trail swings to the left and follows a ridgetop. Ignore the spur to the left at 1.94 mi. **[7]** and turn right. You'll hike into a savanna at 1.97 mi. **[8],** a grassland with interspersed trees. Several expansive views of wooded ridges appear through large openings in the chinkapin oaks. Just after the trail cuts sharply to the left, you'll see an intermittent spring outlet on your right at 2.12 mi. **[9].** After crossing several more small glades and tributaries, Coonville Creek reappears on your left. As you near the trail's end, watch out for a wire cable across the trail at 2.90 mi. **[10],** installed to keep vehicles out of the creek valley. Turn left on the pavement of the picnic loop to finish your hike.

1. Start
2. Tributary crossing
3. Go straight
4. Aquatic scene
5. Glade overlook
6. Coonville Creek crossing
7. Right turn
8. Savanna
9. Intermittent spring
10. Wire cable

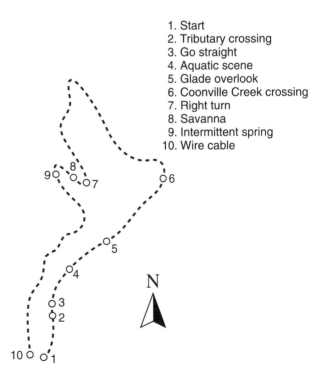

# Swimming Deer Trail 👢👢👢

**Distance Round-Trip:** 3 miles

**Estimated Hiking Time:** 1.75 hours

*"They look like the fragments of a broken up world piled together in dread confusion . . ."—reported description by Sam Hildebrand in 1870 of the Pike Run Hills, his Civil War hideout.*

**Caution:** Be careful at the steep bluff overlooks, where ivy sometimes obscures the bluff edges. Also, smooth rocks on the trail may be slippery because of moist algae and moss.

**Trail Directions:** The trail begins at the south end of the park, at the east end of the campground loop. The trailhead is marked by a signboard **[1]**, behind campsite #30. Follow green arrows on this trail. Start in a lush and shaded bottom of the Big River, which is just to the right. Along with pawpaw are Ohio buckeye, small trees with palm-shaped leaves and leathery, spiny capsules containing three shiny brown seeds. The leaves emerge in early spring, before any other tree, and some people carry the seeds in their pockets to prevent rheumatism. Go straight at .04 mi. **[2]** and turn right at the fork in the trail at .08 mi. **[3]**. Layered dolomite outcrops protrude from the slope on your left. Trees grow so tall in the rich, moist soil that it's hard to see their leaves, but the telltale bark of their trunks reveal towering black walnut, hackberry, and sycamore.

Appearing soon on your right is a slough, which may be dry. As the trail approaches the Big River, the dolomite outcrops on the left turn into bluffs, scenic in their weathered and eroded condition. Listen for the rattle of kingfishers as you near the river and look for startled ducks and herons. Scan the gravel bars and logs for sunning aquatic turtles and snakes, and search the pools for floating gar and carp. At .32 mi. **[4]** turn left, toward a wet-weather waterfall over layered blocks of weathered dolomite. The trail ascends these blocks and continues on the right, climbing a bluff. Stop at .36 mi. **[5]** and enjoy some of the fruits of your labors, as the first of several Big River overlooks comes into view on your right. Look down on sycamore tops next to the ambling river and view the remote hills that hid Civil War guerrillas and moonshiners alike.

The trail winds along the blufftop, offering several overlooks as you go, sometimes at the end of short spurs off the main trail. As you descend to the river level, the trail is crowded by spicebush and white crown-beard. Cross two wooden bridges at .95 mi. **[6]**. The trail widens again as you climb another bluff. Take the small spurs on your right at 1.10 mi. **[7]** through small glades to the highest and best overlooks of all. Sheer cliffs drop to the water, far below, while twisted trunks of ancient cedars cling precariously to the rock face.

The trail and river turn away from each other as the trail curves to the left. On this bend, look for the flattened, long leaves of the blackberry lily, an old homesteader's exotic flower that produces a brilliant orange and blood-red blossom in July. At 1.71 mi. **[8]** look for a small cabin in the woods on your right, now taken over by creepers and critters. After crossing two rocky, intermittent streams, you'll pass some curious trenches in the forest floor at 2.19 mi. **[9]**. Miners dug these pits in the 1700s to recover lead. After crossing another stream, you'll enter an open forest with crisscrossing ravines and a playground of craggy, moss-covered dolomite boulders—perhaps fragments of Sam Hildebrand's "broken up world."

The old, open lead-mining shaft at 2.62 mi. **[10]** is fenced to keep forest wanderers from tumbling in. Some natural sinkholes appear along the trail, too, many of which have filled in with leaves and soil. You'll pass through a final, small glade at 2.89 mi. **[11]**. Turn right when you return to **[3]** to finish your Pike Run Hills hike.

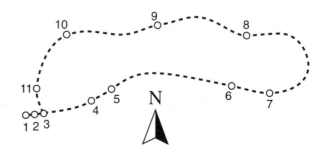

1. Start
2. Go straight
3. Right turn
4. Left turn
5. Big River overlook
6. Wooden bridges
7. Big River overlooks
8. Small cabin
9. Lead-mining trenches
10. Fenced shaft
11. Small glade

# 30.  Washington State Park

- Examine the largest group of petroglyphs in the state—thunderbirds, snakes, and human figures—carved in limestone bedrock between A.D. 1000 and 1600.
- Hike on a rich talus slope noted statewide for its luxuriant and diverse spring wildflowers.
- Catch sight of the eastern collared lizard doing push-ups on a rock or running away on its hind legs like a miniature dinosaur.
- Find hematite pieces on the trail near old prospecting sites.

## Area Information

The cultural, historical, and natural features of Washington State Park fuse beautifully in many ways. Prehistorically, the area was a significant ceremonial site for villagers of the Middle Mississippian culture, evidenced today by three major groups of petroglyphs. Birds, turkey tracks, arrows, and many other symbols carved in flat, limestone sheets may have been part of initiation ceremonies for secret societies. The petroglyphs may have been memory aids for the initiates, who perhaps were required to perform complex sequences of songs and ritualistic rites.

Later, after the petroglyphs became protected as part of Washington State Park, the African-American stonemasons of Company 1743 of the CCC were influenced by the work of these ancient rock carvers, as well as by the natural outcroppings of rock in the park. Between 1934 and 1939, these master craftsmen artfully laid the stone steps of the 1,000 Steps Trail and built Thunderbird Lodge, rental cabins, an octagonal lookout shelter, and a trail shelter that resembles a natural stone outcrop. All their work in the park is listed on the National Register of Historic Places.

Even without its cultural and historical legacy, Washington State Park is remarkable for its natural features and beauty. Expansive limestone glades, rippling with prairie grasses, are home to such uncommon species as Fremont's leather flower and the eastern collared lizard. All the hiking trails and lookout shelters offer outstanding views of the Big River Valley. A 68-acre portion of the park's rich hardwood forests is a designated state natural area. In spring, the north-facing slope of the 1,000 Steps Trail is resplendent with the park system's showiest display of woodland wildflowers.

**Directions:** The park is located eight miles south of DeSoto on Highway 21.

**Hours Open:** The site is open year-round, and the park office is open from 8 A.M. to 4:30 P.M. Monday through Friday.

**Facilities:** A campground, picnic areas, and swimming pool are available. The Big River provides opportunities for fishing and canoeing. Kitchen-equipped cabins may be rented, and a park store operates at Thunderbird Lodge.

**Permits and Rules:** Please stay on designated boardwalks near the petroglyphs to avoid damaging them. Bicycles and horses are not permitted on the trails, nor are cutting implements such as saws and hatchets. Campfires are prohibited. Camping is permitted by backpackers only on the portion of Rockywood Trail that lies west of the campground and swimming pool.

**Further Information:** Park Superintendent, Washington State Park, Route 2, Box 450, DeSoto, MO 63020; 314-586-2995.

## Park Trails

**Rockywood Trail** 🥾🥾🥾🥾—10 miles—This trail features rugged forested terrain, numerous blufftop overlooks, and open, rocky, scenic limestone glades. The trail begins from the northwest side of Thunderbird Lodge parking lot and is marked with orange arrows in a counterclockwise direction.

# Washington State Park

LEGEND

Road
Trail
Boundary

Park Office
Interpretive Center
Restrooms

Dining Lodge
Picnic Area
Shelter

Cabins
Camping
Backpack Camp

Swimming Pool
Overlook
Petroglyph Area

Big River

1,000 Steps Trail

Opossum Track Trail

N

# 1,000 Steps Trail 👢👢👢👢

**Distance Round-Trip:** 1.5 miles

**Estimated Hiking Time:** 1 hour

*I was too busy noticing the abundant celandine poppies, wet-weather waterfalls, and sweeping blufftop vistas to count the stone steps laid by the ambitious CCC stonemasons of the mid-1930s. Are there really 1,000?*

**Caution:** The trail at the bottom will be muddy after a hard rain.

**Trail Directions:** Park at Thunderbird Lodge and begin the trail behind the picnic area at the northeast end of the parking lot **[1]**. You are hiking on the edge of a rich floodplain of the Big River, which is just to your left. On your right is a mature hardwood forest that has developed on broken-down talus—rock fragments eroded from the dolomite bluff on top. The soil is rich here and kept cool and moist on the north-

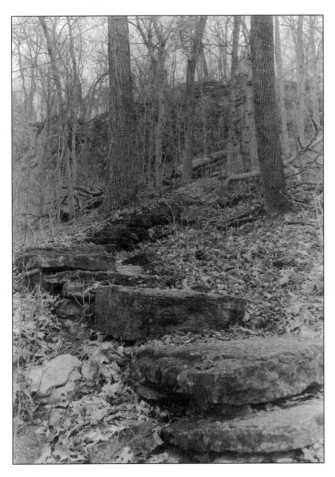

facing slope, which allows vigorous and diverse growth. Many of the trees here are over 100 feet tall and more than 150 years old.

Also abundant here are wet-weather waterfalls **[2]**, the first at .04 mi. Before reaching the main intersection of the trail you'll find three or four more trickling down from the forest slope. Stream water falls down layers of stair-stepped dolomite, covered in mosses and walking fern, while carpets of bluebells, Dutchman's-breeches, and blue-eyed Marys adorn the banks.

At the intersection at .15 mi. **[3]** the stone steps invite you upward. Painstakingly laid over 60 years ago, these steps of native stone now blend beautifully into the forested hillside. Turn right here and again at the top of the steps at the base of the dolomite bluff. At .17 mi. **[4]** the trail takes you left on top of the bluff—the parent rock for the talus. Soon you'll find a scenic overlook of the Big River Valley **[5]** (.22 mi.). At .28 mi. is a native-stone shelter **[6]** built into the hillside, offering another inspiring view.

Walk behind the overlook and away from the river to continue the trail. Turn left at .32 mi. **[7]**, where you see a bent tree on your left. You'll pass a rest room at .45 mi. At .57 mi. is the interpretive center **[8]**, where you can stop in to see exhibits about the petroglyphs in the park. A park office building is here, too, where you can find park information.

Turn left behind the interpretive center to continue. You'll descend more stone steps under some giant bur oaks, sugar maples, and Kentucky coffee trees. Turn left at .90 mi. **[9]**, just before you reach the picnic shelter. Notice the variety of wildflowers and mushrooms here, growing among the big logs in all stages of decay. At 1.26 mi. go straight at **[3]** and enjoy the wet-weather waterfalls again on your way back to the trailhead.

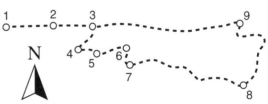

1. Start
2. Wet-weather waterfalls
3. Right turn
4. Left turn
5. Overlook
6. Stone-shelter overlook
7. Left turn
8. Interpretive center
9. Left turn

# Opossum Track Trail

**Distance Round-Trip:** 3 miles

**Estimated Hiking Time:** 1.5 hours

*I'm glad someone named something after the ubiquitous and humble possum. They are quick to "grin" at those who might disturb them, flashing more pretty teeth per mouth than any other mammal in North America. No other animal's footprint more closely resembles a human hand.*

**Caution:** Watch for traffic when crossing the main park road. Use caution near bluff edges.

**Trail Directions:** The trailhead **[1]** is across the road from Thunderbird Lodge, just southwest of the parking lot. Turn right at .02 mi. **[2]**, and soon you'll be hiking next to a shallow forest stream **[3]**, its bed a pleasant jumble of flat sedimentary rocks. Wet areas near the stream are good places to look for the trail's namesake. You cross the stream at .23 mi. **[4]** and then hike up and down its woodland drainages as the trail parallels it. Cross the stream again at .52 mi.

Soon you'll be upon a good exercise hill, where some beautiful dolomite shelves make good company for the trees. Here, among the loose stones of the trail, is a good place to look for hematite, or iron ore. These rocks are dark brown or rust colored and are heavy. Iron and barite were two minerals mined in the area before it became a state park. At .81 mi. are several old prospecting pits **[5]**, now nearly filled in. Turn right at .88 mi. **[6],** just before you get to the parking lot for the swimming pool. Cross a gravel road at .91 mi. and turn right at the intersection at 1.03 mi. **[7]**. The water tower looks bald, foreign, and sterile, sticking above the tree canopy. Walk toward the water tower and go straight when you get under it.

The trail parallels the main park road for a while and crosses it at 1.51 mi. **[8]**. At 1.68 mi. **[9]** turn right. Turn right again where the trail meets the Rockywood Trail at 1.82 mi. **[10]**. The trail goes through some switchbacks, around boulders, across a stream, and up into a glade remnant at 1.94 mi. **[11]**. Note the twisted branches of the chinkapin oaks and the high density of cedars, choking the glade. Glades

sometimes look ragged when restoration practices are first applied, but we must be patient—they respond quickly to cutting and burning of the cedars. Seeds of glade plants may lie dormant for many years, suddenly exploding into bloom in unison when the cedars are removed.

Cross a dirt road at 2.17 mi. and turn right at 2.25 mi. **[12]**. You are suddenly treated to magnificent blufftop views of the Big River Valley and outlying wooded hills. The trail hugs the bluff edge and offers a series of overlooks **[13]** (2.32 mi.). At 2.42 mi. **[14]** is an octagonal stone trail shelter built by the CCC. As you descend the bluff, notice the natural tabletops of weathered dolomite, broken off the face of the bluff. Turn left at the intersection at 2.70 mi. **[15]** and hike directly behind the lodge. Take the wooden bridge over the stream and you'll be back in the parking lot.

| | |
|---|---|
| 1. Start | 9. Right turn |
| 2. Right turn | 10. Right turn |
| 3. Forest stream | 11. Glade remnant |
| 4. Stream crossing | 12. Right turn |
| 5. Prospecting pits | 13. Overlooks |
| 6. Right turn | 14. Octagonal trail |
| 7. Right turn |     shelter |
| 8. Road crossing | 15. Left turn |

# 31. Meramec State Park

- Hike next to a spring stream, wet meadow, glade, pirated stream, two sections of ancient collapsed cave passage, and three cave entrances—all on one trail!
- Feel the cool air emerging from Mushroom Cave, where mushrooms were farmed commercially in the early 1900s.
- Look for your favorite wild edibles on the Natural Wonders Trail—82 different ones have been found there so far.

## Area Information

Meramec State Park is 6,896 acres of forests, savannas, caves, and bluffs along one of Missouri's most beautiful rivers—the Meramec. Its natural communities are diverse, ranging from moist, towering forests to dry, rocky glades. Lush vegetation and a great diversity of trees thrive in the lower elevations, while impressive displays of wildflowers adorn the highest savannas and glades, dotted with twisted and gnarled chinkapin oaks.

The Meramec River almost became Meramec Lake. The U.S. Army Corps of Engineers had already begun construction of a dam on the Meramec River when a public vote in 1978 resulted in the project's deauthorization. Today, the Meramec still flows freely, and several miles of the scenic river and its wooded banks are preserved in the park, providing a haven for the park's abundant wildlife. The Meramec contains the greatest variety of aquatic life in Missouri. Exhibits in the visitor center are designed to interpret this healthy and diverse habitat.

Missouri has nearly 5,500 caves, and 43 of these are hidden within Meramec's expansive forests—more than in any other park in the state. Naturalist-led tours of the largest and most spectacular cave in the park, Fisher Cave, offer the park visitor adventure, outstanding cave scenery, and insight into how caves and calcite deposits are formed. The 90-minute tours are given four times daily during the summer for a small fee.

**Directions:** From Sullivan, travel 3.2 miles south on Highway 185 to the park entrance.

**Hours Open:** The park is open year-round. The front gate is open from 7 A.M. to 10 P.M. daily from April through October and from 7 A.M. to 9 P.M. daily from November through March. The visitor center is closed on Thanksgiving, Christmas, and New Year's Day.

**Facilities:** The park offers a visitor center that includes a 3,500-gallon aquarium, a large campground, an outdoor amphitheater for interpretive programs, cabins, motel, convention center, dining lodge, boat ramp, picnic areas and shelters, play areas, store, and canoe and raft rentals.

**Permits and Rules:** Do not enter any cave without first contacting the visitor center. Some caves require a permit to enter. Pets must always be leashed. Some campsites are reservable while others are not.

**Further Information:** Park Superintendent, Meramec State Park, 2800 South Highway 185, Sullivan, MO 63080; 573-468-6072 (visitor center) or 573-468-6519 (cabin and canoe rental).

## Park Trails

**Wilderness Trail**—10 miles—This trail traverses the most rugged and remote area of the park, including the Meramec Upland Forest Natural Area, the largest undisturbed Ozark chert forest in the state. Eight backpacking camps are found along the trail, which begins across the road from picnic shelter #3.

**Deer Hollow Trail**—1.8 miles—This linear trail, which connects the dining lodge to Fisher Cave, is a good trail to see blooming dogwood trees in late April, fall colors in early October, and white-tailed deer all year long.

**Walking Fern Trail**—.5 mile—This trail takes you next to Indian Cave, through a lush, moist forest, next to a boulder covered with walking ferns, and up onto a dry, upland forest. The trail begins and ends at Fisher Cave.

**River Trail**—.8 mile—This loop trail begins at the southern end of the campground and winds along a slough of the Meramec River.

# Meramec State Park

Cane Bottom

Meramec River

Wilderness Trail Northern Loop

Natural Area

Fern Trail

Wilderness Trail

Deer Hollow Trail

To Sullivan 4 Miles

Bluff View Trail

River Trail

185

To Potosi 25 Miles

185

Natural Wonders Trail

N

LEGEND
— Road
····· Trail
▬ Boundary
▬ Natural Area

Visitor Center

Hickory Ridge Conference Center

Dining Lodge

Park Store

Cabins

Camping

Showerhouse

Trailer Disposal Station

Picnic Area

Picnic Shelter

Trail Shelter

Campers Beach

Amphitheater

Fisher Cave

Old Hamilton Iron Works

# Natural Wonders Trail 🥾🥾

**Distance Round-Trip:** 1.3 miles

**Estimated Hiking Time:** .75 hour

*I had been sitting on a large rock on the glade for about 15 minutes before noticing a rather large, coiled eastern coachwhip snake about six feet away. I admired its braided brown and tan coloring before creeping slowly away, leaving the snake to its morning reptilian business.*

**Caution:** Do not enter any cave without contacting the visitor center for a review of cave regulations and a check for flash-flood possibility.

**Trail Directions:** Before or after your hike, be sure to see the exhibits and the park slide show in the visitor center. Park in the lot for the visitor center and begin the trail at the trailhead **[1]** at the southeast end of the lot. Turn right at the intersection at .08 mi. **[2]**, and you'll soon be hiking under the whispering branches of a shortleaf pine grove. Ignore the spur to the right at .13 mi. **[3]** and go straight, looking for signs of beaver on nearby trees. Elm Spring Creek **[4]** riffles along the trail at .17 mi. Look for beaver here as well as at the beaver pond behind the visitor center. October is the best time to watch for beaver, when their preparations for winter make the nocturnal rodents more active during the day.

Just after you cross a small drainage at .22 mi. you'll find a wet meadow **[5]** on your left. The stream flowing out of Mushroom Cave (passed later on the trail) keeps this area eternally moist, providing a good habitat for burrowing devil crayfish. You may see their mud chimneys near the trail here. Stop by the stream pool at .27 mi. **[6]** and look for camouflaged sculpin fish lying on the bottom and agile water striders skating across the top. You'll also find watercress here and a good patch of spearmint.

Just before you cross a wooden bridge at .44 mi. you'll see an entrance to Camp Cave **[7]**. More accurately, this is an exit to Camp Cave because the water flowing out of it comes from another opening to the cave (encountered later), which acts as a surface stream drain. This is known as stream piracy. Cross the bridge to continue. Climb the hill and find the continuity of the forest broken by a beautiful glade **[8]** (.53 mi.). Layers of the sedimentary dolomite created three levels of the glade, making a three-tiered minidesert, resplendent with prairie dock, shooting star, Indian paintbrush, and purple coneflowers.

At .67 mi. stand at the top of the wooden switchbacks and look down the ravine. This is part of a collapsed cave passage. At the bottom of the switchbacks you'll find the inlet entrance to Camp Cave **[9]**. Hike under the canopy of black walnut, white oak, pawpaw, and dogwood trees on your way to yet another cave opening. Find the yawning maw of Mushroom Cave **[10]** at 1.05 mi., the site of several commercial mushroom farming operations in the early 1900s. Today, wild hydrangea flourish near the cave's outflowing stream, which is always cool enough to refresh hot feet—even in the middle of summer. The minicanyon just across the trail is another section of an ancient, collapsed passageway. On your way back, go straight at the intersection at **[2]** to return to the trailhead.

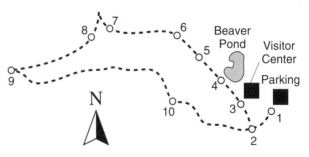

1. Start
2. Right turn
3. Go straight
4. Elm Spring Creek
5. Wet meadow
6. Stream pool
7. Camp Cave outlet
8. Glade
9. Camp Cave inlet
10. Mushroom Cave

# Bluff View Trail 👢👢👢

**Distance Round-Trip:** 1.5 miles

**Estimated Hiking Time:** 1 hour

*Meramec means "big catfish" in the Algonquin language, which says something about the productivity of its spring-fed, rippling waters. With over 100 species of fish and 40 species of mussels, the Meramec River is one of the most diverse aquatic habitats in the United States.*

**Caution:** Sections of the trail contain large rocks and tree roots. Also, be careful near the bluff edges.

**Trail Directions:** Park in one of the parking areas near the dining lodge and find the trailhead **[1]** on the west entrance to the lodge, about 50 yards from the main park road. If you are here on a cold day, look for frost flowers—fragile white ribbons of ice that sometimes flow from the stems of certain plants. Dittany, a mint with small, teardrop-shaped leaves, is one of only three plants in Missouri that can produce frost flowers. Dittany is common on this trail, especially around the twin black oaks at .03 mi.

Turn left at .30 mi. **[2]**, ignoring the small trail on the right. Soon you'll discover a plot of native bluestem grasses taking advantage of the opening in the forest canopy that a powerline provides. In summer, this spot is a colorful jumble of orange butterfly weed, purple prairie clover, and yellow black-eyed Susans.

At .53 mi. **[3]** you will find an unusual octagonal stone building. Built in 1935 by the Civilian Conservation Corps, this trail shelter was used as a model for shelters built in national and state parks in other parts of the nation. Today, it's a good place to stop for a moment, catch your first glimpse of the sparkling Meramec River below, and hear the music of its riffles.

The path to the right goes to the picnic area and picnic shelter #3. Continue the trail to the left and follow the blufftop along the river. At .62 mi. stop at the overlook **[4]** to enjoy the view. In the summer, look for brown softshell "pancake" turtles floating near the surface over deep pools of the river. Swallows elegantly dive and swoop for flying insects over the water by day. Bats replace them as afternoon eases into evening.

Descend to river level and discover a patch of spanglegrass, or wild oats, near the bottom. Look how wide the seeds are. But look closer . . . they are as flat as paper. At .71 mi. follow the trail to the left over a wooden bridge **[5]**, hike through a stand of wild rye (looks like wheat, but the seed grains are farther apart), and it's up you go again to the blufftop. Take the short spur on your right to the overlook **[6]** at .77 mi. and again at .84 mi. **[7]**, where dried, twisted trunks of ancient cedars still cling to the bluff face, and brilliant black-eyed Susans contrast with the dark craggy dolomite rocks found on top.

At 1.03 mi. is another stone trail shelter **[8]**, and the trail meets the River Trail. Go straight to continue the Bluff View Trail. After a few steps, look for bottlebrush grass on both sides of the trail. Bottlebrush grass looks like wild rye having a bad-hair day.

Cross an intermittent stream **[9]** at 1.11 mi., take a few steps, and turn right. Go uphill a short distance and bear right at the intersection at 1.13 mi. **[10]**. Continue uphill and turn left at the next intersection at 1.14 mi. **[11]**. Ignore the path on the left at 1.25 mi. **[12]** and continue straight to complete the switchback and finish the trail.

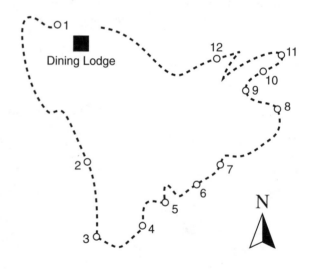

1. Start
2. Left turn
3. Octagonal trail shelter
4. Overlook
5. Wooden bridge
6. Overlook
7. Overlook
8. Trail shelter
9. Stream crossing
10. Right turn
11. Left turn
12. Go straight

# 32.  Onondaga Cave State Park

- See the blue green waters of Onondaga Spring, the only natural entrance to Onondaga Cave.
- Hike next to an oxbow lake—a channel that the Meramec River abandoned.
- See how the red-eared slider got its name.
- Feel reindeer lichens to check the humidity.

## Area Information

Onondaga's human history is every bit as colorful as its speleothems (calcite deposits). Around the turn of the century, several of the cave's early owners intended to remove and sell its splendid calcite, or "cave onyx," but several factors, including a glutted market, prevented these operations. A break came in 1904, when the World's Fair came to St. Louis. Visitors were brought from St. Louis to Leasburg by the Frisco Railroad and then transported by buggies to the cave. For an extra 25¢, visitors could rent clothes to wear on their adventurous cave tour.

Several owners of Onondaga managed the cave as a public attraction, but none was as successful or memorable as Les Dill, who took partial ownership of the cave in 1949. Dill, famous for fabricating tall tales about his show caves, had both a P.T. Barnum-style showmanship and a genuine interest in the cave's natural integrity—a combination that elevated Onondaga as a nationally known show cave.

If a visitor had to choose only one cave in Missouri to explore, Onondaga should probably be it. Recognized as one of America's most spectacular caves because of the great abundance and quality of its speleothems, Onondaga has been designated a national natural landmark, joining the roll of the country's outstanding natural features kept by the U.S. Department of the Interior's National Park Service.

Missouri celebrated 1990 as the Year of the Cave, when it officially recorded its 5,000th cave. Governor John Ashcroft proclaimed Missouri *The Cave State* and encouraged people to become aware of the state's underground mysteries and natural beauty. About this time, the state dedicated the new visitor center at Onondaga Cave State Park, which illustrates and interprets the state's fantastic subterranean world.

**Directions:** From the I-44 Leasburg exit (214), take Highway H southeast for seven miles.

**Hours Open:** The park is open year-round, and the gates to the campground are open from 7 A.M. to 10 P.M. The visitor center is open from 9 A.M. to 5 P.M. daily, March through October, with shortened hours during the other months. The visitor center is closed Thanksgiving, Christmas, and New Year's Day.

**Facilities:** The park offers a visitor center, campground, amphitheater, picnic areas, and boating, swimming, and fishing on the Meramec River. Onondaga Cave tours are given daily, March through October, for a fee. Cathedral Cave tours are given on weekends from Memorial Day to Labor Day.

**Permits and Rules:** Pets must always be leashed. Boats without motors are allowed to be carried onto the oxbow lake, where fishing is allowed. Horses or bicycles are not allowed on the hiking trails.

**Further Information:** Park Superintendent, Onondaga Cave State Park, 7556 Highway H, Leasburg, MO 65535; 573-245-6576.

## Park Trails

**Oak Ridge Trail** 👢👢👢—3 miles—This trail will take you across several wet-weather streams, through an upland forest, and up into some glades that are responding well to recent restoration and management practices. The trail also passes a number of wet-weather waterfalls and a pirated stream. The trailhead is in the campground, next to the playground.

# Onondaga Cave State Park

LEGEND

Road
Trail
Boundary

Visitor Center and Cave Entrance
Picnic Area
Camping
Scout Area
Shelter House
Restrooms
Boat Ramp
Canoe Access
Amphitheater

To Leasburg
and Interstate 44

Park Entrance

Blue Heron Trail

Deer Run Trail

Meramec River

To Steelville, Potosi,
Hwy 8, Hwy E

N

# Blue Heron Trail 🥾

**Distance Round-Trip:** 1 mile

**Estimated Hiking Time:** .5 hour

*While hiking, I kept thinking of the early explorers of Onondaga Cave swimming through the spring and sinking johnboats under the bluff to get in. Today, over a hundred years later, the cave's beauty is still intact, and the tour route is wheelchair-accessible!*

**Trail Directions:** This is a good trail to explore while waiting for a cave tour to begin. The trail begins near the visitor center, in the south end of the parking lot **[1]**. Soon you will see an old river channel on your left. If the wind is blowing across the surface, it may fool you; this channel is no longer flowing. This oxbow lake **[2]** (.05 mi.) was left when the Meramec River cut a new channel and began flowing along a different course. Oxbow lakes, often horseshoe shaped, are most easily identified from aerial photographs.

The trail parallels the lake for most of its length, giving you time to watch for aquatic turtles basking in the sun near the water. Look closely for the red-eared slider, a medium-sized turtle with a patch of red on each side of its head and a propensity for sliding in the water somewhat gracefully when disturbed. At .14 mi. is Onondaga Spring **[3]**, the site of several mills during the latter half of the 19th century. Damming of the spring in the 1880s forced early explorers to enter Onondaga Cave by johnboat through the spring—the cave's only natural entrance. The cave's first artificial entrance is beneath the small concrete roof, just to the left of the spring.

As you continue, look in the forest edge for blooming wildflowers, including toothwort, dogtooth violet, and spring beauties, which sometimes bloom in February. The limestone bluffs and rocky slopes on the right are also home to the graceful columbine, which blooms through July. On the left, the oxbow lake becomes more shallow, until tapering off into a slough. This is apparently a favorite night-time feeding spot for beavers **[4]** (.35 mi.), judging by the number of chewed off trees and sprouts. Here is a good spot to look for the trail's namesake, fishing in the shallows.

At .38 mi. is a rather authoritative boulder of layered, weathered dolomite **[5]**. A form of limestone that contains magnesium, dolomite is relatively soft and is easily eroded. At .45 mi. **[6]**, where the trail meets the blacktop road to the campground, is a good place to turn around and hike back to the trailhead.

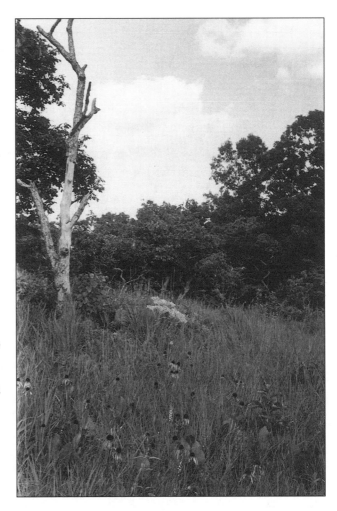

1. Start
2. Oxbow lake
3. Onondaga Spring
4. Beaver feeding area
5. Dolomite boulder
6. Turn around

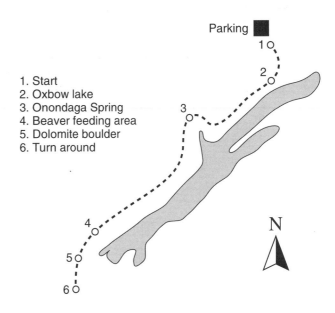

# Deer Run Trail 👢👢👢

**Distance Round-Trip:** 2.5 miles

**Estimated Hiking Time:** 1.5 hours

*You may find yourself on your stomach, like I did, examining the multitude of delicate mosses and lichens up close. You will find green meadows and hummocks, swales, and handsome forests only millimeters high—just inches from your nose.*

**Caution:** Crossing the stream bottom may be difficult after a rainy period. Use caution near the blufftop overlook edges.

**Trail Directions:** The trailhead [1] for the Deer Run Trail is in the campground, between the amphitheater and showerhouse. Parking is available near the playground equipment. Hike toward the amphitheater, then turn left at the intersection at .04 mi. [2]. At the intersection at .09 mi. [3] turn right, toward the forest.

The structure at .40 mi. [4] is the locked entrance to Cathedral Cave, the other show cave in the park besides Onondaga. Tours of Cathedral Cave are given by hand-held lanterns and reveal rooms filled with cave coral, white flowstone, and delicate soda straws. Entire fossilized algae blooms (stromatolites) nearly the size of Volkswagens hang from the ceiling. Walking underneath them makes you feel like a mole, tunneling under the bulbous roots of plants in a garden.

The interesting thing about the old paved road at .60 mi. [5] is that you can hardly see it. Leaves have fallen on it, building soil. Plants are growing in the ever-widening cracks. Trees have closed the gap overhead, while shrubs continually crowd in from the sides. Nature is taking it back. Continue the trail across the road and you'll soon hike next to some small hills covered with mosses and airy puffs of reindeer lichen [6] (.65 mi.). The lichen is lighter green than the mosses, has antler-like tips, and like all lichens, is made up of a fungus and an algae. Reindeer lichen is soft and rubbery in high humidity and wiry and brittle in dry times.

Notice all the cedar trees at .91 mi., announcing the presence of an upcoming glade [7]. Native grasses dominate where there are breaks in the thick cedar cover. The regular hardwood forest canopy resumes as you exit the glade at 1.15 mi. Descend the hill to the stream bottom, cross the wooden bridge at 1.61 mi. [8], and you'll walk under a bent tree [9] at 1.64 mi. Cross a gravel road at 1.72 mi., hike through a cedar-choked glade remnant, and go straight at the intersection at 1.84 mi. [10].

As you climb the hill, you are nearing the bluff edge, and soon the Meramec River will come into view below you. There are several overlooks here. One of the best is at 1.94 mi. [11], complete with gnarly, ancient cedars and views of the forested hills and winding river. At 2.12 mi. cross a foot bridge [12] before taking a final view of the river from a grassy knoll. Turn left at the intersection at 2.25 mi. [13], cross a gravel road at 2.29 mi., and turn right at the intersection at 2.33 mi. [3]. Soon you will be back at the trailhead.

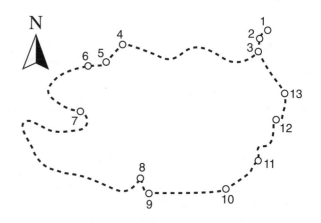

1. Start
2. Left turn
3. Right turn
4. Cathedral Cave
5. Old paved road
6. Reindeer lichen
7. Glade
8. Wooden bridge
9. Bent tree
10. Go straight
11. Overlook
12. Wooden bridge
13. Left turn

# 33. Big Spring

- Witness the beauty and power of Big Spring, the largest single-outlet spring in the nation.
- Look and listen in the slough for the loud, rising whistles of the wood duck, one of North America's most beautiful (and quackless) ducks.
- Stand under some 12-foot-high native bamboo canes (in the grass family) and imagine what it's like to be an insect in your lawn.
- Hike onto blufftop overlooks with vistas of the Big Spring Branch, the Current River, and the rugged horizon of forested Ozark highlands.

## Area Information

Big Spring roars from the mouth of a cave at the base of a towering dolomite bluff. Daily flow records kept at Big Spring since 1921 show an average of 276 million gallons per day. The lowest daily reading, 152 million gallons, was during a dry period in 1956. Maximum flow is estimated to be 840 million gallons per day. Although other spring systems have more total volume, Big Spring is the nation's largest single-outlet spring and among the 10 largest springs in the world. Archaeological excavations in the park give evidence that Big Spring has been a gathering place for people for at least 10,000 years.

Formerly Big Spring State Park, Big Spring is now part of Ozark National Scenic Riverways, managed by the National Park Service. National riverways are natural streams that have recreational, natural, and cultural resources of national significance. Ozark National Scenic Riverways is composed of two rivers—the Current River and the Jacks Fork (a total of 134 river miles). Both rivers are famous for their scenic beauty and offer excellent opportunities for floating, fishing, and sight-seeing. Big Spring flows into the Current River at the CCC Historic District in the park.

About 80,000 acres of riverways land border the rivers and are preserved to help protect the rivers' outstanding health and natural beauty. This riverways corridor includes many springs and caves, historic mills, campgrounds, and hiking and equestrian trails. The riverways also includes 13 natural areas, which are biological communities or geological sites chosen by a panel of experts as the best areas of natural integrity left in Missouri.

**Directions:** From Van Buren, take Highway 103 south for four miles to the park entrance.

**Hours Open:** The park is open year-round. The Ozark National Scenic Riverways headquarters and visitor's information office in Van Buren is open weekdays from 8 A.M. to 4:30 P.M.

**Facilities:** The park offers camping, fishing and boating access, picnic areas, and shelters. The CCC Historic District features a dining lodge and rustic cabins that may be reserved, and offers craft demonstrations of quilting and johnboat building on weekends from May to September. Guided johnboat rides are also offered during summer months from the Big Spring Lodge complex. Canoe and tube rentals are available in Van Buren.

**Permits and Rules:** Because springs are fragile ecosystems, wading, fishing, swimming, tubing, and boating are not allowed in any spring. All these activities are allowed in the Current and Jacks Fork Rivers.

**Further Information:** Superintendent, Ozark National Scenic Riverways, P.O. Box 490, Van Buren, MO 63965; 573-323-4236. Free copies of the *Directory of Missouri Natural Areas* are available by contacting the Missouri Department of Conservation, Natural History Section, P.O. Box 180, Jefferson City, MO 65102; 573-751-4115.

## Other Areas of Interest

**Skyline Drive** is a four-mile loop road that offers at least a dozen scenic vistas of the surrounding Ozark hills. The drive is in the Mark Twain National Forest and is managed by the U.S. Forest Service. Skyline Drive is off Highway 103 and is labeled FR 3280; one access is one mile northwest of the Big Spring park entrance and another is closer to Van Buren State Park. For more information call 573-996-2153.

Located 13 miles north of Eminence, **Round Spring** features a tranquil spring pool set in a natural amphitheater of dolomite rock. A great variety of wildflowers decorates the area in spring and summer. Round Spring also offers a cave, year-round campground, boat access, picnic area, and playground. Cave tours are offered from May until September for a small fee. For more information call 573-323-4236.

# Big Spring

60 → To Van Buren

103

N

Skyline Drive
U.S. Forest Service
(4 Mile Scenic Drive)

103

Skyline
Drive

103

Park
Entrance
No Fee

Big Spring Trail

Giant
Cane
Trail

Current River

LEGEND
— Road
⋯ Trail
— Boundary

Big Spring
Ranger Station
P Parking
Camping
Group Camping
Restrooms
Picnic Shelter
River Access
Big Spring Lodge
Stone Building
Rental Cabins
Amphitheater
Craft Demonstration Area

# Big Spring Trail 👢👢👢👢

**Distance Round-Trip:** 2.5 miles

**Estimated Hiking Time:** 1.5 hours

*We are familiar with rivers, or sections of them at least. We usually see only a short piece of them, or occasionally a confluence. But to witness a river's birth . . . to see it erupt from a hole in the earth is magical. In a way, it seems sheer nonsense.*

**Caution:** For safety, please respect the signs that close a short section of the trail behind the spring. Weathering action on the bluff above the spring occasionally causes rocks to fall onto the trail there.

**Trail Directions:** Both featured trails share a trailhead. Park at a CCC-era stone building on the left side of the road a half mile from the park entrance. The hiking sign pointing to the left is for the half-mile Giant Cane Trail. To begin the Big Spring Trail **[1]**, ascend the 20 sandstone steps among the jumble of moss-covered boulders directly in front of the parking area. The steps fuse with dolomite boulders and tree roots on the trail. You are soon treated to overlooks **[2]** at .07 and .09 mi. The stream closest to you, with unusual aquamarine water and vivid, bright green aquatic plants is the Big Spring branch. Just a few yards beyond, across the narrow ribbon of trees, is the Current River. On the foggy blue horizon are layers of the ancient and worn peaks of the Ozark mountains.

As you ascend, notice the dolomite moss-covered boulders being replaced by lichen-covered chert boulders. Twisted red cedars cling to steep bluff faces on the right, while shortleaf pines tower on the hilltop on the left. The Giant Cane Trail intersects at .18 mi. **[3]**. Go straight to continue the Big Spring Trail. Ignore the small spur at .32 mi. and enjoy the warm feeling in your legs as you continue climbing—you're only halfway to the peak! Ignore the small spur on your left at .60 mi. You'll finally begin the descent at .64 mi. **[4]**.

At 1.25 mi. you'll come upon a small wooded slough **[5]** which is perfect habitat for frogs, sala-

manders, muskrat, and beaver. The trail jogs to the right here and again at 1.28 mi. Turn right at the intersection at 1.31 mi. **[6]** and find a stand of native bamboo **[7]** at 1.42 mi. You can touch the large canes and feel where the leaf blades erupt from the distinctive nodes. Find a patch of horsetail at the base of a boulder at 1.47 mi. **[8]** on your right, where a small spring trickles from the hillside. At 1.64 mi. **[9]** turn right.

At 1.72 mi. walk out onto a sandstone walkway to catch your first views of Big Spring **[10]**. Walk next to the spring and feel the mist in the air. Watch clouds of deep, blue green water billow up and roar among mossy boulders. With an average flow of 276 million gallons per day, this spring is among the 10 largest in the world.

When you get to the closed area behind the spring **[11]**, turn around and walk past the picnic shelter toward the main road. Turn right at the stop sign at 2.07 mi. **[12]**. Just after you cross the bridge, turn right on the stone sidewalk **[13]** at 2.23 mi. and turn left at the first intersection **[14]**. At 2.36 turn right at the fork in the trail **[15]** and soon you'll be back at the trailhead.

| | |
|---|---|
| 1. Start | 9. Right turn |
| 2. Overlooks | 10. Big Spring |
| 3. Go straight | 11. Turn around |
| 4. Descent | 12. Right turn |
| 5. Wooded slough | 13. Right turn |
| 6. Right turn | 14. Left turn |
| 7. Native bamboo | 15. Right turn |
| 8. Horsetail patch | |

# Giant Cane Trail 👢👢👢

**Distance Round-Trip:** .5 mile

**Estimated Hiking Time:** .25 hour

*There's a lot packed into this 15-minute hike—Missouri's largest native grass, a good exercise hill, curly poverty grass, and blufftop overlooks of the Big Spring Branch, Current River, and outlying Ozark mountains, cloaked in layers of blue water vapor.*

**Caution:** Loose gravel on a steep hill makes some unsure footing. Also, some smooth boulders on the trail near the parking lot will be slick after a rain.

**Trail Directions:** Both featured trails share a trailhead. Park at a CCC-era stone building on the left side of the road, a half mile from the park entrance. The Big Spring Trail is straight ahead, up the sandstone steps. To begin the Giant Cane Trail **[1]**, walk to the front of the stone building and continue into the forest.

Just past the stone building, look in the low-lying area on your left at .05 mi. **[2]** for tall stalks of bamboo-like giant cane. Early travelers in Missouri found extensive thickets of cane (*canebrakes*) growing in the lowlands and along streams, with stalks reaching a height of 25 feet and with wood-like, hollow stems two to three inches in diameter. Young shoots and seeds were eaten by Native Americans and early settlers, who also used the stems for fishing poles, baskets, mats, pipestems, and musical flutes. Missouri's largest species of native grass, giant cane's natural range is in the southern counties of the state, where it is becoming uncommon, due to cattle grazing and cultivation of stream valleys.

You'll soon enter a rocky area, where chert blocks lie scattered in the forest and chert gravel accumulates on the trail. Unlike dolomite, which breaks down chemically by the dissolving action of water, chert is very resistant and usually breaks down physically, into smaller and smaller pieces. It accumulates in thin-soiled areas, like the trail, where softer rock has already dissolved away. The trail bends to the right at .12 mi. **[3]** and you'll go up a steep, rocky hill. Shortleaf pine are in their native

range here, and they can tolerate the thin, rocky soils of Ozark upland peaks and slopes. You'll notice more of them among the oaks and hickories as you climb the hill. Around .22 mi. **[4]** you'll find another interesting grass on or near the trail growing in pronounced tufts with lots of dried, curly blades at its base. This is poverty grass, named for its ability to grow in dry, poor soil.

Turn right at the intersection at .30 mi. **[5]** and you'll find yourself near the edge of a bluff overlooking the Current River valley. Views improve as you continue, and you'll arrive at an overlook at .38 mi. **[6]** among some dark gray, craggy dolomite boulders. At your far left, though not visible, is Big Spring. The spring branch, with its characteristic blue-green hues, is the stream closest to you. The Current River is just beyond, its banks lined with white-barked sycamore trees. During flood times, the Current comes up over Big Spring, making the spring branch and the river indistinguishable. Another overlook in just a few steps offers more views of the scenic streams below and the rugged, forested ridges on the horizon. Make your way over an outcrop of boulders of assorted sizes and shapes, and you'll soon return to the parking lot.

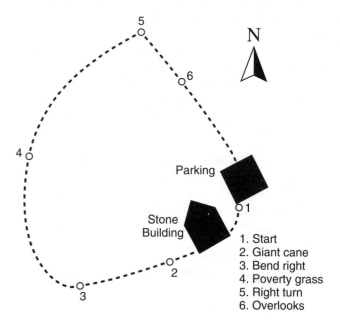

1. Start
2. Giant cane
3. Bend right
4. Poverty grass
5. Right turn
6. Overlooks

# 34.  Peck Ranch Conservation Area

- Climb a 1,300-foot mountain on rocks of all shapes and sizes.
- If the steep climb up Stegall Mountain's rocky side doesn't leave you gasping for breath, the overwhelming views from the top might.
- Hike quietly in the spring and summer to increase your chances of spotting a black bear.

## Area Information

George Peck, a Chicago businessman, bought 19,000 acres along Mill and Rogers Creeks around the turn of the century and established the Mid-Continent Iron Company there. One hundred cords of wood were cut from the rich oak forests each day to fuel the blast furnaces of the smelter. But the iron ore was low grade, and the company soon folded. By 1945, the wild turkey was nearly exterminated in the state, and the Missouri Conservation Department bought Peck Ranch for wild turkey management. This and other acquisitions restored wild turkeys throughout the state.

Peck Ranch consists of 22,968 acres of rugged hills, hollows, limestone and rhyolite glades, and oak-hickory forests mixed with pine. There are 119 ponds, seven caves, and numerous springs. The wilderness-like area supports turkey, deer, bobcats, and an occasional black bear, and eastern collared lizards survive on the largest igneous glade complex in the lower Ozarks. Four state-designated natural areas on Peck Ranch protect a sinkhole pond, a pirated stream, bottomland forests, glades, and scenic waterfalls.

The Ozark Trail is a long-distance trail designed primarily for hikers and backpackers that begins in St. Louis, traverses the rugged and scenic Ozarks, and joins the Ozark Highland Trail of Arkansas. When complete, the trail will be 500 miles long. A 9.5-mile segment of the Current River Section of the Ozark Trail passes through Peck Ranch and features shut-ins, clear streams, scenic forests, and mountaintop panoramas.

**Directions:** From Winona, take Highway H east 5.4 miles to a sign for the area. Take the gravel road (Peck Ranch Road) east another 5.8 miles to a parking lot for the Ozark Trail, on the left. Both featured trails begin from this parking lot.

**Hours Open:** The public hunting area is open daily from 4 A.M. to 10 P.M. The special-use zone (wildlife refuge) is open only during daylight hours.

**Facilities:** Area headquarters are .9 mile south of the Ozark Trail parking lot and offer camping (no hook-ups), rest rooms, drinking water, picnic tables, a short nature trail, a firearms shooting range, and a walk-through archery course. Stegall Mountain lookout tower, open to the public for climbing, can be reached from the Ozark Trail or from a driveway 3.7 miles east of Highway H off Peck Ranch Road. (The driveway to the tower is gated near the top.)

**Permits and Rules:** Bikes and horses are not allowed on the Current River Section of the Ozark Trail. Elsewhere, horses are restricted to vehicle roads and designated trails. Hunting and primitive camping are allowed in designated areas. Free-running pets are prohibited.

**Further Information:** Area Manager, Peck Ranch Conservation Area, Route 1, Box 1395, Winona, MO 65588; 573-323-4249. For more information on the Ozark Trail, call 573-751-2479.

## Other Areas of Interest

**Rocky Falls**, one of the most beautiful waterfalls in the state, is a 40-foot series of cascades over a wide outcrop of pink and purple igneous rocks. The site is in the Stegall Mountain Natural Area and is managed by Ozark National Scenic Riverways, National Park Service. Although no camping is allowed, the site offers picnic tables, grills, rest rooms, and wading. To reach Rocky Falls, return to the intersection of Highway H and Peck Ranch Road. Turn north on H and go 3.4 miles to Highway NN, where you turn right. Go 2.1 miles and turn right at a sign for the area. Go .3 mile and turn left at another sign. This road ends at the parking lot. For more information call 573-323-4236.

## Area Trails

**Current River Section—Ozark Trail** 👢👢👢👢— 30 miles—This section begins at Owls Bend on the Current River and ends on Highway 60, west of Van Buren. The 9.5-mile section that goes through Peck Ranch connects portions to the north, maintained by the Ozark National Scenic Riverways, with the segment to the south, maintained by the Mark Twain National Forest.

# Peck Ranch
# Conservation Area

Mud Spring
Hollow

Stegall
Mountain

No camping
from this point
to next fence

N

← To Hwy. H

Peck Ranch Rd.

Long Hollow

Cane Hollow

1 Rocky Point Glade

1 Bare Rock Glade

1 Mule Hollow Glade

LEGEND

Road

Trail

Fence

Headquarters

Stegall Mountain
Lookout Tower

1 Rocky Point Glade

2 Bare Rock Glade

3 Mule Hollow Glade

P Parking

# Ozark Trail to Stegall Mountain 👢👢👢👢

**Distance Round-Trip:** 4 miles

**Estimated Hiking Time:** 2.25 hours

*Don't be fooled by the common scenes at the beginning of the trail. Stegall Mountain packs a punch, with views from the top that will knock your hiking socks off!*

**Caution:** You will traverse some steep sections with loose rocks. From October through January, special hunts may take place in the area; call ahead to make sure the trail is open. Bring a compass and topo map if you want to extend this hike to the lookout tower.

**Trail Directions:** Park in the lot for the Ozark Trail trailhead and climb the steps over the fence in the northeast corner of the lot **[1]**. Turn left on the gravel road, which is a spur to the Ozark Trail. The gravel road is mostly downhill and lined with several kinds of oaks, hickories, and shortleaf pine. Go straight at the sign for the Ozark Trail on your right at .38 mi. **[2]**, which is the trail to Rocky Point Glade. Soon after crossing a small creek with cardinal flower on its banks, you'll find another sign for the Ozark Trail on your left at .48 mi. **[3]**. Turn left here.

The trail is well marked with Ozark Trail markers, which are green and white or brown and white "OT" signs on trees. Trail markers may tilt to indicate a bend in the trail ahead, and double markers indicate a sharp bend. Though vegetation may crowd the trail near the road, you soon enter a clear, rolling forest. Go straight at the intersection with an old road at .51 mi. **[4]**. The old field on your left at .71 mi. **[5]** is growing back in native grasses. By early fall, this field will be ablaze with bright orange and red sumac and brilliant yellow goldenrod, set against bronze and golden grasses. Watch for turkeys, deer, and other wildlife moving between the oak and hickory forest and the brushy, grassy old field. Deer use old fields to browse on shrubs and grass, while turkeys feed there on grasshoppers and other insects.

As the trail ascends a few rocky hills, shortleaf pine replaces oaks and hickories. Highbush and lowbush blueberry shrubs indicate the acidic soil here. Though lowbush blueberry shrubs (huckleberry) are only a quarter as tall as the highbush, their fruits are much tastier. Cross a gravel road at 1.32 mi. **[6]** and continue on the other side. At 1.57 mi. **[7]**

rocks of all shapes and sizes in hues of red, pink, and dark purple suddenly inundate the trail. From huge boulders to tiny pebbles, red granite and rhyolite of Stegall's core poke through the forest floor at the mountain's base.

You'll now begin a series of switchbacks up Stegall's rocky side, and the trail becomes more difficult. Massive outcrops of red granite, blanketed with green lichen, erupt from the slope amidst grassy glades with leadplant and black-eyed Susans. The trail skirts the base of one red boulder the size of a small house. At 1.82 mi. **[8]** climb on top of this pink granite outcrop and be treated to an unusually expansive view of your surroundings. As remarkable as this vista is, it's only a hint of what's to come.

Continue uphill and you'll reach a vast glade landscape with billowing, smooth igneous bedrock on the surface. If you can resist, wait until you get to the very top of the mountain before taking a look around. At 2.0 mi. **[9]**, among several rock cairns marking Stegall's peak, stop to survey your world. This point commands a stupendous view in a 180-degree sweep. Lesser mountains line up and fall away from Stegall like dominoes, and the blue haze of water vapor melts distant ridges into one another all across the horizon.

If you have leftover hiking energy or if you've been energized by the view, you can follow the peak of Stegall Mountain northwest about three quarters of a mile to the lookout tower, which you can climb for more tremendous views of the Ozark landscape. Otherwise, retrace your steps to complete your mountain hike.

1. Start
2. Go straight
3. Left turn
4. Go straight
5. Old field
6. Gravel road
7. Stegall's red rocks
8. Glade overlook
9. Mountain peak

N

Parking

# Ozark Trail to Rocky Point Glade 👢👢👢

**Distance Round-Trip:** 6.4 miles

**Estimated Hiking Time:** 3 hours

*Hike this trail in the spring or summer to find a jubilee of wildflowers on the glades contrasting with the dark gray dolomite boulders and the fine, arching stems of prairie dropseed grass.*

**Caution:** You will traverse some steep sections with loose rocks. From October through January, special hunts may take place in the area; call ahead to make sure the trail is open.

**Trail Directions:** Park in the lot for the Ozark Trail trailhead and climb the steps over the fence in the northeast corner of the lot **[1]**. Turn left on the gravel road, which is a spur to the Ozark Trail. The gravel road, mostly downhill, is lined with several kinds of oaks, hickories, and shortleaf pine. Turn right at the sign for the Ozark Trail at .38 mi. **[2]**. The trail is well marked with Ozark Trail markers, which are green and white or brown and white "OT" signs on trees. Trail markers may tilt to indicate a bend in the trail ahead, and double markers indicate a sharp bend.

The trail takes you uphill in a beautiful, open forest with black oaks, sugar maples, and tall pines. Flowering dogwood, the state tree, decorates the forest in April and May with snow white blossoms. Maidenhair ferns turn brown and collapse into the leaf litter by October, while ebony spleenwort and Christmas ferns stay green all year long. After you reach the top of this ridge, you'll find an odd, solitary sandstone boulder on your right at .58 mi. **[3]**, covered with small, delicate ferns.

If you're hiking in the fall, you will probably become acquainted with beggar's lice (tick trefoil), which leaves triangle-shaped seedpods sticking to your clothing as you go along. If you collect these stickers and pull them off elsewhere, you are a seed dispersal agent for the plant. These seeds are edible when they are green and puffy (after removing the sticky case) and taste like peanuts. Continue on the chert and sandstone gravel trail, with huckleberries and pussytoes (acid-soil indicators), until you cross a gravel road at 1.06 mi. **[4]**. Continue on the other side. The trail follows the gravel road for a while and is lined with reindeer lichen, dittany, and baby pine trees. With a grassy field on your right, cross an old road at 1.79 mi. **[5]**.

At 2.0 mi. **[6]** the trail takes you down into a ravine, where you hike between two slopes. Look for tracks and signs of deer and other wildlife that use this natural corridor of the forest. You'll pass a talus slope (a collection of rocks that broke off from bluffs or bedrock above and tumbled down) on your left at 2.11 mi. **[7]**. The next slopes you climb are so covered in chert and sandstone gravel that it's hard to believe the trees are anchored in any soil at all. After a prescribed fire, sassafras sprouts light up the forest in fall with bright yellow, orange, and red leaves, splashed against the white gravel.

At 2.71 mi. **[8]** you'll be on a narrow, gravelly ridge with black oaks and hickories. Grassy slopes appear on your right, as well as views of distant wooded ridges. At 3.21 mi. **[9]** you'll find Rocky Point Glade, where craggy, dark gray dolomite boulders stick out from the slope in ledges. Spring, summer, and early fall (depending on the rainfall) will find these glades awash in color, from lemon yellow Missouri evening primrose to deep-purple blazing star. Seven-foot nodding yellow blooms of prairie dock are taller than some of the woolly buckthorn trees, gnarled and stunted in this dry, desertlike environment. To explore two more glades nearby, descend the slope and turn right (west) on the gravel road. The next slope on your right is Bare Rock Glade, and the one beyond that is Mule Hollow Glade, a state natural area. Retrace your steps to return to the trailhead.

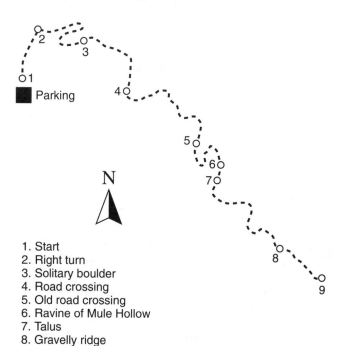

1. Start
2. Right turn
3. Solitary boulder
4. Road crossing
5. Old road crossing
6. Ravine of Mule Hollow
7. Talus
8. Gravelly ridge
9. Rocky Point Glade

# South Central

The south-central region of Missouri is the area south of the Missouri River, west of Highway 19, and east of Highway 65.

## Topography

Topographically, this region can be divided into two areas—the Ozarks and Ozark border. The Ozark Highlands, which cover almost the lower half of Missouri (40 percent of the state), compose the lower 80 percent of the south-central region of Missouri. The Ozarks are an unglaciated area of greater relief and elevation than surrounding areas. The area is characterized by steep topography, thin, rocky, residual soils, deep erosion by streams, and extensive forests. While glaciers, seas, or floods repeatedly covered the surrounding areas, the Ozarks have been an exposed land mass for 250 million years. A distinctive topographic feature in the southwest corner of this region are conical peaks, or knobs, of sedimentary bedrock.

The Ozark border is a transition zone between the Ozarks and the big rivers. In the south-central region of Missouri, this area lies just south of the Missouri River and covers the upper 20 percent of the region. The Ozark border contains rugged hills that resemble the Ozark landscape but also includes more gentle hills and rolling plains. Soils, composed of loess and alluvium, are much deeper and more productive than in the lower Ozarks.

## Major Rivers and Lakes

The Missouri River forms the north boundary of this region. The Osage River, the state's third largest, flows from Kansas and joins the Missouri River just east of Jefferson City. The Union Electric Company of St. Louis dammed the Osage in 1931 forming Lake of the Ozarks, an impoundment of 55,342 surface acres and 1,150 miles of shoreline—the Midwest's largest hydroelectric reservoir. Lake of the Ozarks State Park, Missouri's largest at 17,200 acres, highlights the area's rich natural resources, while the lake area itself has become a highly developed commercial playground.

The White River used to meander back and forth between Missouri and Arkansas but has been dammed to create five reservoirs—three of which lie, at least partially, at the southern end of this region. Powersite dam, built in 1912, created Lake Taneycomo. Bull Shoals Lake is split nearly in its middle by the state line, and Norfork Lake's northern end lies just east of Gainesville.

Other rivers in this region include the Osage Fork of the Gasconade, Gasconade, Maries, and Big Piney. The James, Current, Jacks Fork, and Eleven Point Rivers also have their headwaters here.

## Common Plant Life

The great age and physiographic variety of the Ozarks make it the area of greatest species diversity in Missouri. Deciduous, pine-oak, and pine forests were the main vegetation in presettlement times, and still dominate today. Glade, savanna, fen, and bottomland communities also exist. Dry-mesic chert forests, characterized by white oak, red oak, shortleaf pine, various hickories, and flowering dogwood, are common in this region. Common plants are Virginia creeper, tick trefoil, black cohosh, bedstraw, and Christmas fern.

Although most glade communities in the Ozarks are threatened by aggressive growth of cedar trees because of fire suppression, thousands of these rocky, sunny openings still occur in the forest landscape. Dolomite glades are a characteristic of the Ozarks, and the glades of the White River area are the most notable examples. Grasses dominate, interspersed with stunted trees and shrubs. Wildflowers are numerous and often showy. These include Missouri evening primrose, compass plant, blazing star, prairie dock, black-eyed Susan, silky aster, and yellow coneflower.

Although upland deciduous forest was the main presettlement vegetation in the Ozark border, glade, savanna, marsh, bottomland forest, and even prairie communities existed. Much of the Ozark border has been converted to pastures and crop fields, but fragmented forests and forested bottomlands still persist. Mesic forests are rich, well-developed upland forests where trees reach 90 to 140 feet and the canopy is dense. Deep soils support rich growths of mixed herbs, ferns, and mushrooms. Sugar maple, red oak, white oak, and basswood are distinctive trees in mesic forests; understory species include pawpaw, spicebush, flowering dogwood, and musclewood. Some of the many wildflowers are blue-eyed Mary, spring beauty, Dutchman's-breeches, toothwort, mayapple, wild ginger, purple trillium, and celandine poppy.

## Common Birds and Animals

Birds prevalent in upland forests of the Ozarks include wild turkey, turkey vulture, screech owl, crow, various woodpeckers, summer tanager, ovenbird, parula warbler, black-and-white warbler, red-eyed vireo, and white-breasted nuthatch. Other animals include white-tailed deer, bobcat, gray fox, raccoon, armadillo, wood rat, gray squirrel, chipmunk, black rat snake, and various bats.

While on some of the expansive savannas of the region, watch for the great crested flycatcher, eastern bluebird, prairie warbler, indigo bunting, goldfinch, and kestrel. You may also see the coyote, red fox, ornate box turtle, six-lined racerunner, glass lizard, speckled kingsnake, and yellowbelly racer.

Mesic forests are home to barred owl, whippoorwill, eastern wood pewee, blue-gray gnatcatcher, wood thrush, Kentucky warbler, and Carolina wren. Other animals include white-tailed deer, opossum, three-toed box turtle, spring peeper, pickerel frog, leopard frog, gray tree frog, redbelly snake, and five-lined skink.

## Climate

The south-central region's temperatures average 57 degrees F in spring, 78 degrees F in summer, 57 degrees F in fall, and 31 degrees F in winter. Mean annual precipitation varies from 40 inches at the top of this region to 46 inches at the bottom.

## Best Features

- Rolling, expansive savannas, resplendent with wildflowers
- Desertlike glades with craggy boulders, panoramic views, and six-foot-tall wildflowers
- Large and fabulously decorated caves
- Splendid karst features—springs, caves, natural bridges, pirated streams, sinkholes, and canyonlike collapsed caverns
- Burial mounds and mysterious prehistoric earthworks at Van Meter State Park
- Rich, moist, tall forests of white oak, sugar maple, and basswood
- Rock-bottomed, spring-fed, clear, scenic streams
- Blufftop vistas of endless, densely wooded ridges

# 35.  Grand Gulf State Park

- Hike through a spectacular geology lesson and discover a collapsed cave passage, sinkhole, spring, pirated stream, cave, natural bridge, and wet-weather waterfalls, all on two short hikes.
- From four overlooks, watch a stream splash along, vanish underground, and emerge again in a geological disappearing act called stream piracy.
- See the cave where local Ozark old-timers claimed to have dumped sacks of oats into the draining stream to watch the grains emerge at Mammoth Spring, Arkansas, nine miles away.

## Area Information

The story of Grand Gulf begins in a seemingly un-likely place—the bottom of a warm-water ocean, over 450 million years ago. Here, calcium-rich sediments formed dolomite, the dominant rock found in the area. As the land was uplifted the ocean waters receded, and fresh water began to erode the land-scape. Surface streams carved down through the soft rock, creating fissures and channels in the bedrock. Mildly acidic groundwater dissolved passageways underground, which later became air filled, and a cave system developed.

But the water did not stop there. The erosional forces that formed the cave continued, and at Grand Gulf today is a cave system whose roof collapsed thousands of years ago. The result is a vertical-walled canyon about three-quarters of a mile long, which is often called the Little Grand Canyon. A bit of remain-ing roof forms one of the largest natural bridges in Missouri. Grand Gulf is a national natural landmark.

Like many other geological wonders, Grand Gulf has a long history of public attraction, local pride, and folklore. In 1892, using a boat and candles, scientist Luella Agnes Owen set out to explore the cave, which drains all the water from the gulf. Her account included seeing "small eyeless fish, pure

white and perfectly fearless; the first I had ever seen, and little beauties."

While the sack-of-oats experiment may sound dubious, modern investigators have used dye tracing to confirm that water from Grand Gulf does indeed travel to Mammoth Spring, Arkansas. Today, visitors can still see water winding and eroding its way through the gulf, a testimony to the forces that created it thousands of years before.

**Directions:** Grand Gulf is in south-central Missouri, just a few miles from Arkansas. From Thayer, travel west on Highway W for 6.1 miles to the entrance.

**Hours Open:** The park is open daily from 8 A.M. to sunset, year-round.

**Facilities:** The park offers picnic areas, boardwalks, and four overlooks. Rest rooms are available but water is not.

**Permits and Rules:** Grand Gulf is a day-use park only; camping is not allowed. Stay on the boardwalks and trails to prevent erosion, and always keep pets on leashes.

**Further Information:** Tourist Assistant, Grand Gulf State Park, Route 3, Box 3554, Thayer, MO 65791; 417-264-7600, or call the park office at Montauk State Park, 573-548-2201.

## Other Areas of Interest

After learning about the story of the water at Grand Gulf State Park and seeing the cave where the water enters the earth, why not drive down into Arkansas to **Mammoth Spring** and see where all that water comes out? It's just nine miles south of Grand Gulf on Highway 63. Billowing 850 million gallons of water per day, Mammoth Spring is one of the largest springs in the nation. The site is an Arkansas state park and includes a picnic area, federal fish hatchery, and aquarium. For more information call Mammoth Spring State Park at 501-625-7364.

Grand Gulf State Park

To Koshkonong
3.8 Miles

To Thayer →

W

Grand
Gulf
Sink

Northwest Rim Trail

Grand Gulf

Chasm Loop Trail

N

L E G E N D
Road
Trail
Boundary
Boardwalk

Cave
Natural Bridge
Parking

# Chasm Loop Trail 👢👢

**Distance Round-Trip:** .25 mile

**Estimated Hiking Time:** .50 hour

*Look down the gulf and imagine how the cave would have looked while it was still intact, perhaps as recently as 10,000 years ago. The rock faces you see were here then. So was the water. It was water that dissolved this stone, giving birth to the cave eons ago. And water flows through the chasm today, carving it ever deeper.*

**Caution:** The 130-foot vertical cliffs make staying on the boardwalks and trails a good idea. Also, keep pets on leashes and children in control.

**Trail Directions:** Before you begin, you may want to take the boardwalk on your far right to the overlook over two of the highlights of the park—the Grand Gulf sink and the cave that drains the Bussell Branch stream and Shiloh Spring. This water, a combination of surface drainage and spring water, enters the cave and travels nine miles underground to reemerge at Mammoth Spring, Arkansas.

Begin the trail at the interpretive signs in the northwest corner of the parking lot **[1]**. At .02 mi. turn left to take the small spur to the Grand Junction overlook **[2]**. From here you are looking into the main passage of an ancient cave, the roof of which has collapsed. The giant boulder on the left, covered with bur cucumber vines, constricts the gulf. This point is called the Needle's Eye. The area at the far end, called the Narrows, is where the cave passage ended. Today, a wet-weather stream joins the sink here in an erosional continuum tens of thousands of years old.

Just after you return to the main trail, turn left **[3]** at the intersection at .03 mi. At .05 mi. you will come to Natural Bridge overlook **[4]**, so named not because you look over a natural bridge but because you are standing on one! Because of its resistance to erosion or its architectural soundness, this is a portion of the cave roof that didn't collapse.

At .09 mi. ignore the spur on the right. In a few steps you will come upon the third overlook of the trail **[5]**. Step out onto the overlook and look to your far left. At the end of the chasm are slabs of bedrock, which form a waterfall after a heavy rain. At the base of the falls is Shiloh Spring, which bubbles up for a few feet before disappearing below the surface. It reappears below the overlook, just to the left, where it gurgles and trickles its way into the mouth of the cave in the Grand Gulf sink.

At .15 mi. is a wooden deck and an opportunity for you to take the steps to the bottom of the chasm **[6]**. Choosing this option affords a unique perspective of the gulf as well as adding another boot or two to the difficulty rating for this trail. Take the steps up and walk across the parking lot to complete the trail.

1. Start
2. Grand Junction overlook
3. Left turn
4. Natural Bridge overlook
5. Shiloh Spring overlook
6. Steps to bottom of chasm

# Northwest Rim Trail 👢👢

**Distance Round-Trip:** .9 mile

**Estimated Hiking Time:** .75 hour

*Shiloh Spring stream was cheerily gurgling along far below me, and a tufted titmouse was busy with his spring song the day I was here. But oh, what a different sound these canyon walls must have heard one day long, long ago . . . the day the ceiling came tumbling down.*

**Caution:** Stay on the trail to prevent erosion problems and avoid dangerous drop-offs.

**Trail Directions:** Before you begin, you may want to take the boardwalk to the far right of the interpretive signs for a great view of the Grand Gulf sink and cave. Also be sure to stop at Grand Junction overlook to get an end-view of all the features you will be hiking alongside. This overlook is on a small spur on your left, just after you begin either trail.

Begin the trail at the interpretive signs at the northwest corner of the parking lot **[1]**. When you come to an intersection at .03 mi. look on your right at the beckoning oak **[2]**, silently gesturing the way you should go. Go straight here to continue the trail.

At .04 mi. look down in the bottom of the deep sinkhole on your right and see where the sunken passage meets the still-intact cave **[3]**. At about 200 feet, the cave is in the deepest part of the chasm and acts as a drain for all the water flowing into the gulf. Early explorers of the cave reported finding a large lake inside, as well as blind cavefish, but exploration halted in 1921 when a tremendous storm washed trees and other debris into the gulf, damming the cave a short distance inside the entrance. Recently, a camera-carrying robot named STEVE has been sent into the cave to try to find what lies beyond the flood debris.

Turn left at the intersection **[4]** at .09 mi. Take the small spur at .11 mi. on the left to enjoy the view of the natural bridge **[5]** you were standing on a few minutes ago. With an opening 75 feet high and a span of 250 feet, this is one of the largest natural bridges in the state.

Ignore the spur on your left at .13 mi. and turn left at the intersection **[6]** at .16 mi. At .18 mi. turn right **[7]**. Up to now, the chasm has been fairly yawning on your left as you hike, but you will soon approach the area known as the Narrows, where the collapsed cave passage ends and an intermittent surface stream begins. At .39 mi. take the small spur on your left and see the gravel pit that pirates (drains) the spring stream at this end of the chasm. During heavy rain, runoff from approximately 20 square miles cascades over the smoothed bedrock above the gravel, making a wet-weather waterfall **[8]**. This sometimes turns the gulf into a skinny lake reaching depths of over 100 feet. Most of this water slowly drains through the cave.

At .43 mi. ignore the spur on your left and find the end of the trail at .44 mi. **[9]**. Retrace your steps to make your way back to the trailhead.

1. Start
2. Beckoning oak
3. Cave in sink
4. Left turn
5. Natural bridge
6. Left turn
7. Right turn
8. Wet-weather waterfall
9. End

# 36.  Greer Spring

- Hike in a shortleaf pine and hardwood mixed forest and hear the hushed roar of Greer Spring, over half a mile away.

- Find Christmas ferns in their favorite habitat and experience the sight of a Christmas fern mania.

- Stand next to the "boil" and witness the power of the 220-million-gallon-per-day flow of Greer Spring, Missouri's second largest.

- Why did the walking fern cross the rock? Find the answer at the bottom of the Greer Spring Trail.

## Area Information

You couldn't tell from looking at it now, but Greer Spring has a long history of milling and timbering operations that included dams, turbine waterwheels, and two mill buildings at the spring site as well as a third on a ridge above it. It all started when Samuel Greer bought the spring in 1859, built a gristmill, and began operating the mill powered by water from the spring. After serving in the Civil War, Greer returned home to find that roaming guerrillas had burned his mill and driven off most of his livestock.

Around 1870, Greer rebuilt the mill, constructed a dam, installed a turbine waterwheel, and expanded operations. Greer's mill now could grind grain, saw timber, gin cotton, and card wool—all from harnessing the spring's tremendous power. Greer expanded again in 1883, rebuilding the dam and starting construction on a new roller mill located on the ridge above the spring. A unique cable system was used for transferring power from the turbine wheel at the spring to the new mill on the ridgetop. The mill continued operating until 1920.

Today, visitors to Greer Spring can experience the area in its natural and nearly undisturbed state. This opportunity is the result of good stewardship of the land since 1920, conscientious management by the U.S. Forest Service, who has owned the area since 1993, and nature's incredible ability to renew itself.

**Directions:** From Alton, travel north on Highway 19 for 7.5 miles to the small town of Greer. The entrance to the parking lot for the trail, marked by a U.S. Forest Service sign, is .6 mile north of Greer.

**Hours Open:** The site is intended for day use only and is open year-round from dawn to dusk.

**Facilities:** Rest rooms are available but water is not.

**Permits and Rules:** Camping, hiking, and hunting are allowed on the national forest land surrounding Greer Spring, but no hunting or camping is allowed near the spring or trail. Regulations posted near the trailhead also prohibit shooting, littering, picnicking, horses, ATVs, bicycles, swimming, fishing, boating, glass containers, smoking, night use, pets off leash, and audio devices.

**Further Information:** District Ranger, Eleven Point Ranger District, Route 1, Box 1908, Winona, MO 65588; 573-325-4233.

## Other Areas of Interest

The 53-degree water of Greer Spring rolls down a rock-filled canyon for one mile before entering the **Eleven Point River,** which it more than doubles. The Eleven Point is a national scenic river, part of the National Wild and Scenic Rivers System, and is protected by the U.S. Forest Service. The Forest Service has picnic areas, campgrounds, and boat and canoe accesses along the river. Several outfitters rent canoes. For more information call 573-325-4233.

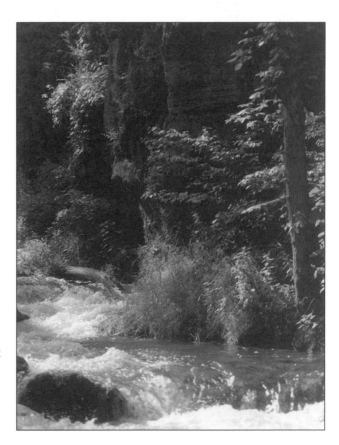

# Greer Spring Trail 👢👢👢

**Distance Round-Trip:** 2 miles

**Estimated Hiking Time:** 1.5 hours

*While over a billion pounds of water billow from Greer Spring every day, its steep valley walls and omnipresent mist create a terrarium you can walk in. Here you'll find mats of water-loving mosses and ferns, tiny trickles of spring water emerging from cracks in the rock walls, handsome jack-in-the-pulpit, and the delicate yellow lady-slipper orchid.*

**Caution:** Watch out for poison ivy along the trail.

**Trail Directions:** The trail begins at the northwest end of the parking lot, near a wooden bench and a regulations sign **[1].** Before you begin hiking, stop here and listen. The slightest breeze will incite a pleasant "Shhhhhh . . . shhhhhh" from the shortleaf pines towering above. In this part of the Ozarks, the shortleaf is in its native habitat. Besides the cedar, it is Missouri's only evergreen tree.

As you begin the trail, notice how the pines intermingle with the hardwood oaks and hickories. Pines often dominate the ridgetops in the area because they can tolerate the thin, drier soils there. Find a wooden bench **[2]** at .19 mi. and a wooden bridge **[3]** at .32 mi. Soon after you cross the bridge, start listening down in the valley for the hushed roar of the 220-million-gallon-per-day flow of Greer Spring, the second largest spring in Missouri after Big Spring on the Current River.

Find another wooden bench **[4]** at a switchback at .48 mi. From the wooden bridge at .59 mi. you can view a Christmas fern mania **[5].** So named because they are green at Christmastime, Christmas ferns are actually green all year round. These shaded, rocky, wooded slopes with acidic, well-drained soils are their favorite habitat. Cross a final wooden bridge at .64 mi. **[6].**

Soon you will come upon an interpretive sign that explains how the nearby rocks were formed by sedimentation. Layers of resistant sandstone were formed between layers of dolomite, which is softer and quicker to erode. As the layers of dolomite dissolved away, the remaining sandstone broke into unusual cubical shapes. You'll see many of these curious cubes here along the trail. At .79 mi. you will find a natural sandstone bench **[7].**

At .87 mi. you can step out onto the stone overlook **[8]** to hear and see the mighty spring. Greer Spring actually emerges from two openings. One is from Greer Spring Cave, on your far left, and the other is from the big "boil" on your right. To descend to the water level, take the steps at the far left of the overlook.

At the bottom at .94 mi. you can feel the water vapor in the air and see the lush vegetation it supports. Here are several species of aquatic plants, watercress, and carpets of thick mosses and liverworts clinging to boulders in the cold spring water. Look on some of the larger boulders and you will find heart-shaped leaves with extremely long tips poking through layers of moss. Look carefully at these walking ferns **[9]** and you'll see tiny plantlets forming at the tips of many of the leaves. These plantlets are what makes walking ferns "walk." Aha! Walking ferns cross rocks to reproduce.

Wading or swimming is not allowed, but you can have fun exploring more wonders of nature near the spring and spring branch before hiking your way back to the trailhead.

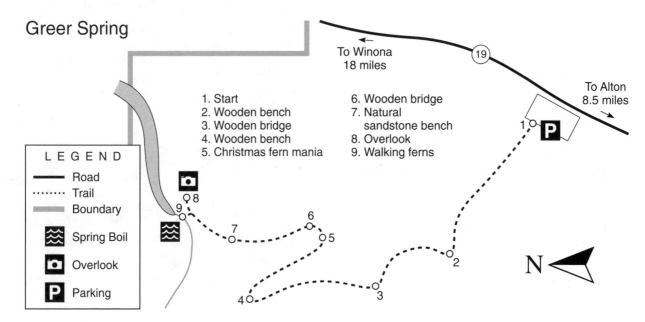

**Greer Spring**

To Winona
18 miles

To Alton
8.5 miles

1. Start
2. Wooden bench
3. Wooden bridge
4. Wooden bench
5. Christmas fern mania
6. Wooden bridge
7. Natural sandstone bench
8. Overlook
9. Walking ferns

LEGEND
— Road
······ Trail
▓▓ Boundary
≋ Spring Boil
📷 Overlook
🅿 Parking

N

# 37.  McCormack Recreation Area

- From a 200-foot-high blufftop overlook view the Boomhole and find out how it got its name in the late 1800s.
- Water, water everywhere! Hike next to a serene forest lake, numerous spring branches, streams, and the Eleven Point River.
- Discover the gum bumelia tree, or woolly buckthorn, which is in the family of trees from which chewing gum chicle comes and looks like big bonsai trees on the blufftop glades.
- Begin and end your hike next to the enchantingly tranquil Lake McCormack.

## Area Information

McCormack Lake Recreation Area is in the Doniphan-Eleven Point District of the Mark Twain National Forest and is managed by the U.S. Forest Service.

Two major features of the area are the Eleven Point River and the Ozark Trail. While the McCormack-Greer Trail connects the McCormack Recreation Area with the Greer Recreation Area and river landing, most of the trail is also a segment of the Eleven Point River Section of the Ozark Trail. The Ozark Trail follows the most scenic and varied route from the St. Louis metropolitan area southwestward through southern Missouri to the Arkansas border and will be 500 miles long when completed. The Eleven Point River, part of the National Wild and Scenic River System, is fed by over 30 springs and provides a cool swim or wade even on the hottest summer days. Picnic areas, boat launch ramps, and campgrounds are located along the river, as well as eight float camps, which are accessible only by watercraft.

Originally established as a bass-rearing pond in the late 1930s, McCormack Lake is now a peaceful setting for camping, resting, or reconvening from an outdoor trip. At the McCormack Lake area alone, visitors can find excellent places for hiking, backpacking, camping (including riverside camping), picnicking, boating (by canoe, kayak, or johnboat), tube floating, fishing, bird and wildlife watching, photography, berry and mushroom gathering, and horseback riding. Plenty of spots are also available to sit down next to a stream and just listen to the forest.

**Directions:** McCormack Recreation Area is 13.3 miles south of Winona on Highway 19. Or, from the south, it is only 5.5 miles north of the Greer Spring Trail on Highway 19.

**Hours Open:** The site is open year-round.

**Facilities:** The area offers developed campsites, rest rooms, picnic areas, fishing, boating on Lake McCormack (by carry-on boats only), and drinking water (except during winter months).

**Permits and Rules:** No firearms may be discharged. No boat motors are allowed. All pets must be leashed. Fires are restricted to fire pits while camping in the developed campground.

**Further Information:** District Ranger, Eleven Point Ranger District, U.S. Forest Service, Winona, MO 65588; 573-325-4233. Especially helpful is the *Taste of the Ozarks* newspaper that includes camping and hiking guides by each district of the Mark Twain National Forest. For more information on the Ozark Trail, contact the Missouri Department of Natural Resources, Ozark Trail Coordinator, P.O. Box 176, Jefferson City, MO 65102; 573-751-2479.

## Other Areas of Interest

**Turner's Mill North Picnic Area** was the site of the town of Surprise and has a spring that was used to power Turner Mill. A large waterwheel still sits in the spring branch. The area is on the Eleven Point River and offers easy access. Next, go 2.1 miles south of McCormack Lake on Highway 19. Turn onto FR 3152 for 6 miles, then take FR 3190 for 3 miles.

**Falling Spring Picnic Area,** a scenic spot and favorite area of photographers, includes a spring, mill pond, old mill, and 100-year-old cabin. Go 3 miles north of McCormack Lake on Highway 19. Turn onto FR 3170 and take FR 3164 to the left for 2 miles. For more information about either area, contact the Eleven Point Ranger District in Winona at 573-325-4233.

# McCormack-Greer Trail

**Distance Round-Trip:** 8.5 miles

**Estimated Hiking Time:** 4.5 hours

*Hike next to boulders carpeted with ferns, lichens, and lush mosses while trailside streams provide you with music along the way.*

**Caution:** You will cross many streams on this trail. At times during high water and floods, stream crossings will be difficult or impossible. Also take care not to hike onto adjoining sections of the Ozark Trail by mistake—it's 500 miles long!

**Trail Directions:** Begin the trail at the south end of the parking lot for McCormack Lake **[1]**. Most of this trail is also a portion of the Ozark Trail, which is marked with green and white "OT" trail markers. Hike next to the lake until you get to the spillway at .22 mi., where you turn left **[2]**.

You can't go far in the Ozarks without coming upon a spring branch or stream, and soon you will find one gurgling and snaking along near the trail. Where the trail crosses a stream at .42 mi. you will also find a beaver dam **[3]**. Cross a dirt road at .48 mi. and continue the trail on the other side **[4]**. You will cross two more streams at .55 and .57 mi. **[5]**.

At .62 mi. you will walk up to a magnificent boulder **[6]**. Make your way along the stream until you come to an intersection at 1.11 mi. **[7]**, where you turn left uphill among some moss-covered boulders.

At the top of the mountain you will find a glade—a rocky, grassy opening in the forest. At 1.52 mi. you will walk out onto the Boomhole overlook **[8]**. Near the turn of the century, the bluff across the river supported a wooden chute. Massive logs cut from virgin shortleaf pine were slid down the chute, plunging into the river below with thunderous booms. The logs floated downriver and were placed on log trains, bound for the mill at Winona.

The trail turns away from the river and passes through the pine-oak forest before treating you to another outstanding overlook at 2.62 mi. **[9]**. From here, descend to the river level and cross a stream. At 3.11 mi. **[10]** turn right at the intersection. At 3.5 mi. the river more than doubles in volume, due to the inflow of the Greer Spring branch **[11]**. About a mile up this branch is Greer Spring.

At 3.88 mi. turn left **[12]**, cross a small stream, and follow the trail under the Highway 19 bridge. At 4.02 mi. **[13]** is Greer Recreation Area, where rest rooms, water, and camping are available. Hike on the pavement, away from the river, and you'll see the trail markers where the trail reenters the forest. Turn left at the intersection at 4.25 mi. **[14]**. When you get to Highway 19 at 4.43 mi. **[15]**, turn right on the road for about 50 yards and pick up the trail on the other side. You'll cross a couple more rocky, singing streams before returning to the intersection at **[10]**. Turn right here. You'll get to experience both overlooks and the other sights all over before returning to the trailhead.

## McCormack Recreation Area

LEGEND

— Road

····· Trail

P Parking

1. Start
2. Left turn
3. Beaver dam
4. Go straight
5. Stream crossings
6. Boulder
7. Left turn
8. Boomhole overlook
9. Overlook
10. Right turn
11. Greer Spring branch
12. Left turn
13. Greer Recreation Area
14. Left turn
15. Road crossing

Eleven Point River

N

# 38. Alley Spring

- See the huge, blue eye of Alley Spring, framed by a natural amphitheater of sheer, smooth bluffs.

- Imagine 81 million one-gallon milk jugs full of water . . . how many bathtubs is that? How many swimming pools is that? It's an average day's flow from Alley Spring.

- Take a tour of the red, three-story Alley Mill— once the center of a turn-of-the-century community and now one of the most photographed buildings in the state.

- Hike next to the chilly waters of the spring branch, beneath overhanging rock ledges, and up to a rocky overlook with a soaring vulture's view of the entire spring valley.

- Bring a mushroom identification book; many mushrooms are so brilliantly colored that they compete with the wildflowers.

## Area Information

The story of Alley begins with its spring, which is Missouri's seventh largest—a round, blue pool about 60 feet across and 30 feet deep, with a 150-foot-deep chasm below it. Every day, Alley gushes around 81 million gallons of water, at a temperature of about 57 degrees year-round. Surrounding the spring pool are tall walls of smooth dolomite, the parent rock from which is carved most caves and springs in the Ozarks. The spring branch flows for a half mile before entering the Jacks Fork, about a quarter mile down North River Road.

In 1894, the Alley roller mill was constructed, which harnessed part of the spring's power to grind flour for local farmers. Farmers sometimes had to wait for days for their turn at the mill, which became a center for storytelling, news exchange, and checker playing. By 1900, a community was flourishing around the mill, with a blacksmith shop, general store, post office, school, and baseball diamond. The mill was expanded to saw lumber and generate electricity. On Sundays and holidays, festivities around the spring included target shooting, amusements, dancing, speeches, horseshoes, and the ever-popular picnics.

Alley Spring, managed by the National Park Service, is part of the Ozark National Scenic Riverways, which includes over 134 miles of the Current and Jacks Fork Rivers. National riverways are natural streams that have recreational, natural, and cultural resources of national significance. Both the Current and Jacks Fork are clean, diverse, scenic rivers, and offer endless possibilities for floating, fishing, and exploring the Ozarks.

**Directions:** From Eminence, take Highway 106 west 5.9 miles to Alley Spring and picnic area, on the right. The campground and river access are .4 mile east of Alley Spring on Highway 106.

**Hours Open:** The spring area, trails, picnic area, and campground are open year-round. Alley Mill is open every day from 9 A.M. to 6 P.M. from Memorial Day through Labor Day. Storys Creek School is open on Friday, Saturday, and Sunday from Memorial Day through Labor Day.

**Facilities:** The site offers free admission and tours of Alley Roller Mill, which serves as an interpretive center. Picnicking is available near the spring; horseback and bicycle riding are available on North River Road; and camping, boating, fishing, floating, and swimming are all available at the campground. Check bulletin boards for scheduled events and programs.

**Permits and Rules:** No wading, fishing, swimming, boating, or tubing is allowed in the spring, but all these activities are allowed in Jacks Fork River. No horses or bikes are allowed on the trails, but both may be ridden on North River Road. The Alley Spring area is closed to all hunting or shooting.

**Further Information:** Superintendent, Ozark National Scenic Riverways, P.O. Box 490, Van Buren, MO 63965; 573-323-4236.

## Other Areas of Interest

Northwest of Alley Spring, **Montauk State Park** features seven springs which are the origins of the well-known Current River. The Missouri Department of Conservation operates a trout hatchery at the park and stocks the river during the fishing season (March 1 through October 31). The park includes a grist mill with most of its original machinery, campground, motel, cabins, restaurant, picnic areas, and a hiking trail. The park is 21 miles southwest of Salem on Highway 119. For more information call 573-548-2201.

# Alley Spring

To Summersville
← 13 Miles

(106)

Alley Spring

N

Overlook Trail

Spring Branch Trail

P

North River Rd.

(106)

To Campground
and Boat Access

Jacks Fork River

LEGEND
—— Road
······ Trail
Ranger Station
Storys Creek School
Alley Mill
Picnic Area
Picnic Shelter
Playground
Restrooms
P Parking
Handicap Parking
Hitching Rail

# Spring Branch Trail 🥾🥾

**Distance Round-Trip:** .75 mile

**Estimated Hiking Time:** .75 hour

*There is something about spring water . . . it often has vapor rising from it, and whether it's boiling from a 30-foot-deep pool or rolling along a 2-foot-deep spring branch, its beautiful, almost eerie, blue green hue is unmistakable.*

**Caution:** Some of the flat rocks on the trail may be slippery because of rainwater and seeps.

**Trail Directions:** Park in the lot for the Alley Spring Mill. The trail begins on North River Road, which is just across the wooden bridge over the spring branch, near the southeast corner of the parking lot. Cross the bridge at the sign that reads "Local Traffic Only," and begin the trail just across the bridge **[1]**, on your left.

Aside from the mill and the historical significance and attractions of the area, the spring and spring branch have a beauty all their own. You probably already noticed the sound of this cool water, pushed along by the millions of gallons emerging from its source, just ahead. The watercress is surprisingly green, and the blue-tinged water obscures its depth. At a bend in the stream at .04 mi. **[2]**, look near the water for a patch of tall, pencil-thin plants that have no obvious leaves. These are horsetails, which represent a family of nonflowering plants that flourished some 400 million years ago, before flowering plants evolved. Just across the trail, you'll find a Carolina buckthorn tree, whose smooth, shiny leaves turn yellow in the fall. Its sweet, edible fruit gives the tree its other name, Indian cherry.

Another interesting tree appears at .07 mi. **[3]**, just to the right of a boulder on your left. This is a musclewood tree, so named for the unusual, musclelike ridges beneath its smooth bark. One of the hardest and strongest woods in North America, it has been used for tool handles, wedges, and golf clubs. Like giant eyebrows of the steep slope on your right, dolomite ledges soon protrude from the hill and hang over the trail. Hydrangea sprouts where water seeps or drips. Alum root and columbine grow up the

bluffs, while Virginia creeper trails from the top. You'll pass some small caves in the bluffs at .12 mi. **[4]**, and both the caves and the bluffs continue nearly to the mill. Notice the island at .16 mi. **[5]**, covered with jewelweed.

After climbing some stone steps, go straight at the intersection at .25 mi. **[6]** and go up some more steps. The water gets louder as it rushes around boulders and islands. The red mill comes into view on the left as the big, blue eye of Alley Spring (.32 mi.) **[7]** appears in front of you. Bur reeds wave in the calmer shallows, a fog persists over the boiling center, and smooth, sheer dolomite bluffs frame the whole scene. Continue around the spring. When you arrive at the mill at .42 mi. **[8]**, turn left and follow a sandstone walkway. Turn right at .45 mi. **[9]**, and go over a wooden bridge. Just across the bridge, turn left, and take the spur on your right at .48 mi. **[10]** to the small, white schoolhouse and peek inside.

Turn right after returning to the sidewalk, and you'll find an interpretive display at the corner of the parking lot at .67 mi. **[11]**, with photos and information on the community that developed around Alley Spring during the late 1800s. Continue on the sidewalk until you reach the "Local Traffic Only" sign at .74 mi. **[12]**, where you turn left to finish your spring hike. The Overlook Trail also begins here, which gives you a different view of Alley.

| | |
|---|---|
| 1. Start | 7. Alley Spring |
| 2. Horsetails | 8. Alley Mill |
| 3. Musclewood | 9. Right turn |
| 4. Small caves | 10. Spur to schoolhouse |
| 5. Jewelweed island | 11. Interpretive display |
| 6. Go straight | 12. Left turn |

# Overlook Trail 👢👢👢👢

**Distance Round-Trip:** 1.5 miles

**Estimated Hiking Time:** .75 hour

*From the overlook, it's easy to imagine the busy general store, the loud blacksmith shop, and the rest of the little town that once flourished far below. What remains is the soft-red mill, and the blue dot of the spring that started it all.*

**Caution:** Small, loose rocks cover the trail on some of the inclines.

**Trail Directions:** Park in the lot for the Alley Spring Mill. This trail shares a trailhead with the Spring Branch Trail. Cross the bridge at the sign that reads "Local Traffic Only" and begin the trail just across the bridge **[1]**.

Go straight on North River Road and pass a few hitching rails for horses and some picnic tables. At .05 mi. **[2]** ascend the stone steps on your left that lead uphill, into the woods. Ignore the spurs on your right and continue on the main trail as it zigzags up the hill. The sudden abundance of little bluestem grass and the opening in the tree canopy signal a glade remnant at .16 mi. **[3]**. As on prairies, flowers bloom on glades from early spring through fall. Wildflowers that bloom in spring are usually short, but later-blooming species grow taller, when they have to compete with the tall prairie grasses. By fall, the yellow flowers of prairie dock, sunflowers, and compass plant may be six to eight feet high!

Unless you visit in winter, you are likely to find mushrooms here in all sizes and shapes, especially after a wet period. Look for bright orange miniature chanterelles, poking through dark green moss beds. Large, candy-apple-red mushrooms are here, as well as smaller ones, lemon yellow and dull green. Oyster mushrooms grow snow white and earlike on rotting logs, while the king bolete looks like a hamburger bun on a fat stalk. Near the top of the ridge, you'll hike through an open forest with some grandpa and grandma white oak trees and several stands of large shortleaf pines. Feel the pine bark. You'll discover that it's made of layers of thin plates that can flake off, making the tree resistant to fires.

Listen for the rushing water of Alley Spring; you'll soon reach a spot on this ridgetop where the sound is funneled up from far below. The vast expanse of the entire spring valley and outlying wooded hills opens in front of you at the overlook at .75 mi. **[4]**. From here, you can see the red mill, which became the center of a thriving community just after the turn of the century. After the overlook, look for coneflowers, blazing star, and rattlesnake master in several more glade remnants on your way downhill. You may also see false foxglove here, a tall plant sometimes so full of yellow flowers that the long branches droop to the ground. The trail makes some switchbacks downhill, and you'll pass a small, wet-weather waterfall at 1.02 mi. **[5]**.

You'll reach Alley Mill at 1.18 mi. **[6]**, which you can tour during open hours. Turn left, in front of the mill, and follow the sandstone walkway. Turn right at 1.21 mi. **[7]** and cross the wooden bridge over a small stream. Just across the bridge, turn left, and pass Storys Creek School and a picnic shelter on your right. At the corner of the parking lot at 1.40 mi. **[8]**, you'll find an interpretive display with photos and information on the turn-of-the-century community that once thrived here and literature on the Ozark National Scenic Riverways. Return to your vehicle here or continue on the sidewalk until you reach the "Local Traffic Only" sign at 1.48 mi. **[9]**, where you turn left to return to the trailhead.

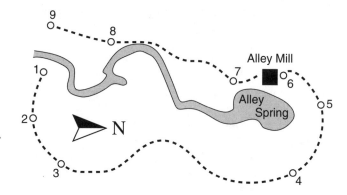

1. Start
2. Stone steps
3. Glade remnant
4. Scenic overlook
5. Wet-weather waterfall
6. Alley Mill
7. Right turn
8. Interpretive display
9. Left turn

# 39. Lane Spring Recreation Area

- Find the odd sandstone Blossom Rock in the forest and make your guess about how it got there.
- Hike on ridgetop glades with magnificent views of the scenic Little Piney Creek Valley.
- See the unusual outlet of Lane Spring, where each day 11 million gallons of water percolate from a loose, sandy bottom, creating strange, circular "boils" of sand.
- Get the feeling of beach hiking, as your boots sink into the soft sand of the trail next to Little Piney Creek.

## Area Information

Lane Spring Recreation Area features a campground, picnic area, and spring on the banks of Little Piney Creek and is one of six recreation sites managed by the U.S. Forest Service in the Houston-Rolla District of the Mark Twain National Forest. Encompassing nearly 200,000 acres in the south-central region of the state, the district provides facilities for camping, picnicking, hiking, horseback riding, fishing, floating, and hunting. Hikers can discover a variety of landscapes—forests with interspersed pine, streams, springs, caves, bluffs, and glades in hilly, rolling terrain.

Unlike many springs that have an obvious outlet or two, the fishhook-shaped spring branch of Lane Spring is an accumulation of dozens of small outlets. These outlets, evidenced by underwater "boils" in the loose sand, range in size from dinner plates to coins. Lane Spring joins Little Piney Creek a short distance downstream from the picnic area. The Missouri Department of Conservation stocks the area with rainbow trout, providing visitors a special fishing opportunity.

The namesake of Lane Spring's Blossom Rock Trail is an unusual mass of sandstone that abruptly juts from the forest floor and has a way of surprising hikers with its sudden presence. The rock's origin is uncertain. One theory is that the sandstone was deposited in a dolomite cave and, because it was

more resistant, remained as the blossom after the cave's walls and roof weathered away. Another theory is that the sandstone is a remnant filling of an ancient sinkhole—a suggestion substantiated by the blossom's roughly circular shape. Blossom Rock is only one of Lane Spring's wonders—come and explore them all!

**Directions:** From the intersection of I-44 and Highway 63 in Rolla, take Highway 63 south 13.2 miles. Turn right at the sign for the area and go 1.3 miles to the parking lot.

**Hours Open:** The site is open daily from 6 A.M. to 10 P.M. The picnic areas are open from 6 A.M. to 9 P.M. only.

**Facilities:** The area offers two campground loops, picnic areas with shelters and grills, rest rooms (but no showers), a playground, and fishing for rainbow trout and other fish in Little Piney Creek.

**Permits and Rules:** A two-dollar parking fee is required for each vehicle per day. (Single campsites are eight dollars.) ATVs and horses are prohibited on the trails. An annual state trout permit is required for possession of trout, and the daily limit is five. State-wide seasons and regulations apply to all other species. All pets must be leashed.

**Further Information:** District Ranger, U.S. Forest Service, Houston/Rolla District, 108 South Sam Houston Boulevard, Houston, MO 65483; 417-967-4194.

## Other Areas of Interest

**Dillard Mill State Historic Site** features a picturesque red mill perched on a bluff that overlooks the clear, spring-fed Huzzah Creek. A small waterfall next to the mill cascades to the millpond below. Dillard Mill was built around 1900 and continued to grind grain until the 1960s. Restored to operational order, it is one of Missouri's best-preserved examples of a water-powered gristmill. Guided tours of the mill are available for a small fee. The site includes picnic areas. The mill is 25 miles southeast of Steelville, off Highway 49. For more information call 573-244-3120.

Lane Spring
Recreation Area

LEGEND
Road
Minor Road
Trail
Lane Spring
Bulletin Board
Picnic Area
Camping
Restrooms
Water
Fee Station
Trash Bin
Parking

Cedar Bluff Trail

To U.S. Hwy. 63
1 Mile

Blossom Rock Trail

Little Piney Creek

N

# Blossom Rock Trail

**Distance Round-Trip:** 1 mile

**Estimated Hiking Time:** .75 hour

*Was the blossom rock still here? What is a blossom rock, anyway? Signs in the parking lot didn't mention it. The first part of the trail yielded no clues. I had written the thing off as an obscure fragment of sketchy local history, when suddenly I was standing before it, and all my questions were answered. So **that's** a blossom rock!*

**Caution:** Stay on the trail to avoid stinging nettles in the creek bottom.

**Trail Directions:** Park in one of several lots between the picnic area and campground loops. The trailhead is across the road from the campground host site.

Begin the trail on a wide, mowed path through a mixed forest on the Little Piney Creek floodplain **[1]**. Two of the dominant plants here have winged stems—wing-stem sunflowers and white crownbeard, both of which may be seven feet tall by summer's end. White crownbeard is one of only a few plants in Missouri that can produce frost flowers—white, delicate ribbons of frost that extrude from the plant's stem near the base. Look for frost flowers after hard freezes, especially early in winter. Among the slippery elm and black walnut trees are sweet gum, which have five-lobed, star-shaped leaves and prickly "gum ball" seed cases.

A small slough, which may be dry, soon appears on your right. Tall hackberry trees block most of the sun, while a subcanopy of pawpaws finishes the job. Cross an intermittent stream at .12 mi. **[2]** and find three musclewood trees just on the other side. Musclewood has some of the hardest wood of any American tree. Its other name, hornbeam, comes from *horn*, meaning hard, and *beam*, an old-world word for tree. Ignore the spur on your right at .15 mi. **[3]**. Look for thin strips of bark that peel off sycamore limbs, fall onto the trail, and crunch like eggshells under your feet. Just after crossing another intermittent stream, turn left at the intersection at .27 mi. **[4]** and go up a rocky hill. Dittany, goldenrod, and asters bloom next to the trail, while a steep ravine plunges on your left. As you climb higher, flowering dogwoods replace pawpaws, and white oaks replace hackberry trees.

The Blossom Rock appears without announcement at .42 mi. **[5]**. Although this 50-foot-high pinnacled mass of sandstone may have been named because it erupts from an underlying bed of dolomite, what is more striking is that it "blossoms" from the forest floor without another rock mass or boulder in sight. Explore the blossom, looking for sunning brown fence lizards and spectacular green "blooms" of spreading lichens. Turn left after returning to the trail.

The trail passes through a dry forest with occasional slabs of sandstone. You'll find some glade remnants on the switchbacks at .45 mi. **[6]**, with blazing star, black-eyed Susans, and wild onions, which produce clusters of six-pointed, star-shaped lavender flowers in late summer. As you complete the last switchback, you'll see sparkling Little Piney Creek below you at .50 mi. **[7]**. Hike on a sideslope, with protruding sandstone and dolomite ledges, and turn left at the bottom of the hill, at .65 mi. **[8]**.

After crossing a small, wooden bridge over a sandy tributary, you'll follow the trail to the right and hike next to the creek, with great views of the stream's clear water and variety of lush aquatic plants. Look in the deep sand on the trail for small, round depressions. These are made by carnivorous doodlebugs (antlion larvae), who make their living by trapping ants and other small insects in tiny pitfall traps. Turn right at .75 mi. **[9]** onto the pavement of the campground loop. Bear right at all intersections of the loop to return to the trailhead.

1. Start
2. Stream crossing
3. Go straight
4. Left turn
5. Blossom Rock
6. Glade remnants
7. Little Piney Creek
8. Left turn
9. Right turn

# Cedar Bluff Trail 👢👢👢👢

**Distance Round-Trip:** 1 mile

**Estimated Hiking Time:** .75 hour

*Hike next to a spring-fed river, past a moist rock garden, and up onto cliff overlooks, where congregations of blooming black-eyed Susans, goldenrod, and asters stand all around you and a rugged and forested world opens in front of you.*

**Caution:** Stay on the trail to avoid stinging nettles and poison ivy in the creek bottom.

**Trail Directions:** Park in the small lot for the trailhead, which is at the end of the paved road, north of the picnic areas. Begin the trail just to the left of the locked gate at the lot's north end **[1]**, and hike on a wide, mowed path through the dense vegetation of the Little Piney Creek floodplain. The trail is shaded by numerous sweet gum trees, whose brilliant yellow and red star-shaped leaves in the fall compete with maples in their beauty. The ruffly leaves at the top of the tallest sycamores find breeze, even on balmy days.

At .07 mi. **[2]** you'll hike next to Little Piney Creek and feel the cool air from its spring-fed waters. Lane Spring contributes its 11-million-gallon-per-day output into the creek just a few yards upstream from here. Notice that the streambed is composed of different substrates—sometimes rock, sometimes gravel, and sometimes sand—providing a variety of habitats for riverine plants and shrubs. As the trail follows the creek, numerous spurs lead to the water's edge, providing opportunities to watch for mink, raccoons, herons, kingfishers, and other wildlife using the stream. Breezes reveal the silvery-white undersides of the leaves of the silver maple, the fastest growing of all maples.

Go straight at the intersection at .35 mi. **[3]**. After crossing a small spring emerging from a rocky ravine, the trail swings to the right, going uphill. At .44 mi. **[4]** is a natural rock garden, where blooming hydrangea adorns the top of some of the craggy boulders, and maidenhair ferns arise from moist crevices. As you climb, the soil becomes thinner, drier, and rockier, and river-bottom species like boxelder and silver maple are replaced by white oak, post oak, and cedar. The trail soon becomes a matrix of roots and rocks.

At .46 mi. **[5]** a glade remnant welcomes you to the top of the bluff. Among the silvery blue prairie

grasses are goat's rue and the surprisingly large leaves of prairie dock. As you hike along the blufftop, several overlooks open on your right, the best of which is at .48 mi. **[6]**. From sandstone ledges, with chinkapin oaks and ancient cedars all around, a tremendous vista of the Little Piney Creek Valley opens before you, in a 180-degree sweep. Look for rattlesnake master and other glade plants near the trail as you continue.

At .61 mi. **[7]** you begin some zigzags down the hill. After crossing a seep (where groundwater flows over bedrock, beneath a thin layer of soil) at .73 mi. **[8]** you'll find an abundance of Christmas ferns, gracefully arching their fronds over the side of the trail. Look in these moist areas for persimmon trees and blue lobelia, a tall wildflower whose blossoms have a two-parted upper lip and three-parted lower lip. Near the bottom of the hill, the ravine on your right becomes a slough, which may hold standing water (watch out for mosquitoes). After crossing a small, wooden bridge, you'll find the pavement of the picnic area at .98 mi. **[9]**, where you turn right to finish your bluff hike.

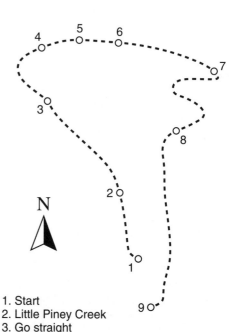

N

1. Start
2. Little Piney Creek
3. Go straight
4. Rock garden
5. Glade remnant
6. Blufftop overlook
7. Descent
8. Small seep
9. Right turn

# 40. Mill Creek

- Hike through a hidden, C-shaped natural tunnel that looks like a cave from each end.

- Discover a wide, shallow spring emerging from the base of a dolomite bluff and riffling into a rocky creek.

- In the middle of a field, find the deep, round, emerald blue eye of Wilkins Spring.

- Stroll on high, breezy ridgetops with sand underfoot and pines overhead.

## Area Information

The Mark Twain National Forest, managed by the U.S. Forest Service, includes 1.5 million acres in southern and central Missouri in a diversity of natural communities and habitats. The forest is managed for multiple uses, including recreation, wilderness, timber, watershed, minerals, and fish and wildlife habitats. Fourteen floatable streams—most of them spring fed, gravel bottomed, and amazingly clear—provide infinite possibilities for floating, fishing, swimming, and boating. Sixteen lakes, ranging in size from 3 to 440 acres, add recreational opportunities. Many of the national forest's campgrounds are located near lakes or streams.

The national forest is divided into seven districts within the state, which are visible on many highway maps as green-shaded blocks. The Houston/Rolla forest district, which is just south of Interstate 44 between Rolla and Fort Leonard Wood, includes nearly 200,000 acres and six recreation sites. Mill Creek, within this district, includes a picnic area and the adjacent Kaintuck Hollow, which features a multiuse trail.

Following explorers like Daniel Boone, many pioneers from the Kentucky and Tennessee region settled in the Ozark hill country. Surely the Mill Creek and Little Piney Creek Valleys reminded some of these early Missourians of their Kentucky homeland. It is believed that "Kaintuck" is fashioned from the Ozark dialectical trend of dropping a syllable here and there to produce a local variation of "Kentucky." The Kaintuck Trail includes multiple loops, which allow options for shorter or longer hikes, and features a 3-million-gallon-per-day round spring, a 175-foot-long natural tunnel hidden in the forest, and a good serving of the area's beauty and solitude.

**Directions:** From Rolla, take I-44 west 7.2 miles to Highway T. Turn left and follow Highway T through Newburg. Turn left on First Street and turn right on Water Street. After crossing the railroad tracks and Little Piney Creek, turn right onto Highway P and travel 3 miles to County Road 7550, where you turn left. Travel 2 miles to the Mill Creek picnic area.

**Hours Open:** The site is open year-round.

**Facilities:** The Mill Creek area offers picnic tables, pit toilets, and an artesian well for drinking water. Fishing and wading are available in Mill Creek. Bikes, horses, and backpack camping are allowed on the Kaintuck Trail. Parking lots are not developed, but horse trailers may be parked in a field .8 mile down the gravel road from the Mill Creek bridge. Picnic tables, primitive campsites, and a pit toilet are available at Wilkins Spring.

**Permits and Rules:** Fishing in Mill Creek is regulated by wild-trout management restrictions, which are posted. No motor vehicles are permitted on the Kaintuck Trail, but bikes and horses are allowed. Backpack camping is allowed at several campsites along the trail.

**Further Information:** District Ranger, U.S. Forest Service, Houston/Rolla District, 108 South Sam Houston Boulevard, Houston, MO 65483; 417-967-4194.

## Other Areas of Interest

**Meramec Spring Park** is in Saint James, just east of Rolla on I-44. The park features trout fishing in a stocked stream and includes a campground (two weeks' notice required), Meramec Spring, trout-rearing ponds, and two museums. Trout fishing season is from March 1 through October 31. Residents and nonresidents can buy daily fishing licenses. For more information call 573-265-7387.

**Painted Rock Conservation Area** consists of 1,490 wooded acres along the Osage River and includes Osage Bluff Scenic Trail. This trail features remnants of a Native American burial cairn, an ancient cedar more than 600 years old, and blufftop overlooks of the Osage River. The area is six miles west of Westphalia on Highway 133 and is managed by the Missouri Department of Conservation. For more information call 573-368-2225.

# Kaintuck Trail—Northern Loops 👢👢👢👢

**Distance Round-Trip:** 9 miles

**Estimated Hiking Time:** 4.75 hours

*Around the old springhouse is a medley of aquatic plants, grasses, and wildflowers, attended by swallowtails, pearl crescents, and hummingbird moths.*

**Caution:** Bring a flashlight if you want to explore in the natural tunnel. Bring a compass and topo map if you choose to extend this hike or explore off the trail. Hunting is allowed in national forests, so wear orange clothing during spring turkey season and throughout the fall. Creek crossings may be difficult or impossible after rainy periods.

**Trail Directions:** From the Mill Creek picnic area, take the first gravel road to the left, just past the picnic area. Cross the Mill Creek bridge and go .4 mile on the gravel road. Park on the side of the road or in the small pull-off on the right for the trailhead.

Begin at the trailhead **[1]** and descend into a creek bottom, where weeds and grass may encroach the trail by late summer. When you reach the gravel-bottomed creek at .13 mi. **[2]**, a tributary to Mill Creek, notice the spring at the base of the dolomite bluff just across the stream. The spring emerges from two wide outlets, riffles through a big patch of watercress (a spring indicator), and flows into the creek. Look for pickerel frogs and southern leopard frogs—both medium-sized spotted frogs that are powerful jumpers. Cross the stream here. Ignore the spur on your right to the campground at .21 mi. **[3]** and follow the trail as it bends to the left.

Ascend a steep hill, with loose rocks on the trail, and you'll arrive on a ridgetop, where breezes pass between the trunks of oaks, hickories, and shortleaf pine. You'll find sparkling sandstone here and a buildup of sand on the trail. Where pine needles have accumulated over the sand, your feet will feel some cushioned relief from the otherwise rocky terrain. Go straight at the spur on your left at 1.47 mi. **[4]** and also at the intersection at 1.62 mi. **[5]**.

Go straight at the intersection at 2.61 mi. **[6]** and turn right at 2.71 mi. **[7]**. Approach the old farm pond at 2.94 mi. **[8]** quietly to watch for deer or other wildlife. After passing a glade remnant, complete with a variety of colorful wildflowers, you'll reach a picnic and primitive camping area. Hike through the picnic area, turn left at the spring pond, and you'll find the round, blue green eye of Wilkins Spring at 3.87 mi. **[9]**. Return to the picnic area and resume the trail on your right, beneath a black locust tree with long, curly seed pods. Turn left at 4.01 mi. **[10]**, where the trail splits from an old road. After winding through an old field, you'll pass another farm pond at 4.18 mi. **[11]**. Hike on a narrow ridge, covered with pines, and turn left at 5.06 mi. **[12]**. Turn right at **[7]** and at **[6]**. This section is a rocky and sandy hike downhill.

At 5.88 mi. **[13]** you are standing on top of the Kaintuck Natural Tunnel! Take the small spur to your left. You can enter the cavelike entrance, hike through the C-shaped tunnel, and emerge at a small campsite at the other entrance. If you don't want to go through the tunnel, return to **[13]** and turn right. Keep bearing right until you arrive at the small campsite near the other tunnel entrance. From the campsite, hike away from the tunnel and ignore the spur on your left. At 6.38 mi. **[14]**, just after crossing two rocky streams, turn left at a small parking area. Turn left on the gravel road at 6.87 mi. **[15]**. Cross the creek and turn left again, just on the other side, at 6.92 mi. **[16]**. While hiking up a steep and rocky hill, look behind you for clear views of the steep, wooded ridge on the other side of Kaintuck Hollow. After hiking through a sandy, old hay field with a small pond, turn right at **[5]** to finish your hike.

## Mill Creek

LEGEND

— Road

······· Trail

⛺ Picnic Area

🏠 Natural Bridge

〰 Wilkins Spring

N

Mill Creek Bridge

7550

Kaintuck Trail

Mill Creek

1. Start
2. Spring and creek crossing
3. Left turn
4. Go straight
5. Go straight
6. Go straight
7. Right turn
8. Old farm pond
9. Wilkins Spring
10. Left turn
11. Old farm pond
12. Left turn
13. Kaintuck Natural Tunnel
14. Left turn
15. Left turn
16. Left turn

# 41. Stone Mill Spring Recreation Area

- Discover an old-growth forest, flower-filled glades, an ancient cedar tree clinging to a cliff, and remarkable vistas on top of a bluff overlooking the Big Piney River Valley.
- See Stone Mill Spring emerging from the base of a bluff and pouring 18 million gallons of water per day over underwater patches of vibrant green watercress.
- Find a historic petroglyph on the blufftop, made by a landowner in 1921.

## Area Information

The Big Piney River, which gets its name from numerous pine-clad ridges and rocky bluffs along its route, begins near Cabool and flows north through Fort Leonard Wood U.S. Army base before joining the Gasconade River. Native Americans lived along the Big Piney and, no doubt, took advantage of its clear and productive waters. The high quality of its water, its gravelly and sandy streambed, and its scenic beauty make the Big Piney ideal for nature watching, fishing, and camping adventures. Numerous good-sized springs make it floatable all year long.

Fort Leonard Wood, a 63,000-acre installation of the U.S. Army located in a richly forested area southwest of Rolla, offers many outdoor recreation opportunities to the public. Fishing is available on several small lakes on the base, as well as on Big Piney River and Roubidoux Creek. Canoe accesses are also maintained on these streams. Stone Mill Spring is periodically stocked with trout from spring through summer. Visitors can camp for free at Big Piney Camping Area, near the East Gate, and numerous sections of the forests are intermittently open for hunting.

Stone Mill Spring Recreation Area is located on Fort Wood and is part of the Big Piney River Recreational and Interpretive Corridor, which is managed by the Natural Resources Branch of the Public Works Department of the base. The corridor features recreational, natural, and cultural resources along several bends of the Big Piney River. All its facilities are open to the public and are within a short drive, canoe trip, or hike.

**Directions:** From exit 161A (St. Robert) off I-44, take Missouri Avenue south into Fort Leonard Wood 4.2 miles to 1st Street, where you turn left. Travel 3.8 miles on 1st Street to a sign for Happy Hollow Picnic Ground, where you turn right. Go 3.4 miles and turn left to cross a narrow bridge over the Big Piney River. Go 1.7 miles (you'll pass a golf course on your left) and turn right at a sign for Stone Mill Spring. Go .7 mile and park in the lot for the spring and trail.

**Hours Open:** Stone Mill Spring Recreation Area is normally open during daylight hours, year-round.

**Facilities:** Stone Mill Spring offers a picnic area with grills, toilet, and fishing in the spring branch and on the Big Piney River.

**Permits and Rules:** Although many resources on the military base are open to the public, training missions often involve live ammunition, and most areas are closed to public entry. Visitors wishing to hunt or fish at the base must first obtain a post sportsman's permit from the Outdoor Recreation Center and must check daily listings for section closings. A post trout stamp is required for fishing in Stone Mill Spring. Bikes and horses are prohibited on the trails.

**Further Information:** Natural Resources Branch, Environment, Energy, and Natural Resources Division, Department of Public Works, Building 2112, Fort Leonard Wood, MO 65473; 573-596-0871. For information on hunting and fishing permits call the Outdoor Recreation Center at 573-596-4223.

## Area Trails

**Miller Cave Trail** 🥾🥾🥾🥾—.2 mile—Miller Cave is one of the largest caves on Fort Wood and offers catacomb-like passages in its entrance and a tremendous view of the Big Piney River valley. To reach the cave, turn southeast (along the river) from the bridge near the golf course and go 1.2 miles to Road TA256, where you turn left. Go 1.4 miles and turn right, just before reaching Training Area #70. Go 1 mile and park on the side of the road. The trail begins on your left.

**Sandstone Spring Trail** 🥾🥾—.04 mile—This short trail begins across the road from the bridge near the golf course and leads to a picturesque spring emerging from the base of a bluff.

# Stone Mill Spring Trail

👢👢👢👢

**Distance Round-Trip:** 1.9 miles

**Estimated Hiking Time:** 1.25 hours

*I scampered up the bluff, counted the wildflowers on the glades, and oohed and aahed at the overlooks, but my favorite was the ancient cedar—growing out of a rock, a twisted veteran and survivor of ice, wind storms, lightning, and untold generations of humans.*

**Caution:** Be careful near bluff edges, especially at the cliff edge near the ancient cedar.

**Trail Directions:** Park in the lot for Stone Mill Spring and find the trailhead marked with a sign at the southeast corner of the lot **[1]**. The first part of the trail is more vertical than horizontal, and you'll quickly gain elevation over the Big Piney River. Climbing a trail over dark gray dolomite boulders and cedar tree roots, you'll find the first of a series of glades at .06 mi. **[2]**. Look closely on the craggy dolomite rocks and you'll find a different sedimentary rock fused on top. The lighter colored rock is chert, which is very resistant to weathering.

Keep climbing among an understory of flowering dogwood and ironwood. Views of the river valley explode in front of you at a glade overlook at .12 mi. **[3]**. You are parallel with tall, wooded ridges on your left and are about the same height as turkey vultures soaring over the vast valley. Look behind you to find a slope covered with flat, tilted slabs of sandstone.

Hike over the sandstone to continue. You'll see ripple marks, left by ocean water lapping on ancient beaches, that make the rocks look like big wash-boards. You are now beneath a stand of shortleaf pine that escaped loggers' saws on this rugged bluff. At .14 mi. **[4]** turn right at the intersection beneath a tall hickory tree, and you'll enter a mature forest with grand white and black oaks. Hike across a ridgetop, where chert gravel accumulates on the trail. Take a look at the odd, bubblelike burl erupting from the forest floor on your left at .29 mi. **[5]**.

Just after turning left at the intersection at .37 mi. **[6]**, you'll see a series of depressions near the trail at .39 mi. **[7]** that resemble sinkholes. Made by neither caves nor foxes, these foxholes were dug by soldiers in training. A wooden bench at .62 mi. **[8]** marks another overlook of the Big Piney, far below. With the overlook in front of you, turn right and walk 12 steps. Look on your left for a boulder with carvings on top at .63 mi. **[9]**. Beneath the lichens you can still make out "Chas. Ramsey 1921." Keep hiking on your right, toward the end of the bluff, and you'll find a bonsai-shaped ancient cedar at .65 mi. **[10]**. Although the age of this tree is not known, some blufftop cedars in Missouri are over 700 years old. With a good view of the river, this is an excellent spot to watch for ospreys in the spring and fall and bald eagles in the winter. Turn left after returning to the wooden bench.

At the end of another ridge, you'll find another wooden bench and overlook at .82 mi. **[11]**. The trail swings right and takes you down to a moist bottom with pawpaws and Christmas ferns. Turn left at the clearing to find Stone Mill Spring at 1.10 mi. **[12]**. Turn right, in front of the bridge, and you'll pass two big pecan trees on your left. Turn left at 1.27 mi. **[13]** over the bridge and hike along the other side. Go straight when you return to the bridge near the spring at 1.41 mi. **[14]**. You'll hike on a gravel road between the Big Piney River and the bluff you just climbed. Go straight at the gravel loop to finish your blufftop hike.

1. Start
2. Glade
3. Glade overlook
4. Right turn
5. Burl
6. Left turn
7. Foxholes
8. Overlook
9. Ramsey petroglyph
10. Ancient cedar
11. Overlook
12. Stone Mill Spring
13. Left turn
14. Go straight

Stone Mill Spring Recreation Area

# 42. Slabtown River Access

- Climb a bluff over the Big Piney River, with a pine forest, sparkling sandstone boulders, and magnificent views of ridges, valleys, meadows, and the river below.
- Bring your tree book to help you identify both moisture-loving trees like river birch, persimmon, boxelder, and musclewood and dry-habitat trees like post oak, blackjack oak, and woolly buckthorn.
- Entertain yourself endlessly, watching the scenic river and its interactive inhabitants.

## Area Information

The Big Piney River begins just north of the Willow Springs District of the Mark Twain National Forest and flows north, through the Houston/Rolla District and Fort Leonard Wood U.S. Army base before joining the Gasconade River. It is the Gasconade's largest tributary. Numerous good-sized springs give the river a good temperature for swimming all summer long and keep the river floatable all year, except during droughts.

The Big Piney is an excellent fishing stream for smallmouth, goggle-eye, sunfish, and catfish, and its gravelly and sandy streambed makes it ideal for gravel-bar camping. Despite its scenic pine-capped limestone bluffs and overall health and natural beauty, it is often overlooked by river users. Without the hoopla of Missouri's more celebrated rivers, the Big Piney offers floaters a quieter place to be on the river. On weekdays and in fall and winter, canoeists may find that they have the river to themselves.

Slabtown River Access, in the Houston/Rolla District of the Mark Twain National Forest, is managed by the U.S. Forest Service. Just east of the popular Paddy Creek Wilderness, with its 17-mile Big Piney Trail and two recreation areas, Slabtown offers the outdoor enthusiast an access and stopover for combination outings of floating, camping, and hiking.

**Directions:** From Licking, travel 4 miles west on Highway 32. Turn northwest on Highway N for 2.2 miles and west on Highway AF for 5.9 miles. Turn left at the sign for the area.

**Hours Open:** The site is always open.

**Facilities:** Besides the boat ramp on the Big Piney, the area also offers a small campground with picnic tables, grills, a pit toilet, and campsites for tents.

**Permits and Rules:** When building campfires near trailheads or developed areas, use existing fire rings. When camping elsewhere in the national forest, select a site away from the trail and use only dead and downed wood for fires. Make sure the fire is cold and scatter its remains before you leave. The section of the river from Slabtown to Ross Access is designated a special smallmouth bass management area, and regulations are posted at these sites.

**Further Information:** District Ranger, U.S. Forest Service, Houston/Rolla District, 108 South Sam Houston Boulevard, Houston, MO 65483; 417-967-4194. *Missouri Ozark Waterways,* available from the Missouri Department of Conservation (573-751-4115), is a detailed guide to 37 major float streams in the Ozarks. It includes maps and describes features and accesses along the way.

# Slabtown Bluff Trail 👢👢👢👢👢

**Distance Round-Trip:** 1.75 miles

**Estimated Hiking Time:** 1 hour

*I stopped along the trail to watch the river, and found it full of life. A northern water snake lazily glided to shore while a smallmouth bass and a goggle-eye became fish statues, suspended below.*

**Caution:** Vegetation crowds the trail along the river; consider wearing long pants.

**Trail Directions:** Park in the lot for the river access. The trail begins near the boat ramp **[1]** and follows the east bank of the Big Piney River, heading upstream. At the trailhead, you'll cross an intermittent tributary that passes through a grove of river birch trees with papery, peeling bark. At .01 mi. **[2]** turn right at the fork in the trail. As you hike along the river, notice the different types of aquatic plants in the transition zone between the water and land.

At .07 mi. **[3]** a pawpaw grove forms a green awning over the trail, and several stump statues (carved by beaver) line the walkway. Keep an eye on the river, watching and listening for the variety of wildlife it attracts. In the morning or early evening, watch for mink and raccoon, cruising along the banks. Anytime, listen for the rattling "chirrrrr" of kingfishers and the startled (and startling) "bwaaaack!" of great blue herons.

After passing through a patch of horsetail, or scouring rush, at .20 mi. **[4]**, you'll find many mois-ture-loving trees like persimmon and musclewood. Pick your way over the talus (rocks broken off from the bluff above) at .32 mi. **[5]** and watch the sun sparkle on a section of riffles in the river. Gaze a while longer at the river—you two will soon part ways. At .80 mi. **[6],** the river bends right as the trail swings left.

As you climb the hill onto the rocky blufftop, bear right at a couple of places where the trail seems to fork. Large dolomite boulders lie scattered about—some weathered into flat-topped pinnacles. By .91 mi. **[7]** you should arrive at the top, where views across the valley begin to open on your left. Species that thrive in drier environments, like sassafras, post oak, and chinkapin oak, become more abundant, and glade remnants dot the top and sideslopes. Spectacular views across the Big Piney Valley open at 1.02 mi. **[8].** Just past the river, far below, is a grassy meadow, surrounded by lush forest. On the opposite ridge are sheer, white bluffs, where black mineral stains drape down their sides like curtains. Downstream, river-bluff faces are pocketed with dark caves.

As you continue, dolomite gives way to sandstone, and shortleaf pines dominate the ridgetop. In rocky outcrops, sparkly sandstone peeks through blankets of green lichens. More vistas open intermittently on your left through gnarly limbs of big oaks and pines. At 1.40 mi. **[9]** you'll begin your descent. You'll hike beneath more pawpaws and sugar maples downhill, where Christmas ferns grow next to the trail. The sound of the Big Piney will meet you again as you approach the trailhead.

**Slabtown River Access**

LEGEND
— Road
······ Trail
— Boundary
⭐ Trail Head
🏕 Camping
📷 Scenic Overlook

1. Start
2. Right turn
3. Pawpaw grove
4. Horsetail
5. Talus
6. Swing left
7. Blufftop
8. Overlook
9. Descent

# 43.  Paddy Creek Wilderness

- Enjoy the peace and tranquillity of a federally designated wilderness.
- Sit on a rocky ledge at the scenic overlook and look down on an arena of treetops.
- Find a small stream creating a wet-weather waterfall over flat sandstone ledges next to the trail.
- In late summer, nibble on huckleberries found on sandy and piney ridgetops.
- Hike alongside crystal-clear and boulder-strewn Paddy Creek, where longear sunfish, smallmouth bass, and chubs hover in its aquarium-like pools.

## Area Information

Paddy Creek Wilderness is within the Houston/Rolla District of the Mark Twain National Forest and became a federally designated wilderness when President Reagan signed Public Law 409 on January 3, 1983. The 7,020-acre area is named after Sylvester Paddy, who began the first logging of the area in the early 1800s, floating timber downriver to St. Louis to help supply a growing need for construction lumber. The area was homesteaded and grazed as open range until the 1930s.

The wilderness is characterized by steep ridges with sandstone and dolomite outcrops, and oak and hickory forests with interspersed shortleaf pine. Big Paddy and Little Paddy Creeks flow through the area and join the Big Piney River just outside the northeast wilderness boundary. A feature of the area is the Big Piney Trail, a 17-mile hiking and horseback trail that explores a good variety of Ozark terrain and connects two Forest Service recreation areas and a trail camp, located just outside the wilderness boundary.

Roby Lake Recreation Area, at the southwest corner, provides a small lake for fishing and is one of three trailheads for the Big Piney Trail. Big Piney Trail Camp, at the northeast corner, is designed primarily as a campground for equestrians. Paddy Creek Recreation Area, just south of the trail camp, is the most developed area near the wilderness and offers a picnic area and campground with tables and fire rings. At all trailheads, visitors to the wilderness are encouraged to practice no-trace, minimum-impact camping and trail use to protect the solitude and natural beauty.

**Directions:** To reach **Roby Lake Recreation Area**, take Highway 17 north from Roby for 1 mile. Turn southeast at the sign for the area on Forest Road 274 and go .9 mile to the parking lot for Roby Lake. **Big Piney Trail Camp** is 2 miles north of Roby on Highway 17 and 5.5 miles down County Road 2800. To reach **Paddy Creek Recreation Area**, take Highway 32 west from Licking for 13.4 miles to Paddy Creek Road, where you turn north. Go 6.9 miles and turn right on Campground Drive. The campground loop begins at the end of the picnic area.

**Hours Open:** The wilderness and its three trailheads are always open. Paddy Creek campground is closed December 1 through March 15, but camping is permitted in the picnic area during that time.

**Facilities:** Roby Lake Recreation Area offers a five-acre lake for fishing, drinking water, a toilet, and a picnic area. Big Piney Trail Camp includes picnic tables, fire rings, a toilet, hitching posts, and a stockwater pond. Paddy Creek Recreation Area provides a picnic area with grills, a toilet, and 23 camping units with tables and fire rings.

**Permits and Rules:** Horses are permitted on the Big Piney Trail but are not allowed in Paddy Creek campground. Bicycles and motorized vehicles are not allowed in the wilderness. Shooting is prohibited in all recreation areas. Boat motors on Roby Lake are restricted to trolling motors. Littering and building "structures" such as rock fire rings or lean-tos in the wilderness are prohibited.

**Further Information:** District Ranger, U.S. Forest Service, Houston/Rolla District, 108 South Sam Houston Boulevard, Houston, MO 65483; 417-967-4194.

## Area Trails

**Big Piney Trail** 👢👢👢👢—17 miles—This hiking, backpacking, and equestrian trail traverses the rugged wilderness landscape and crosses Little Paddy and Big Paddy Creeks. With three trailheads and a connecting link in the middle, this trail offers multiple hiking options.

Paddy Creek Wilderness

N

Slabtown River Access and Tent Camp

Slabtown Bluff Trail

Big Piney River

Big Piney Trail Camp

Paddy Creek Campground

Paddy Creek Trail

Big Paddy Creek

Big Piney Trail

Little Paddy Creek

Slabtown Rd.

Big Piney Trail

Big Piney Trailhead

Roby Lake

Roby Lake Recreation Area

LEGEND
— Road
⋯ Trail
▬ Boundary
★ Trail Head
⛺ Camping
📷 Scenic Overlook
🏕 Picnic Area

# Big Piney Trail

**Distance Round-Trip:** 4.5 miles

**Estimated Hiking Time:** 2 hours

*Even the cadence of your feet on the trail can be numbing to the senses. At the overlook, sit quietly on the sandstone ledge with the plunging valley below you. Listen. You'll hear nothing but the whispers of the pine forest and the animals that live there.*

**Caution:** Depending on the season, the first part of the trail may warrant chigger repellent.

**Trail Directions:** Park in the lot for Roby Lake Recreation Area. Walk north on the driveway (back the way you came) until you find an iron gate in the fence on your right. This marks the Big Piney Trailhead. Go through the gate to begin the trail **[1]**.

To reach the wilderness boundary, just to the northeast, hike through a large, open field of Indian grass, which is up to seven feet tall. Near the end of the field, sumac, locust, and cedar take over the field, and several white oak and post oak wolf trees stand as living witnesses to earlier, different times. At the four-way intersection at .15 mi. **[2]** go straight. At .20 mi. **[3]** you'll come across two iron gates in a fence. Go through the smaller one on the right, and you'll soon find the wilderness trail registration box, which marks the wilderness boundary. Please register before continuing.

The trail now immerses you in a gently rolling, open woods dominated by oaks and hickories. Small drainage streams are relatively frequent and shallow. If you are here in late August or September, look for the first signs of fall in the red-tinged leaves of Virginia creeper and poison ivy. Sassafras is another champion of the fall forest wardrobe, dependably turning bright orange, yellow, and red, while oaks and hickories, still green, wait for favorable weather. At the intersection of the north and south loops of the trail at .73 mi. **[4]**, turn right to begin the south loop. As you hike, look for a variety of woodpeckers attracted to this large, mature forest. When you get a woodpecker in view with binoculars, you'll notice they use their tails as props when they scale tree trunks and do their hammering. Woodpecker tails, with stiff, strong feathers, are specially adapted for this purpose.

Just after passing a shallow pond on your left, you'll hike through a young pine grove at .90 mi. **[5]**. Look closely as you pass and you'll see the straight rows of someone's abandoned pine plantation project. At 1.42 mi. **[6]** the trail takes you next to a wet-weather waterfall over sheets of sandstone bedrock. A little farther downstream, the creek has cut through blocks of rock, creating a miniature canyon, lined with bluffs. Cross the creek just upstream from the waterfall. You'll ascend a dry hill with mounds of reindeer lichen, which always seems to grow together with clumps of pin-cushion moss. Reindeer lichen (also incorrectly called reindeer moss) not only resembles the branching antlers of reindeer but also is a staple food of reindeer living in tundra regions.

The valleys on each side of this ridge suddenly come surprisingly close to the trail, and at 2.0 mi. **[7]** you'll find yourself on a narrowing tongue of a ridgetop. From here, the show begins. Undercut layers of sandstone hang off the steep sides, which drop straight down and become lost in the treetops far below. You are surrounded by pines, which sigh in the breeze. Hike among huckleberry bushes on a trail blanketed with pine needles to 2.15 mi. **[8]**, where you'll find a spectacular view. A wide rock ledge makes a perfect overlook deck, where you can enjoy the panorama and listen to the wilderness. Splendid views continue on the trail until 2.25 mi. **[9]**, which makes it a good spot to turn around and enjoy the views again on your way back to the trailhead.

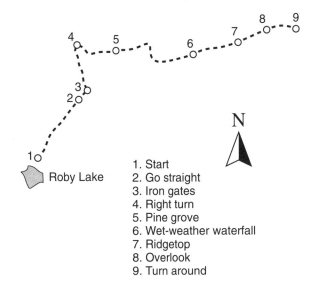

1. Start
2. Go straight
3. Iron gates
4. Right turn
5. Pine grove
6. Wet-weather waterfall
7. Ridgetop
8. Overlook
9. Turn around

# Paddy Creek Trail 👢👢👢👢👢

**Distance Round-Trip:** .85 mile

**Estimated Hiking Time:** .75 hour

*Paddy Creek is a long, stretched-out aquarium. Through its clean, clear water I could see all the vibrant colors of the longear sunfish—bright orange head with iridescent emerald stripes and glowing, red eyes—as beautiful as any angel fish of the coral reef.*

**Caution:** Vegetation crowds the trail along the river; consider wearing long pants. Do not attempt this trail during periods of high water.

**Trail Directions:** Park in the picnic area and walk back to the low-water bridge over Paddy Creek. The trail begins on the east side of the creek, near the bridge **[1]**.

The gray, metal box on your left at .03 mi. **[2]** contains an instrument that monitors the water level of Paddy Creek. Hydrologists from the U.S. Geological Survey use this data for making graphs, models, and for other analysis. As you continue, you'll hike between the creek and some large sandstone boulders that tumbled down from above, almost making it to the streambed. The ridged texture of the boulders is caused by mineral-filled fracture lines that are slightly more resistant to weathering than the rest of the sandstone. Blocky talus (rocks that broke off from bluffs above) continues on the trail at .05 mi. **[3]**, making for challenging hiking. Marginal shield ferns and hydrangea grow on top and between the rocks, creating green, streamside gardens.

Look in the creek for an assortment of Ozark stream fish. While you stand on the bank, sunfish will sometimes rise near the surface, waiting for their chance to slurp terrestrial insects that fall in the water from overhanging bushes. The tan fish with a black vertical bar on their tails are young smallmouth bass, which sometimes follow suckers as they root around on the stream bottom, snapping up uncovered crayfish and aquatic insect larvae.

Hike on top and around boulders, some decorated with delicate ferns and mosses, while others are covered with what looks like green spaghetti, an appearance caused by numerous "walkers" of walking fern. Continue next to the stream until you reach

a large boulder (about the size of a tool shed) that has two flat sides and is tilted on end next to the water (.31 mi.) **[4]**. This chunk of sandstone, before it was cemented by minerals, was sand on the beach. The rippling action of ocean water lapping on the shore created the washboard texture of its flat sides. Remember this rippled boulder; you'll return to it later.

As you begin the spur to the swimming hole, you'll pass a deep hole filled with water on your left at .34 mi. **[5]**, next to a boulder. Whether an old sinkhole or an abandoned creek channel, the hole has been adopted by several frogs. At .43 mi. **[6]** you'll find a gravel beach and a picturesque swimming hole, where the water gradually deepens to a pool at the base of a gray, dolomite bluff. Deep-blue blossoms of lobelia and dayflower surround the beach, and ninebark (a streamside shrub in the rose family) emerges from the gravel. After enjoying a dip, or just the scenery, return to the rippled boulder to continue.

Just upstream from the rippled boulder you'll find a good place to cross the stream. On the other side find the trail and turn right at .59 mi. **[7]**. At a small spring stream at .65 mi. **[8]** is a grove of musclewood (American hornbeam) and persimmon, two trees known for their hard, heavy wood. After crossing another small spring stream, you'll arrive on a gravel road at .77 mi. **[9]**. Turn right here and cross the low-water bridge to return to the picnic area.

1. Start
2. River gauge
3. Blocky talus
4. Rippled boulder
5. Frog pond
6. Swimming hole
7. Right turn
8. Musclewood grove
9. Right turn

# 44.  Lake of the Ozarks State Park

- Visit Missouri's largest state park, explore its 17,203 acres, and discover its stunning array of opportunities for outdoor recreation, education, exercise, and relaxation.

- With a naturalist as a guide and hand-held lanterns to light the way, explore the subterranean beauty of Ozark Caverns.

- Hike the Coakley Hollow Trail, with a boardwalk over a cold, seepy fen and two swinging bridges over spring-fed streams.

## Area Information

Lake of the Ozarks was formed in 1931 as the Union Electric Company of St. Louis dammed the state's third largest river, the Osage, creating a hydroelectric reservoir of 55,342 surface acres and 1,150 miles of shoreline. Two years later, as part of President Roosevelt's New Deal programs, a system of National Recreation Demonstration Areas was developed to convert poor farmland into outdoor recreation areas that could later be transferred to the states. Eighty-five miles of shoreline of the Grand Glaize Creek was identified as a park site, the land was transferred to the federal government, and Lake of the Ozarks Recreation Area was born.

The National Park Service originally managed Lake of the Ozarks. In the 1930s, the Civilian Conservation Corps built six group camps, log cabins, and stone bridges in the park. Most of this work appears on the National Register of Historic Places. The site was turned over to the state in 1946.

Although opportunities for water-based recreation abound at Lake of the Ozarks, the park's natural attractions include a major cave and a variety of hiking trails. In an urbanized hubbub of shopping, lodging, amusements, and entertainment that encompasses the rest of the lake area, the state's largest park is an oasis of natural beauty.

**Directions:** The park's main entrance is at the north end, off Highway 54. From Osage Beach, take Highway 42 east for 3.6 miles. Turn right on Highway 134 and go .5 mile to the park office.

**Hours Open:** The park is open from 7 A.M. to 10 P.M. The park office is open from 8 A.M. to 4:30 P.M. Monday through Friday. The visitor center is open and tours of Ozark Caverns are given from April 1 through October 31; call ahead for hours and tour times, which are variable.

**Facilities:** The park offers swimming beaches with bathhouses, boat ramps, a marina with boat rentals, picnic areas, campground, group camps, camper's store, primitive rental cabins, tours of Ozark Caverns, visitor center, trail center, stables with horses for rent, amphitheater, and an airport. Fishing, swimming, boating, and skiing are available on the lake.

**Permits and Rules:** Bicycles are restricted (besides paved roads) to the Trail of 4 Winds. Horses are restricted to the Trail of 4 Winds and Squaw's Revenge Trail. Backpack camping is allowed on the Woodland Trail, but campfires are prohibited there. Pets must always be leashed. Alcoholic beverages are prohibited on swimming beaches and parking areas.

**Further Information:** Park Superintendent, Lake of the Ozarks State Park, P.O. Box 170, Kaiser, MO 65047; 573-348-2694 (park office) or 573-346-2500 (Ozark Caverns).

## Park Trails

**Woodland Trail** —6 miles—This hiking and backpacking trail features the diverse habitats of Patterson Hollow Wild Area. The trail begins at the trail center, located .5 mile south of the park office.

**Trail of 4 Winds** —6 miles—Open to hikers, bicyclists, and horse riders, this trail features a scenic overlook of a wooded valley and unusual rock formations. The trailhead is on the west side of the main park road, 2 miles from the entrance.

**Fawn's Ridge Trail** —2.5 miles—This trail begins across the road from the picnic area near the stables. The first .5 mile is wheelchair accessible.

**Grand Glaize Trail** —2.5 miles—This trail is in a more remote part of the park and begins just north of the service area between Ozark Caverns and McCubbins Point.

**Aquatic Trail**—This is a unique, self-guiding trail for boaters that interprets 14 natural features along a lake shoreline marked by buoys. Booklets are available at the park office and public beach #1.

# Lake of the Ozarks State Park

To Brumley

To Eldon
To Camdenton

L E G E N D

| | |
|---|---|
| —— Road | 🏠 Trail Center |
| ······ Trail | ✕ Terminal Building |
| ▬▬ Boundary | Store |
| 🏠 Park Office | Beach |
| | Camping |
| | Camper Cabins |
| | Shelter |
| | Picnic Area |
| | Boat Launch |
| | Ozark Caverns |
| | Riding Stables |

N

L.R. 42-18

Lee C. Fine Memorial Airport

42

134

Park

Wild Area

134

Kaiser

McCubbin's Point

Coakley Hollow Trail

Natural Area

A33

Fort Leonard Wood Recreation Area

Camp Rising Sun

54

Camp Red Bud

Camp Pin Oak

Camp Hawthorn

Camp Clover Point

L.R. 54-65

A

Grand Glaize Bridge

Grand Glaize Arm

Lake of the Ozarks

Rocky Top Trail

54

# Rocky Top Trail 👢👢👢

**Distance Round-Trip:** 3 miles

**Estimated Hiking Time:** 1.5 hours

*When I stepped out from beneath the stunted post oaks onto the Rocky Top Glade, I was reminded that glade comes from an Old English word meaning "bright" or "cheerful." Glades have a way of surprising you. As you walk onto them, the temperature goes up, and your spirits will, too.*

**Caution:** Use caution at the edges of the bluff, which is a veritable cliff.

**Trail Directions:** This trail is at Grand Glaize Beach, on the west side of the park. From the park's main entrance, at the north end, take Highway 42 west to return to Osage Beach. From here, take Highway 54 west 4.5 miles, turn left at the sign for Grand Glaize Beach, and follow the signs to the picnic shelter. The trail begins across the road from the picnic shelter.

Begin at the signboard **[1]**. Fill out a registration card at the trailhead before you begin. The trail ascends some craggy dolomite rocks before bringing you to a small glade at .04 mi. **[2]**. Note the thick bluestem grasses, brilliant yellow coneflowers, and the lacy leaves of purple prairie clover . . . but this is only the beginning. Walk through the shade of several gnarly post oaks and you'll emerge onto the trail's namesake—an expansive and impressive glade at .08 mi. **[3]**. Think of the sun scorching the trees right off the top of this ridge, leaving only the thin soil and ridges of dolomite rock. With the trees gone, plants that have adapted to these hot and dry conditions flourish, and Missouri glades are known for their magnificent displays of wildflowers. Step onto the glade and feel the temperature go up. Watch for six-lined racerunners and other lizards zipping in front of you as the trail takes you through this miniature, rocky "desert."

Next, you'll pass through a savanna landscape, a grassland with interspersed trees. Look for rattlesnake master at .48 mi. **[4]**, an erect plant with ball-shaped flower heads and spear-shaped, bluish leaves with bristles along their edges. The plant was once purported to be a treatment for snakebite, and its species name, *yuccifolium*, means "with the leaves of a yucca." At .65 mi. **[5]** turn right, following the sign for

the second loop. After crossing an intermittent stream, turn right again at the intersection at .74 mi. **[6]**. You now enter a dry dolomite forest, with white oak and chinkapin oaks shading hillsides covered with flowering dogwood and dolomite fragments.

At 1.48 mi. a spectacular view of the lake opens before you as you step to the edge of a towering bluff **[7]**. Tiny boats move as if in slow motion, leaving white Vs behind them. Countless fingers of water reach into the shady draws of the forest in all directions. Hike among the scraggly dwarf hackberry trees and nodding gray-head coneflowers of a blufftop glade as the lake views continue all around the bluff edge. After you reenter the forest, you'll hike midslope in a scenic, open woods. On your right, a small cove of the lake tapers to a quiet, secluded point as you hike, affording chances to glimpse fishing herons in the shallows or sunning carp just below the surface.

Turn right when you return to **[6]**. After recrossing the stream, turn right when you return to **[5]**. You'll enter a savanna at 2.55 mi. **[8]**, actually a lower slope of Rocky Top Glade, above you on your left. The lake cove reappears on your right, as leadplant and elephant-ear-like prairie dock grow right down to the shoreline. As the trail swings to the left, at the water's edge, turn left, uphill, on the wide, rocky trail at 2.94 mi. **[9]**, which returns you to the picnic shelter.

N

1. Start
2. Small glade
3. Big glade
4. Rattlesnake master
5. Right turn
6. Right turn
7. Lake overlook
8. Savanna
9. Left turn

# Coakley Hollow Trail 👢👢👢

**Distance Round-Trip:** 1 mile

**Estimated Hiking Time:** .75 hour

*From spring-water streams to arid glades, from lush grasslands to a fen that hides glacial survivor species, this trail would be a winner, even without its two swinging bridges!*

**Caution:** The gate to this part of the park is locked nightly, and closing times vary according to the season. Be sure to check the trailhead or the visitor center for the closing time before you begin the trail.

**Trail Directions:** The Coakley Hollow Trail begins near the Ozark Caverns visitor center, at the south end of the park. From the park's main entrance, at the north end, take Highway 42 west to return to Osage Beach. From here, take Highway 54 west 10.8 miles to Highway A. Turn east on Highway A for 7.1 miles, and turn north at the sign for Ozark Caverns. Follow the signs for the caverns and find the visitor center 1.7 miles north of Highway A. Park at the visitor center; the trailhead is just a few yards from the parking lot.

Before or after your hike, stop in the visitor center, which is also the starting point for naturalist-led tours of Ozark Caverns. Coakley Hollow is an interpretive trail, and self-guiding trail booklets are available from the trailhead or the visitor center. Numbered stations on the trail do not correspond to numbered features in this book. Begin at the sign for the trail **[1]**. You'll feel the sway of the swinging bridge as you hear the trickle of the remarkably clear and picturesque stream below. Later, you can find the origin of this stream at Mill Spring, which is a short and pleasant hike off the park road, .15 mile from the visitor center. Like the temperature of the air inside Ozark Caverns, the temperature of this water, when it emerges from the tiny cave opening at Mill Spring, is a nearly constant 55 degrees, year-round.

Across the suspension bridge, the trail takes you on a sideslope where lichen-covered chert boulders lie scattered between trunks of various types of oaks and hickories. Native Americans often used chert, or flint, to make arrowheads and tools because of its hardness and ability to form fine, sharp edges. Look underneath the boulders near the trail at .27 mi. **[2]** and you'll discover the dens of groundhogs, skunks, or foxes. Christmas ferns and ebony spleenwort, two ferns that stay green all year long, soon line both sides of the trail.

Turn right on the wide, moss-covered path at .52 mi. **[3]** and turn left at .54 mi. **[4]**, following yellow arrows. The steps at .56 mi. go over a seep **[5]**, a wet area caused by water flowing over sheets of bedrock just under the soil's surface. After crossing a bridge under some pawpaw trees, you'll reach a second swinging bridge over a clear stream at .59 mi. **[6]**. Across the stream, you'll enter a savanna (.60 mi.) **[7]**. Native grasses and wildflowers thrive here because of large openings in the forest canopy and the absence of an understory. In the middle of this savanna is a glade (.64 mi.) **[8]**, a rocky, dry opening only suitable for plants and animals specially adapted to this sun-drenched microenvironment.

Turn left at .77 mi. **[9]** at the spur to the remnants of a dam. This pile of rock and earth is all that remains of a dam that channeled the stream to power a grist mill, built here in the 1870s by an Irish settler named Coakley. Turn left after returning to the main trail. At .92 mi. is a boardwalk over Coakley Hollow Fen **[10]**. An unusual type of wetland, fens are boglike areas kept saturated by groundwater that constantly seeps to the surface. To recognize and preserve the special natural community of plants that have adapted to these cool, saturated soils, this four-acre area was designated a state natural area in 1982. The music of a spring-fed stream accompanies you as the visitor center comes into view ahead.

1. Start
2. Boulder shelters
3. Right turn
4. Left turn
5. Seep
6. Swinging bridge
7. Savanna
8. Glade
9. Spur to dam
10. Coakley Hollow Fen

# 45.  Arrow Rock State Historic Site

- Visit Missouri's first state historic site—a little town that was named for a river bluff and became an antebellum powerhouse.

- Bring a tree identification book; you'll see a mixed bag of trees on the Pierre A Fleche Trail.

- Walk around in a living-history river town where many early 19th-century buildings retain their original appearance and most of the town is a national historic landmark.

- Take a tour of the George Caleb Bingham Home, the Old Tavern, and the Courthouse, built in the 1820s. The one-room stone jail, built in 1873, has never held a prisoner!

## Area Information

Arrow Rock's name first appeared in 1732 in French records as *pierre a fleche*, which referred to a nearby bluff along the river that was a landmark to Indians and early explorers. The Osage Trace, an important Indian trail, crossed the Missouri River here. Situated at the point where the main east-west route over land intersected the Missouri River, Arrow Rock became an early crossroads of all sorts.

Before the first settlers arrived, Arrow Rock was associated with the fur trade, Boone's Lick Trail, the Sante Fe Trail, and the Lewis and Clark Trail. In 1808, William Clark wrote in his journal that Arrow Rock was "a handsome Spot for a Town." Settlers from the east prompted a river ferry and increased growth for the town, and its citizens numbered over a thousand by the mid-1800s. Many prominent people became associated with Arrow Rock and played significant roles in the state's history. The town became the state's political power center and remained so until the Civil War.

Today, Arrow Rock is Missouri's grandparent, resting near the center of the state and waiting for people to visit. Many of the buildings look as if they haven't changed since they were built. Walking tours visit buildings throughout the town, most of which is a national historic landmark. The Old Tavern, built in 1834, still offers home-cooked meals to travelers.

**Directions:** Just west of Boonville, on I-70, take exit 98. Turn north on Highway 41 for 13 miles and turn right at the sign for the site.

**Hours Open:** The visitor center is open from 10 A.M. to 4 P.M. Monday through Saturday and from noon to 5 P.M. on Sunday. The campground and lake area close at 10 P.M.

**Facilities:** A visitor center with exhibits, a campground, and picnic areas are available on the site. Fishing and boating (carry-on only) are available at the lake near the campground. Guided tours of the historic buildings are available for a fee. The community offers historic tours, bed-and-breakfasts, antique shops, restaurants, and a summer theater.

**Permits and Rules:** Bikes or horses are not allowed on the trail. Swimming is not allowed on the lake. Pets must always be leashed.

**Further Information:** Site Administrator, Arrow Rock State Historic Site, Highway 41 North, Arrow Rock, MO 65320; 660-837-3330 (visitor center); 660-837-3231 (tours); 660-837-3311 (theater).

## Other Areas of Interest

**Boone's Lick State Historic Site** is the site of the salt-manufacturing business once owned and operated by Daniel Boone's sons, Daniel and Nathan Boone. Recovering salt from natural salt springs, or "licks," the Boones began one of the earliest centers of industry in central Missouri in 1805. A trail leads to the salt springs. The site is 12 miles northwest of Boonville, off Highway 87, on Highway 187. For more information call Arrow Rock State Historic Site.

# Pierre A Fleche Trail 👢👢👢

**Distance Round-Trip:** 1.5 miles

**Estimated Hiking Time:** .75 hour

*Who is this Pierre A. Fleche, anyway?*

**Caution:** Be careful when crossing the paved park roads.

**Trail Directions:** Park in the lot for the visitor center; the trailhead is at the edge of the lot. Begin at the sign for the trail **[1]** and follow the green arrows on this trail. The trail begins in a mixed forest, among Osage orange, hackberry, shingle oak, and cedar. After crossing a couple of intermittent streams, you'll cross a paved road at .12 mi. **[2].**

The trail soon intersects another paved road. WPA workers constructed the European-style, triple-arched, stone bridge in front of you around 1936. Cross this bridge at .20 mi. **[3]** and turn left at the trail sign, just on the other side. Notice the abundant jewelweed, with cornucopia-shaped orange blossoms, in the spring branch.

When you approach a small, wooden bridge on your left, take the spur on your right at .30 mi. **[4].** When you enter the open field of the picnic area, turn left on the pavement and stop at the overlook at .37

mi. **[5].** The ceaseless flow of muddy water below you is the Missouri River, the dominant geographic feature of the region. Descend the hill to your right and reenter the forest at the trail sign. You'll cross a wooden bridge. After passing through a glade remnant, turn left on the wide, mowed path at .54 mi. **[6].** Soon you'll pass the tip of the campground loop. When you reenter the woods, you'll spy a few more trees; here are slippery elm, honey locust, and persimmon.

As the trail begins some switchbacks, notice the unusual contours of the water-sculpted bedrock in the stream crossing at .72 mi. **[7].** The deep Vs of the terrain show the effects of draining water, as well. Go straight at the connecting link on your right at 1.04 mi. **[8].** Take the spur on your left at 1.11 mi. **[9]** to sneak behind some willows and scan the lake for bulging eyes of bullfrogs, pointed snouts of aquatic turtles, and bobbing coots.

Turn left after returning to the main trail and cross a paved road at 1.20 mi. **[10].** As you cross a wooden bridge at 1.28 mi. **[11]** notice the stone slabs on each side of the stream bank—remnants of a *much* older bridge. At 1.4 mi. **[12]** cross a small stream and turn right to find Big Spring, a watering stop for early travelers on the Sante Fe Trail. Turn left on the paved road here to return to **[2],** where you turn left to return to the trailhead.

Arrow Rock
State Historic Site

To Marshall
15 Miles

To Boonville
17 Miles

N

Big
Spring

Pond

Saline County
Cooper County

1. Start
2. Road crossing
3. Stone bridge
4. Right turn
5. Missouri River overlook
6. Left turn
7. Bedrock stream
8. Go straight
9. Spur to lake
10. Road crossing
11. Old bridge
12. Big Spring

LEGEND

— Road
····· Trail
▬ Boundary
–·– County Boundary
🏠 Visitor Center
⛬ Picnic Area

🔺 Camping
🔺 Youth Camp Area
🚽 Trailer Disposal Station
⛺ Shelter
🚻 Restrooms
🚻 Latrine
🚿 Bath House
📷 Scenic Overlook
🌲 Woodlot
⭐ Godsey's Diggings
🏛 Old Courthouse
🏠 Dr. Hall House
🏠 Bingham House
🏠 Old Tavern
🏠 Old Seminary
🏠 Old Jail

# 46.  Van Meter State Park

- Hike on a trail with a 100-year-old cemetery at one end, a 1,300-year-old cemetery at the other, and mysterious, prehistoric earthworks in between.

- Learn about the Missouri Indians, who built their principal village on the steep, loess ridgetops that are now within and near the park, and who gave the state and the river its name.

- View the intriguing and unexplained parallel rows of ditches and embankments at the Old Fort, believed to have been constructed by the Oneota Indians between 300 and 600 years ago.

- Walk around the Burial Mounds—three large, earthen mounds constructed as burial monuments to the dead.

## Area Information

The Missouri Indians were probably living for 300 to 400 years on the loess hills and ridges above the Missouri River before they were noted by the first Europeans who ventured into what is now Missouri. The first historical mention came in 1673, when two Frenchmen, Father Jacques Marquette and Louis Jolliet, drew a map of their village's location and recorded their name as *Oumessourit*, which, loosely translated, means "people of the big canoes." *Oumessourit* evolved into *Missouri*, and so it was that a group of people, a major river, and a state were named.

In the early 1700s, as many as five thousand Missouri Indians may have lived on the ridges in and near the park. The Missouri were described as a friendly and proud people, who farmed, fished, hunted, and gathered their food from the rich floodplain and uplands alike. But the Missouri were not the first people to live here. Although the Old Fort has been revealed to be associated with the Oneota (prehistoric Missouri Indians), the Burial Mounds predate these people, and archaeological research here indicates that Indians may have inhabited this area as early as 10,000 B.C.

When the Missouri lived here the landscape looked very different from how it does now. Prairies or savannas capped many of the ridges, which commanded distant views of the great river valley. Natural marshes, wet prairies, and other rich wetlands covered the vast floodplain.

Today, however, the park offers a peaceful, natural landscape in an urbanizing world. It preserves unusually steep and serrated ridges of loess, as well as rich forests of red oak, sugar maple, and black walnut. Although the park contains a beautiful lake and shady, spacious picnic areas, the most special parts of the park are the sacred ones. Hike up to one of them and imagine the lives of the early Missourians.

**Directions:** From Marshall, take Highway 41 north for 7.3 miles. Turn west on Highway 122 for 4.7 miles to the visitor center, on the right.

**Hours Open:** The park is open year-round from 8 A.M. to 10 P.M. The visitor center is open from 10 A.M. to 4 P.M. Monday through Saturday and from 10 A.M. to 5 P.M. on Sunday. From November through March the visitor center is closed on Tuesday and Wednesday.

**Facilities:** The park offers a visitor center with exhibits and an audiovisual room, a campground, picnic areas, and an amphitheater. Fishing and boating (carry-on only) are available on Lake Wooldridge.

**Permits and Rules:** Strict federal and state laws prohibit the disturbance of archeological sites and artifacts. Digging, or otherwise disturbing the area, is prohibited. Boat motors on Lake Wooldridge are restricted to trolling motors. Swimming is not allowed. Horses or bikes are not allowed on the trails. Do not pick the wildflowers. Pets must always be leashed.

**Further Information:** Park Superintendent, Van Meter State Park, Route 1, Box 47, Miami, MO 65344; 660-886-7537.

## Park Trails

**Lake View Trail** 👢👢—.75 mile—This trail follows the west shoreline of Lake Wooldridge and offers great opportunities to see a variety of wildlife. The trail shares a trailhead with the Loess Hills Trail.

# Van Meter
# State Park

N

Lake
Wooldridge

Lake
View
Trail

Loess
Hills
Trail

Devil's Backbone

Natural
Area

Old Fort
Trail

Missouri
Indian
Village

AD

LEGEND

| | |
|---|---|
| —— | Major Road |
| —·— | Minor Road |
| ···· | Trail |
| ▬▬ | Boundary |
| 🏠 | Visitor Center |
| 🏠 | Research Center |
| ⛺ | Camping |
| ◩ | Shelter |
| ⛰ | Mounds |
| 🚹 | Restrooms |
| P🚹 | Pit Latrine |
| ▣ | Van Meter Cemetery |
| ▦ | Old Fort |

122

# Old Fort Trail 👢👢👢

**Distance Round-Trip:** 2 miles

**Estimated Hiking Time:** 1.75 hours

*After stepping into one of the 3,000-foot-long ditches dug by the early Missouri Indians, I imagined myself helping dig it, sweating, and doing my share with my bison scapula shovel. Then, I tried to imagine why.*

**Caution:** Digging or otherwise disturbing archaeological sites is prohibited.

**Trail Directions:** If possible, stop in the visitor center before your hike; an understanding of the area's history will help you appreciate the prehistoric archaeological sites you will see on this trail. From the visitor center, enter the park and turn right at the picnic shelter, toward Lake Wooldridge. Park in the lot for the Burial Mounds, located 1.3 miles from the visitor center.

Before you begin, notice the earthen mounds to the northeast of the parking lot. The Indians of the Late Woodland period built these as burial monuments to honor individuals with high status. The mounds were probably constructed between 1,100 and 1,600 years ago by people who lived on the loess ridges all around you.

Begin the trail at the wooden gate **[1]**. Look around the gate for wahoo, a shrub with four-lobed seed pods that turn deep red in the fall. Native Americans found many uses for this shrub, including medicine for sores, eye lotion, and wood for arrows. You are now entering Van Meter Forest Natural Area, a 114-acre part of the park designated for its rugged ridges of loess (known as the Pinnacles) and a rich, diverse forest, with remnants of old-growth forest in deep ravines. Continue on a wide roadbed. The tall, spiked wildflower here with star-shaped, blue flowers is tall bellflower, a plant that prefers borders of woods and stream bottoms.

Soon, an expansive field opens before you on this ridgetop. Widely spaced trees and a manicured lawn may make you think you've entered a picnic area, but there are no tables. You have entered the Old Fort (.12 mi.) **[2]**, an archaeological earthwork site with encircling rows of parallel ditches and embankments. Originally thought to be built around 2,000 years ago

by Hopewell people, excavations have revealed that it was built by the Missouri Indians, who lived on these ridgetops as recently as 300 to 600 years ago. Despite being known to scientists as early as 1872, reasons for this massive and complex structure are still unknown. Walk around the Old Fort to appreciate its scale, slowly making your way to its opposite end.

At the south end of the fort take the trail to the far left of the bench you'll find at .36 mi. **[3]**. This trail takes you down from the top of the Pinnacles and skirts some of its steep sides. Notice the dense and diverse understory that thrives in this rich soil. Thick grapevines climb from pawpaw groves to limbs of immense red oak, walnut, and hickory trees. Various wild nuts lie scattered on the trail as if someone spilled a bag of big marbles.

At the bottom of the hill, cross the small, wooden bridge at .80 mi. **[4]** that leads into the picnic area. Before you reach the paved road, turn left and cross the road you drove on to reach the Burial Mounds (.83 mi.) **[5]**. Look for a small asphalt sidewalk leading up a hill into the forest at .85 mi. **[6]** and take this trail. After climbing a steep loess hill, you'll reach the Van Meter family cemetery at the top at 1.06 mi. **[7]**. The Van Meters lived here for a century before donating this land to the state for the park. Return to **[5]**, where you can take the road up the hill to the trailhead, or you can return to **[4]** to retrace your steps through the Old Fort.

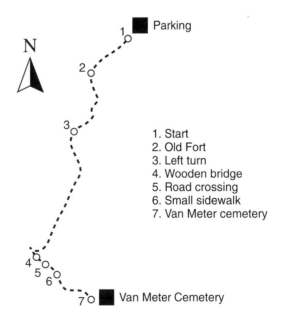

1. Start
2. Old Fort
3. Left turn
4. Wooden bridge
5. Road crossing
6. Small sidewalk
7. Van Meter cemetery

# Loess Hills Trail 🥾🥾🥾

**Distance Round-Trip:** 2 miles

**Estimated Hiking Time:** 1 hour

*You'll see some grapevines as big around as trees, looming through the dark woods and hanging from the limbs of giant red oaks. If you listen carefully, you can hear the faint rustle of the wind in the upper canopy. Down here, there's little breeze to be had.*

**Caution:** Unless you are here in winter, use some repellent for mosquitoes and biting flies.

**Trail Directions:** Park at the end of the main park road, at Wooldridge Lake, located two miles north of the visitor center. This trail shares a trailhead with the Lake View Trail. Begin at the sign for the trail **[1]**, in the corner of the parking lot, and you'll plunge into a junglelike forest. The windblown glacial dust (loess) that covers much of this area is fertile soil that produces immense trees and a dense understory.

At .09 mi. **[2]** you'll cross a small, wooden bridge. Go straight at .16 mi. **[3],** where the Lake View Trail continues on the left. As you cross another bridge, notice the ferns below, with long, gracefully arching fronds. Cat briars and grapevines connect the understory with the overstory, and large pawpaw leaves virtually eliminate the possibility of a ray of sunshine reaching the forest floor. Notice the puffy, yellow green lanterns of American bladdernut, as the trail swings to the left. At .30 mi. **[4]** is a small boardwalk over a marshy area. Notice the jewelweed below, a water-loving plant that produces orange, cone-shaped flowers. Later in the summer, when many plants get older and tougher, deer feed more heavily on jewelweed, which remains soft and juicy.

Go up some steps and enter a higher, more open forest. Notice the alligator-hide-like bark of the persimmon tree. At .68 mi. **[5]**, as the trail bends left, you'll cross two more small boardwalks over a slough area, which may hold some standing water. You'll climb higher again and emerge into the opening of an old field at .88 mi. **[6]**. Now you'll get to see the sun

and feel the breeze again! Look for the iridescent blue indigo bunting. Listen for the dropping-Ping-Pong-ball song of the field sparrow and the buzz of flying grasshopper wings as you hike on a wide, mowed path through this old pasture or hay field, now grown up in sumac, fescue, and blackberry briars. You'll find a bench at 1.12 mi. **[7]**. As you continue, dragonflies zip figure-eights over the trail, and black-eyed Susans and purple ironweed brighten the way.

After you reenter the forest, some views of the lake open on your left. Duckweed covers the coves in the foreground, while the steep, wooded, loess hills frame the lake in the distance. Look for rough-leaved sunflowers and the star-shaped blue flowers of tall bellflower. At 1.75 mi. **[8]** you'll walk out into the clearing of the lake dam. Hike over the dam. At 1.8 mi. **[9]** you'll find a signed intersection with the Lake View Trail; go straight here. Ignore the spur on the right at 1.92 mi. **[10]** and go straight to return to the trailhead.

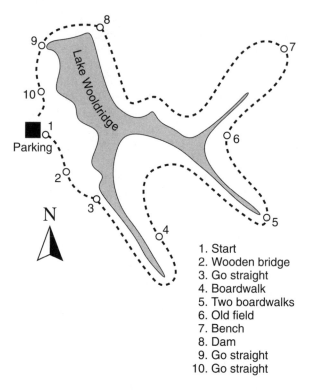

1. Start
2. Wooden bridge
3. Go straight
4. Boardwalk
5. Two boardwalks
6. Old field
7. Bench
8. Dam
9. Go straight
10. Go straight

# 47.  Ha Ha Tonka State Park

- Bring your camera; you'll hike through seas of yellow coneflowers on the finest and largest savanna in the state.
- Survey the world below from the castle ruins perched atop a 250-foot-high cliff.
- See Ha Ha Tonka Spring erupt from the base of a dolomite bluff and fill a surprisingly blue pool with 48 million gallons of water per day.

## Area Information

Nowhere else in the state can you see so many different karst features in such a concentrated area as Ha Ha Tonka State Park. Surface streams cut their way through dolomite bedrock, intersecting and eventually collapsing an immense, ancient cavern system. This collapsed canyon includes sinkholes deep enough to trap cool air where glacial relicts, plants surviving from the last ice age, still thrive.

Ha Ha Tonka is located in a transition area between the prairie landscape farther west and the rugged forested hills to the east. Ha Ha Tonka Savanna is just such a blend of prairie and forest. For centuries, periodic fires shaped this landscape, and early settlers wrote about passing through these "oak orchards" with ease, their wagons and stock unencumbered by brush and thickets. Prescribed fires maintain this highly diverse community of native grasses and wildflowers, sometimes as many as two hundred species on a single acre.

Grandly situated on a bluff overlooking the spring and canyon are the ruins of a European-style stone castle. Native sandstone for the castle was quarried on site. A miniature railroad was constructed to haul the stone, worked by stonemasons from Scotland. No expenses were spared. But in 1906, one year after construction had begun, the castle's owner, Robert Snyder, was killed in an automobile accident. Although the elegant castle was eventually completed, it was gutted by a fire just 20 years later. All that remain today are the ruins, adding their intrigue to Ha Ha Tonka's already interesting landscape.

**Directions:** From Camdenton take Highway 54 west for 2.4 miles. Turn south on Highway D for 1.6 miles to the park's visitor center.

**Hours Open:** The park is for day-use only, year-round.

**Facilities:** Many shady picnic sites are available, and the visitor center features outdoor exhibits. Two courtesy docks are in a cove of Lake of the Ozarks for visitors who arrive by boat, and fishing is available.

**Permits and Rules:** Cave entry in the park is allowed only by permit. Contact the park office for a permit at least one week before desired entry. Camping is allowed only on the Turkey Pen Hollow Trail. Campfires are prohibited in the park. Swimming, fishing, or any access to the water is prohibited in the spring branch. Pets must always be leashed.

**Further Information:** Park Superintendent, Ha Ha Tonka State Park, Route 1, Box 113M, Camdenton, MO 65020; 573-346-2986.

## Park Trails

**Castle Trail** —.5 mile—This trail takes you to the castle's carriage house, some overlooks, and the castle ruins. It begins between the two parking lots for the castle ruins.

**Quarry Trail** —2 miles—This trail starts by the castle and takes you to two old quarries.

**Boulder Ridge Trail** —1.5 miles—This is a little-used trail that passes near large lichen-covered boulders and offers views of the lake. It begins at the parking lot for the lake cove.

**Island Trail** —.75 mile—See remnants of fallen caves, including a precarious block of dolomite known as Balanced Rock. The trail begins at the old mill site, on the Spring Trail.

**Oak Savanna Interpretive Trail** —450 feet—This is a paved trail with four interpretive stops accessible to those with disabilities. It begins at the Turkey Pen Hollow (TPH) trailhead.

**Devil's Kitchen Trail** —1.4 miles—Walk under a horseshoe-shaped cliff and see a cavern opening with a window in its roof. The trail begins at the TPH trailhead.

Ha Ha Tonka
State Park

Lake of the Ozarks

N

River
Cave

Balanced
Rock

Lake of the Ozarks

Whispering
Dell

Spring Trail

Colosseum

Turkey Pen Hollow Trail

LEGEND

— Road
···· Trail
▬ Boundary

🏠 Park Office
🎪 Picnic Area
⛺ Picnic Shelter

⛺ Scout Camp
🚻 Restrooms
🏰 Castle
🚤 Boaters' Access
  To Castle

🌉 Natural Bridge
🍃 Natural Area
〰 Spring
🏛 Post Office

⛲ Drinking
  Fountain
💧 Water Tower
🐎 Stable
⭐ Point of
  Interest

Full View of
Ha Ha Tonka State Park

Area of Detail

Lake of the Ozarks

D

D133

D144

D

⛺

# Spring Trail 👢👢👢👢

**Distance Round-Trip:** 1.5 miles

**Estimated Hiking Time:** 1 hour

*Laughter is a universal human reaction, crossing all generations and cultures. In the Osage language Ha Ha Tonka means "laughing waters."*

**Caution:** The boardwalk steps can be slippery when wet.

**Trail Directions:** Park in the lot across Highway D from the old post office. This trail offers several hiking options; you can shorten it by using a white connector trail or lengthen it by adding the three-quarter-mile Island Trail. The trailhead for the Island Trail is at the old mill site on the Spring Trail.

Begin at the descending steps at the north end of the lot **[1]** and turn left when you reach the bottom. Follow blue arrows on this trail. Turn left at the connector link at .07 mi. **[2]**. At .33 mi. **[3]** the trail brings you onto an open, restored glade. Cedar stumps and fire scars are evidence of the park staff's efforts to remove thickets and restore this special community. Look for the large, lemon yellow flowers of the Missouri evening primrose, which opens in late afternoon and closes with the morning sun. Also look for coneflowers, Indian paintbrush, and snakes and lizards, scurrying away near the trail. Some scenic views soon open on your left.

Pass beneath large, tropical-looking pawpaw leaves after you return to the woods, and a cove of Lake of the Ozarks will appear through the trees. You'll soon pass a parking lot for the lake and a dock to accommodate park visitors who arrive by boat. Turn right at .72 mi. **[4]** onto a paved trail that takes you along the lakeshore. At .87 mi. **[5]** is an old mill site where at least two grist mills stood. One mill burned in 1836, and another was destroyed in 1931 to make way for Lake of the Ozarks. A stone dam and millstone still remain. Here also is the trailhead for the Island Trail. Go straight at the connector at .88 mi. **[6]**.

Keep an eye on the shallow slack water on your left and look for aquatic turtles basking on logs,

sunfish fanning out circular nests with their tails, and dragonflies hovering at intervals between their high-speed maneuvers. The unusually blue water of Ha Ha Tonka Spring pool soon comes into view at .98 mi. **[7]**. Look on top of the cliff on your left and you'll see the castle ruins, which look imposing and mysterious from this angle.

Scramble through a fracture between some boulders at 1.13 mi. **[8]** that create a natural toll gate to the spring (no charge) and you'll find Ha Ha Tonka Spring, Missouri's 12th largest, at 1.16 mi. **[9]**. Until now you might have thought the difficulty rating for this trail was a mistake. Alas, you are facing 316 wooden steps that will lift you 200 vertical feet in no time. Enjoy some breathtaking (if you have any left) views of the spring pool, cliff, castle ruins, and lake cove along the way. At 1.29 mi. **[10]** is an overlook over Whispering Dell sink basin. Formed by the collapse of a cavern roof, it is so named because it contains remnants of caverns capable of transmitting slight sounds along their length. Turn right to continue. Turn right again at 1.38 mi. **[11]**, where the boardwalk ends. You'll come across three forks in the trail at 1.44 mi. **[12]**; bear right at each of them. Ascend the wooden steps on your left at the trailhead to finish your hike.

1. Start
2. Left turn
3. Restored glade
4. Right turn
5. Old mill site
6. Go straight
7. Spring pool
8. Natural toll gate
9. Ha Ha Tonka Spring
10. Whispering Dell overlook
11. Right turn
12. Three forks

# Turkey Pen Hollow Trail 🥾🥾🥾

**Distance Round-Trip:** 5 miles

**Estimated Hiking Time:** 2.5 hours

*" . . . the traveler in the interior is often surprised to behold at one view, cliffs and prairies, bottoms and barrens, naked hills, heavy forests, and rocks, and streams, and plains, all succeeding each other with rapidity and mingled with the most pleasing harmony."* —Henry Rowe Schoolcraft, from Journal of a Tour into the Interior of Missouri and Arkansas in 1818 and 1819.

**Caution:** Savannas and glades are prime chigger and tick habitats. Try wearing long pants and duct-taping your pants legs around your hiking boots before spraying with repellent.

**Trail Directions:** Park in the lot east of Highway D between the parking lot for River Cave and the old post office. While the south loop of this trail was closed in 1998, it would have lengthened the hike by 2 miles. Check with park staff for the status of this loop if you are interested in a 7-mile hike.

Begin the trail at the signboard **[1]**. Bear right at the trail's first fork. Go straight at .06 mi. **[2]** at the intersection with the Acorn Trail. Follow the red arrows for the Turkey Pen Hollow Trail. Turn left at .12 mi. **[3]** where the Devil's Kitchen Trail cuts away to the southwest. Turn right at the intersection at .16 mi. **[4]**.

Soon, the expansive savanna landscape opens before you. The trail goes around the upper rim of a sinkhole at .28 mi. **[5]**. Near the 1 mi. mark, if you are here in May, June, or July, you'll walk through a sea of yellow coneflowers **[6]**. If you feel something pulling on your sock you may have discovered the sensitive brier, a creeping plant about ankle high that resembles a miniature mimosa tree.

Turn left at 1.65 mi. **[7]** at the white spur. After crossing a small stream at 2.05 mi. **[8]** you'll walk uphill onto a glade (2.10 mi.) **[9]**. Situated on these south and west slopes, these thin, rocky soils are the hottest, driest parts of the savanna. Notice the stunted trees. Plants and animals must be specially adapted to thrive on these minideserts. After you cross another stream you'll come across a wet-weather spring in a jumble of rocks on your left (2.32 mi.) **[10]**. After a zigzag in the trail, make left turns at both 2.75 and 2.78 mi. **[11]**. Turn left again at the intersections at 3.04 mi. **[12]** and 3.14 mi. **[13]**.

Be careful—it would be easy to miss the left turn at 3.35 mi. **[14]**. Panoramic views open down the valleys on your left. Go straight at the intersection at 3.70 mi. **[15]**. After a couple more zigzags, turn left at the crossing at 4.25 mi. **[16]** and in a couple of steps turn right. You'll cross under a powerline and meet the Acorn Trail at 4.36 mi. **[17]**, where you turn left to complete your savanna hike.

1. Start
2. Go straight
3. Left turn
4. Right turn
5. Sinkhole
6. Yellow coneflowers
7. Left turn
8. Stream crossing
9. Glade
10. Wet-weather spring
11. Two left turns
12. Left turn
13. Left turn
14. Left turn
15. Go straight
16. Left turn
17. Left turn

# 48. Bennett Spring State Park

- See the big, round, blue spring that the local Native Americans referred to as the "Eye of the Sacred One."
- Hike through a 296-foot-long S-shaped tunnel, one of the state's largest and most beautiful natural tunnels.
- Bring your wildflower book—you may see as many as 45 species blooming at one time on the Savanna Ridge Trail.

## Area Information

Like many other springs in Missouri in the mid-1800s, Bennett Spring's strong and steady flow was seen as free power by early settlers. The spring's 100-million-gallon-per-day output powered a series of grist mills, the most successful of which belonged to Peter Bennett, known for his generous donations of flour to needy families during the Civil War. Area farmers, waiting their turn at the mill, camped and fished in the scenic spring valley.

Built by the CCC in 1937, the triple-arched bridge near the trout hatchery isn't the only major bridge in the park. An even more spectacular bridge, or tunnel, is in the woods about four miles upstream. The Bennett Spring Natural Tunnel, a remnant of an ancient cave roof, is 100 yards long!

Mention Bennett Springs in a group of Missourians and tales of *Salmo gairdneri*, the rainbow trout, are likely to ensue. Although trout are not native to Missouri, the state's numerous springs provide water that is cold enough for trout. Trout were stocked in the Bennett Spring branch as early as 1900, and the first trout hatchery appeared on the site in 1924. One of the state's oldest and most popular parks, the site owes its popularity to its spring. Anglers and their families compose most of the park's visitors.

**Directions:** From Lebanon take Highway 64 west for 11 miles to the park entrance.

**Hours Open:** The site is open year-round from sunrise to 10 P.M. The nature center is open from 9 A.M. to 5 P.M. daily. Sirens audible along the entire spring branch announce the opening and closing of fishing hours, which change seasonally. Trout season is open from March 1 through October 31.

**Facilities:** The park features fishing for rainbow trout in its 1.5-mile-long spring branch. Several campgrounds are available, as well as a nature center with exhibits, swimming pool, dining lodge, rental cabins, amphitheater, camp store, trout hatchery, picnic areas, and a boat ramp on the Niangua River.

**Permits and Rules:** A state fishing license and daily permit required for trout fishing are available from the park store. Fish feeding is allowed in the hatchery's rearing pools near the park store, but only food bought on site may be used. Swimming in the spring branch is not allowed, but anglers may wade. Pets must always be leashed.

**Further Information:** Park Superintendent, Bennett Spring State Park, 26250 Highway 64A, Lebanon, MO 65536; 417-532-4338 (park office) or 417-532-4307 (cabin reservations).

## Park Trails

The park's other trails (except the .25-mile loop behind the nature center) are linear. Hiked together, they total 3.35 miles (one way.) Starting at the spring and going downstream, these are the trails:

**Spring Trail** —.65 mile (one way)—This trail begins at the west side of the spring and follows the spring branch to the hatchery.

**Bridge Trail** —.75 mile (one way)—Begin at the CCC-era triple-arched bridge on the east side of the stream, traverse some oak-hickory woods, and finish at the Oak-Hickory Trail loop.

**Oak-Hickory Trail** —.25 mile—This loop trail begins at the amphitheater and winds through a forest behind the nature center. Access this trail from the nature center or the Bridge Trail.

**Bluff Trail** —.25 mile (one way)—The upper section of this trail climbs a bluff, offers great views of the stream and park, and connects the Bridge and Whistle Trails.

**Whistle Trail** —1 mile (one way)—This trail begins from the upper section of the Bluff Trail, explores a more peaceful section of the stream, and ends at the bridge near the Niangua River.

# Bennett Spring
# State Park

To Hwy. 65
18 Miles

Niangua River

64

Whistle
Trail

Bluff
Trail

Bridge
Trail

Oak-Hickory
Trail

Spring Trail

00

64A

64

To Lebanon
12 Miles

Savanna
Ridge
Trail

Natural
Tunnel
Trail

N

## LEGEND

| | | | |
|---|---|---|---|
| —— | Road | △ Camping | |
| ····· | Trail | Full Hook-up Camping | |
| ▬▬ | Boundary | Sanitation Station | |
| | Office and Park Store | Restrooms | |
| | Motel | Picnic Area | |
| | Cabins | Picnic Shelter | |
| | Dining Lodge | Spring | |
| | Hatchery | Nature Center | |
| ★ | Trailhead | Swimming Pool | |

# Natural Tunnel Trail 👢👢👢

**Distance Round-Trip:** 7.5 miles

**Estimated Hiking Time:** 3.75 hours

*Because of its S shape, the tunnel looks like a cave until you step inside and see the glow of light coming from the other opening. From inside, the entrance looks exotic; Virginia creeper trails from the roof and tropical pawpaw leaves are reflected in the still pools of the tunnel stream.*

**Caution:** Bring a flashlight if you want to explore inside the tunnel; it's dark and rocky in the middle part. Stinging nettles encroach the trail in places, especially on the east loop.

**Trail Directions:** Once in the park, follow the signs for the spring and the trailhead, marked by "TH" signs. Park in the lot for the trailhead, at the end of the road just southeast of the spring.

Begin the trail between the interpretive signs at the parking lot **[1]** and turn left at the first intersection. Follow blue arrows on this trail. You are now on the east loop. The trail soon takes you into a streamside forest, where the vegetation is thick and limbs of black walnut, hackberry, and basswood trees arch over the trail. Just after passing under a grand sycamore tree leaning over the trail, look for a trickle of water falling off a boulder next to the trail on your left. Two water-loving plants are here at .43 mi. **[2]**—jewelweed (a favorite of hummingbirds) and water hemlock (one of North America's deadliest plants). At .59 mi. **[3]** a tiny spring erupts next to the trail on the left.

At .81 mi. **[4]** cross a streambed and resume the trail slightly to your left on the other side. You'll climb a wooded hill with many Christmas ferns and maidenhair ferns before reaching a connector link and wooden bench at 1.07 mi. **[5]**; turn left here. Turn right at the intersection with an old road at 1.17 mi. **[6]** and you'll enter an old field, now grown up with locust trees and lots of blackberries. Purple milkweed and butterfly weed are attended by great spangled fritillaries and black swallowtails.

Just after crossing a gravel streambed, look on your left for some steep bluffs on the side of the ridge. When you see a streambed opening on your right at 1.53 mi. **[7]**, step into the bed to see some dolomite bluffs carved into some fantastic shapes by the stream. These erosional features foreshadow what awaits you at the end of the trail. Turn left at the intersection with the west loop at 1.75 mi. **[8]**. An expansive old field opens on your left, filled with more locusts and blackberries. Turn right at 2.09 mi.

**[9]** at a crossing with an old road. Go straight through two pipeline clearings and bear right at the fork in the trail at 2.47 mi. **[10]**. Turn right at an old road crossing at 2.62 mi. **[11]**.

The trail now parallels a small stream. Just after crossing this stream for the third time, you'll see the black mouth of the natural tunnel yawning through the trees at 3.5 mi. **[12]**. Make your way under some beautiful dolomite ledges dripping with water and wild hydrangea (another water-loving plant) and step inside the opening. Feel the breeze inside the natural wind tunnel and see the calcite deposits on the ceiling and walls. Here's a good place to explore and relax.

Return to **[8]**, which you'll reach at 5.25 mi. Turn left, cross a small stream, and begin an uphill hike. Fern medleys cover some ravine sides. At the top at 5.8 mi. **[13]** are several views of distant wooded ridges and valleys. You'll pass a farm pond and cross a stream before reaching the connector link at 6.34 mi. **[14]**; go straight here. You'll cross another stream and turn right at the intersection at 6.83 mi. **[15]**, joining a section of the Savanna Ridge Trail. Turn right at the intersection at 7.28 mi. **[16]**. Just after passing a house, turn right on the gravel road and cross a concrete bridge. Turn right again at the end of the bridge to return to the trailhead.

1. Start
2. Water-loving plants
3. Tiny spring
4. Stream crossing
5. Left turn
6. Right turn
7. Erosional features
8. Left turn
9. Right turn
10. Bear right
11. Right turn
12. Natural tunnel
13. Overlooks
14. Go straight
15. Right turn
16. Right turn

# Savanna Ridge Trail 👢👢👢👢

**Distance Round-Trip:** 2.35 miles

**Estimated Hiking Time:** 1.25 hours

*I knew I risked a chigger infestation by leaving the wide, mowed path through the old field grown up in acres of blackberry briars. But the shiny, ripe blackberries squished between my teeth like little soft balloons filled with sweet juice, warmed by the June morning sun. The chigger welts would heal, I figured.*

**Caution:** Repellent against chiggers and ticks in the summer is a good idea.

**Trail Directions:** Park in the lot for the trailhead, just southeast of the spring. The Natural Tunnel Trail and Savanna Ridge Trail share a trailhead here. Start between the interpretive signs at the parking lot **[1]** and turn right at the first intersection. Follow green arrows on this trail. Turn left on a concrete bridge at .07 mi. **[2]** and watch for kingfishers perching on dead tree limbs and great blue herons stalking the shallows of this slack water. Turn left again on the trail on the other side at .13 mi. **[3]**.

Just after crossing a small stream turn right at the intersection at .30 mi. **[4]**. Walk uphill into the woods, keeping an eye out for brown mounds of earth about a foot high and two feet wide on the left side of the trail. These are made by mound-building ants, which excavate extensive tunnels underground for their colony. Look for wing-stem sunflowers—yellow-flowered plants about waist-high with wings that run parallel to their main stems. They join spiderwort, Christmas ferns, and black-eyed Susans in an interesting jumble of colors and textures.

Prescribed fires keep underbrush in check and release nutrients back into the forest soil. Wildflowers and native grasses can flourish in areas that are periodically burned, and the diversity of species at .62 mi. **[5]** illustrates this. Among many others here are pale-purple coneflowers, feverfew, and beard-tongue. Rich yellows of two kinds of coreopsis bloom over purple spikes of lead plant. You'll soon reach the connector link at .69 mi. **[6]** where you turn right and cross two small streams. Continue uphill and continue finding wildflowers. Here are sunny ox-eye daisies, pealike blooms of goat's rue, and fragile and slender Deptford pink.

The trail swings to the left and finally takes you downhill. You'll pass through a large colony of bracken ferns at 1.0 mi. **[7]**. Notice that each frond section looks like a separate leaf.

Some overlook views appear through the trees at 1.23 mi. **[8]**. Notice the elephant-ear-like leaves of prairie dock amidst the bluestem grasses in these forest openings. Look for the yuccalike leaves of rattlesnake master near the trail. Turn right at the intersection with the connector link at 1.38 mi. **[9]** and turn left when the trail meets the Natural Tunnel Trail at 1.54 mi. **[10]**.

At 1.95 mi. **[11]** you'll enter an old field filled with thickets of brush and blackberry briars. If you're here in late June or July, you should experience blackberries for yourself—one of Missouri's tastiest wild edibles. The berries start out green before turning red. They're not ripe until they're a deep, dark purple. Turn right when you return to **[4]** to complete your wildflower hike.

1. Start
2. Left turn
3. Left turn
4. Right turn
5. Wildflower display
6. Right turn
7. Bracken fern colony
8. Overlooks
9. Right turn
10. Left turn
11. Old field

# 49.  Hercules Glades Wilderness

- Tarantulas, scorpions, armadillos, and roadrunners? Hiking the glades of southwest Missouri can make you feel you've gone south of the border.
- Find the uncommon smoke tree, and come in June or July to see what makes it smoke.
- Climb 133 steps to the top of a U.S. Forest Service lookout tower for clearer insight into an analogy of the landscape made in 1818.

## Area Information

The White River section of the Ozarks is the region that straddles the border between Missouri and Arkansas in Missouri's southwest corner. Named for the major river that is responsible for carving its famous hilly terrain, the White River section is characterized by steep ridges, deep valleys, conical knobs, and extensive, open glades. When glades occurred on knobs, they were named balds because thin, rocky soils allowed few trees to grow. Natural periodic fires and fires set by Native Americans kept cedars, sumac, and other brush from invading the balds.

The first settlers of the area were primarily old-stock Americans from Appalachia. The Civil War was particularly divisive here and produced an aftermath of vicious feuding and guerrilla fighting. One of the largest and most flagrant vigilante clans that roared through the region in the 1880s was the Bald Knobbers, a part of Ozark culture that serves as a motif for the thriving local tourism industry.

Today, much of the White River valley's original culture and environment has been displaced. Major dams on the river have created Norfork, Bull Shoals, Taneycomo, Table Rock, and Beaver Lakes. Fortunately, Hercules Glades Wilderness is one of several areas designated to preserve a portion of this unique, original Ozark landscape. Hercules Glades is one of seven wilderness areas in Missouri managed by the Mark Twain National Forest, U.S. Forest Service. It has three public trailheads and four interconnected loop trails in addition to the two featured trails.

**Directions:** The area is near the Arkansas border, north of Bull Shoals Lake. To reach the **Coy Bald Trailhead** (west side), take Highway 160 east from Forsyth 10.2 miles to Cross Timbers Road, where you turn left. Go 1.7 miles to the T and turn right. Take an immediate left and go 1.4 miles to the parking lot at Coy Bald. To reach the **Lookout Tower Trailhead** (east side), take Highway 160 east from Forsyth 20.8 miles to Highway 125, where you turn north. Go 7.3 miles and turn left at the sign for the area. Go .2 mile to the parking lot at the tower.

**Hours Open:** The wilderness is always open.

**Facilities:** Picnic tables, grills, and parking for horse trailers are available at both trailheads. The Lookout Tower Trailhead also has a lookout tower, rest rooms, and two primitive campsites.

**Permits and Rules:** Horses and bikes are allowed, but ATVs are prohibited. Hunting is permitted but not within 150 yards of the trail. Campers must observe regulations designed to protect the wilderness beauty. Choose a campsite away from the trail and avoid constructing a fire ring. Cut no standing trees (live or dead), extinguish all campfires, and scatter their evidence before leaving. Leave no litter, trail-marking ribbons, or other evidence of your presence.

**Further Information:** District Ranger, U.S. Forest Service, Ava/Cassville/Willow Springs District, P.O. Box 188, Ava, MO 65608; 417-683-4428. For a map of the entire Mark Twain forest or topographic maps of all seven districts and seven wilderness areas, contact the Forest Supervisor, 401 Fairgrounds Road, Rolla, MO 65401; 573-364-4621.

## Other Areas of Interest

Also in the Mark Twain National Forest, just 2.8 miles south of the lookout tower, the **Glade Top Trail** is a 23-mile scenic driving trail. The Glade Top Trail, Missouri's only national scenic byway, offers vistas of the White River Hills, the Springfield Plateau, and the St. Francois and Boston Mountains. For more information call 417-683-4428.

Dubbed the new Nashville, **Branson** offers a multitude of music shows, shopping villages, water parks, restaurants, and other entertainment attractions, including the theme park **Silver Dollar City**. Branson is 35 miles south of Springfield on Highway 65. For more information call the Missouri Division of Tourism at 573-751-4133.

# Hercules Glades Wilderness

N

Lookout Tower

Pees Hollow

Pole Hollow

Lookout Tower Trail

Blair Ridge

Upper Pilot Knob

Coy Bald Trail

Persimmon Hollow

Devil's Den

Lower Pilot Knob

Coy Bald

Owl Hollow

LEGEND
······· Trail
▬▬▬ Boundary

# Coy Bald Trail

**Distance Round-Trip:** 6.75 miles

**Estimated Hiking Time:** 3.75 hours

*As I was leaving the trailhead, I spied a roadrunner, cocking its head from side to side and strolling along the road ahead. It suddenly stretched out and became all neck and tail, and all hopes of a photograph vanished in about 2.2 seconds!*

**Caution:** Bring a compass and topo map if you plan to extend this hike or explore off the trail. Bring sun protection and extra water. Wear orange clothing during hunting seasons.

**Trail Directions:** Park in the lot for the Coy Bald Trailhead and begin the trail straight across the lot from where you entered **[1]**. Please register at the trail box near the trailhead, and turn left at the intersection at .09 mi. **[2]**. While descending a rocky trail shaded by post oaks, black hickories, and cedars, turn left at the fork at .25 mi. **[3]**. At .56 mi. **[4]** you'll find a campsite on your left, the solid bedrock streambed of Long Creek in front of you, and a white limestone bluff, streaked black by manganese. Notice that each level of the bluff has its own little glade, complete with bluestem grass and blooming wildflowers. Desiccated trunks of ancient cedars cling from the top edge.

Follow the trail to the right, and cross Long Creek. Look for Ozark witch hazel growing in the streambed and flat, gray, flaky pieces of shale among chunks of limestone and chert. Just across the stream, you'll find another campsite under a large white oak at .69 mi. **[5]**. Turn right and cross another streambed. From here, you'll hike through several glades separated by patches of forest. Some glades have cedars, while others are more open. Some are rocky and sloped; others are flat. All of them feature prairie grasses and a surprising variety of wildflowers. Go straight at the three-way intersection at 1.59 mi. **[6]**. Notice the way the bluestem grasses make the round glade at 1.99 mi. **[7]** look blue and green at the same time—just the way the water looks in a big, round spring.

Turn right at the intersection at 2.48 mi. **[8]** and cross Long Creek again, which may be dry. Just across the stream, you'll find a campsite on your left. Turn right here. At 2.64 mi. **[9]** is the trail to the Blair Ridge Road trailhead; go straight. After crossing another dry, rocky, streambed, go straight at the four-way intersection at 2.75 mi. **[10]**. Climb a steep, rocky hill to a glade where sunshine-yellow black-eyed Susans contrast with craggy, nearly black dolomite rocks.

The small pond on your right at 3.20 mi. **[11]** illustrates the ability of cattails to collect soil and eventually fill in shallow ponds. The terrific glade-top views that soon open on your left and right are only previews of what's to come.

Notice the small, bushy trees with oval, wavy leaves at 3.69 mi. **[12]**. These are smoke trees, which are restricted in Missouri to glades and bluffs of a few southwestern counties. The appearance of smoke is from the profusion of hairy stalks that remains on the tree after the flowers have fallen away, in June and July. At 3.76 mi. **[13]** you'll step onto a ridgetop glade over a third of a mile long that offers spectacular vistas every step of the way. On both the left and right, beyond plunging valleys, are distant knobs and balds, some showing horizontal stripes of exposed limestone layers. The foreground is lit up with blazing star, prairie dock, and gum plant. In early summer, look for the saucer-sized, lemon yellow blossoms of Missouri evening primrose. After passing another cattail pond, you'll find another overlook at 5.03 mi. **[14]**, with uninterrupted views of dozens of outlying ridges and deep valleys. On your way back to the trailhead, you'll hike on a sideslope of Coy Bald at 6.28 mi. **[15]**. Turn left at **[2]** to finish your glade hike.

N

1. Start
2. Left turn
3. Left turn
4. Long Creek and bluff
5. Campsite
6. Go straight
7. Round glade
8. Right turn
9. Go straight
10. Go straight
11. Cattail pond
12. Smoke trees
13. Glade overlook
14. Glade overlook
15. Coy Bald

# Lookout Tower Trail 👢👢👢👢👢

**Distance Round-Trip:** 4.5 miles

**Estimated Hiking Time:** 2.25 hours

*" . . . sometimes we crossed patches of ground of considerable extent, without trees or brush of any kind. . . . Frequently these prairies occupied the tops of conical hills, or extended ridges . . . and resembling, when viewed on perspective, enormous sand-hills promiscuously piled up by the winds."—Henry Rowe Schoolcraft, 1818.*

**Caution:** Bring a compass and topo map if you plan to extend this hike or explore off the trail. Wear orange clothing during hunting seasons. Vegetation may encroach the trail near Long Creek.

**Trail Directions:** Park in the lot for the Hercules Lookout Tower. It's okay to climb the tower, which offers superb views of the White River Hills in a 360-degree sweep and provides an appreciation for Schoolcraft's analogy. The trailhead is at the far end of the lot (west end), behind a picnic area. Please register at the trailhead before you begin.

Start your hike on a wide, rocky trail on a ridgetop [1] in a forest of oak, hickory, black walnut, and cedar. All the nut trees attract squirrels, and you are apt to see plenty of them here, thrashing in the upper limbs and chasing each other around trunks. Carolina buckthorn (Indian cherry) fruits will be tinged red, and wild grapes will fall onto the trail in clusters by late summer. After you start descending the ridge on a trail of chert gravel and slabs of dolomite bedrock, take the spur on your left at 1.12 mi. [2] to a curious, human-made collection of stones. Was it a homestead cabin foundation? A Native American burial cairn? Before these young trees crowded in, this site offered a splendid view across a deep valley. After thinking about who, what, or why, turn left on the main trail to continue.

At 1.22 mi. [3] you'll enter a glade that continues for a half mile, downhill, over limestone gravel and bedrock. Unless you are here in winter, you'll find a festival of wildflowers. Among the conspicuous prairie dock, gum plant, and asters, you'll find tiny flowers growing on rock beds with no apparent soil.

Between smoke trees and cedars, you'll see the tallest peak in the area, Pilot Knob, to the northwest. After the glade tapers off into the bottoms of Long Creek, you'll cross an intermittent stream at 1.94 mi. [4] and pass through an old field of tall lespedeza and sumac. Just before reaching Long Creek, turn right at the intersection at 2.20 mi. [5]. In a few steps you'll find another streambed, where you turn right (2.23 mi.) [6]. Hike in the streambed, looking for softball-sized, green Osage oranges, and turn right at 2.26 mi. [7] onto a steep, rocky trail up into the forest.

On your way uphill, look for the blue, lip-shaped blossoms of skullcap, and scratched and burrowed places on the ground made by armadillos. Along with roadrunners (and black bears, to a lesser extent), armadillos are moving into Missouri from their more typical southern range. After passing through another old field with winged elm and persimmon trees, you'll enter a series of glades, interspersed with patches of dry woods. Near the top of the ridge, chinkapin oaks surround a large glade at 3.0 mi. [8], where views of distant ridges and knobs extend from both sides. Blooming onions look like lavender fireworks explosions in the bluestem grass, and flying parades of butterflies attend fields of coneflowers, blazing star, and goldenrod.

Turn right at the three-way intersection at 3.40 mi. [9]. You'll hike on a narrow, dry ridge with blackjack oaks and a shortleaf pine grove. Go straight at the intersection at 4.35 mi. [10] and you'll soon be back at the lookout tower.

| | |
|---|---|
| 1. Start | 6. Streambed |
| 2. Spur to rock collection | 7. Right turn |
| 3. Half-mile glade | 8. Scenic glade |
| 4. Stream crossing | 9. Right turn |
| 5. Right turn | 10. Go straight |

# Southwest

The southwest region of Missouri is the area south of the Missouri River and west of Highway 65.

## Topography

Approximately 10 percent of this region, a narrow band south of the Missouri River, has geologic characteristics like those of north Missouri—an area often referred to as the glaciated plains. Deep soils are formed from loess, glacial till, or alluvium, and the area has gentle terrain.

Farther south, another 40 percent of the region is occupied by the Osage Plains, a distinctive area along the Kansas border that contains remnants of Missouri's once-vast prairies. Soils are composed of sedimentary residuum or shallow loess. Though unglaciated, Osage Plains topography is characterized by gently rolling hills and plains, blending gradually into other areas of Missouri around it.

The southern 50 percent of the region is composed of two distinct sections of the Ozarks. The Springfield Plateau, like the Osage Plains, is unglaciated yet relatively flat. Drainages have not dissected the land deeply, and the terrain is mostly gently rolling hills. The White River section, on the Arkansas border, is more typical of the rest of the Ozarks. The White River and its tributaries have carved deeply into the limestone bedrock, creating a rugged landscape. Long, steep-sided ridges and conical hills, or knobs, characterize the area.

## Major Rivers and Lakes

The Missouri River flows across the north boundary of this region and, as in the other regions, the river strongly influences the soils, terrain, and plant and animal communities surrounding it. Other rivers of the region include the Blackwater, Osage, Little Osage, Spring, and James Rivers. The White River, for which the lower Ozarks section of this region is named, once meandered back and forth between Missouri and Arkansas but has been dammed to create five reservoirs. Not a single mile of the river flows freely in Missouri. Table Rock Lake is the only White River impoundment in this region.

Truman Lake, Missouri's second largest, is a twin of Lake of the Ozarks. Like its twin, it was created by damming the Osage River. With 55,000 surface acres of water, Truman is one of the largest hydroelectric reservoirs in the Midwest and only a few hundred acres smaller than Lake of the Ozarks. The U.S. Army Corps of Engineers designed the reservoir to provide power and recreation opportunities for the public. The dam began generating power in 1979. Other lakes in the region include Pomme de Terre, which offers fishing for northern muskies. A steady southwest wind from the Springfield Plateau seems always to be blowing across 25,000-acre Stockton Lake, making it popular with sailing enthusiasts.

## Common Plant Life

From top to bottom, the majority of the region differs greatly from presettlement times. Agriculture has replaced most of the area's original communities. About 45 percent of the glaciated plains was prairie, but the deep soils and gentle terrain made ideal farming conditions. Only fragments of forest and savanna remain in the northern part of this region. Prairie covered about 75 percent of the Osage Plains before settlement. Streams have shallow valleys and broad floodplains with many sloughs and marshes. Although deeper soils have been plowed for crops, and areas of thinner soil have been converted to pasture, most of the state's remaining prairie is here. The Springfield Plateau is characterized by fragmented forests, pasture, and early successional shrubby habitats, but a few savanna remnants persist. The White River section has deciduous forest mixed with some pine, as well as major glade landscapes.

Prairie grasses like little bluestem, Indian grass, and big bluestem, which may reach six to eight feet tall, dominate the prairies of the Osage Plains. Wildflower types often depend on the bedrock present and amount of moisture, and include tickseed coreopsis, downy sunflower, false dragonhead, gay feather, pencil flower, cream wild indigo, purple prairie clover, Venus's looking glass, birdsfoot violet, and prairie rose gentian.

Savannas are often thought of as transition zones between prairies and forest, where prairie plants grow beneath open canopies of widely spaced trees.

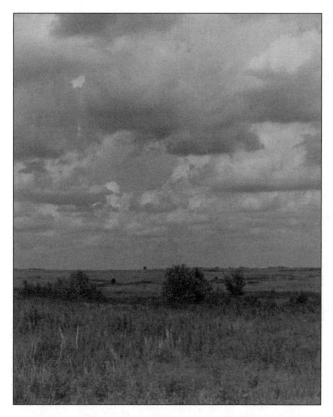

Chinkapin oak, red cedar, and white ash trees, and little bluestem, sideoats grama, and Indian grasses dominate the limestone and dolomite savannas of the Springfield Plateau. Other plants include rattlesnake master, various sunflowers, adder's tongue fern, seneca snakeroot, white prairie clover, rose gentian, and black-eyed Susan.

When glades occurred on the conical knobs of the White River area, they were often called balds because of their relative lack of trees. Dolomite glades of the White River section are dominated by little bluestem, sideoats grama, and prairie dropseed grasses, dotted with stunted, often gnarled, trees and shrubs. The smoke tree may be present. Wildflowers include silky aster, blue hearts, Missouri evening primrose, yellow coneflower, pale purple coneflower, compass plant, rattlesnake master, and prairie dock.

## Common Birds and Animals

The upland prairies of the Osage Plains are home to numerous birds including the prairie chicken, horned lark, northern harrier, dickcissel, upland sandpiper, meadowlark, Henslow's sparrow, grasshopper sparrow, and scissor-tailed flycatcher. Other animals include the coyote, badger, ornate box turtle, glass lizard, bullsnake, prairie kingsnake, crayfish frog, and legions of butterflies. Prairie State Park has also returned a herd of American bison to roam freely in their native habitat of presettlement times.

Birds often living in savannas include the red-tailed hawk, kestrel, indigo bunting, bluebird, red-headed woodpecker, great crested flycatcher, prairie warbler, blue-winged warbler, and goldfinch. Other animals include the coyote, red fox, wild turkey, white-tailed deer, gray squirrel, ornate box turtle, rough green snake, prairie ringneck snake, and fence lizard.

The Bachman's sparrow and roadrunner are two birds largely restricted to dolomite glades in southwestern Missouri. Besides the roadrunner, the glades here are home to several other species of animals like the collared lizard, tarantula, and scorpion, which are typically associated with habitats of the southwestern United States. Other reptiles include the six-lined racerunner, coachwhip snake, western worm snake, copperhead, and western pygmy rattlesnake. The armadillo, another animal associated with the Southwest, is also increasing its range in southern Missouri.

## Climate

The southwest region's temperatures average 57 degrees F in spring, 78 degrees F in summer, 58 degrees F in fall, and 30 degrees F in winter. Mean annual precipitation varies from 39 inches at the top of this region to 43 inches at the bottom.

## Best Features

- Missouri's largest tallgrass prairie at Prairie State Park, complete with fields of wildflowers and roaming bison
- Peaceful, parklike oak savannas, with qualities of prairies of the west and forests of the east
- Exceptional and diverse plant communities on the White River balds
- Animal communities with a southwestern twist in the White River Hills
- Osage Village—the site of 200 lodges where the Osage were living when first encountered by Europeans
- Beautiful spring and the Devil's Kitchen at Roaring River State Park
- The tristate Spooklight

# 50.  Pomme de Terre State Park

- Hike through a restored savanna with interspersed limestone outcrops and glade openings, resplendent with spring and summer wildflowers.

- Come visit the ancient chinkapin and post oaks of the savanna—many have thick, spiraled trunks, craggy limbs, and are over 200 years old.

- For a dramatic view of the lake during any season, hike to the end of a long peninsula to the rocky promontory known as Indian Point.

- Find the remnants of a Native American cairn at the end of a ridged, rocky peninsula.

- Try to fool a muskellunge.

## Area Information

For thousands of years, American Indians lived along Missouri's rivers, where game, shelter, water, and fertile soil were plentiful. French trappers and traders explored the state's rivers in the late 1600s, finding an abundance of beaver, otter, and other valuable furbearers. When the French came to southwest Missouri, they named one of its rivers Pomme de Terre ("apple of the earth") for some plants resembling potatoes that grew on its banks. Now thought to be potato beans or prairie turnips, American Indians used these "apples" for food.

The 1800s brought to the area white settlers, who cleared or grazed much of the prairielike savanna. In the early 1960s, the U.S. Army Corps of Engineers dammed Pomme de Terre River for flood control, forming 7,800-acre Pomme de Terre Lake. Today, the 734-acre Pomme de Terre State Park is leased from the corps. The park is divided into two units, the Hermitage and Pittsburg areas, each of which has a full set of facilities. In total, the park has more campsites than any other Missouri state park. Although the emphasis is water-based recreation, the park is also successfully restoring a savanna landscape to its presettlement conditions.

Northern muskies stocked in Pomme de Terre Lake offer anglers an unusual challenge. These large, toothy game fish add to the lake's more common inhabitants—bass, bluegill, catfish, and crappie.

**Directions: Hermitage Area**—From Hermitage, on Highway 54, take Highway 254 west for 3 miles to Carson's Corner. Turn south on Highway 64 for .7

mile. Turn right at the sign for the park. **Pittsburg Area**—From Nemo, take Highway 64 toward Pittsburg for 2.5 miles. Turn west on Highway 64B for 1.7 miles into the park. (Use Highways 64 and 64B to travel between park units.)

**Hours Open:** The park is open during daylight hours, year-round. The park office (Pittsburg area) is open from 8 A.M. to 4:30 P.M. Monday through Friday, year-round.

**Facilities:** The park offers a large campground, marina (with boat rentals), swimming beaches, boat ramps, picnic areas, and amphitheater. Fishing, boating, and skiing are available on the lake.

**Permits and Rules:** Strict federal and state laws prohibit the disturbance of archeological sites and artifacts. Refrain from climbing on the rock cairns or disturbing them in any way. Alcohol is prohibited on the beaches. Pets must always be leashed.

**Further Information:** Park Superintendent, Pomme de Terre State Park, HC 77 Box 890, Pittsburg, MO 65724; 417-852-4291.

## Other Areas of Interest

The **U.S. Army Corps of Engineers** operates a number of recreation facilities along the lake that primarily feature water recreation and camping. The corps also operates a small visitor center at the east end of the dam. For more information call 417-745-6411.

An interesting half-mile walking tour interprets an American Indian village on top of a hill at **Osage Village State Historic Site.** Bedrock outcrops still bear the signs of use by the Osage for cracking nuts, pounding flour, and sharpening tools. The site marks the location where two to three thousand Osage lived when they first encountered Europeans, around 1700. The site, west of Pomme de Terre, is 2.1 miles west of Fair Haven, off Highway C. For more information call 417-682-2279 (Harry S Truman Birthplace State Historic Site).

**Schell-Osage Conservation Area**, just east of Osage Village, is a wetland wildlife area that includes marshes, bottomland, and upland timber. The area has major concentrations of waterfowl in fall, winter, and spring, and offers hunting, fishing, limited camping, and a 1.5-mile linear hiking trail. The area is owned by the Missouri Department of Conservation. For more information call 417-432-3414.

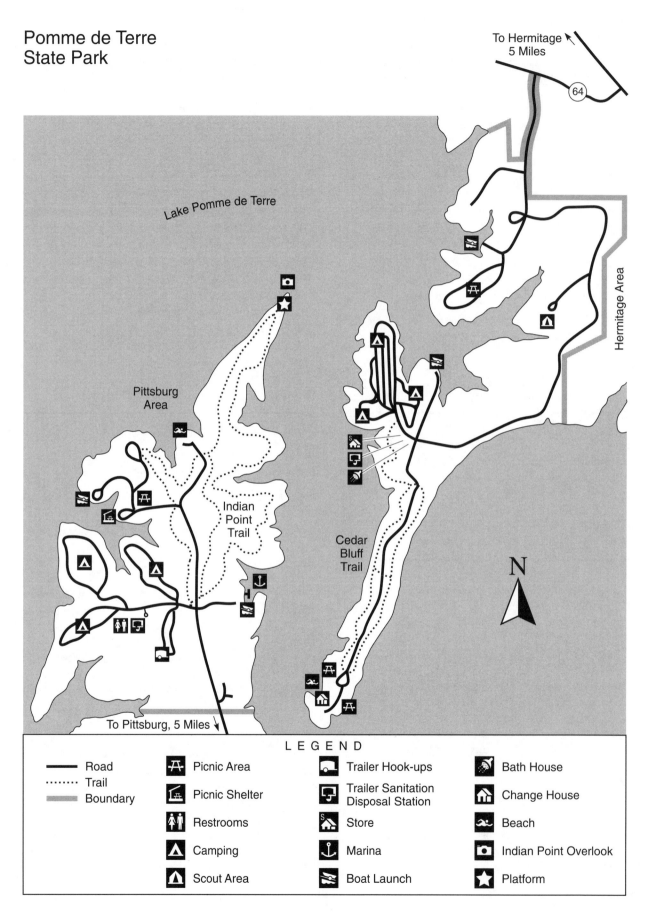

# Pomme de Terre
# State Park

To Hermitage
5 Miles

64

Lake Pomme de Terre

Pittsburg
Area

Indian
Point
Trail

Hermitage Area

Cedar
Bluff
Trail

N

To Pittsburg, 5 Miles

## L E G E N D

| | | | |
|---|---|---|---|
| —— Road | Picnic Area | Trailer Hook-ups | Bath House |
| ···· Trail | Picnic Shelter | Trailer Sanitation Disposal Station | Change House |
| ▒ Boundary | Restrooms | Store | Beach |
| | Camping | Marina | Indian Point Overlook |
| | Scout Area | Boat Launch | Platform |

# Indian Point Trail 👢👢👢

**Distance Round-Trip:** 3 miles

**Estimated Hiking Time:** 1.5 hours

*Settlers wrote in their journals about riding their wagons easily through "oak openings" or open "oak orchards." Natural fires had eliminated most of the understory, leaving widely spaced oak trees above oceans of prairie grasses and herbs.*

**Caution:** This property is owned by the U.S. Army Corps of Engineers and leased to the state park system. Strict federal and state laws prohibit the disturbance of archeological sites and artifacts. Refrain from climbing on the rock cairns or disturbing them in any way. Also, the trail can be difficult to follow in places because of the open nature of the savanna. Try to follow numbered features closely.

**Trail Directions:** This trail is at the southern, or Pittsburg, area of the park. Park in the lot for the trailhead, which is across the road from the campground entrance. Begin at the sign for the trail [1], next to the amphitheater, and go straight, into the savanna [2].

Savannas, which are transition areas between prairie and forest, were once common in Missouri. Today, because of logging, grazing, and conversion to forest, savannas are an uncommon and threatened natural community. The soil is thin here, and sometimes limestone and dolomite bedrock protrude from the surface. Just after passing through a large patch of spanglegrass (with extremely flattened seed heads), you'll cross the main park road at .34 mi. [3]. The savanna is so open that you can see coves of the lake through the trees. Turn right at the trail marker at .60 mi. [4], just before reaching the road. Go straight at the wide, old road intersection at .72 mi. [5].

Notice the barbed-wire fence remnants deeply embedded in an old chinkapin oak, just as the trail bends left at .89 mi. [6]. Big grazers like elk and bison fed on rich savanna grasses in presettlement Missouri. Later, settlers fenced savannas for their cattle. Cross the park road at .92 mi. [7] and go straight at the connector link at .97 mi. [8]. Red cedars join the chinkapin oaks. Fire, which maintains the savanna, often burns off the lower limbs of cedars that are large enough to survive. You'll soon be able to see water on both sides of you as this ridged peninsula becomes narrower.

At 1.38 mi. [9] are the remnants of a Native American cairn. Bluffs or ridgetops like these were often chosen as sites for cairns, which were used for monuments, burials, and landmarks. Archaeological excavations have dated the cairn to the Mississippian cultural period. Go straight at 1.48 mi. [10] to take the spur to the overlook. The breeze starts to kick up as you make your way to Indian Point overlook, which you'll reach at 1.56 mi. [11]. Sunsets are magnificent here, but the view of the lake arms and the island are great anytime. To continue, return to [10] and turn left.

As more views of the lake open on your left, you'll hike through a glade at 1.69 mi. [12], with purple prairie clover, rose verbena, and coneflowers adding their splashes of color. The trail continues through the savanna and follows the shoreline. After crossing two intermittent drainages at 2.09 mi. [13], stay as close to the water as is convenient until you reach a second cairn remnant at 2.39 mi. [14], with buttonbush and several other aquatic plants. Hike around the cairn and pass a large sign on the shore that reads "L2." Soon, you'll pass some ancient, twisted, craggy oaks at 2.61 mi. [15] and see the marina on your left. You'll find some wing-stem sunflowers and rattlesnake master before arriving at the connector link at 2.94 mi. [16], where you go straight. Return to the trailhead just across the park road.

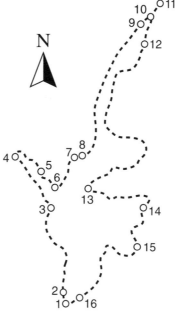

1. Start
2. Savanna
3. Road crossing
4. Right turn
5. Go straight
6. Fence remnants
7. Road crossing
8. Go straight
9. Cairn remnants
10. Go straight
11. Indian Point overlook
12. Glade
13. Two drainages
14. Cairn remnant
15. Ancient oaks
16. Go straight

# Cedar Bluff Trail 👢👢

**Distance Round-Trip:** 2 miles

**Estimated Hiking Time:** 1 hour

*Keep alert—you'll be amazed at the wildlife you can see and hear on this skinny, ridged, wooded peninsula.*

**Caution:** Watch for traffic on the park road; you'll cross it twice.

**Trail Directions:** This trail is at the northern, or Hermitage, area of the park. Park in the lot for visitors, next to the showerhouse. The trail begins **[1]** at the signboard, across the road from the campground entrance.

Begin on a rocky trail that leads down a shaded hill. As a small cove of the lake appears on your right, scan the edges for the largest North American heron, the great blue heron, which stands a full three feet tall. Startled great blues emit three or four loud, hoarse squawks. The green heron, about a third the size of the great blue, feeds along the lake here, too. At .07 mi. **[2]**, near a stand of yellow false foxglove wildflowers, a spur to your right takes you down to a courtesy dock for the park store. Stand on the dock and watch bluegills and green sunfish patrol the water under the dock and near the shore, waiting for unfortunate terrestrial insects to fall in.

Turn right after returning to the trail. You'll wind around some tall lespedeza and buttonbush near the water before emerging onto an open, rocky point at .14 mi. **[3]**. Turn right, toward the lake, for a magnificent overlook. Overhanging dolomite bluffs make up the shoreline on your left, and gentle, wooded hills of the Springfield Plateau line the horizon over the water. Turn away from the lake and into the woods to continue.

In a mixed forest of white oak, post oak, cedar, and sugar maple, you'll reach a trail intersection at .30 mi. **[4]**. Bear right here. The trail takes you about midslope, between the top of the ridge, on your left, and the lakeshore, on your right. Listen for the pileated woodpecker, a crow-sized, shy bird usually heard more often than seen. Its drumming on resonant logs is loud, slow, and softer at the end, and its loud, repetitive call is reminiscent of a monkey's chatter. Notice the twisted trunks of the old chinkapin oaks near the ridgetop. Their wide-

sprawling limbs indicate they grew in a more open setting in the past, having no need to grow tall to compete for sunlight.

At .61 mi. **[5]** go straight at the connecting link. Watch for groundhogs; park staff have noticed they've taken a liking to this peninsula and its surroundings. Another animal you may meet along the trail is the box turtle. If you find one, count the rings on any of the large scales of its shell to find its age—box turtles can live up to 80 years! Males usually have red eyes while females have yellow or brown eyes. You'll hike beneath some shagbark hickories and cedars before emerging into the clearing of the picnic and beach area. Turn left here and cross the park road at .93 mi. **[6]**.

Where the trail is sunny, look closely for the sparkling crystals of quartz in the sandstone. Where the trail becomes sandy and dusty, look for small, bowl-shaped depressions made by ant lions. These small, predatory insect larvae lie at the bottom of each "lion pit," waiting for crawling insects to tumble in. Several clear views of the lake open on your right. If you are here during winter, look for bald eagles soaring over the lake or perching on nearby trees. Just after passing a glade remnant, with gray-head coneflowers, black-eyed Susans, and lots of bluestem grass, go straight at the connecting link at 1.42 mi. **[7]**. A groundhog burrow is on your left at 1.59 mi. **[8]**; approach quietly and you may spy its inhabitant. After crossing the park road at 1.71 mi. **[9]**, you'll return to **[4]**, where you turn right to finish your hike.

1. Start
2. Spur to dock
3. Spur to overlook
4. Bear right
5. Go straight
6. Road crossing
7. Go straight
8. Groundhog burrow
9. Road crossing

# 51. Harry S Truman State Park

- Hike along the top of a limestone bluff with a magnificent overlook of Truman Lake, one of the largest hydroelectric reservoirs in the Midwest.

- Keep your nose open on your glade-savanna hike; the diverse plants in this sun-baked landscape produce a potpourri of aromas as they warm.

- Spy the showy and smelly western wallflower, a plant typical of the southwestern Great Plains and found in no other state park in Missouri.

- Find a patch of prickly pear cactus, which produces large, yellow blossoms in early summer and is the only cactus that grows wild in Missouri.

## Area Information

At birth, Harry Truman, the nation's only president to hail from Missouri, was given the middle initial *S* (but no name) for his grandfathers, both of whose names began with an *S*. Similarly, the state park named for the president serves double duty. Situated near the eastern edge of an area of the state known as the Osage Plains, Harry S Truman State Park contains characteristics of both the prairies to the west and the Ozark forests to the east. The park's prairie elements are visible among its savannas and glades on south- and west-facing slopes, while its Ozark flavor is exhibited in its rugged, dissected hills.

Located on a 1,440-acre tip of a peninsula, the park is surrounded on three sides by Truman Lake, a 55,000-acre reservoir formed by damming the Osage River. The U.S. Army Corps of Engineers designed the reservoir to provide hydroelectric power and recreation opportunities for the public, and the dam began generating power in 1979. The park's peninsula is divided into two sections. The western section contains the park office and campground, while the eastern section is designed as a day-use area for the general public. Both sections cater to the water-recreation enthusiast.

**Directions:** From Warsaw, take State Route 7 north (toward Tightwad) for 6.4 miles. Turn north on Highway UU for 2.6 miles into the park. The visitor center (at Kaysinger Bluff Park, at the east end of the dam) is 1.4 miles west of Highway 65.

**Hours Open:** The park is open during daylight hours, year-round. The park office is open from 8 A.M. to 4:30 P.M. Monday through Friday, year-round. The visitor center is open from 9 A.M. to 6 P.M. daily.

**Facilities:** The state park offers an extensive campground, a full-service marina (including boat rentals), boat ramps, sandy swimming beaches, an amphitheater, and picnic areas. Boating, fishing, and skiing are available on Truman Lake. The U.S. Army Corps of Engineers operates a visitor center with a panoramic view of the lake, interpretive displays, an audiovisual room, a restored homestead site, and a short hiking trail. The visitor center facilities are free to the public.

**Permits and Rules:** Alcoholic beverages are prohibited on all state park beaches and parking areas. Pets must always be leashed.

**Further Information:** Park Superintendent, Harry S Truman State Park, HCR 66, Box 14, Warsaw, MO 65355; 660-438-7711 (park office); 660-438-2423 (marina); 660-438-7317 (visitor center).

## Other Areas of Interest

The **U.S. Army Corps of Engineers** operates a number of recreation facilities that primarily feature water recreation and camping along all arms of the Harry S Truman reservoir. For more information call 660-438-7317.

## Park Trails

**Lakeside Trail** 👢👢👢—.25 mile—This trail begins behind the picnic shelter at the end of the road in the day-use area. It makes a loop next to the lake but is somewhat difficult to follow.

# Harry S Truman State Park

LEGEND

— Road
········· Trail
▬▬ Boundary

🏠 Park Office
🛈 Picnic Area
◩ Shelter
🚻 Restrooms
⛺ Camping
⚓ Marina
🛶 Boat Launch
🏠 Change House
🏊 Beach
🎭 Amphitheater
🌲 Wood Lot
🚮 Trailer Disposal Station
🅰 Fee Collection
🅿 Parking

Lakeside Trail

Bluff Ridge Trail

Western Wallflower Savanna Trail

N

UU

To 7

# Western Wallflower Savanna Trail 👢👢👢

**Distance Round-Trip:** .75 mile

**Estimated Hiking Time:** .5 hour

*Come in May, June, or early July to catch the trail's namesake in bloom. It occurs in no other state park in Missouri. The western wallflower is hard to miss—it's a tall, bright-orange, perfumed show-off.*

**Caution:** Consider sun protection if you are here in the summer; the trail takes you through the savanna and onto a cheerful (but shadeless) glade.

**Trail Directions:** Park in the lot for the trailhead, between the park office and the fee-collection booth for the campground. Begin at the interpretive kiosk **[1]**, which describes savannas and illustrates several savanna and glade plants you are likely to see along the trail. The trail begins on a descending path and introduces you to the savanna right away. Notice the widely spaced oak trees, the lack of understory, and the prairie grasses and plants flourishing between the trees. Natural fires maintained expansive savannas in presettlement times. Because of effective fire suppression in the last century and a half, nearly all savanna landscapes have grown up in successional forests. Prescribed fires are used today to maintain a few remnants of this unique, once-extensive landscape.

At .13 mi. **[2]** the savanna eases into a glade, which is rockier, drier, and more open. Notice that most of the white oaks are replaced by chinkapin oaks, which are shorter, farther apart, and more tolerant of drier conditions. Turn left at .14 mi. **[3]**. Big bluestem grass sometimes turns purple at its ends. Little bluestem's stems are very flat at their base. Look for the dark green, frilly leaves of purple prairie clover and the bright yellow blooms of sunflowers. Some splendid views of the lake open at .18 mi. **[4]**. Notice the trees are more numerous at the lower end of the hill (back to savanna).

Sniff the air as you hike and you'll likely smell the aromas of several sun-warmed mints, grasses, and other plants. If you are here in the summer, you will need no reminder that you are on a glade—sometimes known as a minidesert. Nevertheless, several patches of prickly pear cactus appear at .39 mi. **[5]**. The large, oval part of the cactus is really a thickened stem; its real leaves are only about a quarter of an inch long and fall off soon after the cactus's last growth spurt. Look for the indigo bunting here, a small, brilliant, almost iridescent blue bird that is sometimes mistaken for Missouri's state bird, the bluebird. At .41 mi. **[6]**, just as the trail bends to the right, notice the stand of leadplant, with hairy, gray leaves.

As you reenter the partial shade of the savanna at .50 mi. **[7]**, you are in a good spot to appreciate the gradation of three types of communities. Notice the dense, shady forest on your left, with a developed understory and a lack of ground plants. As you look to the right, the tree canopy opens up and a savanna develops. Looking farther right, a glade is formed in the savanna's rockiest, most open spot. Notice, too, that the communities shift almost imperceptibly. Transition areas like this are often considered savanna-glade mosaics, or complexes. After stepping out into the sunny glade again, you'll return to **[3]**, where you turn left to return to the trailhead.

1. Start
2. Glade
3. Left turn
4. Lake overlook
5. Prickly pear cactus
6. Leadplant
7. Community mosaic

# Bluff Ridge Trail 👢👢👢👢

**Distance Round-Trip:** 2 miles

**Estimated Hiking Time:** 1 hour

*As I was near the blufftop lake overlook, the ominous rumblings in the sky took on a whole new meaning for me because I had just passed a huge oak next to the trail that had literally exploded from a lightning strike only a few days before.*

**Caution:** Watch your step; the trail is home to an assortment of different-sized rocks.

**Trail Directions:** This trail begins in the middle of the camping area, on the park's west side. Park at showerhouse #3; the trailhead is just across the street. Begin at the interpretive kiosk **[1]**, which explains the importance of fire as a tool to maintain habitats like forests, glades, and savannas. An oak forest, for example, can evolve into a maple forest if fire is suppressed. Maples are beautiful in the fall, but provide little food for wildlife and shade out more beneficial trees. Once thought only destructive, periodic fire strengthens natural communities by maintaining their diversity.

Descend a rocky hill beneath a variety of oaks, hickories, ashes, and basswood. As the trail bends to the left at .23 mi. **[2]**, notice the abundance of rock and the absence of almost all trees and plants but cedar. Cedars can flourish in the thinnest and driest of soils, and will quickly take over any rocky area where fire is suppressed, crowding out almost everything else. The huge knots on the chinkapin oak trunk at .31 mi. **[3]** are burls, which are abnormal growths caused by disease or some other injury. Fine-furniture makers cherish burls for their interesting, twisted grain patterns.

After crossing a deep ravine that drains into the lake, on your left, you'll climb a rocky hill with fernlike leaves of lousewort on both sides of the trail. Lousewort produces light yellow flower clusters in April and May and was once thought to be a remedy for lice. The trail swings to the right at the top of the bluff. Views appear through the trees of the lake's blue water and, opposite, white limestone bluffs. Go

straight at the intersection with the connecting link at .50 mi. **[4]**. As you hike along this blufftop, you may notice charred stumps and logs from prescribed fires, which park managers use to achieve the same effects that periodic, natural fires produced in presettlement times. Notice that many of the older trees have broken tops, missing limbs, and lightning scars—evidence of their high exposure here to violent weather.

At .98 mi. **[5]** step out onto the open limestone ledge for a magnificent overlook of the lake. Tributaries to these flooded riverbeds have created scores of quiet coves, pocketed by woods. Some of the coves are still filled with the skeletons of standing timber. If you are here in the winter, scan the trees near the lake and the skies overhead for bald and golden eagles. After passing through another cedar-covered glade, the trail takes you through an open glade at 1.18 mi. **[6]**, where the cedars have been removed and prairie grasses and wildflowers thrive.

At 1.54 mi. **[7]** you'll enter a savanna, with widely interspersed mature trees. You may notice a little charcoal at the base of their trunks, but these oaks, unlike cedars, are resistant to fires. Go straight at the connecting link intersection at 1.65 mi. **[8]** and you'll reach the pavement of the campground loop at 1.72 mi. **[9]**. Turn right here to return to the trailhead.

1. Start
2. Cedar-covered glade
3. Chinkapin burls
4. Go straight
5. Lake overlook
6. Open glade
7. Savanna
8. Go straight
9. Right turn

# 52.  Knob Noster State Park

- Hike through a beautiful, open savanna while searching for striking red-headed woodpeckers, showy prairie wildflowers, and a kaleidoscope of butterflies.
- Learn about savannas as important food-factory powerhouses for wildlife.
- Discover an oxbow of Clearfork Creek—a small but important wetland in the forest.
- Meet a green dragon, face-to-face, next to the trail.

## Area Information

The town of Knob Noster was named in the 1850s for two hills, or knobs, northeast of town. Somebody added *noster,* the Latin word for *our,* and "our knobs" (Knob Noster) stuck. Knob Noster State Park, like Cuivre River and Lake of the Ozarks State Parks, began as a National Recreation Demonstration Area (RDA). The federal government created RDAs in the 1930s by buying poor farmland, restoring it, and developing it for recreation near population centers. From 1936 to 1946, the park was named Montserrat and was administered by the National Park Service. Workers from CCC and WPA programs built two group camps in the park, as well as small lakes, bridges, and several buildings. The National Park Service transferred the 3,567-acre park to the state in 1946.

Although the park's land has greatly healed from its history of poor farming practices, overgrazing, and coal mining, management continues today to restore parts of the area to its presettlement condition. One hundred and fifty years ago, much of the area was a savanna landscape, a prairie grassland with interspersed trees. Savannas provided food for a diversity of wildlife

species. Wide-crowned oaks produced valuable acorns for turkey, deer, and rodents, while providing nest homes for woodpeckers, owls, and small mammals. Tall prairie grasses and forbs provided food for large, grazing mammals, grassland birds, as well as legions of insects. Displays in the park's visitor center explain the role savannas played in Missouri's history and describe the park's progress in restoring some of these valuable natural communities.

**Directions:** From Knob Noster, on Highway 50, take Highway 23 south for 1.2 miles. Turn right at the sign for the park.

**Hours Open:** The site is open year-round from dawn to dusk. The visitor center is open from 9 A.M. to 4:30 P.M. daily.

**Facilities:** The park features a nature center with exhibits and environmental activities for kids downstairs. A campground is available, as well as an equestrian trail and camp, two group camps, an amphitheater, and picnic areas. Fishing and boating are available on several small lakes. Park users may, for a fee, use the Royal Oaks Golf Course, managed by Whiteman Air Force Base. Entry is off Highway 23.

**Permits and Rules:** Horses are restricted to the McAdoo Equestrian Trail. Bicycles are restricted to paved roads and the McAdoo Trail. Boats are allowed on the lakes but must be carried on; motors are restricted to trolling motors. Swimming is not allowed. Pets must be leashed.

**Further Information:** Park Superintendent, Knob Noster State Park, 873 SE 10, Knob Noster, MO 65336; 660-563-2463.

## Park Trails

**Buteo Trail** 👢👢—1 mile—This trail follows the entire shoreline of Lake Buteo, offering scenic views of the lake and opportunities to see a variety of wildlife. The trail shares a trailhead with the Hawk Nest Trail, at the lake's spillway.

**McAdoo Equestrian Trail** 👢👢👢—5 miles—Open to hikers, equestrians, and bicyclists, this trail traverses a variety of habitats in hilly and dissected

terrain. The eastern section of the trail approaches Clearfork Creek in several places. The trail begins 1.6 miles southwest of the visitor center, on Highway DD.

**Opossum Hollow Trail** 👢👢👢—1.5 miles—This trail is a gradual incline during its first half and a gradual decline during its last half. It passes three small lakes and many wolf trees in a crowded forest that was once a savanna. The trail begins at the end of the park road that leads to Morel Lake, 3 miles west of the visitor center, off Highway DD.

# Knob Noster State Park

To Sedalia

23
50

To Warrensburg

N

23

Discovery Trail

Lake Buteo

Buteo Trail

Clearfork Savanna Trail

North Loop Grassland

North Loop Trail

Hawk Nest Trail

Clearfork Savanna

Whiteman Air Force Base Golf Course

Pin Oak Slough Natural Area

Clearfork Creek

Clearfork Lake

Clearfork Grassland

Morel Lake

Redbud Lake

P

McAdoo Equestrian Trail

Sullivan Lake

Opossum Hollow Savanna

Opossum Hollow Trail

Camp Bobwhite

Camp Shawnee

DD

To Warrensburg

## LEGEND
- —— Road
- ········ Trail
- ▬▬ Boundary
- Park Office Visitor Center
- Camping
- Group Camp
- Scout Camping
- Equestrian Camping
- Picnic Area
- Picnic Shelter
- P Parking
- Whiteman Air Force Base Golf Course

# Hawk Nest and Clearfork Savanna Trails 🥾🥾🥾

**Distance Round-Trip:** 2.5 miles

**Estimated Hiking Time:** 1.5 hours

*"The view opens upon boundless and beautiful prairies, dotted with clumps of trees. . . . Clumps of trees, away from any stream or water, is another peculiar feature of this region."* —Ephraim M. Anderson, a Missouri Confederate soldier, describing the Knob Noster vicinity in 1861

**Caution:** Be careful on the lake spillway; algae can make it slippery.

**Trail Directions:** Follow the signs for Lake Buteo, which is just south of the campground, and park in the lot for the lake. This trail shares a trailhead with the Buteo Trail and is marked with a signboard [1] at the lake's edge. Cross an intermittent stream over some large rocks near the lake's spillway. Pass a picnic shelter on your right and continue straight. Just after passing a limestone rest-room building on your right, built in the 1930s by a WPA work-relief program, take the far left trail at .21 mi. [2] at the intersection with some old roads. Take every available left turn on a wide, mowed path. Pass a large, open field on your right and continue on your left. Cross the small, wooden bridge at .41 mi. [3] and enter Clearfork Savanna.

As the trail parallels a small tributary to Clearfork Creek, it skirts the savanna and clearly illustrates its characteristics. Notice that the trees on the left are large and widely spaced. A lack of understory allows prairie plants to grow and lends an open appearance. Contrast the savanna with the habitat on your right, which is a creek bottom with a dense understory of small redbud, ash, and Ohio buckeye trees. Most of the interspersed savanna trees here are white oaks, with the occasional shagbark hickory and black walnut. At .62 mi. [4] you'll cross two small streams. Just after climbing out of the last bottom, look on your left for green dragon, an unusual, larger relative of jack-in-the-pulpit. Its central cluster of shiny, green fruit turns bright red in the fall.

As you continue, listen for the song of the field sparrow, which gets faster at the end like the sound of a Ping-Pong ball dropped on a table. The dickcissel lives here, too. Look for the male, which has a yellow breast with a black bib. Go over two small, wooden bridges at .96 mi. [5]. At 1.3 mi. [6] turn left to begin the Clearfork Savanna Trail, a small loop trail that takes you into the heart of the savanna. Turn right at 1.32 mi. [7]. Deeply cut drainages make for a rolling grassland, with several hill starts and stops facing you at once. The post oak canopy is wide open in places, allowing prairie plants like blazing star and purple prairie clover to thrive among the bluestem grasses. The leaves of the rough-leaved sunflower feel exactly like sandpaper. Turn right when you return to [7] and turn left at [6].

Pick at blackberries as you continue and go straight at the spur on your right at 1.86 mi. [8]. Pass through a patch of spanglegrass and ignore the old road on your left at 2.12 mi. [9], marked with an orange-painted post. You'll reach Lake Buteo at 2.19 mi. [10], where you turn left on a small, wooden bridge. Splendid views of the lake will be interrupted only by bullfrogs hurtling into the water, bluegills sucking hapless grasshoppers from the surface, and dragonflies whirring about. Follow the lakeshore until you reach the dam at 2.35 mi. [11], where you turn right. After making your way across the spillway, turn right to complete your savanna hike.

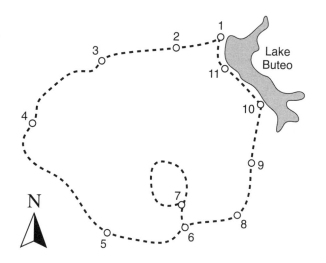

1. Start
2. Left turn
3. Wooden bridge
4. Two stream crossings
5. Two wooden bridges
6. Left turn
7. Right turn
8. Go straight
9. Go straight
10. Lake Buteo
11. Right turn

# Discovery and North Loop Trails 🥾🥾🥾

**Distance Round-Trip:** 2.75 miles

**Estimated Hiking Time:** 1.75 hours

*Several prairie plants are joining the vigorous bluestem grasses in the grassland restoration area. Along with blazing star and sunflowers is sensitive briar, a trailside sock-puller.*

**Caution:** Small, loose rocks make footing unsure on several inclines.

**Trail Directions:** Begin the Discovery Trail on the east side of the visitor center, at the edge of the forest **[1]**. You'll soon cross a small, wooden bridge. At .14 mi. **[2]**, No-Name Creek meanders below you and passes beneath a WPA-built stone bridge on your far right. Several small trees have sprouted from the top of a limestone boulder that has tumbled near the creek bed. As you make your way between the creek on your right and a slope on your left, covered with a variety of oak and hickory trees, notice the trail work—occasional limestone stepping-stones and steps installed by work-relief laborers in the 1930s.

Take the small spur on your right at .24 mi. **[3]** down to the creek. Look for the Louisiana water-thrush, a small, dark brown bird with a streaked breast that spends most of its time on or near stream-beds and bobs its tail up and down almost constantly. You're likely to see aquatic insects and snails scut-tling on the bottom of pools, with a sampling of minnows darting above them. Notice the flat, gray rocks here that crumble in thin sheets. This is shale, a sedimentary rock similar to slate, but softer. Turn right after returning to the main trail.

Keep an eye out for a variety of birds in the canopy and understory. The small trees next to the trail with puffy, yellow-green "lanterns" are American bladder-nut. Turn right at .60 mi. **[4]**. Turn right again at .64 mi. **[5]** immediately after crossing a small, wooden bridge. You are now beginning the North Loop Trail. If you see bright orange yellow, earlike growths on the forest floor, you have probably discovered chantarelle mushrooms, a common summer fungus, especially after a shower. Ignore the connector link at .73 mi. **[6]** and go straight.

No-Name Creek soon appears again on your right, and the trail traverses small ridges dissected by drainage streams. At 1.34 mi. **[7]** is an open grassland restoration area, being managed to return it to its presettlement condition. As much as a third of

Missouri was once covered in prairie, and extensive savannas occurred at transition areas where prairie and forest met. Many trees bordering the grassland here are shingle oaks, with narrowly oval leaves. Settlers split these oaks for siding and roofing shingles.

Turn right at the intersection with a fire road at 1.52 mi. **[8]** and go straight where the connector link joins the trail at 1.75 mi. **[9]**. Bear right, just after crossing a small bridge over an intermittent stream. An abandoned channel of Clearfork Creek appears on your right at 1.81 mi. **[10]**. When streams are allowed to meander, naturally and unchannelized, they provide valuable wetlands, such as this oxbow. Many kinds of amphibians, aquatic plants, and insects need habitat like this to reproduce. Look for the arrow-shaped leaves of arrowhead and the tall, branchy blooms of water plantain.

The trail passes some moist, limestone bluffs on the left. After passing beneath a powerline, you'll cross several small streams as you continue through the mixed, oak-hickory forest. At 2.57 mi. **[11]** you'll enter the campground. Hike straight across the campground loop and reenter the forest at the trail sign at the edge of the woods. Turn right when you return to **[5]** and cross the small, wooden bridge. Keep going straight on this section until you return to the visitor center.

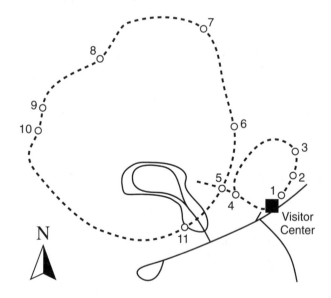

1. Start
2. No-Name Creek
3. Spur to creek
4. Right turn
5. Right turn
6. Go straight
7. Grassland
8. Right turn
9. Go straight
10. Creek oxbow
11. Campground

# 53. Urban Kansas City

- Escape the traffic and telephone and walk in the tranquil gardens of the 17-acre Kansas City Sculpture Park.
- Come hike and feast and frolic in the Plaza, where you can view Italian and American sculptures, shop til you drop, listen to outdoor jazz for free, and indulge in an extraordinary cornucopia of culinary choices.
- Witness Community Christian Church's 1.2-billion-candlepower Steeple of Light, a vision of Frank Lloyd Wright's not realized until 1994.

## Area Information

Like many other cities, Kansas City owes its beginnings to a confluence of two rivers. Fur trappers along the Kansas and Missouri Rivers brought their pelts to the trading post Francois Chouteau established in 1821 where the two rivers join. At this transfer point, settlers outfitted their wagons for the journey to the Far West. Later, the city grew with industries involving wheat, cattle, corn, and one of the largest railway terminals in the country.

In 1922, city planners designed Country Club Plaza as the nation's first suburban shopping district. This outdoor museum of Romantic Spanish architecture and European art has continuously added to its collection since then. Free outdoor concerts are scheduled during the summer and the famous Plaza Lights burn nightly from Thanksgiving through mid-January.

The Nelson-Atkins Museum of Art has extensive collections representing all areas and periods of artistic expression. The Kansas City Sculpture Park, on the museum grounds, was especially designed to exhibit 13 works by Henry Moore, considered one of the greatest sculptors of the 20th century.

**Directions:** The Country Club Plaza hike begins at Mill Creek Park, between J.C. Nichols Parkway, 47th Street, and Main Street in Kansas City. The Nelson-Atkins Museum of Art is bordered by Brush Creek Boulevard (47th Street), Oak Street, 45th Street, and Rockhill Road, just a half mile northeast of the Plaza.

**Hours Open:** Both areas are open year-round. Most of the Plaza stores are open from 10 A.M. to 9 P.M. Monday through Saturday and from noon to 5 P.M. on Sunday. Jazz clubs and many restaurants are open later. The sculpture park is open seven days a week during daylight hours with free admission. The Nelson-Atkins Museum building is open from 10 A.M. to 4 P.M. Tuesday through Thursday, 10 A.M. to 9 P.M. on Friday, 10 A.M. to 5 P.M. on Saturday, and 1 P.M. to 5 P.M. on Sunday. The museum is closed on Mondays and several holidays. Admission is free on Saturdays.

**Facilities:** Facilities abound in the Plaza. The art museum has rest rooms, a restaurant, and a bookstore. Both the museum building and the sculpture park are wheelchair accessible.

**Permits and Rules:** Do not touch or climb on sculptures or wade in the fountains.

**Further Information:** Convention and Visitors Bureau of Greater Kansas City, 1100 Main, Suite 2550, Kansas City, MO 64105; 800-767-7700, or Public Information, The Nelson-Atkins Museum of Art, 4525 Oak Street, Kansas City, MO 64111; 816-561-4000.

## Other Areas of Interest

Almost all the personal possessions are left in place the way the Bentons left them at **Thomas Hart Benton Home and Studio State Historic Site**. Painter of large, dynamic murals, Benton was Missouri's most noted 20th-century artist. Guided tours are available for a fee. For more information call 816-931-5722.

## Area Trails

**Gillham Park Trail** —1 mile—This loop trail is made of recycled roofing shingles. The trail traverses the borders of the park, between West Gillham Road, 47th Street, and Harrison Street. The park is only .18 mile east of the art museum.

**Mill Creek Park Trail** —1 mile—This double-loop trail has a rubberized surface and several fitness stations along the way. Next to the Plaza, the trail offers views of several Spanish-inspired towers.

**Loose Park Trail** —1.2 miles—Travel .9 mile south on Broadway from the Plaza to find the park at the corner of 51st Street and Wornall Road. The trail takes you next to a fountain lake, a Civil War battle site, spacious meadows, and a splendid rose garden.

# Kansas City

N

**LEGEND**

| | |
|---|---|
| ? | Missouri State Info Center |
| ★ | Nelson Atkins Museum of Art |
| 🛍 | Country Club Plaza |
| 🌲 | Jacob Loose Park |
| 🌲🌲 | Mill Creek Park |
| 🌲🌲 | Gillham Park |
| ✕ | Downtown Airport |
| 🐃 | Zoo |

# Country Club Plaza

**Distance Round-Trip:** 1 mile

**Estimated Hiking Time:** 1 hour

*Wear your finest Italian suit when you come to the Plaza, or your shorts or overalls—you'll fit in no matter what you wear. And this is one of the only museums of fine art where you can view the exhibits, talk as loudly as you want, and eat pretzels dripping with mustard at the same time.*

**Caution:** Be careful crossing streets; there are many distractions for pedestrian and driver alike.

**Trail Directions:** Begin the hike at the south end of Mill Creek Park [1], half a mile southwest of the Nelson-Atkins Museum of Art. Free parking is plentiful on the streets and in lots and garages in and around the Plaza. Notice the white Community Christian Church just to the east of the park, on Main Street. Steepleless by day, this church's perforated dome beams the 1.2-billion-candlepower Steeple of Light by night, which reaches several miles into the stratosphere. Originally designed by Frank Lloyd Wright in 1940, the steeple was lit for the first time on December 10, 1994.

Also known as the City of Fountains, Kansas City boasts a variety of monumental fountain sculptures all over town. The J.C. Nichols Memorial Fountain here [2], dedicated to the developer of the Plaza, is probably the city's best known. The four dramatic horsemen, sculpted in Paris in 1910, represent the world's rivers.

Cross 47th Street and J.C. Nichols Parkway. Seville Light [3] (in this intersection) and Giralda Bell Tower [4] (.07 mi.) are replicas of the original structures in Seville, Spain, and set the theme for the Plaza as an open-air public art gallery of Romantic Spanish architecture and European art. Fountains, sculptures, and murals of bronze, marble, and ceramic tile adorn the entire district.

At .09 mi. is Chandler Court [5], one of five courtyards in the Plaza and a great place to meet and relax. Some courtyards are stopping places for the trolley and horse-drawn carriages. Continue west on 47th Street and find an information booth at .16 mi. [6] with helpful people from the Kansas City Convention and Visitors Bureau. After passing the Fountain of Neptune [7] (.19 mi.), originally from Worcestershire, England, cross Central Street and continue west. You'll pass various sidewalk cafes, all with accompanying tempting aromas, while crossing Broadway and Pennsylvania Street.

Turn left on Jefferson Street at .39 mi. [8] and again on 48th Street at .50 mi. [9]. After passing a smorgasbord of specialty shops, including an Irish pub designed and built in Ireland, turn left on Pennsylvania Street. Turn right at Saks Fifth Avenue [10] at .61 mi. and continue east on Nichols Road. You'll pass several fountains, some of which were bought in Italy in the 1920s, before turning left on Wyandotte Street at .90 mi. [11]. Turn right at Chandler Court [5], where you might want to stop in for a cheesecake at the Cheesecake Factory (they have over 40 kinds) before finishing the hike at Mill Creek Park.

1. Start
2. J.C. Nichols Memorial Fountain
3. Seville Light
4. Giralda Bell Tower
5. Chandler Court
6. Information booth
7. Fountain of Neptune
8. Left turn
9. Left turn
10. Saks Fifth Avenue
11. Left turn

# Kansas City Sculpture Park 🥾

**Distance Round-Trip:** 1 mile

**Estimated Hiking Time:** .75 hour

*"Seraphs share with thee knowledge but art o man is thine alone."—Inscription on the northeast end of the Nelson-Atkins Museum of Art*

**Caution:** Please do not touch or climb on the sculptures or allow children to do so.

**Trail Directions:** The park is located on the grounds of the Nelson-Atkins Museum of Art. The hike begins **[1]** at the 17-foot-high badminton shuttlecock at the northwest corner of the museum.

Probably no other single object is a better signature for the art museum, or even for Kansas City, than this four-part sculpture named *Shuttlecocks* **[2]**. Installed in 1994, this was the first outdoor sculpture commissioned for the park. Walk eastward, toward *Rush Hour* **[3]** (.04 mi.), the cluster of bronze people frozen in their walking hurry. Continue toward the 24-foot-high orange *Rumi* and turn right at .09 mi. **[4]** on the herringbone brick sidewalk.

As you round the last corner of the building, the expanse of the 17-acre manicured landscape opens before you. Overall, the exhibits and clusters of trees contrast with the large openness of the south plaza, which imparts its own feeling of peacefulness. Two more shuttlecocks look like they fell from the sky here, adding their touch of humor and playfulness.

Take the spur at .21 mi. **[5]** to view the first piece by British sculptor Henry Moore, the park's featured artist. Moore wanted his sculptures to be seen in nature against rocks, trees, and sky. His works are set in landscapes in more than 20 countries and explore five basic themes: mother and child, the reclining figure, internal and external forms, animal forms, and nonrepresentational forms. After viewing the reclining figure entitled *Hand*, return to the main path and turn right. Several Moore pieces will appear on your left. At *Sheep Piece* **[6]** (.36 mi.) follow the path as it curves left and takes you to *Reclining Connected Forms* **[7]** (.43 mi.) in a private garden. Turn around and bear left to reach *Large Interior Form* **[8]** (.48 mi.), a sentinel over the busy nearby street intersection. Turn around and bear left again. Turn left at the intersection at **[6]**.

Soon you'll reach the big, green, south plaza, a good place to rest, read, or join the shuttlecocks and just sprawl. Continuing the path will bring you to Moore's *Seated Woman* **[9]** (.65 mi.), where you turn right. Turn right again at .83 mi. **[10]** and ascend some steps. Walk toward the main museum entrance, go up the steps, and turn left toward another shuttlecock. In this patio courtyard are two more works by Moore, *Three Park Object* and *Torso*. After viewing these, retrace your steps to **[10]**, where you turn right to return to the parking lot.

1. Start
2. *Shuttlecocks*
3. *Rush Hour*
4. Right turn
5. Right turn
6. *Sheep Piece*
7. *Reclining Connected Forms*
8. *Large Interior Form*
9. *Seated Woman*
10. Right turn

# 54.  Wilson's Creek National Battlefield

- Come to Wilson's Creek and learn about the battle that marked the beginning of the Civil War in Missouri.

- Tour the battlefield where 15,000 soldiers from both sides gathered and more than 2,500 men were killed or wounded.

- See postmaster John Ray's home, one of only two surviving structures on the site from the battle, which was used as a Confederate field hospital during and after the battle.

## Area Information

With civil war imminent, most Missourians favored neutrality, but radical Secessionists and Unionists divided the state, and Missouri's sons quickly filled the ranks of military units that formed everywhere.

The battle of Wilson's Creek was the second major engagement of the Civil War, after Manassas, and marked the beginning of the war in Missouri. The battle here involved 15,000 Confederate and Union soldiers. More than 2,500 men were killed or wounded during the bloody six-hour struggle. The National Park Service manages Wilson's Creek National Battlefield to interpret this important battle, preserve its site, and commemorate the soldiers on both sides who died and are buried here.

**Directions:** From Springfield, take Highway 60 west. Just outside town, take Highway M east for .7 mile. Turn south on Highway ZZ for 1.5 miles and turn left at the sign for the battlefield.

**Hours Open:** The battlefield is open from 8 A.M. to 9 P.M. during summer, until 7 P.M. in spring and fall, and until 5 P.M. during winter. The entire site is closed on Christmas and New Year's Day.

**Facilities:** The site features a visitor center with a museum. Living-history demonstrations and guided tours are also scheduled. A five-mile auto tour route

takes visitors to all the major points on the battlefield. Abundant interpretive signs are located along the way. A biking-jogging route, picnic area, and horseback trails are also provided.

**Permits and Rules:** A two-dollar entrance fee per person is required, up to four dollars per vehicle. Bikes are restricted to the auto tour route, and horses are restricted to authorized horse trails. Using firearms or metal detectors, collecting artifacts, and disturbing buildings, plants, or animals are prohibited. Skates and skateboards are not allowed. Pets must always be leashed. Please acknowledge the memorial qualities of the site and refrain from any activities that might be deemed disrespectful.

**Further Information:** Chief Ranger, Wilson's Creek National Battlefield, 6424 West Farm Road 182, Republic, MO 65738; 417-732-2662.

## Other Areas of Interest

**Bass Pro Shops Outdoor World** is the world's largest sporting goods store. Featuring aquariums, a wildlife museum and displays, waterfalls, and restaurants, the store is Missouri's number-one attraction. The store is northeast of Wilson's Creek, in Springfield, at the corner of Highway 60 and Campbell Street. For more information call 417-887-7334.

**Springfield Conservation Nature Center** is one of four nature centers operated by the Missouri Department of Conservation, and features exhibits, an auditorium, nature programs, and hiking trails. The center is .5 mile from the intersection of Highways 65 and 60, and there is no admission charge. For more information call 417-882-4237.

Hundreds of animals from around the world live at **Dickerson Park Zoo**. The zoo is at the north end of Springfield, at the junction of I-44 and Highway 13. For more information call 417-833-1522.

## Site Trails

**Nature Trail** 👢👢—.5 mile—This trail traverses a mixed forest and crosses an intermittent creek. It includes several loops that begin and end at the picnic area, behind the visitor center.

**Ray House and Springhouse Trails** 👢👢—.5 mile— These short trails connect the only two surviving

structures from the battle. The trails begin at stop #2 on the auto tour route, 1.5 miles from the visitor center.

**East Overlook and Pulaski Battery Trails** 👢👢—.5 mile—These short trails connect the east battlefield overlook with the Pulaski Battery. The trails begin at stop #3 on the auto tour route, 2.1 miles from the visitor center.

# Wilson's Creek National Battlefield

Elm St.
182
To Republic
ZZ

Gibson Mill Headrace

182

111

Edgar Cemetery

Gibson House Site

Route of Union Advance and Withdrawal

Ray Cornfield

Ray Springhouse

Wilsons Creek

Totten's Battery

Bloody Hill

Du Bois' Battery

Sinkhole

Lyon Marker

Pulaski Arkansas Battery

East Battlefield Overlook

Guibor's Battery

Skeggs Branch

194

Sigel's Final Position

Sharp Cornfield

Sharp Stubblefield

Sigel's Second Position

Sigel's First Position

LEGEND

— Road
≡ Unpaved Road
=== Historic Route of Wire Road
····· Trail
▬ Boundary

🏠 Visitor Center
🏠 Edwards Cabin– Price's Headquarters
🏠 Ray House
🏠 Sharp Farm Site
⚙ Gibson Mill Site
★ Point of Interest

N

ZZ

# Gibson Mill Site and Ray Cornfield Trails 👢👢

**Distance Round-Trip:** 1.75 miles

**Estimated Hiking Time:** 1 hour

*The trail reveals an old mill and home site, where the Gibson family crouched in the cellar on August 10, 1861, seeking refuge from the thunderous cannons that shattered the morning air.*

**Caution:** The last half of this trail is in the sun; you may want to bring some protection. Horses are allowed on this section. Stay on the six-foot-wide section of the auto tour route when you hike back to the trailhead and watch out for bicyclists there.

**Trail Directions:** Park in the turnoff for stop #1 of the auto tour route, .8 mile from the visitor center. The trail begins in a prairielike field that was John Gibson's oat field at the time of the battle **[1]**. The Gibsons lived in a cabin near the creek, just ahead, and on the day before the great battle, they found themselves surrounded by 12,000 Confederate soldiers. This spot marks the northern end of the Confederate camps, which extended 2 miles south along the creek.

The trail quickly descends to the wooded corridor of Wilson's Creek. After passing an interpretive sign about Gibson's mill and a wooden bridge, turn right at the intersection at .10 mi. **[2]**. Look for the flaky, peeling bark of black cherry and the lined, orange-tinged bark of Osage orange next to the trail. Osage orange wood was prized by Native Americans for making bows, and, before barbed wire became available, settlers planted the trees as living fences because they grew in impenetrable thickets.

The Gibsons made their living by grinding grain and processing wool with the mill that stood just ahead. To provide a constant supply of water falling on the tall waterwheel that powered the millworks, John Gibson performed an amazing engineering feat—with a shovel and perhaps a neighbor and a mule, Gibson constructed a narrow earthen canal three-quarters of a mile long! The millrace channeled water from a small dam upstream and crossed the creek on a raised trestle. The canal gained elevation over the creek, and when it spilled onto the waterwheel, it was nine feet above the creek. At .30 mi. **[3]**, at an interpretive sign, you can see remnants of this earthen invention.

After crossing a small, wooden bridge, turn right at .35 mi. **[4]** to find the Gibson mill site at .37 mi. **[5]**. In 1966, archaeologists discovered the mill's foundation, waterwheel, gearing, and millstones, as well as evidence that the mill burned sometime after the war. Return to **[4]** and turn right. At .49 mi. **[6]** is the Gibson home site, where a sign explains the 1966 archaeological excavations here. You can still see parts of the home's limestone foundation. Return to the mill site and continue the trail on your left.

As the trail follows Wilson's Creek, look for great blue and little green herons, standing in the water or perching nearby. Watch the trail ahead for rabbits and deer—both animals are plentiful in the recovering savannas and prairies of the battlefield. Just after crossing a small bridge, you'll arrive at a three-way intersection where an Osage orange tree and a walnut tree are growing together (.98 mi.) **[7]**. Turn left here to begin the Ray Cornfield Trail. The only major fighting on this side of Wilson's Creek occurred here. On the morning of the battle, John Ray watched from his front porch as his cornfield became a battlefield and Union forces were driven back across the stream. At 1.07 mi. **[8]**, just after passing a split-rail fence, ignore the spur on your left. As some expansive views open, look on the horizon on your left to see Bloody Hill, scene of the battle's most intense and savage fighting. As you pass through a thicket of wild plum trees at 1.37 mi. **[9]**, notice the animal paths that cross the trail. Turn left on the pavement of the auto tour route at 1.60 mi. **[10]** to return to the trailhead.

1. Start
2. Right turn
3. Millrace remnants
4. Right turn
5. Mill site
6. Home site
7. Left turn
8. Go straight
9. Wild plum thicket
10. Left turn

# Bloody Hill and Wire Road

**Distance Round-Trip:** 2 miles

**Estimated Hiking Time:** 1 hour

*For more than six hours, the armies pounded each other in steady and fierce combat, often at close range. In all, over 80 percent of casualties of the battle fell on Bloody Hill, making it one of the bloodiest fights in the war. Survivors of the battle described the day's relentless heat, blinding clouds of gunpowder smoke, and great heaps of the dead and wounded.*

**Caution:** The last half of this trail is in the sun; you may want to bring some protection. Horses are allowed on this section. Stay on the six-foot-wide section of the auto tour route when you hike back to the trailhead and watch out for bicyclists there.

**Trail Directions:** Park at the turnoff for Bloody Hill, which is auto tour route stop #7, 4.2 miles from the visitor center. Part of this trail is a self-guiding route, and numbered stations along the trail correspond to numbers in a tour booklet, available from the visitor center for 50¢. Numbered stations do not correspond to numbered features in this book.

Near some interpretive signs, begin on a wide, gravel path **[1].** The cannon at .15 mi. **[2]** is in the position the 2nd U.S. Battery maintained during most of the battle. This battery was led by Captain James (Bottle-Nose) Totten, so nicknamed for his fondness for brandy. Cannon projectiles included solid shot, shot designed to explode, and canister shot, which were like giant shotgun cartridges. Despite being outnumbered more than two to one, the Union leader, General Nathaniel Lyon, planned a surprise attack on the Confederates, camped along Wilson's Creek. The intersection at .22 mi. **[3]** marks the spot that Lyon's army of 4,200 men had reached by 6 A.M., advancing from the northwest. From across the creek, to the east, four cannons of the Arkansas battery opened fire on Lyon's army, slowing their advance. Turn left here.

Fierce charges and countercharges came in waves, as the Union desperately tried to hold its hilltop position. After hiking through a glade, with exposed limestone bedrock and prickly pear cactus, you'll reach a stone monument at .31 mi. **[4]** that marks the approximate spot General Lyon fell about 9:30 A.M. while leading the 2nd Kansas Infantry against the Missouri State Guard. "I am killed!" Lyon exclaimed, after a musket ball passed through his chest and he

collapsed into the arms of his orderly. At the three-way intersection at .37 mi. **[5]** turn left. Note the thick forest here. One Iowa private wrote, "The few trees were rather large . . . and everything could be distinctly seen under them." The National Park Service has begun a program of prescribed fires to restore the battlefield to its 1861 landscape of prairie and savanna.

At .55 mi. **[6],** where the trail turns left, you'll see the slope that Southerners attempted to crest three times during the battle, each time suffering heavy casualties. The small cabin at the bottom of the slope marks the site of the headquarters of Confederate general Sterling Price. Price was well liked by his troops, who nicknamed him Old Pap. Turn right at .58 mi. **[7],** and descend to the creek valley. At .85 mi. **[8],** at an iron bridge, turn right. You are now on historic Wire Road, which connected Springfield, Missouri, with Fort Smith, Arkansas, at the time of the battle. You'll soon pass an interpretive sign at the Edwards cabin, where Price was eating his breakfast of cornbread and beef at the time of Lyon's attack.

After Wire Road dips into the welcome shade at the Skegg's Branch crossing, you'll climb a hill. Turn right at 1.31 mi. **[9]** on the pavement of the auto tour route and take the spur on your right at 1.82 mi. **[10]** that leads to Guibor's battery. Captain Guibor assisted the Confederate infantry in their final charge up Bloody Hill by firing four cannons from this spot into the Federal line. Turn right after returning to the auto tour route to finish your battlefield hike.

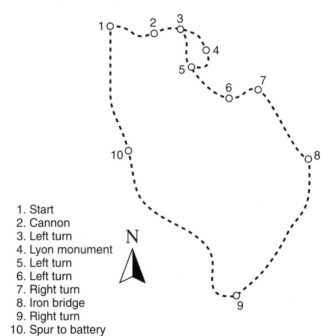

1. Start
2. Cannon
3. Left turn
4. Lyon monument
5. Left turn
6. Left turn
7. Right turn
8. Iron bridge
9. Right turn
10. Spur to battery

N

# 55. Piney Creek Wilderness

- Climb 133 steps to the top of a U.S. Forest Service lookout tower for a soaring vulture's-eye view of the forested, roller-coaster terrain.

- Discover the compass plant, a showy glade wildflower that earned its name from its habit of aligning its lower leaves north and south on sunny days.

- Hike on a natural sidewalk a third of a mile long, with scenic views across a chasmlike valley and blooming glade wildflowers along the way.

## Area Information

Piney Creek is an 8,142-acre wilderness designated in 1980 to be managed by the U.S. Forest Service under the provisions of the Wilderness Act of 1964. Generally, a wilderness must be at least 5,000 acres, basically roadless, and show little evidence of human works. Wildernesses contain no developments, no timber harvesting, no new mining claims, and no use of motor vehicles. Missouri has eight such areas, seven of which are located on the Mark Twain National Forest.

Piney Creek is in the Ava/Cassville/Willow Springs District of the Mark Twain National Forest. The district includes over 200,000 acres in southwest Missouri, where steep ridges and conical hills are often topped with glades, and oak-hickory forests are interspersed with native shortleaf pine. Piney Creek is in the White River section of the Ozarks, named for the major river that straddles the Missouri-Arkansas border and carved the area's rugged landscape. The wilderness protects the entire watershed of Piney Creek, which flows into the James River Arm of Table Rock Lake at the east end of the area.

Several homesteaders lived in the area around the turn of the century and tried to raise cattle, tomatoes, and strawberries on the dry, rocky ridges, but by 1960 there were no permanent residents within the area now designated wilderness. Several animals more typical of the southwest U.S. live here, including armadillos, roadrunners, and tarantulas.

**Directions:** From Cassville, take Highway 76 east 18.3 miles to Table Rock Lake Road 76-6 (FR 2150), where you turn right. Go .8 mile and turn right on a gravel road (#1139) for .1 mile to the Pineview Lookout Tower.

**Hours Open:** The wilderness is always open.

**Facilities:** Picnic tables with grills, rest rooms, and hitching rails for horses are available at the trailhead (north end of area). A lookout tower (maintained for the discovery of wildfires) is also available for climbing.

**Permits and Rules:** Only four people are allowed on the tower at one time. Horses and bikes are allowed on the trails, but ATVs are prohibited. Hunting is permitted but not within 150 yards of the trail. Camping is allowed, but campers should observe regulations designed to protect the wilderness beauty. Choose a campsite away from the trail and avoid constructing a fire ring. Cut no standing trees (live or dead), extinguish all campfires, and scatter their evidence before leaving. Leave no litter, trail-marking ribbons, or other evidence of your presence.

**Further Information:** District Ranger, U.S. Forest Service, Ava/Cassville/Willow Springs District, P.O. Box 188, Ava, MO 65608; 417-683-4428.

## Other Areas of Interest

**Table Rock State Park,** seven miles southwest of Branson, features water recreation on 53,000-acre Table Rock Lake. The park includes a marina, boat rentals, campsites, and a short hiking trail. For more information call 417-334-4704.

**Shepherd of the Hills Fish Hatchery,** one of five trout hatcheries operated by the Missouri Department of Conservation, is at the base of Table Rock Dam, six miles southwest of Branson. The hatchery site offers a visitor center with exhibits, aquariums, and audio-visual presentations, guided tours of the hatchery, a picnic area, wildlife viewing blinds, a boat ramp, and four hiking trails. Adjacent **Lake Taneycomo** receives 80 percent of the hatchery's trout and attracts many trout-fishing enthusiasts. For more information call 417-334-4865.

## Area Trails

Piney Creek Wilderness includes 13.1 miles of trails, most of which are shared by horseback riders. Another trailhead is located on the area's south end;

however, its access road requires a four-wheel-drive or other high-clearance vehicle. To reach the south end, take Highway 76 east from Cassville and turn south on Highway 39. Turn left on Lake Road 39-1.

# Pineview Lookout Tower Trail 👢👢👢👢👢

**Distance Round-Trip:** 3.75 miles

**Estimated Hiking Time:** 2 hours

*You may find yourself leaning from side to side, gasping for breath, and grabbing for saplings as you navigate this rumbly, rocky terrain. It's a good thing the trail's features are so rewarding—this is one of the most challenging hikes in the book!*

**Caution:** Keep your hiking boots laced tightly; numerous sections of the trail are very steep and extremely rocky. Bring a compass and topo map if you plan to extend this hike or explore off the trail. Wear orange clothing during hunting seasons. Vegetation may encroach the trail near Piney Creek.

**Trail Directions:** Park in the lot for the Pineview Lookout Tower. Before or after your hike, be sure to climb to the top of the tower for remarkable and unobstructed views of the surrounding White River Hills region of the Ozarks. Please register at the base of the tower before you begin your hike. The trailhead is at the end of the parking lot (west side) **[1]**.

Begin the trail on a gravelly, narrow ridgetop among oaks, hickories, and interspersed pines. Pine groves dominate the forest in places and fill the air with their fragrance, especially during a warm, sunny afternoon or after a spring shower. The gravel you are hiking on is chert, or flint. If you strike two pieces of this rock together at night, you can see a spark and smell fire. After a quarter mile, the ridge becomes even narrower. Both sides plunge to depths out of view, while steep, dark green hills race up the other side.

You'll find small glades on your way down the slope and many loose rocks on the trail. At .45 mi. **[2]** rosin weed and sunflowers bloom among a series of limestone shelves cascading down the hill. An intermittent stream at .55 mi. **[3]** marks the end of your first descent. Cross the stream, and it's up you go again. You'll quickly be on some more ridgetop glades, where horizontal limestone layers protrude through the thin soil. The trail uses one of these layers as a natural sidewalk at .65 mi. **[4]**, which runs the length of a long ridge and offers some welcome flat terrain. Look for glade plants like coneflowers, prairie dock, and blazing star as several scenic views open across the chasmlike valley on your right.

After the sidewalk ends, you'll descend the slope to the Piney Creek valley. Cross the creek at 1.39 mi. **[5]**. Just after crossing the creek a second time, go straight at the three-way intersection at 1.45 mi. **[6]**. You are now in the Piney Creek bottom, where the vegetation is tall and dense. Cross two intermittent streams and cross Piney Creek two more times at 1.82 mi. **[7]**. Just after passing a pawpaw grove, turn left at the intersection at 2.09 mi. **[8]**.

After crossing Piney Creek again at 2.13 mi. **[9]** (fifth time now?), you'll enter a rocky tributary to the creek at 2.16 mi. **[10]**. Hike about 10 steps to the right in the streambed before finding the trail on the other side. In a few steps, you'll make the last creek crossing at 2.23 mi. **[11]**. After climbing another steep, rocky hill, you'll be back in glade country, with views of sharp, wooded ridges across the deep valley (now on your left). Look for compass plant, a glade wildflower with yellow blooms on long stalks up to eight feet tall. Its rough, deeply lobed lower leaves align north and south on sunny days.

You'll be back on another rocky ridgetop at 2.73 mi. **[12]**. Turn left at the intersection at 2.97 mi. **[13]**. Turn left again at a circular intersection (rotary-like) at 3.33 mi. **[14]**. Soft whispers of breeze in pine tops will accompany you as you return to the tower. Turn right at the intersection at 3.62 mi. **[15]** to finish your rugged and rocky hike.

## Piney Creek Wilderness

1. Start
2. Glade overlook
3. Stream crossing
4. Natural sidewalk
5. Creek crossing
6. Go straight
7. Creek crossings
8. Left turn
9. Creek crossing
10. Right turn in streambed
11. Creek crossing
12. Rocky ridgetop
13. Left turn
14. Left turn
15. Right turn

LEGEND
—— Road
······ Trail
━━ Boundary
🅰 Observation Tower
⭐ Trailhead

Pineview Lookout Tower Trail

James River Arm of Table Rock Lake

N

# 56.  Roaring River State Park

- Visit one of the state's oldest parks, where clear streams have carved deep, narrow valleys between steep, forested knobs and ridges.
- View one of Missouri's most picturesque springs, which emerges from a peaceful cave at the base of a dramatic rock bluff, lined with lush ferns.
- Explore the Roaring River Hills Wild Area, a 2,045-acre undeveloped wilderness that is home to 26 rare or endangered plants and animals.

## Area Information

Roaring River begins quietly. From a shaded cave beneath a high cliff, a deep, blue pool issues about 20 million gallons of water every day. It's not until the river hurries around the boulders of its narrow valley that it begins to roar.

Roaring River's mountainous terrain is part of the White River section of the Ozarks. Weathered bluffs and sheltered forest coves hide caves, seeps, and springs. Clear streams cut through six different rock formations. Many of the park's plants, including yellowwood, Ozark spiderwort, and Ashe's juniper, cannot be found in any other region of the state. Several southwestern species inhabit the park, including armadillos, roadrunners, and the colorful collared lizard. Winter visitors usually see bald eagles perching near the river.

Kansas City and St. Louis residents find the river's rugged and scenic setting the ideal place for fishing retreats. The Missouri Department of Conservation operates a trout hatchery near the spring and stocks the river daily during the fishing season.

**Directions:** Roaring River is in the state's southwest corner. From Cassville, take Highway 112 south seven miles into the park.

**Hours Open:** The park is open year-round. The nature center is open from 9 A.M. to 5 P.M. daily during the fishing season. Opening and closing sirens announce daily fishing hours, which change seasonally.

**Facilities:** The site offers a nature center, fish hatchery, tackle shop and camp store, a new restaurant, motel, gift shop, three campgrounds, swimming pool, amphitheater, rental cabins, a group camp, picnic areas, and a stable for horse rental.

**Permits and Rules:** A state fishing license and a daily permit, available from the tackle shop at the old lodge, are required for trout fishing. Swimming or wading in the river is not permitted. Fish feeding is allowed in the hatchery's rearing pools, but only food bought on-site may be used. Pets must always be leashed. Motel and cabin reservations are required.

**Further Information:** Park Superintendent, Roaring River State Park, Route 2, Box 2530, Cassville, MO 65625; 417-847-2539 (park office); 417-847-2330 (concessionaire); or 800-334-6946 (Department of Natural Resources, Division of State Parks).

## Other Areas of Interest

**Sugar Camp Scenic Drive** is an 8-mile-long gravel road that leads to Eagle Rock and features splendid overlooks of the forested White River Hills, Onyx Cave picnic area, limestone glades, and a view of the White River. The drive is in the Mark Twain National Forest, just south of Roaring River. To begin, take Highway 112 south of the park for 3.4 miles and turn left on FR 197.

**Piney Creek Wilderness,** in the national forest northeast of Roaring River, is 8,000 acres of oak-hickory forest and features five equestrian/hiking trails. The wilderness is about 20 miles east of Cassville on Lake Road 76-6. For more information on either site call 417-847-2144.

## Park Trails

**Deer Leap Trail** 🥾🥾🥾—.4 mile—Beginning on the walkway between the hatchery pools and the spring, this trail climbs limestone bluffs on natural rock and stone steps.

**Fire Tower Trail** 🥾🥾🥾🥾🥾—4.5 miles—This trail explores the Roaring River Hills Wild Area and accesses a state natural area that preserves a remnant of old-growth oak-hickory forest. The trail can be

accessed from the Deer Leap Trail or from the parking area near the stable. The round-trip trail requires a three-quarter-mile hike along Highway F or a shuttle to return to the trailhead.

**Eagle's Nest Trail** 🥾🥾🥾🥾🥾—3.3 miles—This trail follows the river for over a half mile, passes rock bluffs and a patch of sensitive ferns, and ascends to a high, chert ridgetop, clad in shortleaf pines. Middle and lower sections might be seasonally overgrown. The trail begins from campground #2, behind campsite #81.

# Roaring River State Park

LEGEND

| | |
|---|---|
| —— Road | Pool |
| ···· Trail | Picnic Area |
| ▓▓ Boundary | P Wild Area Parking |
| Park Office | Devil's Kitchen |
| Restaurant and Hotel | Hatchery |
| Park Store | Spring |
| Nature Center | Stable |
| Cabins | Lookout Tower |
| Camping | Amphitheater |

Pibern Trail

112

Devil's Kitchen Trail

Eagle's Nest Trail

River Trail

Fire Tower Trail

# Devil's Kitchen Trail 👢👢👢👢👢

**Distance Round-Trip:** 1.75 miles

**Estimated Hiking Time:** 1.25 hours

*The Devil's Den, the Devil's Backbone, the Devil's Sugar Bowl . . . in all, over 80 natural features in Missouri are named after old Beelzebub.*

**Caution:** Several steep hills are covered with small, loose rocks.

**Trail Directions:** Park in the lot for the old lodge, near the hatchery; the trailhead is just across the river. An interpretive brochure for this self-guiding trail is available at the nature center. Numbered stations along the trail do not correspond to numbered features here.

Begin at the sign for the trail **[1]** and hike along a rocky, intermittent stream. On your way to the top of this ridge, you'll come across four types of sedimentary rock—dolomite, shale, limestone, and chert—each at its own level. You'll reach the first level at a three-way intersection at .10 mi. **[2]**, where you turn right on a big slab of dolomite bedrock. As you continue, you'll be able to see geology in action. The bluff on your left is limestone, while the part of the hill you are walking on is dolomite. Because limestone is less resistant than dolomite, the bluff is eroding faster than the trail, creating what is called a bench.

Take the spur on your left at .25 mi. **[3]** to a small cave in the limestone, created when rainwater trickled through cracks in the rock. Many animals in the park, including bats, mice, cave crickets, and even bobcats use shelter caves. Turn left after returning to the main trail and you'll cross the intersection of two intermittent streams. Ignore the spur on your left at the blocky boulders that have broken off the bluff at .45 mi. **[4]**.

At .51 **[5]** is a spur on your right that leads to another small cave across the creek. After heavy rainfall, a small stream flows from this cave's mouth. Turn right after returning to the main trail. As the trail swings left, it takes you to a higher layer of rock. Notice the crunchy, jingling sounds under your feet. This is chert, a very hard rock that collects on trails and in streambeds because it is does not chemically weather as dolomite and limestone do. Several overlooks of the surrounding steep ridges appear through the trees. At the top, at .86 mi. **[6]**, you have climbed 325 feet from the trailhead and are standing beneath native shortleaf pine trees, some of which are 200 years old.

If you didn't see the little spring cave at 1.26 mi. **[7]** or hear its trickling stream, you would probably still find it because of the cloud of frigid air that rolls out of it and hits you in the shins as you hike by. Take a close look at the cave's entrance and you'll see a layer of shale between layers of limestone above and dolomite below. Gray, flaky shale isn't much more than compressed clay, and, as a rock, it is very soft. At 1.36 mi. **[8]** is an odd and interesting array of rocks—the Devil's Kitchen. After several massive limestone blocks broke off the bluff, a layer of shale within the rocks failed to support their weight and caused further sliding. Rocks shifting above were caught by rocks below, forming the kitchen's roof. After exploring the kitchen, turn left on the main trail and turn left at the spur at 1.45 mi. **[9]**. The music of Roaring River will accompany you back to **[2]**, where you go straight to return to the trailhead.

1. Start
2. Right turn
3. Spur to cave
4. Go straight
5. Spur to cave
6. Ridgetop
7. Spring cave
8. Devil's Kitchen
9. Left turn

# Pibern Trail 👢👢👢👢👢

**Distance Round-Trip:** 1.75 miles

**Estimated Hiking Time:** 1 hour

*In 1847, the first land surveyors described the Roaring River Hills as "the steepest description of stony mountains entirely unfit for cultivation." Thanks to a lack of development, this rugged landscape is still home to the striking painted bunting, bobcat, and an occasional black bear.*

**Caution:** Small, loose rocks cover several steep hills.

**Trail Directions:** Park at the turnaround loop at the north end of campground #1 and begin at the sign for the trail **[1]**. After crossing a wide, rocky streambed at the trailhead, you'll hike into a lush grove of spicebush and pawpaw on the other side. In September and October, shiny, bright red berries decorate the limbs of the aromatic spicebush, while green peanut-shaped fruits hang from pawpaw trees. Enormous sycamore and black walnut trees are further indicators of the moist, rich soil here. Just across the stream, gray and white limestone bluffs loom through the trees like cloaked giants, moving in and out of forest shadows.

At .17 mi. **[2]** turn left into the streambed. Wingstem sunflowers on the banks are seven feet tall by late summer, and blooming jewelweed splashes green and bright orange on the mostly white rocks. As you hike in the streambed, layers of overhanging limestone ledges climb the bluff next to the river, evidence of the stone-carving work the water has completed over eons. Just past the ledges, find the trail into the woods on your left. The trail takes you alongside more rock shelves on your left, while another stream valley on your right is filled with blocky boulders, tumbled down from higher bluffs. Even though the boulders wear the dark green mosses of time, they look as if they've been suddenly frozen in their violent and rumbling trip from above.

After hiking uphill and passing some moist, shaded slopes covered with wild ginger and liverleaf, the trail turns left at .24 mi. **[3]**, away from the rocky ravine. Now, the ravine on the left is so deep you can't see the bottom—only the tops of trees. The ridge on your right is so steep you can't see the top—only the fractured, weathered, rocky shelves just above you. Some of the shelves hide small shelter caves, used by chipmunks and mice for homes and food-caching dens. As you continue on this sideslope, you'll find gravelly areas of chert pebbles on the trail. In Missouri, Native Americans made weapons and tools almost exclusively of chert because it is as hard as glass and fractures with fine, sharp edges.

At .68 mi. **[4]**, just before the trail swings to the left, you'll hike beneath grand, towering bluffs, many with shelter caves, overhanging ledges, and interesting eroded shapes. You'll soon descend into another streambed, with many boulders that have broken off from these bluffs. At .85 mi. **[5]** some of the bluffs on your right have weathered into chimneylike pinnacles with flat tops. Look for bloodroot, wild hydrangea, and Christmas ferns crowding around the moisture of small seeps next to the trail.

At .97 mi. **[6]** you'll cross a small, wooden bridge over an intermittent spring emerging from the bluff on your right. From here, you'll descend the hill on a trail full of rocks and tree roots. Ignore the spur to the stream at 1.27 mi. **[7]**. At the intersection at 1.35 mi. **[8]**, with a small building on your right, turn left. After crossing the limestone bedrock of the streambed, you'll emerge into the campground behind site #55. Turn left on the pavement at 1.37 mi. **[9]** to finish your hike.

1. Start
2. Left turn into streambed
3. Left turn
4. Overhanging bluffs
5. Pinnacles
6. Intermittent spring
7. Go straight
8. Left turn
9. Left turn

# 57. George Washington Carver National Monument

- Hike through the forest and next to the streams where George Washington Carver spent his boyhood and shaped his interest in botany.
- Walk through a restored house built by Moses Carver in 1881.
- Learn how to make lye soap.
- Saunter on the banks of a serene spring pond flowing with life, from muskrats, turtles, and bass to dragonflies, minnows, and whirligig beetles.

## Area Information

George Washington Carver was born into slavery in a 14-foot-by-14-foot one-room cabin sometime in the early 1860s on the Moses Carver farm in Diamond, Missouri. Kidnapped by bushwhackers, orphaned as an infant, and plagued by sickness, Carver believed nevertheless that he could achieve whatever he set out to do. On his way to national prominence as one of the foremost scientists of his era, Carver influenced many young people to advance their education or move in a new direction.

Receiving national attention by discovering hundreds of uses for the peanut, sweet potato, and soybean, Carver left a career as a research botanist at Iowa Agricultural College to work with Booker T. Washington at Tuskegee Institute in Alabama, where he taught botany and agriculture. Director of agricultural research at Tuskegee for 47 years, Carver devoted his life to devising better farming methods for poor farmers of the South, who were trying to eke a living from land exhausted by cotton. Carver coaxed farmers away from cotton to soil-enhancing, protein-rich crops such as peanuts and soybeans. By teaching crop diversification and conservation, Carver helped many Southern farmers rise from the enslavement of subsistence farming.

George Washington Carver National Monument, at Carver's birthplace, was dedicated in 1953 to commemorate Carver's life, his work, and his humane philosophy. Carver did his work with its potential benefit to people in mind and was always modest about his success. Concerning success, Carver had this to say: "It is not the style of clothes one wears, neither the kind of automobile one drives, nor the amount of money one has in the bank, that counts. These mean nothing. It is simply service that measures success."

**Directions:** The site is just southeast of Joplin. From Diamond, turn west on Highway V for 2 miles and turn left on Carver Road. Go .7 mile and turn right at the entrance.

**Hours Open:** The visitor center and grounds are open year-round from 9 A.M. to 5 P.M. The site is closed Thanksgiving, Christmas, and New Year's Day.

**Facilities:** The site features a visitor center (free admission) with exhibits and a 30-minute documentary on Carver. A self-guiding trail interprets the area where Carver spent his boyhood. A picnic area is also available.

**Permits and Rules:** Picking wildflowers is prohibited. Fishing, wading, or swimming in the streams or spring pond is not allowed.

**Further Information:** Superintendent, George Washington Carver National Monument, 5646 Carver Road, Diamond, MO 64840; 417-325-4151.

## Other Areas of Interest

What would a trip to the southwest corner of Missouri be without visiting the **Spooklight**? Whether a soft white glow in the distance, a necklace of shimmering lights, or a big, orange ball of fire that silently glides up and down country roads, the Spooklight of the Missouri-Oklahoma line has delighted, intrigued, and mystified residents, visitors, and scientists for over a hundred years.

To find the Spooklight, take I-44 west of Joplin. At exit 4, take Highway 43 south to Highway C, where you turn southwest to the little town of Hornet. From Hornet, turn west on West Hymer Road until it ends at State Line Road. From here, turn .2 mile to the north or .8 mile to the south; the east-west roads (Oklahoma's E40 and E50 Roads) are prime Spooklight viewing spots. For more information look for *Tri-State Spooklight,* a booklet published in the mid-1950s by Juanita Kay, and *Earth Lights Revelation* by English researcher Paul Devereux.

# Carver Trail 🥾

**Distance Round-Trip:** .75 mile

**Estimated Hiking Time:** .75 hour

*"My work, my life, must be in the spirit of a little child seeking only to know the truth and follow it."—George Washington Carver*

**Caution:** Gates to the park are locked at 5 P.M. daily.

**Trail Directions:** An interpretive guide for this self-guiding trail is available from the visitor center for 50¢. Lettered stations along the trail do not correspond to numbered features here.

Begin the trail at the bust of George Washington Carver, just outside the visitor center **[1]**. Carver overcame slavery, becoming an orphan, sickness, violence, and racism to become a world-renowned scientist, educator, and humanitarian. When asked to speak at the commencement at Selma University in Selma, Alabama, on May 27, 1942, Carver read a poem titled "Equipment." Push the button below the bust to hear Carver read the poem in his own voice. Go straight, toward the small log cabin, to continue.

The log cabin at .05 mi. **[2]** marks the site where George was born into slavery sometime in the early 1860s. George lived in a tiny one-room cabin like this one with his mother, Mary, and his brother, Jim, until Confederate bushwhackers kidnapped him and his mother. George was returned, but his mother was never seen or heard from again. After the kidnapping, George and Jim moved into the nearby cabin of their owners, Moses and Susan Carver, who raised them as their own.

George was a sickly child and was relieved of many farm duties, freeing him to spend many hours in the forest, painting pictures of plants on rocks with homemade paints and brushes, and collecting wildflowers for his garden, hidden in the brush. The statue at .13 mi. **[3]** commemorates Carver's boyhood spent here and his intense curiosity about nature, which continued throughout his life. Take the spur on your left to the small spring, where George collected drinking water for the household. Return to the statue and cross the arched bridge to continue.

Turn right at the spring pond at .28 mi. **[4]** to walk around its banks. Williams Spring, which emerges beneath the pond's far end, is named for Moses Carver's niece and her husband, who lived just north of the spring. Walk around the pond until you return to **[4]**, where you turn right. The house at .48 mi. **[5]** was built by Moses Carver in 1881 after a tornado destroyed his cabin and George's birthplace cabin. George never lived in the house but returned during his travels to visit the Carvers. The restored house contains interpretive material and is open to visitors. The V-shaped hopper next to the house was used to make lye soap. The hopper was filled with ashes, water was poured over them, and the lye water was then mixed with hot animal fat to make lye soap. Continue the trail beneath a sprawling oak tree.

After crossing two small streams, you'll find a sign marking the site where Moses Carver planted persimmons at .58 mi. **[6].** Next to the sign, a persimmon trunk remains, with knobby, alligator-hide bark. As you leave the woods, you'll enter a prairie in the process of being restored. At .69 mi. **[7]** is the Carver cemetery, where Moses and Susan Carver are buried, along with many of George's childhood acquaintances. George is buried at Tuskegee Institute. Continue through the restoring prairie to return to the visitor center.

## George W. Carver National Monument

1. Start
2. Birthplace site
3. Statue of young Carver
4. Spring pond
5. Moses Carver house
6. Persimmon grove
7. Carver cemetery

| LEGEND | | |
|---|---|---|
| ⬥3 View of Boy Carver Statue | ⬥8 1881 Moses Carver House |
| — Road | ⬥4 Boy Carver Statue | ⬥9 Persimmon Grove |
| ⋯⋯ Trail | ⬥5 Carver Spring | ⬥10 Walnut Fence Row |
| ★1 Carver Bust | ⬥6 Spring and Pond | ⬥11 Carver Family Cemetery |
| ★2 Birthplace Site | ⬥7 Ash Hopper | ⬥12 Prairie |

# 58. Prairie State Park

- Come and see American bison roaming freely on Missouri's largest remaining tallgrass prairie.

- Hike in a prairie so undisturbed that it contains four state natural areas, each recognized for its exceptional natural qualities.

- Bring your camera—over 400 species of native wildflowers and grasses are found here, as well as 150 species of birds, 25 mammals, and 88 butterflies and moths!

## Area Information

On a hiking trail at Prairie State Park, with infinite waves of grasses and wildflowers and views of grazing bison on gentle hills that roll to the horizon in all directions, it's hard to imagine you are in a remnant of a landscape. But of the 13 million acres of tallgrass prairie that once covered more than a third of the state, over 99 percent is gone.

Luckily, the state's largest remaining tallgrass prairie is preserved today at Prairie State Park. Because glaciers never reached the Osage Plains region of southwest Missouri, the prairies here are older and more diverse than the prairies of the northern glaciated plains. Fortunately, too, 65 to 70 percent of the park has never been plowed, leaving intact the all-important prairie root system, which has taken centuries to develop.

Although bison and elk were eliminated in Missouri in the 19th century, they have been returned to Prairie State Park to live in their natural habitat. Prairie chickens still gather at their booming grounds in April and perform their famous mating rituals. At least 24 other rare or endangered species live here as well.

**Directions:** The park is in southwest Missouri, next to the Kansas border. From Lamar, take Highway 160 west 10.4 miles to Highway 43, where you turn north 4.9 miles to Highway K. Turn west on Highway K 4.1 miles to Highway P. Turn south on Highway P for 2.2 miles and turn left on a gravel road at the sign for the park. Go 1.8 miles to the visitor center.

**Hours Open:** The park is open year-round. The visitor center is open from 8:30 A.M. to 5 P.M. Tuesday through Saturday, and from 1 P.M. to 5 P.M. on Sunday. The visitor center is closed on Monday.

**Facilities:** The park offers a visitor center with interpretive exhibits and a picnic area. Limited primitive camping can be arranged by contacting the park naturalist.

**Permits and Rules:** Before hiking, visitors should stop in the visitor center for information on the location of the bison, which are allowed to roam freely in the park. Fires are restricted in the park, and smoking is not allowed on the trails. Pets are prohibited on the trails and must be leashed when elsewhere in the park. Bikes and horses are not allowed on the trails.

**Further Information:** Park Superintendent, Prairie State Park, P.O. Box 97, Liberal, MO 64762; 417-843-6711.

## Other Areas of Interest

The only Missourian ever elected U.S. president was born in Lamar, 15 miles east of Prairie State Park. **Harry S Truman Birthplace State Historic Site** offers free tours of the Truman home, built between 1880 and 1882. For more information call 417-682-2279.

**Battle of Carthage State Historic Site,** south of Lamar in Carthage, is the site of a Civil War battle in which 6,000 Southern troops forced 1,000 Union soldiers to retreat down the stagecoach road to Sarcoxie. For more information call 417-682-2279.

In Dadeville, east of Lamar, **Stockton State Park** features water recreation on 25,000-acre Stockton Lake, a popular spot for sailing. The park offers camping, a marina, motel, cabins, restaurant, boat ramps, fishing, boating, swimming, and picnic areas. For more information call 417-276-5329.

## Park Trails

**Coyote Trail** 🥾🥾—3 miles—This rolling prairie trail may be partially closed because of a fence for the elk. Check with park staff for the trail's status. The trail may be accessed from the picnic area or from a connector link from the Gay Feather Trail.

**Gay Feather Trail** 🥾🥾—1.5 miles—Named for the tall, spiked, purple wildflower that blooms here all summer, this trail features a diversity of wildflowers and traverses Regal Prairie Natural Area. The trailhead is .9 mile south of the visitor center. The trail is also linked to the Coyote and Drover's Trails.

# Prairie State Park

# Drover's Trail

**Distance Round-Trip:** 2.5 miles

**Estimated Hiking Time:** 1.5 hours

*There is something about the prairie that pulls your gaze outward and upward, and it's hard to decide which is bigger—the sky or the prairie. You get a feeling of freedom in this unusual vastness, and you realize that you are in a very special place indeed.*

**Caution:** Before hiking any trail in the park, stop in the visitor center for information on the location of the bison, which are allowed to roam freely in the park. For your safety, do not leave your vehicle until you have this information. Do not touch the eight-foot-tall electric fence. To use the spur to the back-pack camp, go under the fence only where the electric wires are insulated. Also, unless you are here in the winter, a repellent against ticks and chiggers is recommended.

**Trail Directions:** Park in the lot for the visitor center. Begin at the sign for the trail **[1]**, which is next to the front of the building. At the trailhead, take the left fork of the trail. This trail is named for a type of prairie shepherd, who grazed sheep and cattle on the prairie. Although domestic animals have been absent from the prairie for some time, you will probably see recent evidence of the resident bison. As the trail leads you into an ocean of prairie grasses and wildflowers, keep your senses alert. You'll find that this native prairie is an incredibly diverse and thriving landscape.

The prairie grasses have a way of responding to the wind as if they are part of it. Breezes tease and bend their tops, just as puffs lightly ripple the surface of water. Indian grass, slough grass, and little bluestem grass grow here. By midsummer, look for the "turkey feet" seedheads of big bluestem. Early settlers wrote about prairie grasses growing as tall as a person on horseback, and by fall, several kinds of grasses here will be eight feet tall, with roots just as long. Turn right at the intersection at .08 mi. **[2]**. Look for dozens of dragonflies, skimming the grasstops for mosquitoes and reflecting the sun off cellophane wings. The northern harrier, an endangered bird of prey commonly found here, hunts in a similar fashion, gliding slowly and watching, just over the top of the grass. You may be startled, at any time, by the explosion of northern bobwhites or greater prairie chickens, their wings thumping like tiny helicopters. Watch them glide away and melt into the horizon.

Turn left at the intersection at .31 mi. **[3]** and go straight at the connector link at .35 mi. **[4]**. Notice how much taller the plants grow where the trail dips into shallow draws. As you hike, you'll pass entire fields of wildflowers, in a kaleidoscope of colors and shapes. Look for the gray, heart-shaped leaves of ashy sunflowers, the pealike pods and white blossoms of wild indigo, and the tall, purple, upright spikes of blazing star, shining like beacons in the emerald seas of grass.

Go straight at the four-way intersection at .94 mi. **[5]**. The broad, shallow valley in front of you, lined with shrubs and small trees, is that of East Drywood Creek, the state's most outstanding prairie stream. Look for red-winged blackbirds, perched on top of shrubs, and cliff swallows, swooping and diving overhead. Just after passing through a patch of coneflowers and leadplant, go straight at 1.15 mi. **[6]** at the spur on your left. If you find a bare, bowl-shaped depression in the prairie, you have discovered a bison wallow—a spot where bison, especially bulls, roll on the ground for dust baths when it's dry and mud baths when it's wet.

Turn right at 1.40 mi. **[7]**, just before reaching a tall electric fence. Turn right again at the intersection at 1.46 mi. **[8]**, turning away from the fence. Go straight at a four-way intersection and go straight at the connector link at 1.85 mi. **[9]**. As the waves of wildflower colors wash on each side of you, watch for large, green katydids and razzing, rattling cicadas that start up from the grass, flutter downwind, and land, rather awkwardly, on plant stalks. At the spur on your left at 2.26 mi. **[10]**, turn right, toward the visitor center. Turn right at the fork in the trail at 2.31 mi. **[11]** to finish your prairie hike.

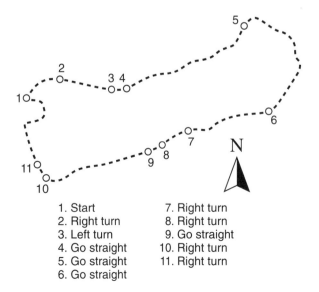

1. Start
2. Right turn
3. Left turn
4. Go straight
5. Go straight
6. Go straight
7. Right turn
8. Right turn
9. Go straight
10. Right turn
11. Right turn

# Path of the Sky People and Sandstone Trails 🥾🥾

**Distance Round-Trip:** 6.5 miles

**Estimated Hiking Time:** 4 hours

*The prairie is a barrage of entertainment. Between sweeping vistas, animated cloud formations, and resplendent seas of wildflowers are endless streams of displays, interactions, and interruptions from a multiplicity of the prairie's creatures.*

**Caution:** Cross the electric fence only at the trail crossing, where the wires are insulated. Please do not trespass on private property, which borders the Tzi-Sho Natural Area on three sides. Also, unless you are here in the winter, a repellent against ticks and chiggers is recommended.

**Trail Directions:** From the visitor center, turn south on Township Road for 1.3 miles. Turn east on Central Road for 2.6 miles and park in the lot for the Tzi-Sho Prairie Natural Area, on your left. *Tzi-Sho* (pronounced "tissue") is the Native American word for "Sky People," one of the grand divisions of the Osage nation. This trail takes you through two of the four natural areas in the park—the Tzi-Sho Prairie and the East Drywood Creek Natural Areas, both distinguished natural tallgrass prairies. This hike is a combination of two trails that present many options for shorter (or longer) hikes.

Begin at the sign for the trail **[1]**, in the corner of the parking lot, and bear left at the trailhead. If you are here in the morning, you'll see and hear a tremendous variety of wildlife. Watch for scissor-tailed flycatchers, perched on powerlines or on the open prairie. Their long, streaming tails help them maneuver in flight. Upland sandpipers are summer residents, and the rare prairie chicken lives here all year long. As vast prairie vistas open in front of you, scan the skies for northern harriers and other hawks, and watch for the heads of deer, foxes, and coyotes bounding through the prairie grasses.

Turn left at .80 mi. **[2]** to begin the Sandstone Trail. Notice the islands of sumac, often with singing birds perched at their tops. In the right proportion, these islands are important shelter and nesting areas for many animals. Park managers use prescribed fire to keep sumac and other shrubs from taking over the prairie. The musical songs of meadowlarks often accompany you as you hike, and the squeaky trills of tiny sedge wrens sometimes come in stereo, on both sides of the trail. Watch for the olive-headed Henslow's sparrow, and listen for the "tick, tick, bzzzzzzz" of the grasshopper sparrow.

At 1.01 mi. **[3]** turn right on the gravel road for a few steps and crawl under the insulated electric fence on your left to continue the trail. Here, American feverfew, wild indigo, and flowering spurge, whose five-lobed white flowers are just over a quarter-inch long, paint entire fields white. Other fields are yellow with goldenrod, splashed purple with ironweed and blazing star. Turn right at the three-way intersection at 1.57 mi. **[4]**. After passing some large sandstone slabs, go straight at the connector link at 2.21 mi. **[5]**. Soon you'll see some persimmon groves and the small sandstone ledges that border East Drywood Creek. Look around on the trail for the burrows or the dried shells and pincers of prairie crayfish. In spring or fall, look for striking yellow-headed blackbirds.

Turn left at 2.84 mi. **[6]**, at the spur to the backpack camp, and turn left at 2.91 mi. **[7]**, at the connector link to the Drover's Trail. The trail soon approaches East Drywood Creek Natural Area, recognized for its healthy prairie stream and its diverse life. After descending into a small, rocky draw, the trail swings to the left. After crisscrossing the creek several times, go straight at the connector link at 4.35 mi. **[8]**. Here, you'll find two ponds on your right, left over from the days when cattle grazed this part of the prairie. Watch here for ducks and other wildlife using the ponds. Turn right after returning to **[4]** and turn left at **[2]**. You will now hike the other half of the Path of the Sky People to finish your prairie hike.

1. Start
2. Left turn
3. Road-fence crossing
4. Right turn
5. Go straight
6. Left turn
7. Left turn
8. Go straight